INTERPERSONAL EXPLORATIONS IN PSYCHOANALYSIS

INTERPERSONAL EXPLORATIONS IN PSYCHOANALYSIS

New Directions in Theory and Practice

EARL G. WITENBERG, EDITOR

BASIC BOOKS, INC., PUBLISHERS
New York

© 1973 by The William Alanson White Institute of Psychiatry, Psychoanalysis and Psychology

Library of Congress Catalog Card Number: 75-174819
SBN: 465-033857
Printed in the United States of America
Designed by Vincent Torre

73 74 75 10 9 8 7 6 5 4 3 2 1

CONTENTS

CONTENTS

AFFILIATIONS OF AUTHORS

EARL G. WITENBERG, M.D.
Director, William Alanson White Institute of Psychiatry, Psychoanalysis and Psychology

DAVID E. SCHECTER, M.D.
Director of Training, William Alanson White Institute of Psychiatry, Psychoanalysis and Psychology
Fellow, Training and Supervising Analyst, William Alanson White Institute of Psychiatry, Psychoanalysis and Psychology
Associate Clinical Professor of Psychiatry, Albert Einstein College of Medicine, New York City
Associate Attending Psychiatrist, Bronx Municipal Hospital Center, New York City

ERNEST G. SCHACHTEL, J.D.
Fellow, Supervisory and Training Analyst, William Alanson White Institute of Psychiatry, Psychoanalysis and Psychology
Adjunct Professor of Psychology, New York University, Postdoctoral Program, Department of Psychology
Fellow, American Psychological Association
Fellow, American Association for the Advancement of Science

MAURICE R. GREEN, M.D.
Supervising and Training Analyst, William Alanson White Institute of Psychiatry, Psychoanalysis and Psychology
Associate Clinical Professor, New York University Medical Center
Member, Medical Board of Roosevelt Hospital, New York City
Executive Committee, Academy of Psychosomatic Medicine
Steering Committee, New York State Academy of Family Physicians

ERICH FROMM, Ph.D.
Trustee and Fellow, William Alanson White Institute of Psychiatry, Psychoanalysis and Psychology
Director of Psychoanalytic Training, University of Mexico

BENJAMIN WOLSTEIN, Ph.D.
Training and Supervising Analyst, William Alanson White Institute of Psychiatry, Psychoanalysis and Psychology

Clinical Professor of Psychology, Adelphi University
Supervisor of Psychology, Graduate School of Humanities and Social
    Sciences, Yeshiva University
Lecturer, New School for Social Research

SILVANO ARIETI, M.D.
Member of the Faculty and Supervising Analyst, William Alanson White
    Institute of Psychiatry, Psychoanalysis and Psychology
Clinical Professor of Psychiatry, New York Medical College
Editor-in-Chief of the *American Handbook of Psychiatry*
Editor of *The Journal of the American Academy of Psychoanalysis*

GERARD CHRZANOWSKI, M.D.
Training and Supervising Analyst, William Alanson White Institute of
    Psychiatry, Psychoanalysis and Psychology
Associate Clinical Professor of Psychiatry, New York Medical College
Medical Director, Bleuler Psychotherapy Center

EDGAR A. LEVENSON, M.D.
Director of Clinical Services, Fellow, Training and Supervising Analyst,
    William Alanson White Institute of Psychiatry, Psychoanalysis and Psy-
    chology

JOHN L. SCHIMEL, M.D.
Associate Director, Fellow, Training and Supervising Psychoanalyst, William
    Alanson White Institute of Psychiatry, Psychoanalysis and Psychology
Associate Clinical Professor of Psychiatry, New York University Medical
    Center

JOSEPH BARNETT, M.D.
Faculty Member and Supervising Analyst, William Alanson White Institute
    of Psychiatry, Psychoanalysis and Psychology
Secretary, American Academy of Psychoanalysis

RUTH MOULTON, M.D.
Chairman, Council of Fellows, Training and Supervising Analyst, William
    Alanson White Institute of Psychiatry, Psychoanalysis and Psychology
Assistant Clinical Professor of Psychiatry, Columbia University
Associate Attending Psychiatrist, New York State Psychiatric Institute and
    Hospital

LEOPOLD CALIGOR, Ph.D.
Co-Director of the Union Therapy Project, Faculty Member, Training and
    Supervising Analyst, William Alanson White Institute of Psychiatry, Psy-
    choanalysis and Psychology
Clinical Professor and Supervisor of Psychotherapy, Postdoctoral Program in
    Psychotherapy, Adelphi University
Advisory Committee, Michigan Health and Social Security Research Institute

AFFILIATIONS OF AUTHORS

MILTIADES ZAPHIROPOULOS, M.D.
Trustee, Fellow, Training and Supervising Analyst, Co-Director, Union Therapy Project, William Alanson White Institute of Psychiatry, Psychoanalysis and Psychology
Associate Professor of Psychiatry, New York School of Psychiatry
Consulting Psychiatrist, Grasslands Hospital, Valhalla and United Hospital, Port Chester

OTTO ALLEN WILL, JR., M.D.
Faculty, William Alanson White Institute of Psychiatry, Psychoanalysis and Psychology
Honorary Member, William Alanson White Psychoanalytic Society
Medical Director, Austen Riggs Center, Inc.
Clinical Professor, Department of Psychiatry, Cornell University

ERWIN SINGER, Ph.D.
Training and Supervising Analyst, William Alanson White Institute of Psychiatry, Psychoanalysis and Psychology
Professor, City College of New York
Visiting Professor of Psychology, Graduate School of Arts and Sciences, New York University

RAYMOND SOBEL, M.D.
Certificate in Psychoanalysis, William Alanson White Institute of Psychiatry, Psychoanalysis and Psychology
Professor of Psychiatry, Dartmouth Medical School

CHARLES CLAY DAHLBERG, M.D.
Fellow, Training and Supervising Analyst, Research Psychiatrist, William Alanson White Institute of Psychiatry, Psychoanalysis and Psychology
Clinical Associate Professor of Psychiatry, New York University Medical Center

STANLEY FELDSTEIN, Ph.D.
Research Affiliate, William Alanson White Institute of Psychiatry, Psychoanalysis and Psychology
Professor of Psychology, University of Maryland, Baltimore County

RUTH MECHANECK
Research Assistant, William Alanson White Institute of Psychiatry, Psychoanalysis and Psychology

JOSEPH JAFFE, M.D.
Fellow, William Alanson White Institute of Psychiatry, Psychoanalysis and Psychology
Associate Professor of Clinical Psychiatry, College of Physicians and Surgeons, Columbia University
Chief of Psychiatric Research, Department of Communication Sciences, New York State Psychiatric Institute

ROLLO MAY, Ph.D.

Fellow, Training and Supervising Analyst, William Alanson White Institute
of Psychiatry, Psychoanalysis and Psychology

Lecturer, New School for Social Research

Adjunct Professor, Graduate School of Arts and Sciences, New York University

LEON EDEL, D.LITT.

Faculty, William Alanson White Institute of Psychiatry, Psychoanalysis and
Psychology

Citizens Professor of English, University of Hawaii

Henry James Professor of English and American Letters, New York University

Pulitzer Prize

INTERPERSONAL EXPLORATIONS IN PSYCHOANALYSIS

PSYCHOANALYSIS TODAY
Earl G. Witenberg

THE CHAPTERS IN THIS BOOK, most of them delivered at the twenty-fifth anniversary symposium of the William Alanson White Institute, have in common the psychoanalytic training institute of their authors. Though representative of the thinking at the institute, they are not institute positions. The institute has only one position: As an association of behavioral and social scientists it is dedicated to the understanding of man in order that he might better cope with the fantastic problem of being simply human. Since any source of information in the service of this goal is evaluated, the essays are diverse, ranging from Arieti's chapter on "The Interpersonal and the Intrapsychic in Severe Psychopathology" to Jaffe's on "Structural Foundations of Linguistic Behavior." To some extent this diversity reflects the beginning maturity of psychoanalysis. The reader may begin at any point and read in any direction as these chapters cover a wide range of topics—each a significant statement of where things are. Perhaps one of the more interesting developments is the shift from the pathological to the normal as psychoanalysis seeks to uncover the concomitants of healthy psychic growth.

Where does the study of man begin? From the moment of conception one may postulate an entire range of influences to which a fertilized egg will be exposed. The influence of the prenatal environment on the growing fetus is well documented, and the newborn infant is a unique set of genes that has interacted with a unique prenatal environment to produce an infant who at birth is different from any other. Wide individual differences among infants are observed right from birth. Since infants differ in their responsiveness to various modes, it is now useful to regard the individual as emerging earlier in life than was previously assumed. Sometimes the behavior of the mother is contingent on that of the child. An infant who refuses to be coddled will elicit a particular kind of response, in a particular kind of mother, to which he will then react. Dr. Daniel Stern, of Columbia University, has filmed a mother's response to the eye-aversion movements of her fraternal twin infants. One infant, responding to the mother's head movements and the like, fixed his gaze on her for a longer period than did his twin, who had a shorter attention span and averted his gaze more rapidly. As a result, the mother's attitude toward the twins differed, and each was endowed by her with a different set of attributes (whom he was like and such). What the infant does, then, arouses certain emotions in the mother which are related to her past experiences but triggered by the child's action. The relationship between mother and child is one of continuous reciprocity, so that the act of the child influences the mother, who influences the child, and so on. Development proceeds in this fashion, and increasingly complex responses are required of the infant as he adapts to his environment: Cognitive growth and language development are affected by the quality and amount of reciprocal stimulation between parent and child.

We are concerned, then, with the development of the infant's perceptual systems (eyes, ears, skin) and with the response of significant individuals to the emergence and maturation of innate capacities. Here, at the borderline of the biological, the nature of reciprocal relationship is stressed. The emotional aura that surrounds the organ systems (mouth, anus, genitals) will by no means be ignored. But we have moved from a psychology that blamed the parents toward a viewpoint that seeks to understand total units of interaction. The nature of the environment and its facilitating or noxious quality is crucial in the development of personality.

The dictum that most of personality is fixed by the age of five has been modified to show that personality changes occur throughout life. The way the individual relates to changes in environment, both personal and social, may be determined by a repetition of childhood patterns; but the response may be a new one, a new integration depending on a different perception of factors. Man is an act not a fact, from birth until death.

The task for the analyst is therefore more complicated than it was twenty-five years ago. From the moment of birth the persistence of the infant as a person is pervasive. Developmental theory has postulated a complex series of interactions that precludes any view of the patient as an organism that is merely lived by life. Like analysis itself, the patient is always evolving and always incomplete. Analytic interpretation can no longer imply that the individual is nothing but a repetition of past occurrences.

The practice of psychoanalysis today in America bears little resemblance to its practice twenty-five years ago. There are manifold reasons for this radical change. Freud's discovery of the importance of unconscious motivation and the eventual universal acceptance of its significance changed the nature of the presenting difficulty for which people came for treatment. Substituted for the hysterical symptoms, which had been so common in Freud's day, were character problems, feelings of ennui, alienation, meaninglessness. Difficulties in living had supplanted the paralysis and blindness. A changing society with its emerging technology was alienating man from himself and from others. Computers and automation had reduced him to numbers, an atom bomb had terrorized him, and a swiftly changing value system prevented his retreat into the illusory haven of familiar ways. Whatever the sphere, values of the marketplace predominated. The emphasis on more and more consumer and material goods created an increasing disparity between achievement and satisfaction: The more one had, the less was one satisfied because there was more to be had.

Among the analysts who first articulated these changes on the basis of their clinical work and the theories that derived from it were Sullivan, Fromm, Thompson, Horney, and Fromm-Reichmann. Sullivan, working intensively with schizophrenic patients at Shepard & Enoch Pratt Hospital, realized that he could not utilize libido theory and its dogma. Freud felt that schizophrenics could not be analyzed, and Sullivan found that they were indeed not suitable patients for classical analysis. Sullivan's clinical experience led him instead to the field of the interpersonal, and on the basis of his observations he developed a theory of personality founded on what goes on, both real and fantasied, between people. Sullivan formulated a classification of experience (proto-, para-, and syntaxic) showing the importance of each mode in the development of the individual. He laid great stress on the significance of language in individual development. Thompson, Fromm, and Horney stressed the character types formed by various cultures and pointed out the cultural determinants of, for example, the psychology of women.

This by no means begins to represent the wealth of knowledge being added to early psychoanalytic theory both by psychoanalysts and other social scientists. The library of experience that has accumulated over the years enables today's analyst to study development and to formulate goals in a way that was not possible thirty years ago. Each psychoanalytic treatment is a unique experience, so that in a sense one begins anew with each patient. But for Freud and for the early analysts this was true in a more fundamental way; each patient was virtually a research project to be studied by a single rigidly and precisely defined method. Psychoanalysis has ceased to be a single, defined procedure, and analysts need no longer begin at the beginning.

As psychoanalytic knowledge accumulated, it became evident that certain difficulties begin at certain stages in life and continue in an untoward way. Today, therefore, in the first contacts between patient and analyst a detailed history is taken with a developmental scheme in mind so that the particular eras where things went astray can be identified. The patient is an active participant in this process, and he joins forces with the analyst at the start. At one time it was thought that the personality was fixed by the age of five or six and could be modified only through analysis or by an intense interpersonal situation outside the analysis. It is recognized now that for a very few people trauma or deprivation has arrested their development so that no further maturation takes place. But for most people the invidious factors do not result in a complete developmental arrest. There are, therefore, uneven factors (in cognition, emotional growth, and interpersonal relationships) within the person in the development of his capacities so that analysis too proceeds in an uneven manner. At one point the process is educational; at another the focus is on anxiety gradients so that the need for dissociation will be relieved. There may be emphasis at one point on the way the person relates currently to others and at another on the historical roots of the behavior. Increasingly, there is an interest in the specificity of understanding. The context (both reality and fantasy) within which certain behavior or feelings is felt is studied intensely. A person is not viewed as an angry or rigid person but as one who is angry or rigid only at certain points. The examination of the specific context in which behavior (oral, cognitive, and so on) and emotions arise leads to the patient's experiencing himself as the unique person he is. There no longer is the automatic assumption that a one to one relationship exists between early childhood experience and adult neurosis. A much more complex relationship with intervening variables is assumed.

Freud called dreams the "royal road to the unconscious," and he used them to get at what he called "drive factors," relating the analysis of the dream to the infantile experience. There has since been increasing emphasis on the ego operations and the transactions of the individual as manifest in the dream. The change in the nature of dreams as the person proceeds in treatment is also scrutinized. One might say that the interpretation of dreams now is more complicated than it was and that the analysis of the dream is related more to the current therapeutic task of the analysis.

Interpretation, that is, the explication of current attitudes and behavior in terms of the past, used to be considered the analyst's chief and most powerful tool. Today the analyst's knowledge of unconscious determinants is taken for granted, and the focus is on the nature of the relationship (both real and illusory) with the patient. The analyst moves toward developing a cooperative relationship with the patient by a careful inquiry into his feelings and attitudes. This inquiry serves to stimulate the curiosity of the patient so that he becomes an active participant in his own treatment. The specific context within which feelings, attitudes, fantasies, and dreams arise are investigated in great detail so that the unique aspects of the individual become apparent. Treatment proceeds with a prevailing respect for the security operations of the patient, in an effort to keep his self-esteem as high as possible. The style and context of questions and statements are attended to closely. A patient who does not offer information freely or easily would twenty-five years ago have been called withholding. It is more useful to recognize that such a defense operation may have arisen from the child's need to protect his privacy and to point out the continuing desire for privacy on the part of the patient. This enables the patient to begin to see that what at one point was necessary for protection of his self-esteem and became automatic is now a matter of choice for him. If you tell a patient that he is withholding, he thinks you think less of him, and he thinks less of himself. If you tell him he is being very private, he can face the reasons for his being private without any loss of self-esteem. "Why" questions are avoided because of the blaming involved in their formulation. In other words, the emphasis is on encountering the patient without less-

7

ening his self-esteem. The implicit direction in these formulations is toward an emotional experience that expands the awareness of the person so that he may become more alive and better integrated. The atmosphere created by the continuous understanding and acceptance of the patient's fantasies, thoughts, and feelings is such that the patient feels safe enough to reveal his inner life. With the increasing revelation he gains the strength through understanding that increases his self-esteem toward the goal of knowing himself as well as the analyst knows him.

Reality factors in the patient's life, such as occupation, marital status, the presence or absence of children, are taken into consideration. For many borderline characters the presence or absence of a helping person in the environment will determine the limits of the therapy. A particular economic situation may dictate the manner in which treatment proceeds. There would be a deemphasis on any factors that might increase untoward regression in the treatment of a patient with a family to support. The information from family and small-group studies enables the analyst to see more clearly the impact of the individual on other people in his environment. It also facilitates knowing or fantasying with a high degree of accuracy the nature of the familial environment within which the person grew.

Though there is no effort to artificially increase the dependency or transference reactions of the patient it must be clear that the direct experience of the transference in therapy is the unique opportunity for correcting distortions. However, largely as a result of Sullivan's formulations, the decisive role of the analyst's total personality in the process and outcome of therapy has become an ever-present consideration, so that the analyst must be careful to distinguish between transference reactions and those reactions to him that are evoked by the person he is. The role of the style of the personality, the character traits, the fantasy life of the analyst, his wishes, hopes, fears, and values are all considered an integral part of treatment, though these are neither verbalized nor made explicit unless they interfere with the increasing self-awareness of the patient. Hence, these factors are not permitted to intrude on the treatment process in an unknowing way. The reward for the analyst is the pleasure of seeing the patient grow and develop, and any other narcissistic gains are considered inappropriate and inadvisable. When other narcissistic gains intrude they should be made explicit.

Psychoanalysis Today

The patient of twenty-five years ago could reasonably expect to have the same kind of treatment experience as that of his friends. He viewed treatment as a procedure in which he would lie down, say what comes to his mind, and clarify the roots of his problems. Today's patient finds himself in the presence of an expert who engages him in a meaningful relating of the issues that are troubling him and the atmosphere in which they arose.

The notion of magic in psychoanalytic treatment has disappeared with the increasing dissemination of the facts of psychoanalysis. Patients come with varying degrees of understanding about psychoanalytic theory, but very few any longer come prepared to be passive recipients of a treatment. The patient comes not to have something done to him but to learn how to be curious about himself. Guided by the skillful questioning of the analyst, the patient becomes interested in what motivates him to do even the simplest thing. He learns to view himself as an object, to stand away from himself and observe himself saying and doing certain things. Relating an experience, he relives it, attending to nuances previously ignored and observing the relationships between past and present. As expanding awareness brings additional aspects of the self into focus, those factors that inhibited or promoted growth are studied closely, and the patient is free to choose his direction.

The interplay ("the ballet") between patient and analyst is crucial in determining the process of the therapy. As the analysis proceeds, the patient becomes disturbed by feelings directed toward the analyst, some precipitated by the actual participation (or nonparticipation) of the analyst and some having minimal basis. Exploration of the latter throws light on distortions from the past, and the examination of issues in the presence of the analyst helps the patient to the extent that the analyst does not respond in the same way as the people around him do. As the patient notes his progress in important areas of living, he can relate more freely, speak up to his boss, and cope better with difficulties that arise in relationships within his own family; he becomes aware that there are seemingly intractable problems in him. In the face of progress, certain central issues remain. They keep being repeated, and they keep being reported.

An example of this process is a man who keeps running away from intimate relationships with women. He has worked through his own identity as a male with other males, he is able to be emotionally separate from his father with whom he had been symbiotically tied, yet he is unable to resolve the issue with women. To be sure he has made progress in this area. He is now living with a woman, having arrived at this point from an earlier "inability" to sleep the night through with his sex partner. He no longer views women as interchangeable, indistinguishable one from the other. But the core problem persists. In the beginning, the panic at continuing intimacy was ascribed to something the woman was doing or demanding. He responded with retreat, sexual fantasy, and acting out with another woman. Now he realizes that the panic arises without any overt or covert demand on the part of the woman. As these phenomena unfold, the patient sees the analyst as being constantly accepting and curious, and he is more able to accept himself. He can identify his particular tastes in women with certain developmental epochs and can recognize that what he calls his adolescent behavior is associated with earlier perceptions and thoughts. He recalls the secrets he was keeping, even from his chums, in preadolescence. His father's verbal and nonverbal attitudes toward women become explicit. As the cognitive, perceptual, and affective experiences are integrated, he feels an evenness, a wholeness of himself and his experience; he feels free to choose whether he marries or not. This working-through process occurs because of the constant effort at understanding put forth by both participants. Patient and analyst have gradually developed a mutually respectful eye-level relatedness with an ability to collaborate on the task at hand.

The patient's self-acceptance enables him to relate in a more productive and creative way to others, be it socially or professionally. His heightened awareness of himself and others will help prevent the noises of the past from intruding on the present. The analytic approach will continue to be useful long after treatment has ended, and the ameliorative atmosphere of the consulting room will become a part of all future relationships.

Freud's use of the blank mirror metaphor as a dictum for the role of the analyst attempted to encourage the projection of transference feelings so that they could be studied scientifically by the two participants. It was a way of formulating a theory of development and a way of observing ontogenesis. However, the indiscriminate use of this technique limited eligibility for analysis to a very small percentage of patients, and the discouraging therapeutic results led to the development of a broader role for the analyst, and eventually to a far wider range of treatable persons. Though the clinician needs a theory, a tangible order of abstract thought that can be applied and yet be flexible, any theory suffers from presenting a complicated human being from one point of view. Any single theory of human development will determine and, hence, limit what the analyst expects of the patient. As the analyst tailors treatment to suit his patient, so may the patient choose an analyst who seems to be compatible with his needs. The choice of analysts was more limited twenty-five years ago, but this was as much a function of number as of point of view. The patient's preoccupation with the personality of his analyst—the style, the manner, the values—was more likely to be examined in terms of his pathology than in terms of what is now considered to be the reality of the situation. Not only has the impact of the analyst been shunted into awareness but the impact of the real psychoanalytic situation as well, so that regular times, fees, and the like are seen as appropriate concerns. Today's patient is quite knowledgeable as regards his choices, and he takes pains to exercise them. In the humanizing of the analyst the patient has become more human.

The chapters in this volume are representative of the work of people who engage in this impossible profession. They are efforts to better understand the factors that make people the complex beings they are.

PART ONE

Developmental
Observations

AN ESSENTIAL INGREDIENT for any psychoanalytic theory or therapy is a theory of the development of an individual. This evolution is viewed as the outcome of and the interplay among several factors: inborn capacities, motivations, maturational factors, acculturation, and the impact of anxiety on the affective, perceptive, and cognitive life of the individual.

Theories are under constant revision because of new methods of collecting data, new perspectives on previously recognized data, and new ways of collating material. The three chapters in this section demonstrate ways in which the knowledge about the growth of a person is derived. The first, by David E. Schecter, illustrates the fruits of using the method of direct observation within the context of the natural family. This method brings into sharp focus the significance of mutually playful social roles and makes it vital to add this model to the tension-reduction model used by Sullivan and Freud et al. to explicate development. Playful activities as ends in themselves are seen then as important in development. In addition, Schecter throws new light on the emergence of stranger anxiety during the first months of life.

Ernest G. Schachtel describes different attitudes (or styles) of attention. This attitude of the mind cannot be separated from the motive or interest in the service of which the attention is used. There are different varieties of attention (or inattention); these may be distinguished from one another. In this chapter Schachtel describes two: open, integrative attention and isolating attention. Like all attitudes, these have a distinct experiential quality; they also determine one's experience of one's self and of the world. They determine what and how one experiences. There are different qualities of attention. The isolating attitude typical of the obsessional is characterized by a

15

broad scanning with a narrow focus; he searches a relatively wide area with a narrow and intense focus, looking for danger, for "mistakes," and the like. Schachtel describes allocentric attention knowing the other (person, painting, living creature) as the appropriate attitude of the analyst in listening to the patient. It is to know the person, not to know about him. He correlates a number of sources to develop a theory about the origins of attitudes of attention. He hypothecates its origins early in infancy. He stresses the importance of tension-free periods in the development of attitudes of attention. He compares and contrasts his formulations with those of the workers in ego psychology and those of Jung and Fromm.

Maurice R. Green comes to a perspective on dreams that emphasizes metaphor and the problematic rather than the symbol and the drive. He sees children's dreams as closely related to the imaginative free play of early childhood in its use of metaphors and symbols. He demonstrates that the clinical significance of children's dreams have to be measured against maturational factors, a normative developmental cognitive gradient. He suggests the devising of phase-level projective techniques to better differentiate between normal developmental issues and pathological ones. The use of a cognitive spectrum along lines suggested by Piaget, Sullivan, Werner, and Bruner is proposed to further refine measures of maturation.

On the Emergence of Human Relatedness

I would like to present to you some aspects of the development of the
social bond between human infant and parent during roughly the first
nine months of life and also to consider some of the major psychological threats to this bond arising during this period. Aside from the interest intrinsic to developmental considerations, I hope to at least
indicate the relevance of developmental research to the theory and
practice of psychoanalysis. The source of our data derives mostly from
the literature of infant research, including impressions from our own
Child Development Project,[1] in which we are observing and assessing
longitudinal ego developments of "normal" infants up to the age of two
years, largely in the context of their natural family settings.

The psychoanalytic theory of infancy had, in the main, originally
been cast from the reconstructions of the psychoanalyses of neurotic
adults or older children (for example, see Klein, 1937) and from re-
trospective extrapolations from the body of theory itself. During recent years the growth of developmental psychology has opened up
enormous new resources for a psychoanalytic understanding of man,
resources of direct observation that had not previously been available
to pioneers of theory construction, including Freud and Sullivan
(1953, pp. 222–223). At the same time, developmental psychology,
with all the riches of its research findings, is very much in need of the
holistic frame of reference that psychoanalytic conceptions can potentially provide. Even more specifically for the practicing therapist, I
would suggest that any significant finding concerning the developments of the social bond will have potential application (of course, on
different levels of complexity) in understanding the psychoanalytic
situation, especially in regard to the primitive and often sticky issues
we meet in the context of transference-countertransference phenomena.

A brief review of psychoanalytic perspectives on the development
of the social bond to mother is in order. Freud properly emphasized
the helpless quality of the newborn infant whose survival depends on

17

the ministrations and need gratifications by his mother. He postulated a primary sucking instinctual drive that was "anaclitic" in nature, since it "leaned on" what he then referred to as the self-preservative ego instincts (Freud, 1953). The object of the sucking drive was seen as the breast, the social bond to mother being developed largely through a secondary psychological dependency consequent to repeated cycles of gratification through reduction of need tensions, primarily oral ones. It could be shown that most analytic authors, even Sullivan and Erikson, retain, in essence, the idea of a secondary psychological dependency based on tension reduction as the prime motivation for the human social bond. However, the latter authors began to point to other types of interactions between mother and child as a further source of social attachment.

Somewhat in contrast to the above analytic observers, the Balints (Balint, 1953), Suttie (1952), Fairbairn (1952), and Bowlby (1958) suggested a primary object-seeking tendency in the infant (not orally dominated) from the time of birth. Of these writers, Bowlby most specifically postulated mechanisms (derived from ethological models) by which the primary attachment to mother is mediated. These mechanisms were referred to as "component instinctual responses" made up of "species-specific behavior patterns" determined by heredity and emerging within specific developmental periods during the first years of life. The five instinctual responses suggested consist of sucking, clinging, following (both visual and locomotor), crying, and smiling. Bowlby stressed that certain internal and external conditions have to be fulfilled before these behaviors are activated and that their evolutionary function is species survival, largely through their evocation of the protective and nourishing mothering one. Bowlby's introduction of ethology was also set forth as an attempt to further unhook psychoanalytic theory from the reductionist preoccupation with oral drive theory; however, as Bowlby (1958) himself stressed, his theoretical model was to retain but update Freud's (1953) original schema of component instincts. Notwithstanding the emphasis placed on the specific conditions needed to activate the responses, when instinctual responses are presented as primary in the causal order of priorities, there is an illusion of a rock bottom explanation. The danger is that such an instinctual view eclipses the perspective in which human development can be understood as a function of *epigenetic ego developments*, which are nothing less than an interactional outcome of heredity, maturation, and the organization of experience, including learning by conditioning and from sign-laden relationships with significant persons in the environment.

I believe that the controversy that has ensued between primary and secondary attachments (Bowlby, 1958, 1960) is largely spurious because in human development it is, at least at present, practically impossible to separate out the primarily innate from the experiential, owing to the fact that early infantile experience tends to become organized or patterned and, presumably, immediately begins to have its effects on later development. Even the study of identical twins is fraught with methodological difficulties in separating out the innate from the experiential (Benjamin, 1962). The ethologists themselves have largely abandoned the idea of an entirely innate origin of instinct-based behavior; Schneirla and Rosenblatt (1961), for example, in their studies of cats showed the influence of early learning and complex mother-kitten interaction on the eventual biopsychological mother-child relationship.

That the *feeding experience* constitutes one of the basic infantile roots of social attachment is not in question. However, as both Erikson and Sullivan took great pains to emphasize, sucking and feeding activities are embedded in a complex relationship between infant and mother, involving subtle mutual adaptations to signs and signals going far beyond the oral drive and oral zone per se. The evidence points to the conclusion that the nature of the infant's bond to his mother cannot be reduced to the vicissitudes of oral drive and experience, as important as these must be.

The significance of *contact comfort* early in the life of the infant is dramatically demonstrated time and again when the crying infant quiets on being picked up and held, at first by any caretaker, but after a few months most effectively by the mother. We presume that tactile, pressure, thermal, kinesthetic, and probably olfactory receptors are all involved in the experience of being held. Harry Harlow's (1958) work dramatized the importance of tactile experience in infant macaques who apparently preferred artificial terrycloth mother surrogates to wiremesh lactating surrogates. The infant monkey used the cloth surrogate as a base for exploration and, when afraid, sought it out and clung to it. Though Harlow had reason to conclude that contact comfort was more important than feeding as an antecedent to social attachment, we must remember that under natural circumstances these two modalities are not dissociated or in competition but in fact would tend to reinforce each other in the formation of the social bond and are organized into a whole experience. Harlow's later work, in fact, demonstrated that infant monkeys reared on artificial surrogates suffered severely in their social and sexual development. In general, any inferences to humans from infrahuman species carry their risk, though the relevance of such inferences for early infantile development may be of a somewhat higher order.

As important as contact comfort and tactile stimulation must be to the primary bond, it should be noted that there appear to be significant individual differences among human infants in the degree to which close physical embrace is accepted, sought out, and enjoyed. On the basis of interviews with mothers over the first eighteen months of their infants' lives, Schaffer and Emerson (1964) studied a group of infants who could be differentiated into cuddlers and noncuddlers. The authors concluded that the noncuddlers were not primarily frustrated by maternal deprivation but rather, as a group, were innately more advanced and more active motorically, and, at the same time, they tended to resist restraint of movement including restraint consequent to close physical contact. Of course, a vicious circle may be set in motion if the mother responds to a baby who is not partial to cuddling by feeling personally rejected; the mother may then not avail herself of alternative modalities of loving her baby, a consequence that would lead to mutual privation. As therapists listening to a patient's history of contactual coldness on the part of his mother when he was a child, we should remember that individual differences in children—and not only a mother's malevolence—can contribute to a complex interactional outcome.[2]

We have noted that mothers use various forms of tactual stimulation, such as stroking, patting, rubbing, predominantly in purely playful contexts or as part of a caretaking procedure. At times the stimulation can be most sensual and seductive, producing a highly excited response in the infant, for example, when the baby's genitals and anal area are anointed with a soothing cream. However, I am not aware of any careful observational study that would indicate the fate of such stimulations (or of their absence) on later developments in the child.

I shall not consider in this presentation the tendency of the infant to literally cling to mother, (Rheingold and Keene 1965; Bowlby, 1958), nor the vicissitudes of his need for tactile stimulation (Shevrin

d Toussieng, 1965); however, tactile experiences, cravings, and ha-
bituations are obviously of prime importance in the development and
conflicts of interpersonal intimacy and not infrequently become—
overtly or covertly—burning issues in the transference-countertransference situation.[3]

Social Stimulation and Reciprocal Interaction as a Basis for Social Attachment

The thesis I wish to pursue here is that *social stimulation and
reciprocal interaction, often playful and not necessarily drive connected or tension reducing, constitute a basis for the development of
specific social attachments between the infant and others.* To trace
the beginnings of the phenomena that eventually become social it
would be of interest to report some findings in the development of the
distance receptors [4]—vision and audition—not because I believe they
are more important than the other senses but rather because they contribute specifically new knowledge concerning the early anlagen to
social development.

In contrast to what one was taught not so many years ago, the visual apparatus is apparently relatively ready to begin functioning soon
after birth. Tauber and Koffler (1966) demonstrated the optokinetic
nystagmus reaction to movement in newborns; Wolff and White
(1965) observed visual pursuit of objects with conjugate eye movements in three- to four-day-olds; Fantz (1958) described more prolonged visual fixation on more complex visual patterns as against simpler ones during the early weeks of infancy. Of course, we cannot
know the quality of the infant's subjective perceptual experience but
only the fact of a discriminating visual motor response. Only in a
loose manner of speaking may we conclude that infants "prefer" complex stimulus patterns.

The normal face was similarly "preferred" to comparable head
shapes with scrambled features in infants from one to six months
(Fantz, 1961). Spitz (1946b) had already shown that up to the third
month a baby would smile at a ferocious Halloween mask much as he
did to the human face when both were presented in full face. Spitz
(1946b) and, separately, Ahrens (1954), in a most detailed analysis,
were able to demonstrate that the infant appeared to smile in re-

21

sponse to a "sign gestalt," at first centering around the two eyes and later becoming more differentiated to include the mouth. A number of observers have also noted the development of preferential visual fixation and visual following of mother from three months onward, a phenomenon that has been understood by some (Tennes) as one of the first signs of a specific "libidinal investment" in mother as against others. Concurrently, from around age four months, there is a decrease from the peak incidence of socially indiscriminate smiling to any person and an increasing selectivity in the smiling response in favor of familiar persons, especially mother.

Wolff (1963), through careful observation and experimentation, discovered that as early as the third week in the infant's life the specifically human stimulus of a high-pitched voice elicits a smile more consistently than any other stimulus. The voice also serves to reduce the infant's fussiness as well as evoke a smile. Our own experience, as well as that of others, indicates that a most effective way of evoking a smile in an infant from the second month onward is by a social approach consisting of a smiling, nodding face with accompanying musical vocalizations and moving lips, that is, with the cumulative potency of various modalities. Of course, it may be argued that by this time the human face has become associated with other forms of gratification and thus represents a conditioned stimulus. But, as Rheingold (1961) rightly pointed out, the animated human face of itself constitutes a most fascinating visual spectacle for the infant: There is a complexity of contour, shiny moving eyes as well as a constant subtle series of expressive changes activated by the facial muscles. Despite an almost infinite potential for variation in patterning of facial expression over time, providing the elements of novelty and complexity that appear to fascinate infants (and grownups), there is an overall continuity in the facial gestalt that permits recognition and pleasureful anticipation.

These observations would point to the probability that the infant is equipped innately with the capacity for a smiling response, a capacity that is evoked by a set of key releaser stimulus configurations, such as the human face gestalt, which become effective at certain phases of development. This point of view on the smiling response does not exclude a complementary one that regards the response, once elicited, as being immediately open to various influences of learning, including conditioning and increasing emotional investment in the recognition of familiar persons. Several workers have experimentally demonstrated that one can reinforce the infant's smiling response by responding to his smile with a smile or tend to extinguish the smile by failing to respond to it. Rheingold, Gewirtz, and Ross (1959) and Weisberg (1963) similarly demonstrated that an infant's vocalizations can be markedly increased by the adult's social responsiveness in contrast to conditioning by contingent nonsocial responses, such as a doorchime.

There is, by now, a mounting volume of evidence [5] that *the crucial variables in determining the outcome of social responsiveness in the potentially healthy infant are the patterned social stimulations and responsiveness of the significant persons in the environment.* Without adequate social (including perceptual) stimulation, as for example, in blind and institutional infants, deficits develop in emotional and social relationships, in language, abstract thinking, and inner controls. Barring social traumata and deprivation, which unfortunately are not rare, nature and culture would seem to guarantee reciprocal responsiveness by the fact that healthy adults, and especially mothers, find the infant's smiles and vocalizations irresistible; they apparently must respond.[6]

It is this responsiveness—reciprocal, sensitive, sometimes imitative, familiar in pattern, but sparked with novel variation—that characterizes human relatedness increasingly from the first months onward. By six to seven months, the infant who is being enjoyed by his parents spends a good part of his day in social interactions involving mutual regard (sometimes with intense eye to eye contact), mutual smiling, and vocalizations, with or without tactile and kinesthetic stimulation, modalities combined in various forms. Many of these patterned exchanges become idiosyncratically personal, whereas others represent traditional social play, such as presemantic vocal conversations, repetitive social approach, and response with or without nuzzling, jiggling, or jouncing; postural games of lifting and lowering, "upside down" and "airplane"; and, most dramatically, the game of peek-a-boo.[7] Some of these playful sequences have begun by the third or fourth month of life and proliferate in variety in the ensuing months.

We note that each mother and infant couple seems to have its favorite form of play at a given stage of development. In some couples the baby is given maximal opportunity to actively respond and/or initiate; in others he is coerced into the position of a relatively passive recipient of stimulation, which may excite him to the point of painful distress. On the other hand, some mothers, more withdrawn or depressed, remain passive and wait disappointedly in expectation of being stimulated and entertained by their infants. Some of the variables involved in a systematic study of the patterns of reciprocity include the infant's and mother's sensitivity and activity levels, their initiatory tendencies, mother's need to dominate versus facilitate her child, the nature of her personification of her infant, her anxiety level, her fear of spoiling the child through play, and so on. These latter maternal tendencies could be studied as patterns comprising "maternal styles." A prominent feature of "maternal style" would include the mother's capacity to enjoy and respond to her infant's activity, including his developmental progressions. The maternal variables are stressed here for the moment since social reciprocity in the infant is given largely as a potentiality, not an actuality, at birth. In this sense *reciprocity must be induced,* and the earliest foundation is laid down during the first few months of life when mother responds to physiologically based needs (hunger, cold, sleep) and functions as a protector from inner and outer stimulation, as well as a provider of perceptual stimulation.

Through reciprocal playful experiences the infant comes to anticipate and learn that he can evoke a social response even when he is not hungry, cold, wet, or in pain. With this develops a sense of social potency and trust that is qualitatively different from the urgent need-tension experience in the sense that the child can produce not only relief of tension but, indeed, positively stimulating and playful patterns of response in relation to a human partner, as well as with objects.[8]

Social playfulness as a relatively autonomous dynamism has, with exceptions,[9] been neglected by psychoanalysis. Its importance for humans has precisely to do with the fact that it is somewhat apart in quality from all other forms of activity. In a sense it originally appears as purposeless [10] as far as apparent survival and security needs. At least in infancy, playfulness seems to encompass its own ends and, perhaps more than any other situation, constitutes a remarkably easy vehicle for the mutual exchange of affectionate and exuberant affects. The pleasure of primitive social play—as in music, dance, and sexual experience—would seem to be, in part, linked to a rising and falling pitch of excitement through repeated rhythmic responsive interchanges between partners.[11] There is something peculiarly unde-fended, open and sharing, disarming and exhilarating in the genu-inely playful experience. At the same time, and for these very reasons, it can constitute an embarrassment or threat for older children and adults who have had to develop excessive armoring against playful affects and activity that, after all, are not in the service of a grim real-ity principle that values mainly behavior whose ends relate to sur-vival, future gain, and the rescuing of self-esteem. Hard adult hearts can be melted by the animation of the infant's smiles, vocalizations, and eager wrigglings, which are read by the responsive adult as "Please answer me" or "Come play with me." The adult identifies, in part, with the infant's poignantly "dumb" attempts to make contact, to evoke a response and indeed, if not too dissociated or depressed, the adult is charmed into a response. When the parent is incapable of responding to the infant he is at the same time often unable to re-spond to that part of himself that yearns for contact and the evoca-tion of a response. We see in early reciprocal stimulation and re-sponse the precursors to all human communication, including eventual courtship patterns, the "invitation to the dance." Observed from the outside, reciprocal play appears to involve the utmost of focal attention and absorption of the two partners, a kind of sacred ritual on which one dare not intrude. With the emergence of social reciprocity the infant gains a new degree of human status, now being perceived as a psychological and social, as well as a physiological creature. At the same time a new kind of parental pride appears; the mother's self-esteem is validated by her feeling that she has suc-ceeded in helping her baby to become socially human. At this stage of development fathers often report that they can, for the first time, relate meaningfully to their infants and feel less excluded from the maternal-infant dyad.

Social playfulness, if it is to remain truly playful, cannot endure under conditions of social domination. For example, if the infant is overwhelmed by stimulation, he becomes distressed, and the play au-tomatically comes to an end. In this sense we can see that *mutual playfulness is a model of freedom and spontaneity in human related-ness*. If one were pressed to seek an evolutionary purpose in social play, I would suppose that it prepares the individual and group for communication, language, and collaboration and provides a means of overcoming destructiveness through playful aggression.[12]

The internalization of "good" reciprocal relationships comes to be organized, eventually, as part of "good-me" and "good-(m)other," and contributes to the sense of one's own potency and self-esteem. With the internalized confidence that one can evoke a response, the child is freed to "be alone in the presence of mother," as Winnicott (1965) put it, a phase that prepares him for separations from mother's physical presence for longer periods and without undue anxiety, thereby enabling the child to do his "own thing." However, there is evidence from Piaget's (1954) work that the six-month-old functions cognitively on a magically omnipotent level—Piaget's (1954, p. 229) stage 3, "magico-phenomenalistic causality"; that is, he associates all happenings causally to something he alone does. Of course, this omnipotent sense, to the extent it exists for the infant, must be frequently frustrated since everything he wants does not always happen. The resulting frustrations contribute to the child's sense of the realistic limits of his powers, as well as to the differentiation of his self and the other. We see cognitive evidence of this development toward the end of the first year when the infant searches for the causal agent outside of himself, for example, within the mechanism of a toy or by eliciting the help of an adult in making the toy work (Piaget's stage 5). It is remarkable how early—literally during the first days of the infant's life—parents begin to walk a delicate tightrope on the issue of the baby's omnipotence. They are torn between fostering a sense of social potency and a fear of "spoiling" the child by overly responding to him, lest they encourage a tyrannical willfulness.[13]

We can only mention here the relevance of social reciprocity, if not playfulness, to the therapeutic situation. Underlying the semantic exchanges between two persons collaborating in the therapeutic endeavor, each has his own expectation (at times a demand) of what should constitute the structure of the social interactions in therapy: Who shall begin to talk? How much? What affects and ideas shall be reciprocated? Many patients bitterly complain that psychoanalysis is artificial or unreal because it lacks a mutuality that is naturally expected when two people collaborate. The patient, especially when he may be in a partial regression in response to the analytic situation itself, will experience a *deprivation of responsiveness* from the analyst which may be variously expressed as tactile, verbal, or facial unresponsiveness or felt as a lack of sharing of intimate affects or of knowledge concerning the analyst's identity. Our point here is that even though the patient may be revealing "transference neurotic demand-ingness" or "efforts to control the therapy," the analytic situation for patient and therapist in fact constitutes a radical rupturing of patterns of responsive interaction that have had their fundamental structuring way back in infancy. And so the patient complains that the analyst is a shadowy "creep," an unfathomable stranger whom he dare not trust. How we cope with this issue in therapy is an entirely different matter.

The Special Attachment to Mother and Threats to Its Integrity

Given the particular family system that characterizes our society it is possible to demonstrate that there is an increasingly discriminating recognition of and emotional attachment to the mothering figure with whom the child develops a peculiarly intense specific relationship by the second half of the first year and throughout the second and third years, only gradually waning in intensity during the subsequent few years. Whereas in the third month the infant smiles and vocalizes with apparent pleasure to both mother and stranger, he may, at the presentation of a face mask, become apprehensive or sober. After four months he tends to respond with an immediate broad smile to mother's social approach whereas he may soberly (and sometimes apprehensively) study the face of the stranger before he warms up, and even then with a less enthusiastic and a stiffer smile. By the seventh or eighth month he may reveal clear differential responses to mother as against others in being held or soothed, in being played with or simply approached.

Toward the end of the first year and during the second year, the child develops the capacity to mentally ("internally") *represent* his mother when she is absent from the perceptual field and endows this representation with qualities of increasing permanence and objectivity. He comes to realize that mother continues to exist and may return, or not return, when she is absent. The toddler has made mere beginnings in recognizing that mother and others have feelings, wishes, and intentions that are separate and different from his own; for many of us this achievement may involve a lifetime struggle. Mother comes to be represented symbolically now, by her name or by

one of her possessions. The child can internalize and actively repro-
duce his parent's behavior and attitudes as we see in his deferred imitations and even more stable identifications which may be revealed in
his behavioral style and dramatic play (Schecter, 1968). The relative
constancy of the attachment to mother is attested to by the fact that
she usually continues to be preferred and sought after though she
may be a source of frustration, disappointment, and even cruelty.
However, the achievement of constancy is, at times, unstable, and as
we know from our work with adults, it is subject to breakdown under
stress or regression. For this reason knowledge of the stages through
which constancy of the maternal image evolves is not only of relevance developmentally but also in understanding some common
breakdowns of interpersonal relatedness that may occur at any stage
of life and, more specifically, in the therapeutic relationship.[14]

The clearest threat to the mother-child attachment is *separation*.
Whereas the younger infant may have cried in apparent protest at the
disappearance of any stimulating social partner, by seven to eight
months his protest appears to be related to a specific attachment to
one or more persons. By eleven to twelve months, the separation reaction rises to a peak of intensity. We have all seen healthy well-
functioning babies (usually of smaller families) who when they are
left by the mother even with a familiar person cry inconsolably until
the mother's return. (Importantly enough, this happens much less frequently when the infant is the one who is leaving.) It would appear
that the intensity of the child's attachment, if measured by the criterion of his protest response, correlates with (1) the tendency of the
mother to respond quickly, (2) the degree of her stimulation of the
child, and (3) the amount of interaction between them (Schaffer and
Emerson, 1964a).[15] Intensity of attachment is also heightened by illness, fatigue, fear, a strange environment, a recent separation or, following a period of increased social stimulation, for example, a doting
relative. *Habituation* to various forms of stimulation—sensory, erotic,
and social—would appear to play a greater role in determining various qualities of relatedness (including what clinicians refer to as
"stickiness") than we have previously considered. There is an analogy
here to the general syndrome of addiction, a sense of well-being at
optimal level of input or availability of response, and acute psychic
pain on withdrawal of social presence or a certain quality of stimulation. A familiar scene at a park bench is the whimpering toddler

plucking at his mother's skirt seeking to get her attention as she engages a friend in conversation; her eyes are not then available to him. Research studies that address themselves to the variables of frequency, intensity, duration, and modality of social experience in infancy may yield some etiological understanding of various outcome possibilities in character development, including tendencies toward sociability, self-reliance, clinging, or withdrawal. We do not mean to assign causal priority to mother or to child behavior since it is a clear possibility that some mothers who respond quickly or stimulate their babies a good deal may do so in part as a function of the strength of the infant's demands. Not only may infants reveal apparent individual differences in their need for social and sensory stimulation but the particular developmental schedule of achievements may free one child to entertain himself much sooner than another. I am thinking of a specific young infant whose newfound capacity to bring objects to his mouth helped free a grateful mother from the bondage of constantly carrying or entertaining her complaining baby. Concurrently, her role (for other reasons as well) shifted from one of *stimulator* to *facilitator* and *mediator* of the baby's experience. Of course, we also know of mothers who cannot control their inner need to socially dominate the child's experience even when he is capable of self-initiated manipulations and explorations of his world. Though a good deal of attention has been given to weaning from breast and bottle, there is much to be discovered about the patterns of "weaning" from the various levels and varieties of habituation in the infant-mother interaction.[16]

A second form of infantile anxiety has received much less attention in analytic theory and practice than separation anxiety; I refer here to what Benjamin (1963) has described as *infantile stranger anxiety*. Phenomenologically, the reaction to the stranger runs the spectrum of behaviors from no apparent reaction, through sobering of the face, expressions of mild apprehension or wide-eyed staring, a freezing (inhibition) of motor and expressive behavior, aversion of visual gaze, clinging, quivering of the lips, to outright terrified screaming and panic behavior. Indelibly imprinted on my memory is a young toddler who froze in an uncomfortable crouched position in the presence of strangers for twenty minutes before he began to loosen up and become mobile. Whereas Freud (1964, p. 169) and Spitz (1957, p. 54) considered this "eight-month anxiety" to be based on the same dynamic found in separation anxiety, that is, the fear of object loss, Benjamin (1963) reported some most intriguing differences. Though stranger and separation anxieties are related dynamically and correlate positively statistically, there are babies showing high separation anxiety but low stranger anxiety as well as vice versa. Stranger anxiety can occur whether or not mother is present, whereas separation reactions occur in the absence of mother, whether or not anyone else is present. Also, the average and peak times of onset were different for each type of anxiety, occurring somewhat earlier for stranger anxiety.[17] Benjamin assumed that stranger anxiety, though sharing a common root with separation anxiety (fear of object loss), had, in addition, a relatively independent source of anxiety based on the infant's *fear of the strange,* which is seen even before the anxious response to the stranger per se. For example, the two- to four-month-old may become apprehensive when confronted with strange objects or sounds or when he is handled in other than his accustomed manner. *An apprehensive response may also be aroused in the young infant by altering an anticipated gestalt pattern through the addition of unfamiliar elements or by the omission of some apparently crucial familiar element.* For example, we have noted that for some infants the visual presentation of a smiling nodding adult face without the accustomed accompanying vocalizations may evoke an apprehensive look. When vocalizations are added the infants would relax and smile giving the impression of closure of the anticipated familiar gestalt.[18] In a similar vein, humming or a falsetto voice excluding the visual presentation of the human face could produce fearful reactions which disappeared once the face was brought into view (Benjamin, 1963). We have also noted that to both the face mask and the stranger the infant may be alternately sober or apprehensive, then smiling, then apprehensive once more. He may respond with apprehension to a variety of alterations of the facial gestalt, such as the placing of pads over the eyes, the forbidding expressions of a frown with vertical (as against horizontal) forehead creasing (Spitz, 1965, pp. 88–96) or with changes in mother's appearance (new hat, glasses, or haircurlers). The expression around the adult's eyes seems to be of particular importance to the infant, which fits in with Wolff's (1963, p. 122) observation of the infant's tendency to search out the eye area and make eye to eye contact before smiling at the face presentation.[19] All these signs of increasing perceptual discriminations of alterations in the facial gestalt, including the discrimination of negative affect expressions, predate and probably constitute the precursors to the appearance of infantile stranger anxiety in Benjamin's sense.[20]

It now becomes abundantly clear how stranger anxiety is of crucial relevance to what has been considered a *third form* of infantile anxiety, namely, *the anxiety that is induced in the infant by the anxiety of the mothering one* through an as yet unknown mechanism that has been referred to as empathic linkage (Sullivan, 1953) or as contagion (Escalona, 1953, p. 46). It is our speculation that *when the mother is anxious or distressed she appears as both familiar and strange to her infant.* We know that by six or seven months the infant has come to recognize and discriminate his mother from others, as we see from the greater eagerness of his smiling response to her at this time. We assume that he has a positively endowed memory of a gestalt experience of mother, including her facial and vocal physiognomy, as well as the qualities of her touch and probably body scent. We would speculate that the child, through repeated pleasurable experiences, anticipates seeing, hearing, and feeling the familiar good mother and is shocked, baffled, and disorganized when the strange elements of her frown, tight lips, and vocal alterations are presented simultaneously with her recognizably familiar elements. It is possible that in addition to the shock of strangeness there may be a primitive neurophysiologically based affectomotor imitative reaction on the infant's part, but this latter suggestion still begs rather than supplies the necessary understanding of empathic induction of anxiety.

Some behavioral evidence for the infant's experience of the mother as both familiar and strange is seen in the appearance of the infant's *anxious smile* (Benjamin, 1963, p. 134), which is in effect a condensation of both positive and negative affect. We had the occasion to observe this reaction in an eight-month-old child who was being scolded for repeatedly activating her mechanical walker toward the television set. The observers were gripped with the importance of this new event, mainly because of the poignancy of the child's facial expression as she questioningly stared at her mother. While a tight smile hovered over her lips, her eyes appeared apprehensive and puzzled. She had frozen in her tracks, but finally moved on toward the television set once more as soon as mother's forbidding expression softened to a smile. Many parents become aware at such times of a momentous change in the previously innocent relationship, once the disapproving and forbidding modalities come into operation, especially when there is conflict and anxiety about expressing oneself in this fashion.

If it is true that the child experiences his disturbed or anxious mother as both strange and familiar at the same time, we would imagine that this would lead to inner confusion, undermining the child's capacity to trust not only his mother (and intimate others) but also his very own anticipations, perceptions, and judgment, that is, his self. As Claparede (1956) described, the experience of recognition itself contributes to a sense of "me-ness," to the sense of one's own self and its continuity. In the proper dosage, state, and stage of development, the infant can assimilate, and indeed seeks out, *novel experience*. The *strange experience* goes beyond the novel in the sense that the organism cannot at first adequately assimilate or cope with the new or conflicting elements. One might say that the infant then suffers from a disorder of recognition ("dys-recognition"), and later, a recognition of his failure to recognize, which makes it difficult for him to anticipate his future. In this partially and temporarily disorganized state he freezes (inhibition), not being able to put himself into relationship with spontaneous or trusting confidence, a state that lays the basis for later active mistrust. We assume, with Sullivan, that good and bad feeling experiences become polarized into the safe or dangerous, familiar or strange, friend or foe. One of the paradoxes of the infant's relation to mother is that she who is most familiar and capable of evoking trust and euphoria is, at the same time, associated with anxiety and mistrust. Nevertheless (and here I disagree with Sullivan) the mother has the power to neutralize certain forms of anxiety in her infant, if she is not too anxious, by familiar and now symbolically reassuring behavior, such as the playful interchange, the calm smile or embrace, or the nursing breast, each of which can have a healing reorganizing potential for the infant.

One of the mother's principal functions—besides her biologically nourishing and protective ones—is to *mediate* for and with her child the new and the strange objects, sounds, and people in the environment. We see the origins of the *magical blessing* when the mother, for example, can undo the child's fear of receiving a new toy from a stranger by simply touching and handling the toy or by offering it to the child herself. In the presence of such a scene the observer has an uncanny sensation of witnessing a ceremony of purification through the detoxification of the strange, anxiety-laden elements connected with toy and stranger. Somewhat similarly, the mother mediates relationships to strange people; she smiles and talks to the stranger and keeps him toned down vocally or at an appropriate distance. The mother can thus actually as well as symbolically remove some of the noxious elements of the stranger and gradually *help render the strange into that which is engagingly novel or even familiar*.[21]

If the mother reacts to her child's stranger or separation anxiety with anxiety and a wounded self-esteem, often because she feels she has failed in her mothering, she may be unable to mediate the infant's anxiety and unable to help in overcoming it with her protective counter-anxiety behavior. Instead, as we have seen not infrequently, she may react with disappointment and embarrassment, scold the child or even force a continued proximity to the stranger. Separation and stranger anxiety are developmental crises that could be public health issues; parents are wounded less when they know that their child's anxiety derives not only from pathogenic aspects of parenting but is a common phenomenon that may be predicated, in part, on new ego capacities, such as the development of perceptual discrimination.[22]

What has been described here in rather detached objective terms as stranger and separation anxieties constitutes the very essence out of which the later nightmares, monsters, and psychic vulnerability arise. So terrifying are the threatening strange-bad images, both real and imagined, that the child, certainly by the second year, becomes highly motivated to avoid these experiences and instead tries to evoke the good-familiar image of the parent who protects, mediates, and magically dispels threats from the outside.[23] There are thus a number of developments that coalesce toward increasing the infant's anxiety at the end of the first year: his increased vulnerability to separation and stranger anxiety; his new relationship to parents who actually forbid, scold, punish, and communicate anxiety; his probably emerging capacity to project his own hostility onto beloved persons, adding to the burden of the already ambivalent significance they have for him. Moreover, the child during his second year, with his new capacity to mentally represent ideas and affects, becomes able at the same time to elaborate through fantasy and play dramatic confrontations between himself and the good and bad witches, increasingly in the context of the family drama.[24]

Conclusion

We have suggested the central role that reciprocal social stimulation and responsiveness, especially of a playful variety, provide as a basis for human attachment. There is reason to expect that, aside from the extreme of institutionalized infants who have been studied in some detail, a vast number of infants in many societies are deprived of the quality of stimulation that we have attempted to describe here. The consequent effects on the capacity to form enduring mutual social relationships as well as on the development of learning and mastery are as yet to be adequately researched. There have been observations indicating that socially and economically deprived and disorganized parents, even though they might provide "good enough" caretaking, tend to offer their infants inadequate social and playful experience. The animated adequate social output by parents derives from the emotional surplus that we associate with well-being, and so it is likely to be the first to suffer when parents themselves—of any social class—are deprived or depleted. *I believe the propagation of defects of early development constitutes one of the widespread human crises of our time* since the relation between such defects and subsequent personal and social pathology is more than merely speculative at this point of our knowledge. An analogous physical deficiency syndrome, such as malnutrition or avitaminosis, is allowed to be perceived with greater moral consternation, largely because it is a lesser threat to the established social order in that its solution can be dealt with on a more mechanical basis.

The second theme explored in this chapter is the development and close interrelationship of the various forms of infantile anxiety, separation, stranger, and empathically induced anxieties. These anxieties threaten the primary bond itself and must be mastered sufficiently to allow subsequent individuation from the primary bond lest distorted defenses and secondary bonds become necessary to mask the failure of individuation. Once anxiety becomes a prominent experience in the infant's life, the need to avoid experiencing it, and later the related propensities to shame and guilt, become society's most effective vehicle by which its values and structure are maintained.

On the Emergence of Human Relatedness

NOTES

1. Dr. Sibylle Escalona, Director, Dr. Harvey Corman, Codirector, Albert Einstein College of Medicine of Yeshiva University. The opportunity for this study was made possible by a grant from the National Institute of Child Health and Human Development.

2. See also the work of Thomas, Chess, Birch, and M. Hertzig (1960) pertaining to the influence of individual temperamental differences in children on the parent-child relationship.

3. It is interesting to remember that during Freud's earliest days of psychotherapy he would touch the forehead of his patients; now there exist an assortment of therapies that encourage touching, holding, or embracing as primary healing agents. The introduction of touching, kissing, and kinesthetic experience into religious liturgy has been urged at the World Council of Churches Assembly in Sweden (*The New York Times*, July 24, 1968) as a means of bringing people together from a state of loneliness and alienation. I mean to make clear here that the tactile modality remains fundamental to the social bond throughout the life cycle with varying degrees of erotic valence.

4. See Walters and Parke (1965).

5. See the classic studies of Spitz (1946a, p. 113), Bowlby (1952), Goldfarb (1947), and the more recent observations of Provence and Lipton (1952), Schaffer and Emerson (1964a, 1964b), and Rheingold (1956).

6. As an observer of infants, one experiences a distinctly "unnatural" feeling —one of tension and frustration—in foregoing social play, especially when the infant focuses directly on you, expecting or even demanding a social response. Withholding of response may constitute an occupational source of tension in psychotherapists. I believe this may be a researchable hypothesis, which, however, is not meant to indicate a specific therapeutic solution.

7. See Kleeman's (1967) excellent description and analysis of this particular form of play. Kleeman did not reduce peek-a-boo to the mastery of separation anxiety or to tension reduction, but saw it also in its own right as "a form of interaction, play, a social game pleasurable to infant and adult. It represents a mutually responsive communication with a love object whose attention the infant thus gains . . ." (p. 261). He also gave a familiar example of how a seven-month-old would use the peek-a-boo game in the middle of a nursing, "as a playful stall to engage the mother" (p. 244).

8. We suggest the hypothesis that with a secondary deprivation of relatively enduring reciprocal social dynamisms, including playfulness, children and adults will appeal for a response by re-creating and communicating the urgent need tensions that have been successful in bringing about a response. Hence, hunger, pain, and later in life various expressions of anxiety, hypochondriac fears, psychosomatic conditions, acting out, and even compulsively working one's heart out can be understood, in part, as *an appeal for responsiveness that has had no alternatively stable and successful pathway.*

9. Note in this connection, Fromm, Suzuki, and de Martino (1960); Schachtel's (1959, pp. 55–68) critique of the pleasure principle; Sander (1964); Spitz (1963).

10. This idea derives from conversations with Erich Fromm.

11. Compare Freud (1961, p. 160).

12. However, the playful spirit can also constitute a threat to society since spontaneity tends to run counter to social constraint. Play is adaptively harnessed

in school years to games with rules and proscriptions that tend to match the models and values of a given society. To "play" grimly in competitive sports or in war games is generally highly valued in our society. To be playfully responsive and open, especially to the stranger, tends to be highly suspect in any society that fosters distrust of the outsider. Nevertheless, genuine play, whether with words, metaphors, ideas, sounds, or design, is the basis for culture. For an illuminating philosophic discussion of this subject see Huizinga's (1955) *Homo Ludens*.

13. In our family observations some of us have been impressed by the relationship between the parental attitudes in child-rearing and the parent's personification of the child, including the image of his child's socioeconomic, occupational, and characterological destiny. There are probably significant ethnic and class, as well as individual, differences in the variable that may be referred to as the fear of spoiling or the taboo against omnipotence, determined in part by what station in life the child is being prepared for consciously and unconsciously. I suspect that such a variable could only be studied in depth by the rather formidable combination of direct family observation and psychoanalysis of the parents.

14. The above schema is oversimplified, since in reality there is not necessarily just a single person to whom the child is attached, but often a hierarchy of preferred persons, with father or grandmother a not infrequent frontrunner beside mother. In 4 percent of Schaffer and Emerson's (1964a) cases, at seven months fathers constituted the sole "specific object of attachment," and in a majority of instances fathers were, or soon became, a joint specific object of attachment.

15. Except for the extremes these findings cannot be directly translated into what is "good" or "bad" in child-rearing. The matter is too complex.

16. Separation reactions in therapy are a common enough experience, but I believe that they are often inadequately worked through because of the intense primitive anxiety they generate in both patient and analyst. Besides the more apparent reactions to the analyst's leaving for vacation or illness, a detailed study of a week in the life of an analysand (and analyst) may reveal well-defended but profound reactions to those particular days on which there are no sessions, as well as to silences during the sessions. In the adult and, as we see more clearly during the second year of life, separation also takes on multi-determined symbolic meaning, becoming associated with feelings of abandonment, rejection, hostility, and diminishing self-esteem.

17. Compare Schaffer and Emerson's (1964a) apparently contradictory results, presumably owing to the use of different criteria.

18. The experimental observations noted here have not been systematically carried out on a significant number of infants to allow us to infer how common such reactions are.

19. Harry Stack Sullivan (1953, pp. 222–223) took special pains to discredit the understandably magical and mystical significance that most people (schizophrenics in particular) attribute to the power of the eyes, to being looked at, and, we would add, to intense eye to eye contact.

20. Wells Goodrich (1969) suggested there may be a value in considering two different kinds of stranger anxiety. One would be based on the experience of the strange gestalt before object constancy had been achieved. The second would occur after the achievement of object constancy and would appear after separation anxiety during the latter part of the first year.

21. The therapist has a similar function in fostering the patient's movement from the familiar and "embedded" (Schachtel, 1959, pp. 48–49) into new areas previously avoided owing to their association with anxious affects. In effect the

therapist is a mediator who looks with the patient into the dark areas of the strange and unknown. Somewhat as in early maternal mediation of the strange, the therapeutic alliance and investigation gradually detoxify the noxiously dissociated areas of the patient's life.

In a clinical seminar (October 1968), Dr. Otto Will beautifully described how he responds to the schizophrenic's separation and stranger fears by making himself known and familiar to the patient. He might see the patient every day and orient him as to the basic elements and continuity of the therapist's identity, for example, by reminding the patient that the therapist is still Dr. Will, even when he appears tired or is wearing a new suit.

22. The whole area of public health application of child developmental issues is fraught with great opportunity but also with dangerous pitfalls, since any apparently objective information, once dispensed, will be processed according to the individual character, problems, and distortions of each parent as well as child health worker.

23. The above considerations are obviously connected with the origins of certain varieties of religious striving. Sullivan's self-system (1953, p. 109), the antianxiety dynamism, is based on the desirability of being good-me and avoiding experiences of anxiety. This conception, as fruitful as it is in understanding the psychiatric phenomena concerned with anxiety, should not be equated with a conception of the self, whose motivations cannot be reduced to the bringing forth of tenderness or the avoidance of anxiety.

24. I have attempted to describe some of these later developments in "The Oedipus Complex: Considerations of Ego Development and Parental Interaction" (Schecter, 1968).

REFERENCES

Ahrens, Rols. "A Contribution to the Development of the Recognition of Physiognomy and Mimicry." *Zeitschrift für Experimentelle und Angewandte Psychologie* 11 (1954): 412–494, 599–633.

Balint, Michael. *Primary Love and Psychoanalytic Technique.* New York: Liveright, 1953.

Benjamin, John D. "Some Comments on Twin Research in Psychiatry." In T. T. Tourlentes, S. L. Pollack, and H. E. Himwich, eds., *Research Approaches to Psychiatric Problems.* New York: Grune & Stratton, 1962.

———. "Further Comments on Some Developmental Aspects of Anxiety." In Herbert S. Gaskill, ed., *Counterpoint.* New York: International Universities Press, 1963.

Bowlby, John. *Maternal Care and Mental Health,* 2nd ed. Monograph Series, no. 2. Geneva: World Health Organization, 1952.

———. "The Nature of the Child's Tie to His Mother." *International Journal of Psycho-Analysis* 39 (1958).

———. "Grief and Mourning in Infancy and Early Childhood." *Psychoanalytic Study of the Child* 15 (1960).

Claparede, E. "Recognition and 'Me-Ness.'" In David Rapaport, ed., *Organization and Pathology of Thought.* New York: Columbia University Press, 1956.

Escalona, Sibylle. "Emotional Development in the First Year of Life." In M. Senn, ed., *Problems of Infancy and Childhood.* New York: Josiah Macy Jr. Foundation, 1953.

Fairbairn, W. Ronald D. *Psychoanalytic Studies of the Personality.* London: Tavistock, 1952.

Fantz, Robert L. "Pattern Vision in Young Infants." *Psychological Record* 8(1958):43–47.

——. "The Origin of Form Perception." *Scientific American* 204(1961):66–72.

Freud, Sigmund. "Three Essays on the Theory of Sexuality" (1905). *Standard Edition.* Vol. 7. London: Hogarth, 1953.

——. "The Economic Problem of Masochism" (1924). *Standard Edition.* Vol. 19. London: Hogarth, 1961.

——. "Inhibitions, Symptoms and Anxiety" (1926 [1925]). *Standard Edition.* Vol. 20. London: Hogarth, 1964.

Fromm, Erich; Suzuki, D. T.; and de Martino, Richard. *Zen Buddhism and Psychoanalysis.* New York: Harper, 1960.

Goldfarb, W. "Variations in Adolescent Adjustment of Institutionally-Reared Children." *American Journal of Orthopsychiatry* 17(1947):449.

Goodrich, Wells. Personal communication.

Harlow, Harry F. "The Nature of Love." *American Psychologist* 13(1958): 675–685.

Huizinga, Johan. *A Study of the Play Element in Culture.* Boston: Beacon, 1955.

Kleeman, James A. "The Peek-a-Boo Game." *Psychoanalytic Study of the Child,* 22 (1967).

Klein, Melanie. *The Psycho-Analysis of Children.* Trans. Alis Strachey. London: Hogarth, 1937.

Piaget, Jean. *The Construction of Reality in the Child.* Trans. Margaret Cook. New York: Basic Books, 1954.

Provence, Sally; and Lipton, Rose C. *Infants in Institutions: A Comparison of Their Development with Family Reared Infants During the First Year of Life.* New York: International Universities Press, 1952.

Rheingold, Harriet L. "The Modification of Social Responsiveness in Institutional Babies." *Monographs of the Society for Research in Child Development* 21, no. 63 (1956).

——. "The Effects of Environmental Stimulation upon Social and Exploratory Behaviour in the Human Infant." In B. M. Foss, ed., *Determinants of Infant Behaviour.* Vol. 1. New York: Wiley, 1961.

——; Gewirtz J. L.; and Ross, W. H. "Social Conditioning of Vocalizations in the Infant." *Journal of Comparative Physiological Psychology* 52(1959):68–73.

——; and Keene, Geraldine C. "Transport of the Human Young." In B. M. Foss, ed., *Determinants of Infant Behaviour.* Vol. 3. New York: Wiley, 1965.

Sander, Louis W. "Adaptive Relationships in Early Mother-Child Interaction." *Journal of the American Academy of Child Psychiatry* 3(1964).

Schachtel, Ernest G. *Metamorphosis: On the Development of Affect, Perception, Attention, and Memory.* New York: Basic Books, 1959.

Schaffer, H. R.; and Emerson, Peggy E. "The Development of Social Attachments in Infancy." *Monographs of the Society for Research in Child Development* 29, 3(1964). (a)

——; and Emerson, Peggy E. "Patterns of Response to Physical Contact in Early Human Development." *Journal of Child Psychology and Psychiatry* 5(1964):1–13. (b)

Schecter, David E. "Identification and Individuation." *Journal of the American Psychoanalytic Association* 16(1968).

——. "The Oedipus Complex: Considerations of Ego Development and Parental Interaction." *Contemporary Psychoanalysis* 4(1968).

On the Emergence of Human Relatedness

Schneirla, T. C.; and Rosenblatt, J. S. "Behavioral Organization and Genesis of the Social Bond in Insects and Mammals." *American Journal of Orthopsychiatry* 31(1961).

Shevrin, Howard; and Toussieng, Povl W. "Vicissitudes of the Need for Tactile Stimulation in Instinctual Development." *Psychoanalytic Study of the Child* 20(1965).

Spitz, René A. "Hospitalism: A Follow-up Report." *Psychoanalytic Study of the Child* 2(1946a).

———. "The Smiling Response: A Contribution to the Ontogenesis of Social Relations." *Genetic Psychology* 34(1946b):57–125.

———. *No and Yes.* New York: International Universities Press, 1957.

———. "Life and the Dialogue." In Herbert S. Gaskill, ed., *Counterpoint.* New York: International Universities Press, 1963.

———. *The First Year of Life.* New York: International Universities Press, 1965.

Sullivan, Harry Stack. *The Interpersonal Theory of Psychiatry.* New York: Norton, 1953.

Suttie, Ian. *The Origins of Love and Hate.* New York: Julian Press, 1952.

Tauber, Edward; and Koffler, F. "Optomotor Response in Human Infants to Apparent Motion: Evidence of Innateness." *Science* 152(1966):382–383.

Tennes, K. Personal communication.

Thomas, A.; Chess, Stella; Birch, H.; and Hertzig, M. "A Longitudinal Study of Primary Reaction Patterns in Children." *Journal of Comprehensive Psychiatry* 1(1960).

Walters, R.; and Parke, R. "The Role of Distance Receptors in the Development of Social Responsiveness." In L. P. Lipsitt and C. C. Spiker, eds., *Advances in Child Development and Behavior.* Vol 3. New York: Academic Press, 1965.

Weisberg, Paul. "Social and Non-social Conditioning of Infant Vocalizations." *Journal of Child Development* 34(1963):377–388.

Winnicott, D. W. "The Capacity To Be Alone" (1958). In D. W. Winnicott, *The Maturational Processes and the Facilitating Environment.* New York: International Universities Press, 1965.

Wolff, Peter. "Observations on the Early Development of Smiling." In B. M. Foss, ed., *Determinants of Infant Behaviour.* Vol. 2. New York: Wiley, 1963.

———; and White, Burton L. "Visual Pursuit and Attention in Young Infants." *Journal of Child Psychiatry* 4(1965).

On Attention, Selective Inattention,

and Experience: An Inquiry into

Attention as an Attitude

Attention is a prerequisite for conscious experience; inattention limits experience. In Freud's (1953, p. 593) words: "Becoming conscious is connected with the application of a particular psychical function, that of attention." [1] Attention always is intentional in the sense of intending or being directed toward its objects whether these be things, persons, feelings, ideas, or the like.[2] But the specific manner in which it "intends" or is directed to its object varies a great deal. Attention is not always the same, nor is inattention.[3] They may occur on different occasions in the service of dealing with different situations; but they may also in the course of development gel into habitual ways of attending and not attending, normal as well as pathological. They can be described as different attitudes of attention. Usually, people automatically use different attitudes of attention for different purposes. One can observe in oneself and in others shifts from one such attitude to another and also the fact that, while one such attitude prevails, it excludes or sometimes conflicts with other attitudes. It is possible to describe the experiential quality of these attitudes themselves as well as the kind of experiences of world and self they are likely to facilitate or else to make difficult or inaccessible.

In the following I shall first deal with attention as an attitude of the mind, an attitude that I believe cannot be separated or isolated from the motive or interest in the service of which attention is used without endangering our understanding of attention. This implies that there exists a variety of attitudes of attention, attitudes in attending, and that one kind of attention is different from other kinds of attention. Second, I shall illustrate this with two examples of such different attitudes of attention. I shall designate them as isolating attention and open, integrative attention. I shall briefly describe these two types of attention, speculate on some of the interests or motives underlying them, and try to sketch in, very crudely, the different kinds of experience they lead to. Third, I shall relate these two attitudes to the development of attention and experience, contrasting early infantile attention and experience with what replaces it and what survives of it, especially on the more differentiated level of the adult mind.

I am aware that in limiting my remarks to two attitudes of attention I am omitting others, among them the important problem of the attention and selective inattention of the person whose main defense is repression. But though the relation and the differences between repression and isolation pose interesting problems concerning attitudes of attention, the discussion of these problems would go beyond the scope of this chapter.

Attention as an Attitude of Mind

William James (1931, p. 402), with his great gift for keen observation and telling expression, has circumscribed in one sentence the whole area in which the problems I want to talk about are located: "My experience is what I agree to attend to." This concise formulation can and has to be understood on more than one level. Not only is such agreement not always voluntary but also very often we think that we agree to attend to something but when it comes right down to it we do not attend or we attend in a very limited, perhaps biased way, to this or that aspect of the object of our attention but not to others. James's "agreement to attend" to something, this precondition for what we call conscious experience, covers a wide range of phenomena. Experience depends not only on agreeing to attend but also on the quality of such attending, not only on that one attends but also on how one attends. The variety of qualities of different acts of attention becomes apparent when we raise the questions: Attention to what? For what motive, purpose, intention? With what or which of our various sensory, intellectual, emotional capacities and sensibilities for attending? How intensely, relaxedly, fleetingly? The list of such questions could be extended and refined further.

The answers to these questions are not independent from one another. The question as to what I am attending concerns not only the object of attention but also what aspect of the object I am attending to. Both the choice of object and the emphasis on a particular aspect to which, or perspective from which, I am attending to the object depend on the intentionality of the act of attending. The intensity and type of interest in the service of which attention is used will decisively affect the quality of attention. Similarly, the questions as to which capacities and sensibilities are employed in the act of attending, to what degree, in what proportions, and in what structural constellation will depend partly on the current interest and motivation underlying the act of attention, partly on personally characteristic, habitual attitudes of attending. These, in turn, may be determined by more enduring structures of motivation. They may also be determined by innate dispositions toward certain attitudes of attention.

The concept of a variety of attitudes of attention is related to, but not identical with, the concept of different ways of deployment of attention or, in the language of psychoanalytic ego psychology, deployment of attention cathexes. Though this—and especially the latter term—suggests that the same amount of energy (hypercathexis) may be deployed in different ways by different people or by the same person at different times, the concept of attitude suggests qualitative differences in different attitudes of attending. Such attitudes are either temporary or more lasting mental structures. If more lasting, that is, if individually characteristic, habitual ways of attending, they can be subsumed under Goldstein's (1939, pp. 340–366) concept of preferred behavior. George S. Klein's concept of "cognitive controls" described by Gardner and associates would be an example of a more enduring type of such structures.[4] The question whether the qualitative differences between such structures can be reduced to quantitative differences in the deployment of attention cathexes and countercathexes I leave to others to decide. The answer to this question is not necessary for the purposes of this essay, and I doubt whether the question itself is a promising one for our understanding of mental functioning, at least insofar as such understanding concerns the different ways of experiencing of different persons, their reactions to such experience, and the psychotherapeutic endeavor to help them to resolve or cope with the difficulties arising from their experience and their reaction to it.

I have mentioned elsewhere [5] that acts of focal attention exclude the not attended parts of the field from focal awareness. This fact, of course, has always been well known. Freud (1957, p. 167) refers to it when he writes that "at any given moment consciousness includes only a small content." This is obvious in terms of the objects of attention. When I pay attention to the table on which I write, I cannot at the same time pay attention to the picture hanging on the wall. But even when two or more objects are in my field of vision I can pay focal attention to only one of them at any one moment of time.[6] The same applies to focal attention to ideas.

But when we turn from the object of attention to the attitude of attending, the exclusion phenomenon characteristic of focal attention takes on a different, less obvious, more complex, more far-reaching, and more comprehensive significance. This change in viewpoint opens up two significant areas. One concerns the rigidity as opposed to the flexibility of attitudes of attending, the rigid maintenance of one attitude of attention as contrasted with the capacity to shift, flexibly, from one kind of attitude to another. The latter can be a matter of employing the kind of attention most suitable to a given task or purpose. But it can also be a matter of the oscillation of different types of attention over quite short periods of time while attending to the same object.[7]

The other area that comes into view when we study the exclusion phenomenon as it takes place in different attitudes of attention concerns the general problem of coexistance of different attitudes; of predominance of one attitude over another; of shifts of attitude and concomitant shifts in predominance; of suppression or repression of one attitude in favor of another. Neurologically, these problems are probably linked to the fact that in any directed, coordinated act the inhibiting functions of the nervous system are at least as important as the activating ones. Psychologically, I believe that there is a continuum rather than abrupt differences between the ways in which the predominance of one attitude over others is achieved in the functioning of man. This continuum may extend from such phenomena as, for example, the automatic and ubiquitous neglect (exclusion by not taking seriously) of all the sensory data that would interfere with object constancy, a neglect that is vital for man's perceptual orientation in his environment, to the repression of strivings and attitudes incompatible with the particular adaptation or maladaptation of a person to his interpersonal environment.[8] Parts of this continuum are primarily known to us from attitudes other than attention. To indicate part of the range of these phenomena I want to mention the conscious exclusion of certain attitudes and behavior in interpersonal relations and the gradual transition from conscious exclusion to the temporary repression of such attitudes in certain social situations. Some of the examples of forgetting given by Freud in "The Psychopathology of Everyday Life" have to be understood as the temporary repression of an attitude owing to the experienced pressure of the conventional requirements of a social situation and the anxiety connected with the possibility that the repressed attitude might become apparent. Conscious exclusion (suppression) of an undesirable attitude and its temporary repression are two end points of a continuum. This continuum extends from a free judgment that an attitude is undesirable or inappropriate, over a feeling that it would be impossible to say or do such and such in a given situation, to actual temporary repression.

Two Attitudes of Attention:
Isolating and Open Attention

I want to illustrate what I have said about the variety of attitudes of attention with two examples: the attention of the isolator (isolating attention) and a contrasting attitude, that of attention open toward its object. One of the data concerning attention and discussed in the literature is the difference between a broad and a narrow deployment of attention. This distinction refers to the size of the field (external or internal) or the number of objects or parts or aspects of an object covered by the beam of attention. The individually typical broad or narrow extension of attention deployment has been conceptualized by Gardner and his coworkers (1959, p. 47) as the scanning control principle. The difference between extensive and narrow deployment of attention seems to be a primarily quantitative one, a difference between the ranges covered by attention. One of the findings of Gardner et al. (1959, pp. 46–47, 136) was that "extreme isolators tend to be broad scanners" but that on the other hand not all broad scanners are isolators. The word "isolator" is used in the sense of Freud's concept of isolation as the characteristic defense of the obsessive-compulsive. In order to understand the meaning of this finding it is useful to consider the typical attitude of attention in the broad scanning characteristic of the obsessive-compulsive, the experiential quality of this kind of attention. Freud noted how difficult it is for the obsessional person to free associate. He wrote (Freud, 1964, p. 121) about the obsessional: "While he is engaged in thinking, his ego has to keep off too much—the intrusion of unconscious phantasies and the manifestation of ambivalent trends. *It must not relax, but is constantly prepared for a struggle" in Kampfbereitschaft).*[9] The obsessive personality tends to be constantly on his toes, hyperalert, always watching out for something. The battle he has to be prepared for at all times is not only a battle against his own thoughts and feelings but a battle on two fronts: the other person, the environment, is one; his own person is the other. In relation to others he has to be ready to avoid any danger from the world outside and to parry, like a fencer in a duel, any possible attack from others and to detect any fault or mistake in them; but he must be equally or even more on the alert and watchful about himself, about any fault or mistake in himself, about what he says or does or is, or hopes or fears he is. On a conscious or semiconscious level, the dangers he fears are dangers seen from the perspective of his pessimism and distrust; the attacks he fears often have to do with blame and rejection; he is preoccupied with potential blame, self-justification and fault-finding, fault in others and in himself. He is hypercritical of others and of himself. His attention has the quality of vigilant attention, vigilant toward both the environment and himself. In both directions it is the opposite of an attention open and receptive toward its objects.[10]

The underlying reason for the tensely vigilant quality of the obsessive's attention is that he lives in a world pervaded by a sense of uncertain danger and risk. In some this sense of precariousness is more or less conscious; in others it is more covert. Though it always, of course, has its roots in the interpersonal sphere, some experience it mainly there, whereas others manage to isolate it from its source and experience it primarily in relation to the world in general, to daily routines, to things, to technicalities of their work, and in such well-known phenomena as excessive preoccupation with orderliness, exactness, and the like. But even where it is consciously related to people, it is often isolated from its real source and experienced mostly with regard to minute questions of etiquette and similar details of behavior, both in the other person and the self. The real source of the uncertainty, precariousness, and doubt in the obsessive-compulsive's life, as Angyal (1965, pp. 156–189) pointed out, is to be found in his pervasive confusion whether the other person and the world in general are friendly or hostile, accepting and approving or rejecting and blaming. This doubt originates usually in relation to a parent whose behavior is such as to make it difficult or impossible for the young child to experience any understandable and reliable pattern of acceptance or rejection, hence interfering with the development of trust and reasonable certainty. And it makes it equally impossible for him to know whether he is good (lovable) or bad (unlovable). This, in turn, leads to increased self-doubt and self-rejection because his resulting distrust, resentment, and anger "prove" that probably he is bad. Though it is true that the obsessive has isolated the strong affects connected with the painful experiences of the described uncertainties and fears about the other and himself, this does not mean that he is without affect. Indeed, his preparedness for battle, described by Freud, and his extreme vigilance are characterized by intense affect. His readiness to fight about logical points and his search for the right rules are intensely emotional. If he has been described as lacking in emotion, this is probably owing to the fact that the things about which the obsessive person gets upset or which are of such great importance to him seem insignificant, absurd, or puzzling to the observer, who is much more impressed with the obsessive's cold and unemotional attitude to what to most people are the important human events and feelings. These the obsessional cannot face and hence has to neutralize by the defense of isolation. Often, the unconscious meaning of being "right" about what seems to others an unimportant detail or issue is to him that he is and has to be irreproachable, so that he be spared the painful and repressed possibility of feeling unacceptable.

I mention these aspects of the obsessive's world not only because of their dynamic relevance but also because they account for another aspect of his attitude in attending: the narrow and sharp focus of his attention. This may seem at first glance a contradiction to his broad scanning. One might think that the obsessive preoccupation with minutiae of living or with minute technical details, in other words the pedantic quality in the obsessive approach to life and his concern with remote or minor "dangers," would exclude a broad sweep of attention. It is, indeed, this pedantic quality, the obsession with the smallest details, with orderliness, punctuality, ritual, exactness, that has struck most clinical observers.[11]

In research conducted at the Menninger Foundation Schlesinger

(1954), following Freud's ideas about the defense of isolation and its relation to concentration, assumed that the isolator is an extreme focuser and that in such extreme focusing awareness is narrowed and irrelevancies are shut out of experience. Later Gardner et al. (1959, p. 47) found that "the focuser is broadly aware of many aspects of the stimulus field because he is constantly scanning the field." The seeming contradiction is resolved, I believe, as soon as we realize that the isolator, the obsessive, does his broad scanning with a narrow focus.[12] He does not take in the overall scene, nor the global quality of a particular object, but his attention searches a relatively wide area with a narrow and intense focus, looking for danger and cautionary cues, for mistakes and the like, similar to a searchlight with a narrow and strong beam that scans the environment, not to make visible its quality but, for example, to discover enemy soldiers hidden in it.[13]

Thus, we can understand the unconscious intentionality of the combination of broad scanning with a narrow, intense focus characteristic of the isolator who can rarely look at something but is usually constrained to look for something, because he feels endangered in so many situations in life. But, as we have heard, not all scanners, not all people who scan broadly, are isolators. This raises the question of the quality and attitude of attention in the nonisolating scanner. Probably there is a variety of such attitudes. I want to briefly describe one that is characterized by openness toward the world and the objects of attention.

If we want really to know the quality of an object, whether it be a person, a work of art, a tree, a landscape, an animal or a large object such as a region, a society or culture we must be able not to look for something, not to look from the perspectives of our preconceptions and biases but to be as openly receptive with all our sensibilities as possible. I doubt that anyone can do this completely because we are all inevitably caught in the perspectives of our time, culture, and personality. But we can approximate such openness toward the object. This open attention does not concentrate on any one aspect but scans all aspects of the object; it does not scan with a narrow and intense but a wide focus and with a relaxed rather than tense and warding off concentration.[14] Such scanning is in the service of a global perception, of global knowing, rather than in the service of wanting to know this or that about the object. I want in no way to minimize the importance of knowing about the objects of this world, which is a fundamental task of science. Indeed, a long immersion and interest in such knowing about the object is the precondition of knowing the object. It distinguishes the global knowledge of the adult from the global experience of the infant. It is globality on a highly differentiated level of experience.

The motive underlying such open attention does not have any particular, partial purpose; it is the wish to relate to the object, to know it as it is, out of interest in the object. There are many different kinds of interest, but the type of interest I am describing here does not want to use the object but to experience it, to know it fully by relating to it. I shall call it "allocentric interest." [15] I believe that the attitude inherent in such interest is akin to the attitude of love, of a love that accepts and affirms the object as it is and does not want to use it for any partial purpose. Such interest always implies respect for the integrity of the object as it is.[16]

I am describing here an idealtypus of attention, in Max Weber's sense, that is to say, a model or construct that empirical men may approach at times, but obviously cannot and do not want to maintain in all their pursuits and, even when they do relate to somebody or something in this way, usually can only approximate. However, this fact does not diminish the great importance for man's development of this attitude and of this kind of attention and interest. It underlies such words as "philosophy" and "philology," the love of wisdom and the love of words. Though these words are still current, their meaning is almost lost or in most scientific thought is frowned on, rejected, or dismissed with a condescending shrug at its supposed irrelevance.

Such open attention implies that whatever details are taken in they do not distract from or obscure the global quality of the object, be it a person, human face, plant, or landscape. Also, though such attention concentrates on its object it does not isolate it from the rest of the world; it sees implicitly in one person all of mankind, in one tree or animal or crystal all of nature. As William Blake says,

> To see a World in a grain of sand
> And a Heaven in a wild flower
> Hold Infinity in the palm of your hand
> And Eternity in an hour.

Open attention is objective, object-centered, but not neutral in the sense of indifference. Indeed it is possible only if the whole person with all his sensibilities and thought is open toward the object in the act of attention. This implies that he is open also toward himself, non-repressive, since otherwise he cannot attend fully.

Goethe (1853, vol. 3, p. 189) expressed the difference between an intellect looking for faults and an intellect combined with what I would call allocentric interest: "Ill-will and hatred restrict the observer to the surface even though they be joined by discernment. But discernment allied with benevolence and love will penetrate world and man; indeed it may hope to arrive at the sublime."

The capacity for open, allocentric attention and interest is of particular importance for the task of the psychotherapist and psychoanalyst and for their relation to the people they try to help. Indeed, it is related to a well-known, specific topic in psychoanalysis, namely, Freud's recommendation regarding the analyst's attitude in listening to the patient. Freud (1958b, p. 111) urged not to try to remember anything in particular or especially but to listen to everything with the same evenly suspended attention (*gleichschwebende Aufmerksamkeit*). For most people, at least in my limited experience with myself and those I have supervised, this is not an easy task. Many listen with their theoretical and diagnostic preoccupations or with their plan of treatment in mind and overlook what may differ from these. Or they listen with their countertransferential notions about what the patient ought to be like to suit their ideas of the most desirable adaptation to society or their ideal of what man should be like. They may feel exasperation if the patient is not at all like that, or impatience if he does not seem to want to be like that or not be in a hurry to change. Or they watch, like a detective, to jump at the patient's faults, that is, at where he deviates from the analyst's preconceptions. And so forth. All this, of course, is apt to get into the way of open attention, of evenly suspended attention that wants to see the other person as he really is. I do not believe that such evenly suspended attention has to be neutral or the analyst like an impersonal mirror. Rather, I believe that with it go and should go acceptance of and respect for the patient as he is, attitudes that are an integral part of genuine interest in and open attention to the patient and to any other object of such attention.

Development and Attention

If isolating attention becomes the predominant attitude of attending rather than being used flexibly, only where it is appropriate for the specific purpose and situation, it will have a severely limiting and repressive effect on the person's experience, in addition to its being a constant strain on the isolator. Exactly what is being shut out from experience by the isolating attitude, by its vigilant scanning with a narrow and onesided focus, will become more apparent if we consider this attitude in relation to the normal development of human awareness and experience from early infancy to adulthood. I shall limit myself to a few salient aspects of this development.

Our notions of the mental state and the experiences of the newborn and the infant are inevitably quite speculative. They become somewhat less so the more they move away from the earliest into later infancy and early childhood. But, as I have pointed out in another context,[17] the radical change in the modes of experience from infancy and childhood to adulthood makes it impossible to remember more than at best a few fragments from the earliest period of our lives. Nevertheless, systematic infant and child observations carried out in the last thirty or forty years have furnished some clues for speculation; current work, no doubt, will provide many more.

I want to start out with a basic assumption that, I think, has validity for all developmental phenomena in plant and animal life. This assumption is that the seed and the fertilized egg carry in them all the potentialities for the unfolding of the basic qualities, functions, capacities, and organization of the plant or the living creature and that we cannot assume that any basic human capacity is not present in its Anlage, that is to say, as a potential in the fertilized human egg. This would include, among others, the capacities for attention, sensing, perceiving, feeling, and thought. It would exclude the notion that attention and thought are superimposed, drafted on as it were by the requirements of reality on a creature striving only for nondirectional tension discharge. This does not, of course, negate the fact that some of these functions have a different timetable of development and maturation than others, nor that the social environment has a large impact on the way in which these capacities develop and are used. It would only imply that their precursors, or Anlagen, are already present in the embryo and at birth. Nor does it mean that from the perspective of the theory of evolution (rather than ontogenesis) the high development in man of thought and of those aspects of attention, perception, and differentiated feeling that are specifically human and closely related to his capacity of thinking may not have occurred because it enabled him to adapt in a much more flexible, inventive, and open way to a great variety of environments than even the primates, his nearest relatives.

Development proceeds in increasing differentiation and reintegration on the new levels of differentiation. In adult man, we find a great variety of degrees and qualities of differentiation and of more or less successful reintegrations. Attention undergoes a radical change in this process of differentiation, and in adult man we find preferred attitudes of attending and not attending, which are integrated more or less successfully in his total personality structure and which serve more or less adequately the functions of flexible attention to the environment and to the self.

The words "attention" and "attend" derive from the Latin "attendere," which means literally "to stretch to," hence to direct one's mind or energies to something. Thus, they imply direction, a directed function. In the newborn we find not yet consciously directed activity. I have described elsewhere focal attention as actively directed attention that is a relatively late development, whereas attention aroused by the impinging environment or by internal sensations appears earlier. Perhaps, in speculating on the newborn's dawning consciousness we should speak of a precursor of attention rather than of attention proper. How should we imagine this precursor of attention, this earliest mode of experience? And what is its relation to the other mental functions of that stage? I think there is today fairly wide agreement, especially in the psychoanalytic literature, that in early infantile experience there is no subject-object distinction and that no distinct and fixed differences between different objects of the environment exist for the young infant.[18]

I need not go into the many reasons and observations that support this assumption. But if we take it seriously, it makes no more sense to say that the newborn and infant have only inner sensations than to speak of their perceiving something in the outer world. The newborn must have some kind of awareness of sensations, and not only of those arising from internal stimuli, such as hunger, but also from external ones, such as light, noise, movement, cold and warmth, tactile stimuli, and so on. Otherwise he could not respond to them as he does during his relatively brief periods of awakeness, for example, by turning toward or away from impinging stimuli and by responding with distress or signs of comfort or attraction to them.[19] Just as there is no "without" for the newborn and young infant so there is no "within"; the experience of the newborn is not differentiated as to the origin of whatever sensations he feels. The young infant's experience probably is best characterized as consisting of "vital sensations," a term coined by Werner (1948, p. 96), who describes them as "devoid of objectivity . . . , psychophysically undifferentiated and [involving] pervasive bodily reactions to the stimuli." [20] Sullivan (1953, p. 252) described these earliest experiences as consisting of "instantaneous records of total situations." This description emphasizes the comprehensiveness and globality of the experience, an undifferentiated globality in which, however, occurs a fusion of a great many elements which have not been perceived separately but, all together, have resulted in the vital sensation.

What are the elements that enter into these vital sensations, this fused, global experience that occurs in the vital sensation? In Freud's model, earliest experience is governed exclusively by the pleasure-unpleasure principle, is lacking in sensory quality, and consists of the attempt to abolish all excitation caused by internal drive needs and external, impinging stimuli. But though the infant's tendency to abolish excitation and return to a state of quasi-intrauterine embeddedness is very apparent once one agrees to pay attention to it and though it is the predominant aspect, it is not the only aspect of his experience and behavior. That the unpleasure principle could monopolize for a long period the psychoanalytic view of the earliest developmental phase may be owing to several factors. One is the great explanatory power of this discovery for the infant's behavior. That it does have this power is owing, in turn, to the fact that the sudden transition from intra- to extrauterine life does confront the young and helpless organism with a sudden and tremendous task of readaptation which, outside of sleep, inevitably creates more occasions of distress than of comfort or pleasure. Another factor may be that it requires careful and sustained, direct observation to notice the first, fleeting appearances of positive pleasure, that is, of the attempt to prolong rather than abolish certain types of stimulation, and the first flickerings of what looks like a precursor of the effect of interest. The fact that discomfort and unpleasure often prevail during the first weeks or months does not mean that the infantile organism is not already equipped with and beginning to use an Anlage that, in healthy development, will turn it increasingly toward rather than away from its environment, provided that the human environment is welcoming, affirmative, and in a position to provide the necessary care.

This view, which I have developed in more detail elsewhere, in part parallels that of post-Freudian psychoanalytic ego psychology whose proponents assume that the ego is not just a later offshoot of the id but that it develops together with the id from a common, undifferentiated matrix. It differs from ego psychology in that it does not share the libido theory nor the drive reduction theory as the mainsprings of human behavior. Similarly, some theoreticians interested especially in ego psychology have recently made the attempt to dispense altogether with the economic aspects of Freud's theory and to eliminate the concepts of force and energy and thus implicitly the drive reduction model.[21]

The exclusive sway of the pleasure-unpleasure principle in Freud's model of the earliest stage of infantile development is conceived by him as excluding sensory quality. According to him (Freud, 1958a, p. 220), only with the advent of the reality principle is consciousness attached to those sense organs that are directed toward the external world while in the preceding stage only the qualities of pleasure and unpleasure were of interest to consciousness. I seriously doubt this. Instead I am inclined to assume that the vital sensations of the early infantile period, though not differentiating between the pleasure-unpleasure feeling, on the one hand, and sensory quality, on the other hand, differ in total quality not only along the pleasure-unpleasure gradient but also in their total, fused quality depending on the particular sensory stimulus that causes them. Though this sensory quality probably is not experienced as separate and distinct, it must affect the total quality of the vital sensation. The great physiological difference between, say, pangs of hunger and exposure of the skin to a cold draft makes it very unlikely that they are experienced as the same kind of unpleasure. To be sure, they are both unpleasant, but in very different ways. Though the infant does not discriminate between them in the sense of any notion of what they are, the vital sensations caused by hunger or by cold are unlikely to be of the same total quality. Also, the vital sensation caused by a cold draft on the baby's skin is likely to feel different from that caused by a scratchy blanket or from seeing a striking contrast of dark and light. It would seem to me that pleasure and unpleasure are already abstractions from the fused totality of vital sensations into which different sensory experiences also enter, not as separate entities but as contributing to the fused quality of the total experience. The fact that the infant has no concepts or words for these feelings and does not know what causes them does not imply that they may not feel differently to him. It seems more likely to me that there is considerable variety of vital sensations, a qualitatively different variety of feelings of comfort and discomfort in addition to the quantitatively different degrees of comfort and discomfort, pleasure and unpleasure.

Werner described the syncretic quality of vital sensations and spoke of the synesthetic level of this kind of experience and of a "sensorium commune," an undifferentiated sense, as the primitive basis for the development of the specific phenomena of sense. But this does not mean that there are not qualitative differences between even such syncretic, vital sensations. In Werner's (1948, p. 97) words, it only means that "vital sensations occasioned by stimuli directed to the different senses are . . . more closely related to each other than are the objective perceptions caused by these stimuli." Also, certain senses are more likely than others to lead to synesthetic sensations. Thus, taste and smell are usually experienced synesthetically also by adults. The synesthetic experience of taste and smell is a good example in adult sensory experience of the fusion not only of two sensory modalities (three, if the tactile sensations caused by the texture of food are included) but also of the fusion of sensory quality and pleasure or unpleasure. Though this experience is likely to be more differentiated than the infant's it can perhaps serve as an experiential example of something analogous to and not too remote from it, though more limited and circumscribed.

Thus, in addition to the subject-object fusion (or, more precisely, the absence of any subject-object distinction) and the tendency toward synesthetic, sensory experience, the vital sensations are also characterized by the fusion of sensory quality and pleasure or unpleasure feeling. This fusion is characteristic of what I have called (Schachtel, 1959, pp. 81–165) the autocentric mode of perception, which predominates during the early phases of development, as contrasted with the later, predominantly allocentric, mode of perception. In other words, though we are wont to distinguish between what we see or hear and how we feel about it, whether we find it pleasant or unpleasant, in the vital sensations sensory quality and pleasure-unpleasure feelings tend to be inseparably fused, as they still are often in the autocentric (so-called lower) senses in the adult, for example, in taste, smell, or physical pain.

The vital sensations constitute felt experiences of the infant, probably the predominant mode of his early experience. His awareness, in the at first relatively short periods of awakeness, may be described as a fluctuating sequence of such experiences. What, later, is distinguished as one's feeling about what one perceives or experiences is at this stage an integral and indistinguishable part of the total sensation. It is fused with sensation and hence closely tied to the sensory and comfort-discomfort sphere.

A mode of experience characterized by the prevalence of vital sensations is by no means chaotic, since each vital sensation is structured by its predominant feeling (sensation) quality. William James's (1931) notion that the infant's mind shows a "blooming, buzzing confusion" is owing to an adultomorph perspective. Confusion can exist only where there is experience and awareness of a multitude of objects, ideas, perceptions, and so on. It is the polar opposite of an ordered universe of the mind with a more or less coherent and structured organization of a great many data of experience. Confusion cannot exist where there is not a great variety of objects and data available to the mind. The early infantile mind does not have the kind of differentiated perception or a corresponding organization of memory which is the condition for the multitude of distinct data that can lead to confusion.[22]

Can we speak of attention at all in this earliest stage of development? If the vital sensations are the prototype of experience at this stage, it seems more appropriate to say that consciousness is in the grip of, or dominated by, the vital sensations than that it attends to them in the sense of directed attention. We might speak of passive attention. However, during those brief periods of awakeness in which the infant is relatively free from need tensions and discomfort we can observe—in some infants already on the first day of life, in most during the first month—that they gaze at something for some time. To be sure, they do not "decide" to look at something; their gaze is caught by something. But, already during the first weeks of life, they do show clearly that some visual aspects of the environment seem to be more interesting to them than others. They show this by prolonged gazing. Attention gripped passively seems to change, on these occasions, into attention sustained.[23] It is likely that such gazing can be

55

described also as a vital sensation. But it lacks the peremptory quality of those vital sensations in which the unpleasure-discomfort quality is predominant. Perhaps these brief tension-free periods of awakeness, thanks to the absence of peremptory pressures of discomfort, pain, and need tension, permit a shift from the strong predominance of the comfort-discomfort range in the vital sensations to an increased significance of sensory quality.

The comprehensive and undifferentiated globality of earliest experience is superseded by increasing differentiation. This differentiation takes place both in the child's experience of the external world and in the increasing differentiation of needs, thought, perception, and feeling. In the external world this development enables man to see and explore an enormous variety of objects. But it also leads to a remarkable differentiation of needs, modes of thought, modes of action, varieties and tones of feeling, modes of perceiving and of attending. A great many of these differentiations can be described as different attitudes within the areas of needs and impulses, thinking, acting, feeling, attending. This differentiation would indeed lead to chaos and confusion if it were not accompanied by reintegration on the new, more highly differentiated levels. Such integration is as necessary for the increasingly differentiated inner needs, capacities, and functions as it is for the meaningful perception and comprehension of the increasingly differentiated environment, the external world. The individual varieties of such more or less integrated functioning and of the resulting personal experience of the environing world—the individual *Umwelt*—interlock with and are inseparable from each other. The personal quality of each individual's world, long known to poets and writers, became the object of systematic thought and investigation in the work of such biologists as Jakob von Uexküll (1949; von Uexküll and Kriszat, 1956) and, later, in the detailed descriptions, inspired by phenomenological thought, of the *Umwelten*, the worlds characteristic of various types of mental pathology as represented by individual cases.[24]

Jung, (1933, p. 547) in his typology, emphasized the importance of the predominance of certain functions. He distinguished the functions of thought, intuition, sensation, and feeling, and he asserted that it is always only one of these functions with which man orients himself in and adapts to reality.[25] I do not agree with some of what he said or implied about the quality and functioning, and especially about the strict separation of these functions. But he had the significant insight that the relative importance and use of different functions in different people plays a decisive role in their approach to and view of the world, even if we may disagree with his selection, definition, and view of the mutual relations of the four functions singled out by him. They are forerunners of the already mentioned concepts of cognitive style and cognitive control, concepts more rigorously defined and with what seems to me a sounder empirical and theoretical basis. I believe that the concepts of cognitive style and cognitive control and the concept of habitual attitudes of attention are relevant for the constitution and structure of personal experience and *Umwelt*.

Though these implications are not mentioned in the experimental work of Gardner and his associates, (1959, 1960) they are implicit in Shapiro's (1965) concept and description of neurotic styles. Each attitude of attention, each cognitive style, each neurotic style, just as each mood, affects and structures the personal *Umwelt*, temporarily while it prevails or more lastingly if it is a more enduringly prevalent attitude or style.

The development of focal attention leads to a radical change in the nature of awareness and consciousness. The most striking change, of course, is the emergence of what we usually call reality, that is to say, the world of a great variety of different objects, perceived as existing independently and separate from the perceiver and also separate and different from one another. This changed world corresponds to the changed function and quality of attention. It is the most impressive phenomenon connected with this change, so impressive that often we are inclined to think of attention only as attention to the phenomena of the environment, its countless objects, the people in it, what they do and say, and so forth. The frequent injunction to pay attention usually means to pay attention to something specific in the environment. Even Freud, who did more than anybody else to draw our attention to what goes on within ourselves, was inclined to think of attention as purely related to the exploration of the external world. Thus, he wrote (1957, p. 220): "A special function was instituted [in the course of development] which had periodically to search the external world in order that its data might be familiar already if an urgent internal need should arise—the function of *attention*." [26] Such a view of attention seems at first glance natural since adaptation to the external world is the main task of man, as of any organism. But such adaptation is always adaptation of the person to the world and, furthermore, not just to single objects in the world but to the world, the *Umwelt* as a whole. Hence, both the relation of oneself to the world and the meaning and relations of any particular object within the context of the total environment are highly significant objects of attention, too, the neglect of which can exact a high price in maladaptation and damage. Different attitudes in attending differ especially with regard to how they meet or neglect any of these tasks. If any one of these attitudes more or less monopolizes the individually characteristic forms of attention, this is likely to be a significant factor in and symptom of either maladaptation and dysfunction or of other restrictions of awareness.

The developmental process of differentiation and reintegration extends in man over a long period of time and, in degrees varying in different people, may continue even after man has reached chronological and biological adulthood. What was inseparably fused in the newborn's and young infant's mind becomes increasingly differentiated, separated and distinct. This involves a great expansion of awareness but also some loss because some of the elements entering into the early instantaneous records of total situations may be lost when attention becomes more focused, just as any global impression usually is in some respects richer (in others poorer) than even the most thoughtful account we can render of it in the distinct categories at our disposal in language and articulate thought. Language is the most important factor in this development. Words and the concepts represented by words enrich and make possible differentiated perception and thought. But their labeling function also restricts their meaning and tends to isolate the object to which a word refers from its context. However, words can have not only a labeling but also an evocative function, especially as they are used in poetry. This evocative function refers to the global sphere and its inexhaustible content. Thus, too great emphasis on the labeling function of words may lead to a loss or impoverishment of the richness of experience. Other elements of the early total, vital sensations may suffer the fate of repression if they cannot be integrated in the development and adaptation of the infant and child.

Two factors play a particularly significant role in replacing, during the course of development, the earlier, primitive forms of global experience of total situations. They are the free play of attention and the mature capacity for global attention and perception. The free play of attention [27] is a decisive factor in the ability to become aware of the many different aspects of each object and of its relations to other objects and to oneself; it is a prerequisite for the integration of these many aspects in the total perception of the object and of its relations to other objects and to oneself in one's grasp of a total context.

The development of focal attention not only permits the perception of distinct objects but also changes the quality of global perception and experience. The primitive globality of the infant's experience is different from the adult's global perceptions which presuppose a long process of differentiation and reintegration and show both differentiation and globality. One among many possible illustrations of what I mean is the development of the perception of the human face. The global experience, say, of a one-week-old infant being held by his mother, from all we know, does not include a perception of the mother's face, though the infant usually gazes at it while nursing. Rather, his global experience of this situation may be the comfortable (or uncomfortable) total feeling of being held while nursing into which a great many sensory data enter without, of course, being distinguished or noticed, separately, by the infant. When, usually from the third month on, though often much earlier, the infant responds with a smile specifically to the human face, it does not matter whether it is the face of the mother or of a stranger or even a piece of cardboard cut in the shape of a human face. Nor does it matter what the expression of the face is like: It can be terrifying or friendly, it can be an immobile Halloween mask or the mobile human face; to all of these the infant is likely to respond with a smile (Spitz, 1946, esp. pp. 77–87). This means that only the overall shape and the grossest features of the face, regardless of its expression, are perceived by the infant and evoke the smile. If we jump from here to adult perception of and reaction to the human face we find, of course, that the adult's perception takes in many more distinct features of the human face than the infant's and that, in particular, the expression of the human face is a decisive factor in the perceiver's reaction to it. However, many, probably most, people would find it hard to say what specifically it was about the face that gave it such and such an expression, beyond perhaps the general feeling that it was something about the mouth and/or the eyes.[28] We may call such global perception intuitive or, to use a phrase coined by Polanyi (1967, pp. 4–7), knowing more than

59

we can tell. He uses the example of our recognition of a person's face among a thousand others, yet being unable to tell how we recognize it. He considers such perception as the most impoverished form of what he calls "tacit knowing." Yet, such recognition of a face or the understanding of a facial expression presupposes the perception of very subtle features and is very different, indeed, from the kind of sensory qualities involved in the global, vital sensations of the infant.

The capacity for such global perception and global knowing is essential for the full human capacity for experience, whether it be in relation to a face, a person, the tone and inflection of words spoken, to the character of a room, of a landscape, or of a melody, to the atmosphere and crosscurrents in a gathering, or to a work of art. This capacity is underdeveloped or interfered with in the isolator. This is consistent with the earlier described attitude of attention characteristic of the isolator who looks and listens with a narrow, intense focus for something rather than at or to something or somebody. The isolator is isolated from the global sphere. He interferes, in fact, though unconsciously, with the globality of his "apparatus for experience," as Rorschach has called it, that is to say, with his capacity for global reception, reception with the fused power of all his sensibilities. And by looking for something, he separates or isolates a certain aspect of the object of his attention from the total, the global object. The impaired capacity for global perception and experience is a significant factor in the often described impairment of the obsessive's failure to perceive or misperception of emotional attitudes in others and in himself. Such attitudes usually find expression in the total behavior and feeling of the person in both gross and subtle changes affecting the total person. Hence, global attention and perception, rather than attention narrowly focused on however many and however exact details, is important for the sensing and for the articulate grasp of other people's attitudes as well as for becoming aware of one's own feelings. The obsessive's preoccupation with "objective," provable detail separates what belongs together and hence gets in the way of his ability to see the whole, the overall picture.

Similarly, the free play of attention is restricted in the isolator. Though he scans broadly, his scanning seems to exclude the perception of a great deal of his own and others' feelings and attitudes while focusing on objective details and on proof and disproof; hence also the characteristic restriction of his "free association." Needless to say, not all obsessive-compulsive personalities are selectively inattentive to the global sphere and to the expressions and the experience of affect to the same degree and under all circumstances. Some obsessives have a keen perception, for example, of other people's personality and attitudes as long as they remain spectators and the other person remains a passing stranger. But in significant interaction with another person this changes, and the characteristic defense of isolation and the described restrictions of attention and perception take over.

I have used the concept of globality with reference to the object of experience, attention and perception, and also with reference to the subject's apparatus for experience, for attending. Isolation affects both perceiver and percept, the experiencing person and the object as experienced by him. Freud described the subjective side of the isolator's experience when he defined the defense of isolation as the separation of idea from affect. In this observation he touches implicitly on the original unity of cognition and affect, a unity that, I believe, persists in attenuated and sometimes not so attenuated form much more throughout life than we are usually aware of, at least focally, explicitly aware of. This unity or fusion of cognition and affect is usually more apparent in global perception than in preoccupation with detail. In relation to people and to nature, if we have not become blind to her, global perceptions are as a rule tinged with affect. This does not mean necessarily that they are not objective. If we are not aware of this I think it is partly because interest is often not considered as an affect, and usually not mentioned where affects are described.[29] The more encompassing reason for the relative neglect of the role of affect altogether, and especially of affect in cognition lies, as Gardner Murphy (1965, p. 145) pointed out, in "the fragmentation of man . . . and the reluctance to see the affective life . . . [as] a vital aspect of the confrontation of and the adaptation to the environment."

He refers to the fragmentation and the lack of integration in modern research about man, which, I believe, in turn is owing to and part of the isolating and fragmenting tendencies in our society. These affect all of us whether or not we came into this world with an innate predisposition toward the mode of isolation as a defense or adaptation to the environment. Some examples will illustrate this socially generated isolation and blindness to the global field. I think that there are not many people who could bring themselves to kill or maim with their bare hands another human being provided they would experience him as akin to themselves, as a human being like they are. But propaganda and prejudice isolate them from this experience. Furthermore, modern technology allows a man to press a button that will cause the death and mutilation of untold thousands while he is isolated from and protected against the experience of his deed. An example from a different sphere of life concerns the increased emphasis in higher education on the training of highly skilled specialists and the concurrent neglect of the humanities. A third is the unheeding exploitation of nature for the sake of profit, without regard to the increasingly apparent damage, which continues even now when man himself begins to feel, painfully, what this is doing to his life and well-being. All these are examples of man's fragmentation and alienation from himself, from his fellow men and from nature.

Let me conclude with what I consider to be signs of a reaction against these destructive tendencies: in the field of science the increasing awareness of the necessity for interdisciplinary exchange and research which attempts to overcome the inevitable blindness of the specialist and, more important, the increasing awareness that the pursuit of scientific and technological "progress" is bound to lead to disaster unless it is coupled with the serious concern to serve a more humane way of life; in the area of human relations such phenomena as the recent interest in sensory awareness training and in attempts to relate to others more meaningfully in encounter groups; the protest of the hippies against a way of life that has lost any meaning. Whatever one may think of these and similar phenomena I have no question but that they are symptoms of the discontent with a civilization that isolates and alienates man from his total self, from his fellow men, from nature, and thus fails to give meaning to his life. They are to be welcomed insofar as they represent honest attempts to overcome some of the results of this alienation even though they are insufficient to deal with and change its causes.

NOTES

1. "Application" does not render fully Freud's word "Zuwendung," a noun for which there is no English equivalent and which means "turning toward," thus emphasizing the intentionality of all acts of attention. "Application" is equivalent to the German "Anwendung," which is synonymous also with "use" (*Gebrauch*).

2. The intentionality of attention and consciousness is a major focus of the

On Attention, Selective Inattention, and Experience

thought of Brentano and Husserl. Psychoanalysis has taught us that there is also unconscious intentionality.

3. I am using Harry Stack Sullivan's term "selective inattention" as a concept comprising the various defenses, such as repression and isolation, serving to eliminate past experience from conscious awareness and to prevent current experience from reaching awareness.

4. Compare Gardner, Holzman, Klein, Linton, and Spense (1959) and Gardner, Jackson, and Messick (1960), both with further references.

5. Ernest G. Schachtel, *Metamorphosis: On the Development of Affect, Perception, Attention and Memory* (New York: Basic Books, 1959), chap. 11.

6. "One" object, in the sense of this discussion, can consist also of a group of objects, such as a cluster of trees.

7. For a discussion of short-term oscillation between more receptive and more active attitudes of attention in the microgenesis of perceptions see Schachtel (1966, pp. 58–61). For a discussion of the flexibly adaptive versus the rigid control of different kinds of attention deployment (attitudes of attention) see Gardner et al. (1959, esp. pp. 53–66).

8. Von Weizäcker (1950, p. 20) designated as "negative achievements" (negative *Leistungen*) the various forms of neglecting perceptual data that would interfere with our object perception and noted that these negative achievements formally resemble what psychoanalysis designates as repression. The formal similarity consists in the fact of exclusion of certain data from awareness or, at least, from focal awareness. The difference between these automatic negative achievements and repression consists, among other things, in the role of anxiety in repression.

9. Italics mine—E.G.S. Actually, in my experience, many obsessives can free associate in the sense of not following a directed, logical trend of thought and saying what comes to mind. But their free association usually does not wander along the lines of emotional connections, which would be analytically fruitful free association, but precisely because of their defense of isolation seems to wander away from any such connections, hence usually is not very useful for psychoanalytic work. If it does produce relevant unconscious material the obsessive is likely to deny strenuously any personal significance of such material.

10. See also Shapiro's (1965, pp. 24–30) description of the obsessive-compulsive's style of attention.

11. Compare Freud's and Abraham's descriptions of the anal character.

12. This is also the view of Wachtel (1967, p. 418).

13. This quality of obsessive attention has been noted also by Shapiro, who wrote: (1965, p. 28): "It is not that [obsessive-compulsive people] do not look or listen, but they are looking or listening too hard for something. . . ."
See also Shapiro (1965).

14. I believe that there are two qualitatively different types of concentration. The main characteristic of one is that it is effortful. It has been described by Rapaport (1951, pp. 715–716). Very often the main effort has to do with the need to ward off distracting internal or external interferences. The relaxed concentration I am referring to is not bothered, as it were, by such interferences; it is composed, collected without being experientially effortful. It is probably more frequent in the East than in the West, since some Eastern religions and philosophies are particularly concerned with developing this capacity. It could perhaps be described as egoless attention, in the popular rather than psychoanalytic sense of ego. Compare, for example, Herrigel, (1953).

15. Compare to Schachtel (1959, pp. 177–183, 220–228), where the concept of allocentric attitude and allocentric perception is discussed more fully.

16. In this I am in agreement with some aspects of Fromm's (1956, 1957) views of man's love and knowledge of man. I believe, however, that the kinship of allocentric interest and attention with love applies also to man's relation to nature, particularly to living creatures.

17. E. Schachtel, "On Memory and Childhood Amnesia." *Psychiatry*, 1947, 10: 1–26; reprinted in E. Schachtel, *Metamorphosis*, chapter 12.

18. I use the word "object" in its general meaning, not in the rather unfortunate psychoanalytic usage denoting a person who is the object of libidinal or other strivings. Where I refer to the traditional psychoanalytic meaning, "object" will be put in quotes.

19. For a more detailed discussion of the newborn's responses to external stimuli and their later development, see Schachtel, *Metamorphosis*, chapter 7, pp. 116–165. This kind of awareness of sensation seems to be present to some extent already before birth, though in utero visual and many other stimuli are absent. For example, the embryo responds in its later stages of development to sudden loud noises with movements, probably of distress.

20. Werner's (1948, p. 96) account is limited to the sensations arising from stimuli received by exteroceptors. But we can extend it to those mediated by the interoceptors and proprioceptors, such as muscular, kinesthetic, and visceral sensations.

21. For my view of this development see Schachtel (1959, esp. pp. 3–77). For the usual view of Freudian ego psychology see Hartmann, Kris, and Loewenstein (1946). Freud (1964) himself, in one of his last papers, had already expressed the view that ego and id are originally one and that there are innate ego qualities. For the recent attempts to eliminate altogether the economic viewpoint of Freud's theory, the concepts of force, energy, and the implied drive reduction model see Holt (1967, pp. 4–6 et passim).

22. From a different starting point and from detailed observation of infant behavior, Wolff (1966) arrived at similar conclusions.

23. See Schachtel (1959, pp. 116–126) and the more recent observations of Fantz (1958, 1961) and of McCall and Kagan (1967). For an interpretation of Fantz's experimental results, different from his, see Schachtel (1966, pp. 153–154).

24. For the phenomenological descriptions of the worlds of various kinds of psychopathology compare especially the writings of Ludwig Binswanger, Erwin Straus, E. Minkowski, V. E. von Gebsattel.

25. By "sensation" Jung means what we usually call veridical perception, the *fonction du réel*, which, surprisingly, he considers together with intuition (and in contrast to thinking and feeling) as an irrational function, since sensation, according to him, does not work with judgment but with "mere perceptions, without evaluation or interpretation." See Jolan Jacobi (1943, esp. pp. 10–11) for a brief presentation of Jung's views, approved by Jung.

26. Italics mine.—Ed. Compare also J. Strachey's (1957, p. 192, n. 1) remarks on Freud's views on attention.

27. For the fundamental significance of play, especially the free play of attention, in the development of man's grasp of reality see Schachtel, (1959) in Schachtel (1959, esp. pp. 270–276).

28. The enormous complexity of the problem of facial and other expression and of the perception of these expressions is illuminated by Karl Bühler (1933),

with an excellent critical survey of the literature and history of physiognomics and expressive features in general. The theory of misperception of human expression has yet to be written.

29. For a notable exception to this, see Tomkins (1962, esp. pp. 336–369).

REFERENCES

Angyal, Andras. *Neurosis and Treatment*. New York: Wiley, 1965.

Bühler, Karl. *Ausdruckstheorie*. Jena: Gustav Fischer, 1933.

Fantz, Robert L. "Pattern Vision in Young Infants." *Psychological Record* 8(1958):43–47.

———. "The Origin of Form Perception." *Scientific American* 204(1961):66–72.

Freud, Sigmund. "The Interpretation of Dreams" (1900). *Standard Edition*. Vol. 5. London: Hogarth, 1953.

———. "Formulations on the Two Principles of Mental Functioning" (1911). *Standard Edition*. Vol. 12. London: Hogarth, 1958. (a)

———. "Recommendations to Physicians Practising Psychoanalysis" (1912). *Standard Edition*. Vol. 12. London: Hogarth, 1958. (b)

———. "The Unconscious" (1957). *Standard Edition*. Vol. 14. London: Hogarth, 1957.

———. "Inhibitions, Symptoms, and Anxiety" (1926). *Standard Edition*. Vol. 20. London: Hogarth, 1964.

———. "Analysis Terminable and Interminable" (1937). *Standard Edition*. Vol. 23. London: Hogarth, 1964. Pp. 216–253.

Fromm, Erich, *The Art of Loving*. New York: Harper, 1956.

———. "Man Is Not a Thing." *The Saturday Review*, March 16, 1957.

Gardner, Riley W.; Holzman, Philip S.; Klein, George S.; Linton, Harriet; and Spense, Donald P. "Cognitive Control." *Psychological Issues* 1, no. 4(1959).

———; Jackson, Douglas, N.; and Messick, Samuel J. "Personality Organization in Cognitive Controls and Intellectual Abilities." *Psychological Issues* 2, no. 4(1960).

Goethe, Friedrich. *Maximen und Reflexionen: Sämtliche Werke*. Stuttgart: Cotta'scher, 1853.

Goldstein, Kurt. *The Organism*. New York: American Book Company, 1939.

Hartmann, Heinz; Kris, Ernst; and Loewenstein, Rudolph M. "Comments on the Formation of Psychic Structure." *Psychoanalytic Study of the Child* 2(1946):11–38.

Herrigel, Eugen. *Zen in the Art of Archery*. New York: Pantheon, 1953.

Holt, Robert R., ed. "Motives and Thought." *Psychological Issues* 5, nos. 2–3(1967).

Jacobi, Jolan. *The Psychology of Jung*. New Haven: Yale University Press, 1943.

James, William. *The Principles of Psychology*. New York: Holt, 1931. Vol. 1.

Jung, Carl C. *Psychological Types*. London: Kegan Paul, 1933.

McCall, Robert B.; and Kagan, Jerome. "Attention in the Infant: Effect of Complexity, Contour, Perimeter, and Familiarity." *Child Development* 38(1967):939–952.

Mullahy, Patrick. "A Theory of Interpersonal Relations and the Evolution of Personality." In Harry Stack Sullivan, ed., *Conceptions of Modern Psychiatry*. New York: Norton, 1953.

Murphy, Gardner. "Discussion." In Silvan S. Tomkins and Carroll E. Izzard, eds., *Affect, Cognition, and Personality*. New York: Springer, 1965.

Polanyi, Michael. *The Tacit Dimension*. London: Routledge & Kegan Paul, 1967.

Rapaport, David. *Organization and Pathology of Thought*. New York: Columbia University Press, 1951.

Schachtel, Ernest G. *Metamorphosis: On the Development of Affect, Perception, Attention, and Memory*. New York: Basic Books, 1959.

———. *Experiential Foundations of Rorschach's Test*. New York: Basic Books, 1966.

Schlesinger, H. J. "Cognitive Attitudes in Relation to Susceptibility to Interference." *Journal of Personality* 22(1954):354–374.

Shapiro, David. *Neurotic Styles*. New York: Basic Books, 1965.

Spitz, René A. "The Smiling Response: A Contribution to the Ontogenesis of Social Relations." *Genetic Psychology Monographs* 34(1946):57–125.

Strachey, James. *Standard Edition of the Complete Psychological Works of Sigmund Freud*. Vol. 14. London: Hogarth, 1957.

Tomkins, Silvan S. *Affect, Imagery, Consciousness*. Vol. 1. *The Positive Affects*. New York: Springer, 1962.

von Weizsäcker, Victor. *Der Gestaltkreis: Theorie die Einheit von Wahrnehmen und Bewegen*, 4th ed. Stuttgart: Georg Thième, 1950.

von Uexküll, Jakob. *Niegeschaute Welten: Die Umwelten meiner Freunde* (1936). Berlin: Suhr Kamp, 1949.

———; and Kriszat, Georg. "Streitzuge durch die Umwelten von Tieren und Menschen." *In Rowohlts Deutsche Enzyklopadiea*. Hamburg: Rowohlt, 1956.

Wachtel, Paul L. "Conceptions of Broad and Narrow Attention." *Psychological Bulletin* 68(1967):417–429.

Werner, Heinz. *Comparative Psychology of Mental Development*, rev. ed. Chicago: Follett, 1948.

Wolff, Peter H. "The Causes, Controls, and Organization of Behavior in the Neonate." *Psychological Issues* 5, no. 1(1966):91–94.

Maturational Factors in Children's Dreams

We have come a long way from the time of the early psychoanalysts who saw motives as basically biological motors analogous to the steam engines of that period that pushed the individual in one or two directions on which the whole structure of personality was subsequently elaborated. Sex and aggression were the principal engines of the personality then. Today, almost all theories of personality posit a multiplicity of motives as enduring elements of personality, even though there are differences concerning the number of different motives that should be conceptualized, the degree of their generality, and the nature of their relations to one another.

In psychoanalysis during the 1930's and the 1940's, Harry Stack Sullivan described as fundamental primary motives, in addition to the genital lust and the hunger, thirst and temperature requirements, separate primary motives for sleep, for body contact, for knowledge or information, and for effective body activity competence. Today we would add the need for novelty among others. Even the classical Freudian psychoanalysts have begun to revise their formulations in consonance with the contributions of ego psychology, which argues for an ego that has separate origins and development, with its own functions and motives.

Today we see motives less as sources of energy or motors that push the organism than as governors or intervening variables in time that direct and modify the organism's behavior in relation to various goals. Within this conception, then, we have room for the intrinsic motivational factors of neuromechanisms, chemical and physiological states, and developmental and maturational factors, as well as the interpersonal products of cues, signals, previous experiences, learning, field conditions, and values.

Feelings are an awareness—conscious, of course—of our position at any one time in terms of the competing and collating motives at work in our life. Though the feeling by definition is conscious, its reference, implications, and sources may be dissociated, unnoticed, or not yet susceptible to conscious cognizance. We use the word "feeling" not only to refer to the relative consummation of any one or more of our motives, intentions, or purposes but to refer to our cognizance of a problem, situation, or formal organization of a complex pattern when it is not yet ready for clear communication. We speak of "having the feel" of a situation, or even with a memory that is not clear enough to communicate precisely, we may say that we "have a feeling of it." The dream mode is not necessary for the expression of these feelings, but the metaphor, in whatever state of consciousness one might be, has long been favored for this purpose. Aristotle said that from metaphor we can best get hold of something fresh or new, and that liveliness is especially conveyed by metaphor. The great linguists Max Muller and Otto Jespersen have both demonstrated that metaphor was the most vital principle of language, and perhaps even of all symbolism.

Jean Piaget (1951, pp. 182, 205) said

the child's conscious thought is the first datum, first in the form of sensory-motor activity and intelligence, then as thought which is semi-socialized but still preconceptual and imaged, and whose higher intuitive activities, aided by social life, produce the operation of reason. Parallel with this development . . . appear either imitation, the simple image, etc., or play and dreams with "unconscious" symbolism at the extreme pole (the symbolism being unconscious to the extent to which egocentrism, which is at its maximum in dreams, leads to the suppression of the ego's consciousness of itself). . . .

[I]n their symbolic structure, as well as in their content, children's dreams seem to be closely related to symbolic play . . . in play, material substitutes of all kinds which make it easier to imagine the object are used as symbols, while in dreams the object must be represented by a mental image or by another image symbolizing the same object. Thus in one of the dreams the image of a watering can symbolizes urination, while in the corresponding game (play) a real watering can will have been used.

The forced, involuntary periodic rhythm of dreaming often presents us with a great variety of metaphor in its manifest content. Free from the requirements of action and communication, the sleeping person, in the quiet insulation of his dream, can confront his feelings in a relatively crude, emotionally vivid way. It has been demonstrated (Green, Ullman, and Tauber, 1968) that more or less similar thematic content tends to occur in daydreams, in free association, and in the dreams of the night, as well as in the thoughts that can be experienced without the vividness of the dream at the other stages of sleep. However, the dream mode, because of its greater privacy, immediacy, intensity, and potential richness, shows the defensive and cognitive style of the person even more clearly than other forms of emotional expression. For example, people who tend to deny their feelings will tend to forget their dreams; hysterical individuals show more rapidly shifting forms and alterations; and obsessive-compulsive persons, as one might expect, show constriction and perseveration. Dreaming, an involuntary activity, shows the problematic and conflictful areas of the personality more than it does the competent and resourceful aspects. People rarely experience their skill and talent in dreams; even after a triumph, they are more likely to dream of the problem than the achievement, to dream of the nonexistent failure that was risked than to celebrate their success in their dreams.

The cyclic variations in the depth of sleep during the night are an opportunity for the individual to confront some challenge to the continuity of his habitual way of life wherein cognitive preparation for reinforcing neurotic illness patterns may occur or, on the other hand, preparation for healthy change may take place. Dreaming involves a process of self-confrontation, concerned not with intelligibility and referential meaning of a given aspect of experience but rather with the felt reactions derivative of that experience. This has more in common with the aesthetic mode that represents feeling uniquely than with our flat-footed scientific or discursive mode that represents facts with conventional and public accuracy. Given a situation involving unknown operating causes, a personal myth is created through the use of familiar and manipulatable imagery. This myth and its expression in imagery have to be understood not only in terms of disguise but also as a statement of a problem, the answer to which is not within the sleeper's awareness; at the same time, it can also be an effort at mastery, once the problem has been explored longitudinally in its connection to events in the past and horizontally in its relationship to current areas of personality strengths and weaknesses. Thus, we have come to a perspective on dreams that emphasizes metaphor and the problematic rather than symbol and drive.

However, just because the dream is sometimes a state of relative activation of attention to inner strangeness or to inner feelings of threats to one's self-esteem or security in some way does not mean that this same state of activation and metaphorical conceptualization of feeling necessarily and always, or even frequently, is insightful or revealing. In fact, some people pay no attention whatever and rarely if ever notice their dreams. It is characteristic of the economy of living organisms, and particularly of the resourcefulness of the human one, to use similar structures for many functions; certainly dreaming can and has been used in many ways—prophecy, medical diagnosis, prediction of a winning horse, or just the sheer fun of it. In other words, just because the dreams of patients who are engaged in psychotherapy so often seem to be so valuable in revealing the truth about themselves and their life, and show their interest and dedication to this difficult and arduous task of self-confrontation, it does not follow that all dreams are valuable in this insightful way.

It seems that there is considerable evidence for Piaget's thesis that the dreaming mode or, as he preferred to call it, the ludic mode, can be equated, in the use of symbols and metaphors, with imaginative free play, the makebelieve, let's pretend world of early childhood. The very young children "know" more in their body movement pantomimes of the world about them than they are able to formulate and conceptualize in either imagery or language. Actually, in working with young children, one can often find out much more from their play activity than one can from their dreams, as Melanie Klein and Susan Isaacs indicated. Dreaming and play activity both, according to Piaget, have predominantly assimilative and integrative functions whereby the individual preserves his historical continuity, assimilating new experiences to the old, and maintains his preparation for the future.

Piaget recognized that many of these imaginative constructions of dream and play in childhood become dissociated from awareness or, in Freudian terms, repressed from conscious attention. However, like William James, Piaget did not draw such a hard line, as Freud did, between the unconscious and the conscious processes. He described six categories of dream and play representation that are most likely to have nests of meanings that vary from conscious reference to marginal awareness to complete unawareness. These include bodily activities such as sucking, eating, sexual play, spitting, and excretion; interpersonal activities such as rivalry, love and aggression; anxieties regarding childbirth; fears and traumas; punishment or self-punishment; and straightforward transformation of physiological sensations such as a watering represent a desire to urinate or eating a pebble representing a pain in the stomach.

Maturational Factors

Dreaming has its developmental aspects, as do any functions or activities of the human organism. The psychoanalytic literature on the subject has, for the most part, ignored developmental changes. Unfortunately, this literature, in general, has been dominated by the tendency to either defend or refute Freud's hypothesis of infantile sexuality and wish fulfillment.

As we have seen, the delicate interweaving of human capacities with the experiential interpersonal responses occurring with mothering ones and strangers begins soon after birth. With the recent work that has been accomplished in cognitive and perceptual development, and in the psychophysiological study of sleep, we now have a larger frame of reference in which the various psychoanalytic theories, including our interpersonal one, can be understood.

How do these developmental studies affect our interpretation of the child's dream experience? Let us look at the material to see if we can draw some parallels with spontaneous storytelling Rorschach responses and obtain a normative and developmental perspective.

Associated with dreaming and with the rapid eye movement (REM) stage 1 electroencephalogram recording, there is a marked increase in excitement of the central nervous system with, at the same time, a sharp drop in the body tone of the large skeletal muscles. It is as though the body was being prepared for peak activity while the inhibition was complete on any possible large movement. The heart rate and respiratory rate are elevated and irregular, and there is a considerable increase in the fine body movements of the fingers, feet, hands, neck muscles, and so on. It is almost as though there was a conflict at the somatic level between excitatory impulses that are going out to all the parts of the body and inhibitory impulses that prevent any large body movement from occurring—like a restrained alertness.

The newborn has 55 to 80 percent of his sleep spent in something like the so-called active sleep or REM period that is familiarly associated with dreaming in later life. Unlike adults, the newborn shows gross body movements, writhing of the limbs, and facial twitchings during REM sleep (Korner, 1968). There is also an erection cycle in males that occurs from only 9 percent to 75 percent of the time in REM sleep of infants. Sucking movements and smiling movements occur about 50 percent of the time during the REM sleep of infants. By the time the infant has reached the sixth to eighth month, these REM periods average about 30 percent of the sleep time. Roffwarg, Muzio, and Dement (1966) offered what seems to be the most tenable hypothesis so far to account for this. They postulated that the increased REM activity is very important in facilitating the maturation of the central nervous system. It may also involve preparation for the more complex cognitive activity of metaphoric or ludic imagination as described by Piaget. This accords with Peter Wolff's (1967) hypothesis about the autonomous regularity of sucking, smiling, and grasping rhythms as preparations for more complex motor and cognitive performance.

Awakenings of children two to four years old during these REM periods elicit clear narratives of visual dreams. Two-year-olds recall dreams on 30 percent of the awakenings from REM sleep. The content of the dreams referred to play activities, animals, and television, for the most part. (Kohler, Coddington, and Agnew, 1968).

Karl Leonhard described a dream of a little girl two years old who awoke during the night crying, "Auto hurt. Dido [her brother] hurt." The mother reassured the little girl that her brother was quite all right, and she smiled and went back to sleep again; this seemed to be a clear carryover from an accident that happened in the car shortly before this dream.

Piaget described a dream of a two-year-old girl that her doll which she had lost had come back; four months later the same little girl dreamt about a lady that she liked very much whom she had not seen for a while. He also described a dream of a boy two and one-half years old that a friend of his was at the water spray, and a little girl he knew was there, too. This referred to an experience involved in his play during the day.

However, not all dreams of this age are pleasant. Piaget described the same little girl dreaming of a lady who was singing very loudly and frightening her. She expressed the feeling that she was scolded by the lady in telling the dream. Another night she dreamt that it was dark and suddenly she saw a lady who frightened her. We know how much the two-year-old, especially, is involved with the challenges of autonomy and the need for discipline and structure.

Many years ago I was deeply impressed by a little two-and-one-half-year-old girl, very bright, who was brought to me because she was pulling out her hair. She was a bright, vivacious, winning child who would not or could not say anything much about what she was thinking or feeling when she did this. However, what impressed me so much was the contrast between her doll play and her other communication. In her play with the family of dolls among a variety of behavior that described the home situation, she particularly had the mother doll take the pants off the father doll and put them on herself. Then the mother doll, wearing the father doll's pants, would flush herself down the toy toilet. This is a metaphor of a high order but a metaphor that could not be translated to the little girl. In other words, verbalizing for the girl that her mother felt bad or that her mother wanted to be the man of the house or "wear the pants" in the family was empty to the child. She knew the mother was quiet and did not feel good at times, and could verbalize that when pressed; she knew the mother was irritable and fought with the father at times, and she could describe their shouting at each other. Tauber and Green (1959) indicated how much more one takes into the spectrum of these prelogical cognitive processes than one can be aware of, and the recent work of Bruner, Olver, Greenfield, et al. (1969) elaborated this even further.

Bruner et al. described three ways of knowing or representing experience for future reference or recall—enactive representation, ikonic representation, and symbolic, conceptual, or relational representation. The enactive is earliest and might explain the doll play of this little two-and-one-half-year-old girl who could represent her experience of her family through the actions of the dolls whereas the images of her dreams or spontaneous speech were much less intimate and much more prosaic. Incidentally, independent probing with the mother confirmed strong suicidal tendencies, a wish to flush herself down the toilet, so to speak. The girl's hair-pulling stopped when the mother's depression lifted.

The ability to communicate with actions where imagery and words are limited is also illustrated by Bruner's description of the uneducated Wolof child from Africa who could by his movements discriminate several different colors from one another in an appropriate context when his language had no words for these color distinctions. Perhaps there are even constitutional and temperamental affinities for one or the other mode of representation. Certainly dynamic factors play a large part.

The implications for therapy might be that some experiences of great import in development may only be accessible through some kind of somatic experience or body movement expressions. As Freud and Wilhelm Reich early pointed out, some muscle tensions themselves may be partly an expression of dissociated experience that had never become assimilated and integrated with the more mature thought processes.

It is interesting to compare the dreams with the Rorschach responses reported in this age group of two to three years (Ames, Learned, Metraux, and Walker, 1952). The Rorschach responses between the ages of two to three are apt to be general impressions such as a tree, a doggie, or a kitty. At this age the Rorschach is not a useful tool for measuring or revealing much about the child. Any attempt that is made to specify the response only confuses matters. A child is very suggestible and, at the same time, does not have clear boundaries between what he sees, what he thinks he is supposed to see, and what is simply interesting to him at the moment. This applies to dream reports as well. By three years of age the responses are a little more elaborated. They will say, "It looks like a turtle; that's how they walk." Magical notions, repetition, stereotyping, interest in the cards and blots themselves, such as asking, "Who painted this red?" are typical of this age.

In spontaneous storytelling (Pitcher and Prelinger, 1963), the same thing holds. A little boy two years and eight months tells the story: "A little boy fall. He went like this. [Falls down] Boy go car. Car got all broken. All fixed." Another boy a year older makes up the story, "A truck and he got crashed. He got crashed in the front right there. Then he went back home. He crashed up again. Then he went home."

There is a movement, as Piaget, Sullivan, Werner, and many others described, in the development of perceptual and cognitive processes, from an emphasis on motor representation and sensorimotor coordination in early infancy toward ikonic representation and imagery later, and then toward freedom of imagery from immediate action and testing, and finally the operational symbolic processes of abstract relations. As one can see from the dreams, the Rorschach blots, and the spontaneous storytelling, these young children two or three years old experience their inner world, as well as the outer one, in terms of global impressions to minimal cues, in terms of concrete, simple attributes, autistically centered around their own sensation and position. Children at this age, that is, two- to three-year-olds, often cannot tell the difference between the dream as private experience and the dream as shared experience. They might even ask someone who had been in the dream if that person remembered what had happened, asking them to fill out the rest of the dream. In fact, I remember witnessing an argument between one little girl and her older sister. The little girl insisted that the sister had been present in this dream event, and the sister, with equal vehemence, insisted that she had not been there.

By five years of age, children are experiencing about 20 percent of their sleep in the REM stage 1 dreaming sleep. A girl four years, nine months, described the following dream: "I dreamt a witch killed me, then another witch killed him and made me alive." Dreams of boys are more directly aggressive as are their play and spontaneous stories. A six-year-old dreamt, "Teacher had to hit me [on the wrist] because I was too noisy." Boys of greater mental age showed more imagination, greater word count, and greater extension in time and space of the dream content. There was also a tendency to a more active dream role with increased mental age (Foulkes, Pivik, Steadman, Spear, and Symonds, 1967). DeMartino (1954) showed this applied in the reverse direction to mental retardates. There was no significant correlation, however, in the Wyoming study between dream content and their performance on the Children's Apperception Test (CAT) except that strong repressive tendencies on the CAT were positively correlated with constriction in the content of the dreams.

Spontaneous storytelling reported by Pitcher and Prelinger (1963) shows similar properties. For example, this is a story made up by a boy of five years three months: "A kind of machine with wheels and a pusher and a hook. It can push gravel, dirt, snow. Once it went out in the snow and it plowed snow."

Sex-role differences are exemplified in the subject content of these dreams: Boys dream more of machines, guns, and sports; girls dream more of fairy tales, play, and household activities.

At about the age of five to seven, there is more concern with the distinction between real and unreal, between magic, dreams, pretensions, disguises, who does what to whom, what is the cause, and what is the effect. The five-year-old brings out more animals in his stories as well as in his Rorschach responses and his dreams.

The speech of five-year-olds has a very rich, colorful, refreshing quality to it, as Bruner et al. (1966) pointed out, because of its preco-cious grammatical syntax in comparison with the very little knowl-edge and understanding that the child has of the world about him. The Russian psychologist Kornei Chukovsky (1963) was fascinated with this quality of children's speech. He described several anecdotes to illustrate how the child tries to make sense with his limited experi-ence. For example, a five-year-old girl came to the cemetery with her mother and suddenly saw a drunkard walking unsteadily along the bushes. "Did this uncle just dig himself out of his grave?" she asked.

Another five-year-old girl witnessed a train running over a pig and killing it. A few days later she saw another frisky live pig and ex-claimed ecstatically, "The pig glued herself up again."

Drawings show a much cruder gradation of differentiation than the child's dreams and stories, which probably reflects his limited level of visual motor coordination at this age. The drawings of children be-tween two and three years of age are usually simply an ellipse with eyes, often the nose and mouth indicated, and perhaps some lines out from the ellipse to indicate feet or arms. (It is interesting to note, as Shapiro did, that this ellipse with eyes is the same visual gestalt de-scribed by Spitz for the six weeks' smiling response.) It may even be upside down. Between three and four, there is usually no neck shown, but you may have two circles, one for the head and one for the body. And the sticks coming out of these circles for arms and legs may have little things added on to them for fingers, hands, and feet. There may also be lines indicating hair. By four to five years of age the arms are attached to the shoulder level of the body; the body is more elon-gated, arms and legs begin to show some solidity, and accessory de-tails may begin to appear, such as pockets, buttons, and hats. It is not until after five that we begin to get significant details, such as pupils, eyebrows, a neck, and an attempt to make a more interesting picture (Shapiro and Stine, 1965).

In summary, the first five years of life may be characterized as one of intimate dependency in a small life space. Growth of the personal-ity occurs in what Bruner describes as the three basic modes of knowledge: (1) knowledge through action; (2) knowledge through im-aging; and (3) knowledge through conceptual relations. These phases correspond roughly to Sullivan's phases of experience from prototaxic (discontinuous global totalities of action) through parataxic (crude generalizations from similarities and differences) to syntaxic (refined abstraction and operational conceptions). The first five years are mostly based on action and imaging, with rudimentary, global conceptual relations that develop gradually. More precise and logical conceptual relations, described by Bruner and Piaget, begin to emerge more fully in the juvenile and preadolescent period of life at school with peers at the same time that the syntaxic mode of interpersonal experience develops. But the capacity for the syntaxic and extended formal logical thought develops most strikingly in adolescence and later.

During the first five years there also emerges a formulation of a personified self, that is, an identity who is acting, who is imaging and imaged, and who has some awareness of the relationship of dependency, of being one who is in need, who is widely concerned with the comings and going of others and with his own movements in this space of the urban or rural home with the figures of parents, siblings, and strangers.

The experiential world of the child changes between two and five years from concrete, immediate events having very short durations in time and a very literal context in space limited more or less to the vicinity of the home; it changes to a larger representation, which is more elaborate, containing a greater variety of characters doing things in which there is greater duration and in which the child sees a larger variety of objects, persons, and detail in which much more is communicated to him of the world outside the home. The older child will see television characters, comic strip heroes, and family members who represent qualities more than actual entities. This gradual development from personal to conventional language and references and from the immediate, concrete, and specific to the more removed, a little more general, a little more stereotyped, occurs in all aspects of the child's conceptual and communicative life. These oversimplified, stereotyped patterns of good mother–bad mother, good teacher–bad teacher, and so on characterize what Sullivan called the parataxic mode of experience, which predominates during these years of early childhood.

The child's relationship to time is also gradually differentiated (Goldstone and Goldfarb, 1966). The child discriminates morning from afternoon before the age of four; but does not communicate about clock time with much accuracy until about age seven. The days of the week are named correctly by five, and the months unfold several years later. The way time is experienced in dreams and in psychopathology should be viewed against this developmental continuum.

In the period between five and seven years there is a very big change in the life of the child. This is the age at which children begin to go to school and to move away from the small, bounded world of the immediate family to a larger universe of siblings, teachers, peers, and strangers in a much larger and infinitely more complicated space. Ames et al. (1952) stated that during this transitional period children of both sexes have many more frequent nightmares. The high rate of nightmares gradually decreases, according to Ames, until by eight years there are few nightmares. However, in a study of children's dreams (Foulkes et al., 1967) by the electroencephalogram monitoring technique, done in a small university town in Wyoming, thirty-two boys were studied from age six to twelve, and there was no greater frequency of nightmares among the six-year-olds than among the twelve-year-olds. Twenty percent of the dreams were described as bad, and these did not occur more frequently in the early part than in the late, nor did they occur more frequently in one age group than they did in another. Madeleine Rambert (1949), a child analyst and student of Piaget, collected about seventy dreams of French children ages six to twelve. She found that more than 50 percent of the dreams were anxiety dreams but were not more frequent in the six to ten age than in the ten to twelve period. Of course, neither her group nor the Ames group were monitored by the electroencephalogram. Perhaps only unpleasant dreams were noticed and reported in the earlier age group of the Ames study. This would suggest that the pleasant dreams are more easily forgotten. Future research will help clarify this.

The dreams of the group from six to nine show a greater degree of personal activity in the dream in contrast to a mere witnessing of events happening. The dreamer may experience himself as an agent or see himself as an agent in the dream. For example, a boy in the Wyoming study (Foulkes et al., 1967) at seven years eleven months had the following dream: "I was just playing baseball. I was the catcher . . . and the pitcher. There were lots of other kids on our team. I threw a curve ball. It was a good dream." An eight-year-old little girl who enjoys dressing up in her mother's clothes and playing at being a teenager reported the dream that she is all dressed up like her mother and having many friends to her house and feeding them cookies. However, a very disturbed little boy of eight, who was in therapy, dreamt a more passive and fantastic dream of being put in the bath to be washed and wrung out through the mangle and then hung up on a line to dry.

The vigorous play of the eight-year-old is also reflected in the Rorschach test with strong movement responses of holding something, fighting, dancing, standing, and color responses of splashed blood, spilled paint, and burning fire. Popular conventional responses of butterflies, birds, and animals predominate.

As the individual grows older and becomes more absorbed in the larger world of acculturation, convention, and socialization in school and society, his dreams, both in the Ames et al. (1952) study as well as in the Wyoming study (Foulkes et al., 1967), seem to be mostly everyday, matter-of-fact, pleasant experiences with occasional unpleasant dreams or more fantastic dreams related to stories, television, radio, movies, and emotional problems.

By the time that eight years is achieved and the child is well along into school and into the early relationships with peers, the type of communication whereby personal and fantastic material freely flows into the more conventional, and everyday type of observation no longer takes place. The imaginary let's pretend play becomes more restricted. As Harry Stack Sullivan pointed out, the juvenile may be heavily penalized for this type of verbal behavior in Western culture. There is less and less imaginary play (it becomes too "childish"), and there is more game playing—sports, cards, and other competitive games. Dreams, too, may become more conventional and prosaic, except for the dream reports of seriously disturbed children, children in treatment, or especially imaginative and creative children.

The dreams of boys in the ten- to twelve-year-old group, according to the Wyoming study (Foulkes et al., 1967), contain more human figures, fewer animal figures, more friendly activity, and more than twice as many grownup women strangers as the dreams of the younger boys. There is no comparable data on girls, but drawing from my clinical experience, they are more intimate and more related to aspects of femininity, peer-group activity, and mother-type figures as the boys' dreams are more related to masculinity and to activities with peers and fathers. For example, a boy eleven years seven months dreams of riding his bicycle with a group of his boy friends in the country and getting lost. A girl of ten years two months dreams of her parents being away while she has a great time playing with her girl friends.

Conclusion

We can now try to appreciate the clinical significance of dreams against a normative developmental cognitive gradient. It raises more questions than answers, but provokes us again to see how rich and rewarding dream research may be. Clinically, we see that the manifest content of dreams, the spontaneous stories, the makebelieve play, the Rorschach responses, all show certain parallels reflecting the maturational level of cognitive and expressive capacities. It remains for future research to spell out the differences at each age level among these various subjective modes for specific individual expression of conflicts, aims, defenses, self-esteem, and so on.

Using dreams the way we do in psychoanalysis is a specific skill that is taught and acquired. This is reflected in the way which various schools of psychoanalysis shape the style and content of the dreams of patients.

In studying dreams of adults we have found it useful to see what developmental task is approached in the dream. This is also appropriate for children's dreams. Dreams can be used in therapy very early in childhood, even though I personally prefer the play technique. However, Melanie Klein made verbal interpretations of the reported dream to very young children and followed it up in the interpretation of the subsequent play activity. Anna Freud encouraged children to make their own interpretations and reported that it is much easier to do this with children than with adults. Recently, Markowitz and Seiderman (1963) were presenting drawings of children's dreams to their parents and finding fruitful dynamic responses.

Nonetheless, there is an urgent need for the same kind of painstaking observations that Dr. Schecter and his colleagues have done with mother-infant transactions. Foulkes et al. (1967) have shown us that the electroencephalogram monitoring technique can be applied to children. Now it remains for us to formulate challenging hypotheses that can be tested by these new methods. Certainly the simplistic dichotomies of primary and secondary processes must be discarded in favor of a much more richly differentiated cognitive spectrum along the direction set by Piaget, Sullivan, Werner, and Bruner. Primary-process thinking is said to characterize the hidden meaning of dreams of latent content; the primitive representations of drives in the unconscious, particularly forbidden sexual and aggressive ones; and the organization of these primitive representations according to the so-called laws of the unconscious first formulated by Freud (1955, p. 608). However, it may not be the drives and unconscious conflicts with the pleasure principle that are the issue but the normative developmental sequences of various levels of cognition. For example, body movement or inactive representation cannot deal with the same complexity and simultaneity of events as the visual or ikonic mode of representation. When one is dealing with a highly charged, highly polarized anxiety situation, say of a phobic experience, one must discriminate between the all-or-nothing quality that is a manifestation of an over simplified ikonic representation into all good versus all bad and the all-or-nothing quality as an overdramatized, hysterical manipulation. All this, of course, may be going on simultaneously and in much greater complexity. We can now explore a wider variety of dissociated feelings than psychosexual and aggressive ones hidden in the dreams of children. We can also give greater weight to the interpersonal problems of simply growing up in a given family and society.

Certainly from the data we have so far gathered, we are no closer to the id, full of oral, anal, urethral, and so on representations in the dreams of early childhood than we are at any other age. The dreams of children, like the dreams of adults, represent disguised dissociated problems and feelings, as well as the everyday experiences readily available to conscious recall and concerned with the phase-specific tasks of development with all its hopes and fears, joys and griefs, and banalities.

Perhaps with further research we can determine which projective techniques are most suitable at particular developmental levels, distinguish between normative and clinically significant manifest content, and illuminate the representation of motives and affect developmentally along the continuum of sleep to waking mentation.

Freud said, "The interpretation of dreams is the royal road to a knowledge of the unconscious activities of the mind." By analyzing dreams we can take a step forward in our understanding of the composition of that most marvellous and most mysterious of all instruments. Only a small step, no doubt; but a beginning. As the dream reminiscences of disturbed patients and his own memories provided Freud with that powerful "small step" of dream interpretation in classical psychoanalysis, so now may the laboratory and developmental studies of dreams lend a further impetus to a developmental and interpersonal theory for psychoanalysis today.

REFERENCES

Ames, Louise Bates; Learned, Janet; Metraux, Ruth W.; and Walker, Richard N. *Child Rorschach Responses*. New York: Hoeber, 1952.

Bernstein, Isidor. "Dreams and Masturbation in an Adolescent Boy." *Journal of the American Psychoanalytic Association* 10(1962):289–302.

Blanchard, Phyllis. "A Study of Subject Matter and Motivation of Children's Dreams." *Journal of Abnormal and Social Psychology* 21(1926):24–37.

Bruner, Jerome S.; Olver, Rose R.; Greenfield, Patricia M., et al. *Studies in Cognitive Growth*. New York: Wiley, 1966.

Chukovsky, Kornei. *From Two to Five*. Berkeley: University of California Press, 1963.

DeMartino, Manfred F. "A Review of the Literature on Children's Dreams." *Psychiatric Quarterly Supplement* 29(1955):90–101.

———. "Some Characteristics of the Manifest Dream Content of Mental Defectives." *Journal of Clinical Psychology* 10(1954).

Despert, J. Louise. "Dreams in Children of Preschool Age." *Psychoanalytic Study of the Child*, 3–4 (1949): 141–80.

Erickson, Milton H. "On the Possible Occurence of a Dream in an Eight-Month-Old Infant." *Psychoanalytic Quarterly* 10(1942):382–384.

Esman, Aaron H. "The Dream Screen in an Adolescent." *Psychoanalytic Quarterly* 31(1962):250–251.

Foulkes, David; Pivik, Terry; Steadman, Helen S.; Spear, Paul S.; and Symonds, John D. "Dreams of the Male Child: An EEG Study." *Journal of Abnormal Psychology* 72(1967):457–467.

Freud, Sigmund. *The Interpretation of Dreams*. New York: Basic Books, 1955.

Furman, Erna. "Some Features of the Dream Function of a Severely Disturbed Young Child." *Journal of the American Psychoanalytic Association* 10 (1962):258–270.

Goldstone, Sanford; and Goldfarb, Joyce L. "The Perception of Time by Children." In Aline H. Kidd and Jeanne L. Rivoire, eds., *Perceptual Development in Children*. New York: International Universities Press, 1966. Pp. 443–86.

Green, Maurice R.; Ullman, Montague; and Tauber, Edward S. "Dreaming and Modern Dream Theory." In Judd Marmor, ed., *Modern Psychoanalysis*. New York: Basic Books, 1968. Pp. 146–88.

Harley, Marjorie. "The Role of the Dream in the Analysis of a Latency Child." *Journal of the American Psychoanalytic Association* 10(1962):271–288.

Maturational Factors in Children's Dreams

Harms, Ernest, ed. *Problems of Sleep and Dream in Children.* New York: Macmillan, 1964.

Kohler, William C.; Coddington, R. Dean; and Agnew, H. W. "Sleep Patterns in Two-Year-Old Children." *Journal of Pediatrics* 72(1968):228–233.

Korner, Anneliese F. "REM Organization in Neonates." *Archives of General Psychiatry* 19(1968):328–340.

Markowitz, Irving; and Seiderman, Stanley. "An Investigation of Parental Recognition of Children's Dreams: Preliminary Report." In Jules H. Masserman, ed., *Science and Psychoanalysis,* vol. 6. New York: Grune & Stratton, 1963.

Piaget, Jean. *Play, Dreams, and Imitation in Childhood.* New York: Norton, 1951.

Pitcher, Evelyn G.; and Prelinger, Ernst. *Children Tell Stories.* New York: International Universities Press, 1963.

Rambert, Madeleine L. *Children in Conflict.* New York: International Universities Press, 1949.

Roffwarg, Howard; Muzio, Joseph N.; and Dement, William. "Ontogenetic Development of the Human Sleep-Dream Cycle." *Science* 152(1966):604–618.

Root, Nathan N. "Some Remarks on Anxiety Dreams in Latency and Adolescence." *Journal of the American Psychoanalytic Association* 10(1962):303–322.

Shapiro, Theodore; and Stine, John. "The Figure Drawings of Three-Year-Old Children," *Psychoanalytic Study of the Child* 20(1965):298–309.

Sperling, Melitta. "Neurotic Sleep Disturbances in Children." *Nervous Child* 8(1949):114–22.

Stern, Max M. "Pavor Nocturnus." *International Journal of Psycho-Analysis* 32(1951):302–309.

Tauber, Edward S.; and Green, Maurice R. *Prelogical Experience.* New York: Basic Books, 1959.

Wellisch, E. "Dreamy States in Children with Apparent Recession and Approach of Objects." *British Journal of Medical Psychology* 25(1952):135–147.

Wolff, Peter H. "The Role of Biological Rhythms in Early Psychological Development." *Bulletin of the Menninger Clinic* 31(1967):197–218.

PART TWO
Theoretical Contributions

THEORIES OF PSYCHOANALYSIS have frequently become dogma and hence ways for narrowing fields of vision rather than devices for opening new vistas. This has been particularly true when they have attempted to explain the nature of man. After all, theories are made by individuals who are products of their philosophical, social, economic, and cultural milieus. They are, to varying degrees, culture bound. Theories are therefore in need of continuing revision, amplification, and transformation.

The four chapters in this section are ongoing efforts in this area. Erich Fromm begins with an analysis of the philosophical, social, and anthropological determinants of Freud's concept of man. He hypothecates the origin of the libido theory in the mechanistic materialistic view of man. He shows the Eros-Thanatos models of the 1920's as originating in the biological-vitalistic thinking of that time and as a result of the pessimism following World War I. The constant struggle between rationality and irrationality is highlighted by Freud, but his patriarchal bias led him to denigrate women and children.

Benjamin Wolstein tells us that the structure of psychoanalytic inquiry is science; the accomplishment of the therapeutic experience is art. Successful treatment is dependent on the discussion of genuine problems in living and not on metapsychology. Psychoanalytic inquiry may be structured on the basis of different levels of data, starting from empirical observations and extending to higher levels of definitions, explanations, and transformations to make unconscious phenomena conscious.

Silvano Arieti adds data usually labeled intrapsychic to the interpersonal framework. For him psychopathology results from the failure of integration of interpersonal situations with the self. He illustrates this with discussion of the simple psychopath, the paranoid schizophrenic, and the psychotic depressive.

Gerard Chrzanowski concludes the section with an effort at clarifying and modifying some aspects of interpersonal theory. He wants the ecological model and particularly the family model to be stressed rather than the dyad; he adds the cognitive styles of the individual and the possible constructive aspects of anxiety as factors in interpersonal theory.

In summary, the chapters illustrate how theories are the products of culture-bound men and how philosophical, physical, and social science discoveries and social changes influence psychoanalytic theories. This makes it vital to have ongoing studies, to create new theories, to modify old ones, and to keep the discourse going.

Freud's Concept of Man
and Its Social Determinants

Freud was a liberal critic of bourgeois society in the same sense in which liberal reformers in general were critical. He recognized that society imposes unnecessary hardships on man, which are conducive to worse results rather than the expected better ones. He saw this unnecessary harshness operating in the field of sexual morality, which led to the formation of neuroses that, in many cases, could have been avoided by a more tolerant attitude. (Political and educational reform are parallel phenomena.) But Freud was never a radical critic of capitalistic society: He never questioned its socioeconomic bases, nor did he criticize its ideologies, with the exception of those concerning sexuality.

It is important to point out first that Freud, rooted in the philosophy of humanism and enlightenment, starts out with the assumption of the existence of man as such, universal man, and not only man as he manifests himself in various cultures, man about whose structure generally valid and empirical statements can be made. Freud, like Spinoza before him, constructed a model of human nature on the basis of which not only neuroses but all fundamental aspects, possibilities, and necessities of man can be explained and understood.

Freud saw man as a closed system driven by two forces: the self-preservative and the sexual. (Freud used the word "sexual" in an enlarged sense that comprised basically all sensuous desires.) The latter are rooted in chemophysiological processes moving in a phased pattern. The first phase increases tension and unpleasure; the second reduces the built-up tension and in so doing creates that which subjectively is felt as pleasure. Man is primarily an isolated being, whose primary interest is the optimal satisfaction of both his ego and his libidinous interest. (Neurosis is the result of a failure to synthesize the two interests.) Freud's man is the physiologically driven and motivated *Homme machine*. But, secondarily, man is also a social being, because he needs other people for the satisfaction of his libidinous and also his self-preservative drives. The child is in need of mother (and here, according to Freud, libidinous desires follow the path of the physiological needs). The adult needs a sexual partner. Feelings like tenderness or love are looked on as phenomena that accompany, and result from, libidinous interests. Individuals need one another as means for the satisfaction of their physiologically rooted drives. Man is primarily unrelated to others, and is only secondarily forced, or seduced, into relationships with others.

Freud's *Homo sexualis* is a variant of the classic *Homo economicus*. It is the isolated, self-sufficient man who has to enter into relations with others in order that all may mutually fulfill their needs. The needs of *Homo economicus* are economic ones which find their mutual satisfaction in the exchange of goods on the commodity market. The needs of *Homo sexualis* are physiological, libidinous ones, which normally are mutually satisfied by the relations between the sexes (the love and marriage market). In both variants the persons essentially remain strangers to each other, being related only by the common aim of drive satisfaction. This social determination of his theory by the spirit of the market economy does not mean that the theory is wrong, except in its claim of describing the situation of man as such; as a description of interpersonal relations in bourgeois society, it is valid for the majority of people.

To this general statement a specific point must be added with regard to the social determinants of Freud's concept of drives. Freud was a student of the physiologist von Brucke, who was one of the most distinguished representatives of mechanistic materialism, especially in its German form. This type of materialism was based on the principle that all psychic phenomena have their roots in certain physiological processes and that they can be sufficiently explained and understood if one knows these roots.[1] Freud, in search of the roots of psychic disturbances, had to look for a physiological substrate for the drives; to find this in sexuality was an ideal solution. This solution corresponded to the requirements of mechanistic-materialistic thought as well as to certain clinical findings in patients of his time and social class. It remains, of course, uncertain whether those findings would have impressed Freud so deeply if he had not thought within the framework of his philosophy; but it can hardly be doubted that his philosophy was an important determinant of his theory of drives; this

90

implies, also, that one will approach his findings with a certain skepticism if one thinks on a different philosophical basis; this skepticism refers not so much to a restricted form of Freud's theories, according to which in some neurotic disturbances sexual factors play a decisive role, but rather to the claim that all neuroses and all human behavior are determined by the conflict between the sexual and the self-preservative drives.

In still another sense does Freud's libido theory mirror his social situation. It is based on the concept of scarcity; it is assumed that all human strivings for lust result from the need to rid oneself from unpleasureful tensions, and not that lust is a phenomenon of abundance aiming at a greater intensity and depth of human experiences. This principle of scarcity is characteristic of middle-class thought. It is a classic trait, whether we think of Malthus, Benjamin Franklin, or an average businessman of the nineteenth century. It would lead too far to discuss here this principle of scarcity and the virtue of saving.[2] What it says is essentially that the quantity of all commodities is necessarily limited, and hence that equal satisfaction for all is impossible because true abundance is impossible, that scarcity is, in fact, the most important stimulus for human activity.[3]

In spite of its social determinants, Freud's theory of drives remains an important contribution to the model of man. Even if the libido theory as such is not correct it is, let us say, a symbolic expression of a more general phenomenon: that human behavior is the product of forces that, though usually not conscious as such, motivate him, drive him, and lead him into conflicts. The relatively static nature of human behavior is deceptive. It exists only because the system of forces producing it remains the same, and it remains the same as long as the conditions that mold these forces do not change. But when these conditions, social or individual, do change fundamentally, the system of forces loses its stability and with it the apparently static behavior pattern.

With his dynamic concept of character, Freud raised the psychology of behavior from the level of description to one of science. Freud did for psychology what the great dramatists and novelists did in artistic form. He showed man as the hero of a drama who, even though he be only of average talent, is a hero because he fights passionately in the attempt to make some sense of the fact of having been born. Freud's drama par excellence, the Oedipus complex, may be a more harmless, bourgeois version of forces that are much more elementary than the father-mother-son sexual triangle described by it; yet Freud sensed the dramatic quality of the child's conflict by giving it the name of a myth.

This theory of desires dominated Freud's systematic thinking only until the 1920's. After 1920 a new phase of his thinking began, which constituted an essential change of his concept of man. Freud postulated a new opposition instead of the one between ego and libidinous drives, namely, that between life instincts (Eros) and death instinct. The life instincts, comprising both ego and sexual drives, were placed opposite to the death instinct, which was considered to be the root of human destructiveness, directed either toward the person himself or the world outside. These new basic drives are constructed entirely differently from the old ones. First, they are not located in any special zone of the organism, as the libido is in the erogenous zones. Furthermore, they do not follow the pattern of the hydraulic mechanism—increasing tension → unpleasure → de-tension → pleasure → new tension, and so on—but they are inherent in every living cell and operate without any special stimulation. Eros has the tendency to unite and to integrate; the death instinct has the opposite tendency, that toward disintegration and destruction. Both drives operate constantly within man, fight and blend with each other, until finally the death instinct proves to be the stronger and has its ultimate triumph in the death of the individual.

This new concept of drives indicates essential changes in Freud's mode of thinking, and we may assume that these changes are related to fundamental social changes.

The new concept of drives does not follow the model of materialistic-mechanistic thinking; it can, however, be considered as a biological-vitalistic oriented concept, a change that corresponds to a general trend in biological thought in those years. More important, however, is Freud's new appreciation of the role of human destructiveness. Not that he had omitted aggression in his first theoretical model. He had considered aggression to be an important factor that, nevertheless, was subordinated to the libidinous drives and those for self-preservation. In the new theory destructiveness becomes the rival of, and eventually the victor over the libido and the ego drives. Man cannot help wanting to destroy, for the destructive tendency is rooted in his biological constitution. He can mitigate this tendency to a certain point, but he can never deprive it of its strength. He is confronted only with the alternative of directing his destructiveness either against himself or against the world outside. He has no chance of liberating himself from this tragic dilemma.

There are good reasons for the hypothesis that Freud's new appreciation of destructiveness has its roots in the experience of World War I. This war shook the foundations of liberal optimism which had filled the first period of Freud's life. Until 1914 the members of the middle class had believed that the world was rapidly approaching a state of greater security, harmony, and peace. The "darkness" of the Middle Ages seemed to lift from generation to generation and in a few more steps, so it seemed, the world, or at least Europe, would resemble the streets of a well-lighted, protected capital. In the bourgeois euphoria of the *belle époque* one forgot easily that this picture was not true for the majority of the workers and peasants of Europe and even less so for the populations of Asia and Africa.

The war of 1914 destroyed this illusion, not so much the beginning of the war, as its duration and the inhumanity of its practices. Freud, who during the war still believed in the justice and victory of the German cause, was hit at a deeper psychic level than the average, less sensitive person. He probably sensed that the optimistic hopes of enlightenment thought were illusions and concluded that man, by nature, was destined to be destructive. Precisely because he was a reformer,[4] the war must have hit him all the more forcefully. Since he was no radical critic of society and no revolutionary, it was impossible for him to hope for essential social changes. Hence he had to see the causes of the tragedy in the nature of man.[5]

Freud was, historically speaking, a figure of the frontier, of a period of radical change of the social character. Inasmuch as he belonged to the nineteenth century, he was an optimistic enlightenment thinker; inasmuch as he belonged to the twentieth century he was a pessimistic, almost despairing representative of a society caught in rapid and unpredictable change. Perhaps this pessimism was reinforced by his grave, painful, and life-threatening illness, an illness that lasted until his death and that he bore with the heroism of a genius, perhaps also by the disappointment over the defection of some of his most gifted disciples—Adler, Jung, and Rank; however this may be, he could never recover his lost optimism. But, on the other hand, he neither could nor probably wished to cut himself entirely loose from his previous thinking. This is perhaps the reason why he never resolved the contradiction between the old and the new concept of man. To be sure, the old libido was subsumed under Eros; the old aggression, under the death instinct. But it is painfully clear that this was only theoretical patchwork.[6]

Aside from the aspect of man as a being driven by conflicting drives, there is another of great importance for Freud's model of man: the dialectics of rationality and irrationality in man. The originality and greatness of Freud's thought becomes particularly clear at this point. As a successor of the enlightenment thinkers Freud was a rationalist who believed in the power of reason and the strength of the human will; he believed that social conditions, and especially those prevailing in early childhood, were responsible for the evil in man. But Freud's genius made him sense, even before World War I, the drastic changes that were to manifest themselves clearly only later. He had already lost his rationalistic innocence, as it were, at the beginning of his work and had recognized the strength of human irrationality and the weakness of human reason and will. He fully confronted himself with the opposition between the two principles and established dialectically, a new synthesis. This synthesis of rationality and irrationality was expressed in his concept of the unconscious. If all that is real were conscious, then indeed man would be a rational being, for his rational thought follows the laws of logic. But the overwhelming part of his inner experience is unconscious, and for this reason is not subject to the control of logic, reason, and will. Human irrationality dominates in the unconscious. Logic governs in the conscious. But, and this is decisive, the unconscious steers consciousness, and thus the behavior of man. With this concept of the determination of man by the unconscious, Freud, without being aware of it, repeated a thesis that Spinoza had already expressed. But though it was marginal in Spinoza's system, it was central in that of Freud.

Freud resolved the opposition not in a static way in which he would have allowed one of the two sides to prevail. If he had declared reason to be the victor, he would have remained an enlightenment philosopher; if he had given the decisive role to irrationality, he would have become a conservative romantic, as so many significant thinkers of the nineteenth century were. Though it is true, he thought, that man is driven by irrational forces—the libido and, especially in its pregenital stages of evolution, his ego—his reason and his will are also not without strength. The power of reason expresses itself in the first place in the fact that man can understand his irrationality by the use of reason. Thus he founded the science of human irrationality—psychoanalytic theory. But he did not stop at theory. By the fact that a person in the analytic process can make his own unconscious conscious, he can also liberate himself from the dominance of unconscious strivings; instead of repressing them, he can negate them, that is, he can decline their satisfaction and control them with his will. This, so Freud thought, is possible because the grownup has as an ally a stronger ego than the child. Freud's psychoanalytic therapy was based on the hope of overcoming, or at least restraining, the unconscious impulses, which, working in the dark, had previously been outside of man's control.

Historically speaking one can look at Freud's theory as the fruitful synthesis of rationalism and romanticism; the creative power of this synthesis may be one of the reasons why Freud's thinking became a dominating influence during the twentieth century.

The fruitfulness of the synthesis becomes very evident in the two most important defections from Freud, that of Adler and that of Jung. Both exploded the Freudian synthesis and returned to the two original oppositions. Adler, rooted in the short-lived optimism of the lower middle classes, constructed a one-sided rationalistic-optimistic theory. He believed that the innate disabilities are the very conditions of strength, that with intellectual understanding of a situation, man can liberate himself and make the tragedy of life disappear. Jung, on the other hand, was a romantic who saw the sources of all human strength in the unconscious. He recognized the wealth and depth of symbols and myths much more profoundly than Freud, whose views were narrowed down by his sexual theory. Their aims, however, were contradictory. Freud wanted to understand the unconscious in order to weaken and control it; Jung, in order to gain an increased vitality from it. It was the interest of the unconscious that united the two men for some time, without their being aware that they were moving in opposite directions. Though they had stopped on their way for a while, in order to talk about the unconscious, they fell under the spell of the illusion that they were proceeding in the same direction.

Closely related to Freud's synthesis of rationality and irrationality is another one, the synthesis of the conflict between determinism and indeterminism of the will. Freud was a determinist; he believed that man is not free because he is determined by the unconscious, the id, and the superego. But, and this but is of decisive importance for Freud, man is also not wholly determined. With the help of the analytic method he can gain control over the unconscious. Man is not free and yet his task is to gain an optimum of freedom. With this position of alternativism,[7] which resembles in its essence those of Spinoza and Marx, Freud accomplished another fruitful synthesis of two opposite poles.

Did Freud recognize the moral factor as a fundamental part in his model of man? The answer to this question is definitely in the negative. Man develops exclusively under the influence of his self-interest, which demands optimal satisfaction of his libidinal impulses, always under the condition that they do not endanger his interest in self-preservation (the reality principle). The moral problem, which traditionally has been that of the conflict between altruism and egoism, disappeared in Freud's thinking. Egoism is the only driving force, and conflict exists only between the two forms of egoism, the libidinous and the material. It hardly needs to be proven that Freud, in this view of man as basically egotistical, followed the concepts of bourgeois thinking. Nevertheless, if one were to say that Freud simply denied the existence of conscience as an effective element in his model of human nature, one would not be correct. Freud recognized the power of conscience, but he explained conscience, and in so doing deprived it of all objective validity. His explanation is that conscience is the superego, which is a replica of all the commandments and prohibitions of the father (or the father's superego) with whom the little boy identifies himself when, motivated by castration anxiety, he overcomes his Oedipal strivings. This explanation refers to both elements of conscience: the formal one, that is, the how of conscience formation, and the substantial one, that is, which norms are contents of conscience. Since the essential part of fatherly norms and the fatherly superego is socially conditioned, or to put it more correctly, since the superego is nothing but the personal mode of social norms, Freud's explanation leads to a relativization of all moral norms. Each norm has its significance, not because of the validity of its contents, but on the basis of the psychological mechanism by which it is accepted. Good is what the internalized authority commands, and bad what it prohibits. Freud is undoubtedly right, inasmuch as the norms believed in by most people as moral are, to a large extent, nothing but norms established by society for the sake of its own optimal functioning. From this standpoint his theory is an important critique of existing conventional morality, and his theory of the superego unveils its true character. But one may assume that he did not intend this critical aspect of the theory and that it may not even have been conscious to him. He did not give his theory a critical turn, and he could hardly have done so because he was little concerned as to whether there are any norms the contents of which transcend a given social structure and correspond better to the demands of human nature and the laws of human growth.

Yet it would be doing Freud an injustice if we left it at that. Here, as so often, Freud transcended the framework of his own thinking and pointed to new possibilities, without being aware of it. In order to show this with regard to the problem of ethics we must return once more to Freud's theory in order to extract from it a thought it contains only implicitly. Freud assumed that character is determined by the various libidinous levels of development. He postulated the development from primary narcissism, that is, total unrelatedness, to oral-receptive, oral-sadistic, and anal-sadistic up to the genital level, which in principle is reached around puberty. He assumed that the fully developed mature person leaves the pregenital levels essentially behind him and his character is determined mainly by the genital libido. This scheme is primarily an evolutionary scheme of the libido, and of the resulting relatedness to the world, which has no obvious reference to values. Nevertheless, it is not difficult to recognize that implicitly it represents a scheme of values. The adult mature person, the genital character in Freud's sense, is capable of love and work, whereas the pregenital character is one that has not fully developed and is in this sense crippled. The clinical data of psychoanalysis make this much clearer than the theory. The oral-receptive person is a dependent, and the oral-sadistic, an exploitative character. The anal-sadistic character is that belonging to a person who enjoys the submission and suffering of others, and who is at the same time an avaricious, hoarding person. Only the genital character has reached full independence. He respects and, as Freud sometimes says, loves the other person. Precisely because the pregenital fixations are an expression of unsolved libido problems, they tend to foster the development of the neurotic character. What matters here is the fact that in Freud's evolutionary scheme (as also in many others) there is a hidden scale of values. The genital character is more highly developed than the pregenital. He is desirable and represents the goal, and hence the norm, for the development of character. For Freud, therefore, the anal-sadistic character, for instance, is not a value-neutral variation but the result of a failure in the normal process of development. Seen in this light we find that the hidden value scale in Freud's scheme of the libido and character is not too different from the humanistic scale of values; independence, respect for others, and love are better than dependence, avarice, and sadism.

One cannot talk about Freud's anthropology without discussing two special cases: (1) man and woman and (2) the child.

For Freud only the male is really a full human being. Woman is a crippled, castrated man. She suffers from this fate and can be happy only if she overcomes her castration complex by the acceptance of a child and husband. But she remains inferior also in other respects, such as being more narcissistic and less directed by conscience than man. This strange theory, according to which one half of the human race is only a crippled edition of the other half, has two sources. One was Freud's theory of sex. It followed in its premises the ideas of the Victorian period, which were that only the male has strong sexual desires and satisfactions, that the woman's desires are mainly those for the bearing and upbringing of children—and to serve the man. Freud gave a clear expression of this Victorian idea when he wrote "the libido is masculine." The belief in this Victorian concept of the woman as being without her own sexuality was only one expression of the extreme patriarchal concept of the natural superiority of the man over the woman.[8] The male, in patriarchal ideology, is more rational, realistic, responsible than the female, and hence destined by nature to be her leader and guide. How completely Freud shared this point of view of his society follows from his reaction to the demand for political and social equality of women expressed by J. S. Mill, a thinker whom Freud deeply and profoundly admired in all respects. With regard to Mill's views on this point, Freud wrote that here Mill is simply "crazy" and that it is unthinkable for him (Freud) to imagine that his beloved bride should compete with him on the marketplace, instead of allowing herself to be protected by him.

Freud's patriarchal bias had two further serious consequences for his theory. One was that he could not recognize the nature of erotic love, since it is based on the male-female polarity which is only possible if male and female are equals, though different. Thus his whole system is centered around sexual not erotic love. Even in his later theory he applies Eros (the life instincts) only to the behavior of living organisms in general but does not extend it to the male-female dimension.

The other equally serious consequence was that Freud overlooked for the largest part of his life completely the primary tie of the child (boy and girl) to the mother, the nature of motherly love and the fear of mother. He could conceive the deeper tie to mother only in terms of the Oedipus situation when the little boy is already a little man for whom mother is not any more a strong power but a sexual object like for father and who is afraid only of father and not mother. Only in the last years of his life did Freud begin to see this primary tie though by no means in all its importance.[9]

It seems that aside from the repression of his own strong fixation to his mother, Freud's patriarchal bias did not permit him consciously to consider the woman-mother as the powerful figure to which the child is bound.[10] It is an example of the negative effect of orthodoxy that almost all other analysts accepted Freud's theories of sexuality and the secondary role of mother in spite of the overwhelming evidence to the contrary.

Here, as everywhere else, pointing to the connection between the theory and its social determinants, of course, does not prove that the theory is wrong; but if one examines the clinical evidence carefully, it does not confirm Freud's theory. I cannot discuss it in this context; a number of psychoanalysts, starting with Karen Horney's pioneering work with regard to this point, have presented clinical findings that contradict Freud's hypothesis.[11]

Summarizing, it might only be said that Freud's theory of women, though always imaginative and fascinating by its logic, seems to contain only a minimum of truth, probably because Freud was so deeply imbued by his patriarchal bias.

Freud's picture of the child is quite a different matter. Like the woman, the child also has been the object of oppression and exploitation by the father throughout history. He (or she) was, like slave and wife, the property of the man-father, who had "given" him life, and who could do with him whatever he liked, arbitrarily and unrestrictedly, as with all property. (The institution of the sacrifice of children, which was so widely spread through the world, is one of the many manifestations of this constellation.)

Children could defend themselves even less well than women and slaves. Women have fought a guerrilla war against the patriarchate in their own way; slaves have rebelled many times in one form or the other. But temper tantrums, refusal to eat, constipation, and bed-wetting are not the weapons by which one can overthrow a powerful system. The only result was that the child developed into a crippled, inhibited, and often evil adult, who took revenge on his own children for what had been done to him.

The domination of children was expressed, if not in brutal, physical, then in psychic exploitation. The adult demanded from the child the satisfaction of his vanity, of his wish for obedience, of the adaptation to his moods, and so on. Of especial importance is the fact that the adult did not take the child seriously. The child, one assumed, has no psychic life of his own; he was supposed to be a blank sheet of paper on which the adult had the right and the obligation to write the text. (Another version of "the white man's burden.") It followed from this that one believed it right to lie to children. If one lies to adults one has to excuse it in some way. Lying to the child did not require any excuses, because after all, the child is not a full human being. The same principle is employed toward adults when they are strangers, enemies, sick, criminals, or members of an inferior and exploited class or race. By and large, only those who are not powerless have the right to demand the truth; this is the principle applied in all more highly developed societies in history, even though it was not the ideology.

The revolution of the child, like that of the woman, began in the nineteenth century. One began to see that the child was not a blank sheet of paper, but a highly developed, curious, imaginative, sensitive being in need of stimulation. One symptom of this new appreciation of the child was, in the field of education, the Montessori method. Another was the much more influential theory of Freud. He expressed the view, and could prove it clinically, that unfavorable influences in childhood have the most aggravating consequences for later development. He could describe the peculiar and complicated mental and emotional processes in the child. He emphasized particularly the fact that was generally denied, namely, that the child is a passionate being, with sensuous drives and fantasies, which give his life a dramatic quality.

Freud went furthest in this radically new appreciation of the child when he assumed in the beginning of his clinical work that many neuroses have their origin in acts of sexual seduction of children by adults, and particularly their parents. At this moment he became, so to speak, the accusor against parental exploitation in the name of the integrity and freedom of the child. However, if one considers the intensity of Freud's rootedness in the patriarchal authoritarian system, it is not surprising that he gave up this radical position later on. He discovered that his patients had projected their own infantile desires and fantasies onto the parents in a number of cases, though in reality no such seduction had taken place. He generalized these cases and came to the conclusion, in connection with his libido theory, that the child was a little criminal and pervert who only in the course of the evolution of the libido matures into a "normal" human being. Thus, Freud arrived at a picture of the "sinful child," which as some observers have commented, resembles the Augustinian picture of the child in essential points.[12]

After this change, the slogan was, so to speak, "the child is guilty"; he gets into conflicts because of his drives, and these conflicts, if poorly solved, result in neurotic illness. I cannot help suspecting that Freud was motivated in this change of opinion not so much by his clinical findings, as by his faith in the existing social order and its authorities. It seems that this suspicion is supported by several circumstances, primarily by the categorical fashion in which Freud declared that all memories of parental seduction are fantasies. Is such a categorical statement not in contrast to the fact that adult incestuous interest in children, including their own, is by no means rare?

Another reason for the assumption of Freud's partisanship in favor of parents lies in the treatment of parental figures, which is to be found in his published case histories. It is surprising to see how Freud falsifies the picture of parents and attributes qualities to them that are clearly in contrast to the facts presented by himself. As I have tried to show in the example of his case history of Little Hans, Freud mentioned the lack of threats on the part of his parents who are allegedly fully concerned with the welfare of the child, when in fact threats and seduction are so clearly present that one has to shut one's eyes in order not to see them. The same observation can be made in other case histories.

The interpretation of Freud's change from being an advocate of the child to a defender of the parents, is indirectly supported by the testimony of Sandor Ferenczi, one of Freud's most experienced and imaginative disciples. Ferenczi, who never wavered in his loyalty to Freud and his school, was caught in a severe conflict with Freud during the last years of Ferenczi's life; Ferenczi had developed ideas that deviated from those of Freud in two important points, and Freud reacted with such sharpness that he did not shake hands with Ferenczi at the last visit the latter made him (de Forest, n. d.). The one deviation that interests us less in this context was the thesis that the patient needs, for his cure, not only interpretation but also the love of the analyst. (Love is understood here in a nonsexual, nonexclusive sense.) The other and more important deviation in this context was Ferenczi's thesis that Freud had been right after all in his original view, that in reality adults were in many instances the seducers of children and that it was not always a matter of fantasies rooted in the child's instinctual life.[13] Aside from the importance of Ferenczi's clinical observation, one has to raise the question as to why Freud reacted so violently and passionately to this deviation of Ferenczi. Was it a matter of something more important than a clinical problem? It is not too farfetched to suppose that the main point was not the correctness of the clinical theory but the attitude toward authority. If it is true that Freud had withdrawn his original radical critique of the parents, that is, of social authority, and that he had adopted a position in favor of authority, then indeed, one may suspect that his reaction was owing to his ambivalence to social authority and that he reacted violently when he was reminded of the position he had given up, of, as it were, his "betrayal" of the child.

The conclusion of this sketch of Freud's picture of man requires a word on his concept of history. Freud developed the nucleus of a philosophy of history, although he had not intended to do this in a systematic form. At the beginning of history, we find man without culture, completely dedicated to the satisfaction of his instinctual drives and happy to that extent. This picture, however, is in contrast to another, which assumes a conflict already during this first phase of complete instinctual satisfaction. Man must leave this paradise precisely because the unlimited satisfaction of his drives leads to the conflict of the sons with the father, to the murder of the father, and eventually to the formation of the incest taboo. The rebellious sons gain a battle, but they lose the war against the fathers, whose prerogatives are now secured forever by "morality" and the social order (here too, one may think of Freud's ambivalence toward authority).

Freud's Concept of Man and Its Social Determinants

While in this aspect of Freud's thinking a state of unrestricted instinctual satisfaction was impossible in the long run, he developed another quite different thesis. In it, the possibility of this paradisical state is not denied, but it is only assumed that man cannot develop any culture as long as he remains in this paradise. For Freud, culture is conditioned by the partial nonsatisfaction of instinctual desires which lead, in turn, to sublimation or reaction formation. Man, then, is confronted with an alternative: total instinctual satisfaction but barbarism or partial instinctual frustration but cultural and mental development of man. Frequently, however, the process of sublimation fails, and man has to pay the price of neurosis for his cultural development. It must be emphasized that for Freud the conflict that exists between drives and civilization and culture of whatever kind is in no way identical with the conflict between drives and capitalistic or any other form of "repressive" social structure.[14] This cannot be otherwise because Freud only applied the consequences of his theory on instincts to history.

Freud's sympathies are on the side of culture, and not on that of the paradise of primitivity. But nevertheless his concept of history has a tragic element. Human progress necessarily leads to repression and neurosis. Man cannot have both happiness and progress. In spite of this tragic element, however, Freud in these concepts still remains an enlightenment thinker even though a skeptical one, for whom progress is no longer an unmixed blessing. In the second phase of his work, after World War I, Freud's picture of history became truly tragic. Progress, beyond a certain point, is no longer only bought at great expense. It is in principle impossible. Man is only a battlefield on which the life and death instincts fight with each other. He can never liberate himself decisively from the tragic alternative of destroying others or himself.

Freud tried to mitigate the harshness of this thesis in an interesting letter to Einstein on the theme "Why War?" after World War I, but in the essential point Freud, who called himself a pacifist at that time, did not allow himself to be seduced either by his own wishes or by the embarrassment of expressing deep pessimism in the decade of new hope (1920–1930); he did not change or prettify the harshness of that which he believed to be the truth. The skeptical enlightenment philosopher, hit by the collapse of his world, became the total skeptic who looked at the fate of man in history as unmitigated tragedy.

Freud could hardly have reacted differently; his society appeared to him as the best possible one and not capable of improvement in any decisive way.

At the end of this sketch of Freud's anthropology I should stress that one can understand the greatness of Freud, that of the man and that of his work, fully only if one sees him in his immanent contradictions and as bound, or chained, in his social situation. If one believes that all his teachings in almost fifty years are not in need of any fundamental revision, or if one wants to make a revolutionary thinker of a tragic reformer, one may say something that appeals to many, for different reasons. I doubt that it furthers the understanding of Freud.

NOTES

1. The dependence of Freud's theory formation on the thinking of his teachers has been described by Peter Ammacher (1962). Holt (1965) summarizes approvingly the main thesis of this work in the following: "Many of the most puzzling and seemingly arbitrary turns of psychoanalytic theory, involving propositions that are false to the extent that they are testable at all, are either hidden biological assumptions or result directly from such assumptions, which Freud learned from his teachers in medical school. They became a basic part of his intellectual equipment, as unquestioned as the assumption of universal determinism, were probably not always recognized by him as biological, and thus were retained as necessary ingredients when he attempted to turn away from neurologizing to the construction of an abstract, psychological model."

2. See Fromm (1932).

3. This is specifically the philosophy based on the nineteenth-century mode of production. With the emergence of the second industrial revolution based on cybernation, the idea of unlimited production begins to conflict with the older idea of scarcity. Up to now one has avoided the full confrontation with this contradiction in several ways: the first by channeling such a large part of industrial production into the field of armament, and recently space travel, that consumption of useful goods is much more restricted than would otherwise be necessary; second, by building in obsolescence and channeling consumption in such a way that the affluent part of the population practices waste, while the nonaffluent and poorer part continues to live under the principle of scarcity. Aside from this, by building up the fantasy of unlimited consumption, almost the whole population remains psychologically wedded to the philosophy of relative scarcity, because it can never buy everything the image makers say is necessary for happiness. As a result, while merely technically speaking, there is abundance and waste, socially and psychologically, most people still live in the psychology of material or psychological scarcity.

4. See, to this point, Fromm, *Sigmund Freud's Mission* (1959).

5. Freud expressed this new pessimism very succinctly in *Civilization and Its*

Discontents (1962) where he portrays man as lazy and in need of strong leaders.

6. In *The Heart of Man* (1964) I have tried to connect Freud's death instinct with the theory of anal libido. In a yet unpublished manuscript on the causes of human destructiveness, I have analyzed the relation between sexuality and Eros in Freud's system.

7. See the discussion of alternativism in *The Heart of Man* (Fromm, 1964).

8. The full understanding of this patriarchal ideology would require a more detailed discussion. Suffice it to say here that women constitute a class dominated and exploited by men in all patriarchal societies; like all exploiting groups, the dominant males have to produce ideologies in order to explain their domination as being natural, and hence as necessary and justified. Women, like most dominated classes, have accepted the male ideology, though privately they often carried with them their own and opposite ideas. It seems that the liberation of women began in the twentieth century, and it goes together with a weakening of the patriarchal system in industrial society, though complete de facto equality of women, even today, does not exist in any country. The basis for the analysis of patriarchal/matriarchal societies was laid by Bachofen (1859), and the whole problem can hardly be understood fully without a knowledge of Bachofen's work. See the translation of his selected writings (Bachofen, 1967).

9. See the excellent paper by John Bowlby (1958).

10. For the same reason Freud ignored also Bachofen's rich material on mother right, which is one of the most important sources for the understanding of the child's tie to mother.

11. See also Ashley Montagu's writings on this problem.

12. For instance, Robert Wälder, one of the most learned and uncompromising representatives of Freudian orthodoxy.

13. A detailed description of this conflict is found in Fromm's *Sigmund Freud's Mission*.

14. Herbert Marcuse, who presents Freud as a revolutionary thinker and not as a liberal reformer, tried to give a picture of a state of complete drive satisfaction in a free, in contrast to a "repressive," society. Quite regardless of the validity of his construction, he failed to state that in this point he negates an essential part of the Freudian system. A statement about this contradiction would have indicated how questionable this picture of the revolutionary Freud is.

REFERENCES

Ammacher, Peter. *Psychological Issues* (1962).

Bachofen, J. J. *Das Mutterrecht.* 1859.

——. *Myth, Religion, and the Mother Right.* Princeton, N.J.: Princeton University Press, 1967.

Bowlby, John. "The Nature of the Child's Tie to Mother." *International Journal of Psycho-Analysis* 35(1958):355–372.

de Forest, Izette. Personal communication by one of Ferenczi's students and friends.

Freud, Sigmund. *Civilization and its Discontents.* New York: Norton, 1962.

Fromm, Erich. *The Heart of Man.* New York: Harper, 1964.

——. *Sigmund Freud's Mission.* New York: Harper, 1959.

——. "Psychoanalytic Characterology and its Significance for Social Psychology." 1932.

Holt, Robert R. "A Review of Some of Freud's Biological Assumptions and Their Influence on His Theories." In Norman S. Greenfield and William C. Lewis, eds., *Psychoanalysis and Current Biological Thought*. Madison: The University of Wisconsin Press, 1965.

The New Significance
of Psychoanalytic Structure

Psychoanalysts are becoming more interested in their structure of inquiry. This new significance of psychoanalytic structure springs from various sources, and I shall mention some below. But the discovery of order among processes and patterns in any field is neither a magical nor a final resolution of its problems, not even in our age of instant communication and technology of full exposure. Excitement of discovery quickly gives way, instead, to slow and steady checking and refinement of the new instrument of knowledge over a long period of time in many different contexts of inquiry. William James once remarked that the truth of an idea does not immediately register its cash value. Psychoanalysts always face this developmental lag in their daily efforts at transforming unconscious into conscious experience, but they have long faced it in their intermittent efforts at clarifying the structure of psychoanalysis and thereby simplifying its fundamentals for therapeutic purposes.

Psychoanalytic self-knowledge is a difficult and uncommon achievement, requiring patient and intensive exploration. Two external factors, today, are threatening to make it even more so. First, the insights of psychoanalytic inquiry are being widely and superficially used with some success yet without personal experience in many other psychotherapies: supportive, hypnotic, goal-oriented, client-centered, and drug therapies in addition to group, milieu, family, and community therapies. Second, the established metapsychologies of psychoanalysis are putting arbitrary restraints on the psychological vision of today's patient who appears less blocked than earlier Freudian and later neo-Freudian patients about sexual and adjustive functions; he suffers less from unsatisfied biological needs and failed social securities than from blockages of psychological freedom and personal fulfillment or, as he reports them, from being "anxious and depressed" and "just plain miserable."

I

These external factors alone might not, perhaps, have motivated serious concern with the significance of psychoanalytic structure. But in the recent past, psychoanalysts have also become more aware of the limits and possibilities of a basically psychological therapy. To what extent is it really biological as the instinctual Freudians believed, or really sociological as the cultural and environmental neo-Freudians believed, or even really linguistic as the grammarian non-Freudians began to teach? And to what extent, above all, do perspectives on metapsychology make psychological differences? In response, psychoanalysts tried to define the features of psychoanalysis that are internal to its psychological inquiry and specific to its psychotherapeutic objectives. And in so doing, they also had to reconsider the nature of psychoanalysis as science.[1]

Until the late 1940's, each perspective on metapsychology was taken exclusively and used separately. There were Freudians, Adlerians, Jungians, Rankians, and so on, each hoping to keep the psychoanalytic experience entirely within its special perspective. In their outlines, separatism in metapsychology far outweighed unity in psychology.[2] They did not quarrel, for example, over whether anxiety is a definition of the same order as transference and resistance, or over how transference, resistance, and anxiety interweave with counteranxiety, counterresistance, and countertransference in the actual psychoanalytic experience and how these interweavings are to be studied. They actively disagreed, rather, about the basic interpretation of psychological disturbance, and each in his own way founded and defended his instinctual dialectics, struggles for power, archetypes of the collective unconscious, conflicts of pure will, and so on. Quite naturally, each saw success as the patient's acceptance of his interpretive slant; each saw failure as his inability to trace it in the patient's unconscious experience. They built these metapsychologies along parallel lines, and crossing them automatically exposed the maverick to prejudice and dispute about the true psychoanalytic character of his therapy.

Among internal sources of this new significance of psychoanalytic structure, then, the conflicts among established metapsychologies are major. Obviously, all psychoanalysts could produce positive results without instant and mysterious conversion to their special perspectives on metapsychology. But if they actually did something else, what was it? Even before this new concern with structure, Clara Thompson (1950, pp. 242–243) observed that "many patients achieve deep and lasting insight under or in spite of the various doctrines taught them if in the interpersonal experience with the analyst the patient's genuine problems in living have been explored." In the context of her observation "interpersonal" refers to the more general and common sense of two persons and what goes on between them. The second sense of it in current psychoanalytic discussion refers to Harry Stack Sullivan's psychiatry and to the distinctive metapsychology he built to interpret it. It is in the first sense, here, that she emphasized the "interpersonal" in psychoanalysis. Because it may be used in both senses, the only way to avoid probable confusion is to specify whether "interpersonal" qualifies an "experience" or a "doctrine." It follows that the psychoanalytic inquiry, rather than the various doctrines taught, defines the psychoanalytic experience. In other words, a structure of inquiry defines this experience of therapy by its orders of observation, definition, transformation, and explanation in psychology, not by its order of interpretation, metaphor, myth, or slogan of metapsychology. This does not mean that psychoanalytic psychology is, or ever strives to be, free and clear of metapsychology; no therapeutic experience ever becomes whole and terminable unless the two move forward in tandem. But it does mean that any perspective on metapsychology, including Harry Stack Sullivan's, may also apply to experiences in other psychological therapies and to experiences in living anywhere else.

To be clear and effective, psychoanalysis has to give up the supremacy of perspectives on metapsychology. Its structure of inquiry, rather, leads to its experience of therapy. This structure is based on both empirical observation and definition and systematic transformation and explanation, by and through which interpretive metapsychology enters this experience. With an open and radical pluralism at the interpretive order, then, it is possible to place established and evolving perspectives in an overall mapping of the psychoanalytic field. Discriminating against none and related to all, the experience of psychoanalytic therapy is no longer the exclusive property of any single metapsychology, traditional or current. Its explanatory range is now defined, instead, by empirical and systematic orders of the structure of psychoanalytic inquiry.

On this new mapping of the psychoanalytic field, pinpoint a fact and a fulfillment. First is the stubborn fact that symbols of unconscious experience always have more than one interpretation; if there's a will there's a way is still true about them because they are suggestive and may be stretched to cover many different processes and patterns. And second is fulfilled respect for everybody's right to make judgments of beliefs, values, and ideals; no psychoanalyst can accept less because the psychology of these judgments, alone, does not make or break them.

All interpretations of unconscious experience follow from the interpreter's, psychoanalyst's or patient's, philosophy of experience. They follow from his system of beliefs, values, and ideals. Historically, it was only after the psychoanalytic experience became independent of exclusive ties to instinctual dialectics that other equally programmatic perspectives could be set forth. Many metapsychologies now exist. There are the very well formulated—instinctual dialectics, struggle for power, the collective unconscious, pure will, and so on; the less formal mysticisms and existentialist irrationalisms; the very individual and impressionistic points of view that do not lend themselves to institutionalization as a school, group, or movement. But when the psychoanalyst's metapsychology is no longer dominant and the patient's acquires equal respect, the situation loses its one-way simplicity. For no matter what a particular psychoanalyst happens to believe and live, it is clear that his patient may have perspectives that best express and affirm his own lived experience. This new diversity is especially relevant to the present stage of our social history and cultural development. Just consider, for a moment, the wide gap between the preatomic and atomic generations, and little more needs to be said. Enforced by a revolution in automated technology, new electronic communications, new frontiers in outer space and exploding populations on earth, rising expectations in political and economic security, the urgency of unity among all races, colors and creeds, this gap cuts all the way down to the roots of our experience. And because social and cultural change is now so swift and unprecedented, the established systems and symbols of beliefs, values, and ideals do not articulate the meanings they once did, and genuine new ones are not yet found and set in personal experience. Above, I suggested the main implication of this for the psychoanalysis of today's patient: an open and radical pluralism at the interpretive order of metapsychology.

II

Given this state of affairs in contemporary metapsychology, it is necessary to look elsewhere in psychoanalysis for its distinguishing features as interpersonal experience. A number of approaches already exists to point the way. They all reorganize and refine the internal structure of psychoanalysis and differentiate it from other structures of psychotherapeutic inquiry. But each one also reflects the special interests of its maker: one a general psychological theory, another a special view of human nature and development, still a third the terms and conditions of psychoanalytic inquiry and experience. The first maps a general psychoanalytic theory of human psychology, from the experimental laboratory to learning theory to developmental psychology to change in awareness, and then separates it from a special clinical psychoanalytic theory whose success or failure is not considered scientific and does not, therefore, modify the general theory (Rapaport, 1960). The second designs a grid coordinating the elements of psychoanalytic theory and therapy for a special perspective on metapsychology without, however, making room for the perspectives of other psychoanalysts and patients (Bion, 1963). The third outlines a structure that is directly clinical in origin and function yet also open to traditional as well as evolving metapsychologies (Wolstein, 1967). I list these approaches not to compare them, since I have already done so elsewhere, but only to illustrate types of approach to the problem of structure in recent psychoanalytic research. I turn, now, to a brief sketch of the third one.

A structure of inquiry guides the selection and organization of terms and conditions that demarcate psychoanalysis. The orders of this structure are:

(1) observation of gross experience
(2) definition of operational terms
(3) postulates of transformation
(4) theory of explanation
(5) perspectives on metapsychology

These orders bridge (1) presented psychological problems and (2) definitions of transference, resistance, anxiety and counteranxiety, counterresistance, countertransference to (3) postulates of genesis and function, structure and dynamism, immediacy and reflection, and (4) theory of unconscious experience. All these are supported by (5) perspectives on metapsychology of both participants. (1) and (2) are empirical, (3) and (4) are systematic and theoretical, while (5) is interpretive and speculative. (4) states the leading explanatory principle of all psychoanalytic inquires and (1) through (5) set off the experience of psychoanalytic therapy, as an integrated process, from experiences of other psychotherapies.

Following this sketch, how does the psychoanalyst proceed? To put it schematically: At (1), he makes detailed observations of selected processes and patterns of problems his patient presents in the experiential field of therapy. At (2), he introduces two sets of definition, one of his patient and one of himself, to specify distortions in perception, disturbances in awareness and difficulties in living. At (3), he adopts three pairs of postulates, for his patient and himself, by which to transform the defined observations. At (4), he applies the theory of unconscious experience to both the original and the transformed observations in order to explain them. And at (5), both participants may interpret these psychological problems and resolutions, together with almost any other aspect of living they find interesting, in accordance with one or several perspectives on metapsychology. (1) through (4) guide procedures that psychoanalysts share by virtue of the experience they seek and explore with patients, whereas (5) embraces all doctrines of the many psychoanalysts and patients undertaking this inquiry to have this experience.

In this structure, the distinction of psychology from systems of beliefs, values, and ideals may be drawn for interdisciplinary purposes between (4) and (5). This distinction makes it possible to avoid confusing psychological with philosophical inquiry and to avert the lifeless repetition of moralistic and adjustive exercises. Even apart from interdisciplinary purposes, it is clear that systems of beliefs, values, and ideals are present and continuous in every phase of the psychoanalytic experience through each order of the psychoanalytic structure. But the point of placing them at (5) is to emphasize the essential line differentiating the empirical and systematic from the interpretive and speculative operations. In no way does the planning of this structure imply, however, that psychoanalytic patients consider judgments of metapsychology less significant than judgments in psychology, only that they have to learn why these two sorts of judgment are not interchangeable and cannot be reduced to each other.

The New Significance of Psychoanalytic Structure

As the empirical and systematic orders, (1) through (4) are necessary for the structure of psychoanalytic inquiry. But they do not suffice for the experience of psychoanalytic therapy, as this also requires a reconstructive movement to (5). Not for any reason of pure logic or scientific elegance is a fifth order therefore added to the structure. It is added for the factual reason that psychoanalysts and patients all have metapsychologies—more or less aware, more or less formal—that are present and continuous in the shared experience because they themselves are. But (5) is in no sense a substitute for (1) through (4). There is nothing new, of course, in the suggestion that perspectives on metapsychology, philosophies of life, slogans for action, and metaphors of the ineffable affecting the psychoanalytic experience are the essentials of psychoanalytic inquiry. But underlining the distinction of (1) through (4) from (5) may help to sharpen the difference between inquiry and therapy in a new way. That is, only those aspects of (1) that are defined at (2) can then be transformed at (3) and explained at (4); other aspects of (1) that are metapsychological belong at (5), however, because they provide the systems of beliefs, values, and ideals in which inquiry gives form to therapy. I make the distinction this way in accordance with a special perspective at (5), affirming philosophies of humanism, science, democracy, and also, therefore, psychoanalytic metapsychologies concerned with individuality, truth, and freedom.

Recall, here, that science and art are not the same, and it may further illuminate the distinction of (1) through (4) from (5). For structure of psychoanalytic inquiry is science, accomplishment of its therapeutic experience art. No matter how closely an artist follows the known structure of his medium the outcome of his efforts in some unique ways is, finally, the outcome of his induplicable self. The psychoanalyst's aim as scientist, on the other hand, is to clarify his structure of inquiry in order to discover common features in the various therapeutic experiences arising from it. And this defines his field. He finds gross experience in the field of therapeutic inquiry consisting of a complex of observable processes and patterns that continually interweave. Under the selective conditions of his inquiry, he may define some as recurrent and covariant, of these some as genuine or distorted, others as vague or irrelevant. After frequently observing and defining them, he may then try to transform and explain them, making possible new observations of gross experience. He can do this because transformations and explanations, while systematically related to one another, are also empirically rooted in observations and definitions of the shared experience.

There are many intriguing aspects of the relations of (1)-(2) and (3)-(4), but they extend beyond the theme of this chapter. Consider, however, a major question in any psychoanalytic inquiry. How do therapeutic results satisfy requirements of the structure when we still have no sure way of knowing in advance which observations are most relevant to a particular phase of the inquiry or to a later application of the overall structure? This sort of question is best answered at later stages of the work, but, even then, it is not always clear that the patient needs answers to close his own experience of therapy or seeks them to satisfy criteria of his psychoanalyst's structure of inquiry. At present, the answer remains a matter of therapeutic art.

To summarize this brief sketch of psychoanalytic structure: A psychoanalyst tries to explain selected observations at (1) by appropriate

TABLE 5–1
Symbols of Representation

ORDERS OF PSYCHOANALYTIC INQUIRY				
EMPIRICAL		SYSTEMATIC		INTERPRETIVE
OBSERVATION	DEFINITION	POSTULATION	THEORY	METAPSYCHOLOGY
(1)	(2)	(3)	(4)	(5)
transference	transference	genesis	unconscious	Freudian
t_n	t	G	experience	$[M_1]$
			U	
resistance	resistance	function		Adlerian
r_n	r	F		$[M_2]$
anxiety	anxiety	structure		Jungian
a_n	a	S		$[M_3]$
counter-	counter-	dynamism		Rankian
anxiety	anxiety	D		$[M_4]$
ca_n	ca			.
counter-	counter-	immediacy		.
resistance	resistance	I		.
cr_n	cr			.
counter-	counter-	reflection		.
transference	transference	R		.
ct_n	ct			$[M_n]$

statements of (2) through (4) and, with his patient, tries to interpret them at (5). This structure is scientific because it retains roots in empirical observation while producing systematic explanation. As a matter of practical convenience, its terms may be symbolically represented and worked with (see Table 5–1 and Wolstein, 1967, chap. 4). But the inquiry does not then become either purely symbolic or simply deductive. (4) is linked to (2) through the transformational mediation of (3), (3) to (1) through the definitional mediation of (2), (5) to (1) through (4) through the interpretational mediation of the particular participant's systems of beliefs, values, and ideals. No chain of systematic deduction, however, is capable of demonstrating the existence of processes and patterns that, at some point in the inquiry, cannot also be empirically observed and defined. This has been clear since David Hume's argument against necessary connection, on which Immanuel Kant based his critique of pure reason and from which Georg Hegel projected his dialectic of appearance and reality. Even the most rigorous systematic operations without empirical consequences, putting it briefly, fail to establish knowledge about anything in particular beyond themselves.

III

Is psychoanalysis a science? The answer is, for the present, a qualified yes. When, more than eighty years ago, a few Viennese psychotherapists began to work in comparative isolation, neither the question nor the answer was relevant. These pioneers did not stop long enough to ask it of their rapidly expanding field of inquiry, let alone answer it to the critical satisfaction of scientists and philosophers then on the sidelines. Courageously and quite directly, they simply used the best structure of inquiry they could produce to explore psychological problems live. As the new psychoanalytic therapists began to publish, however, those on the sidelines began to grow curious about this new psychological inquiry. Gradually, academic psychologists and philosophers of science became involved with evaluating its methods and results. And they found them flawed on such grounds as empirical reliability of results, intrapsychic focus of methods, and interpretive truth of its singular metapsychology. But like some contemporary critics, they also failed to appreciate the qualitative requirements of direct inquiry into psychological problems. Because psychoanalysis did not justify itself in accordance with experimental and mathematical standards of the physical sciences, they treated it as the proverbial stepchild and denied it scientific status.

Yet it is mainly because the scientific status of psychoanalysis is a philosophical question that it is here answered with only a qualified yes. Its implications for philosophy of science are clear: either to outline a unified structure that includes psychoanalysis among the sciences or to set general distinctions among the major sciences that make room for psychoanalysis as an independent, self-corrective inquiry. Awaiting further clarification of this, psychoanalysts must be content to continue elaborating their structure of inquiry and leave its philosophical status to philosophers of science. Between a current philosophical view of the nature of science, however, and a working structure of psychoanalytic knowledge, to the extent that both are free of absolute conventions, the choice need not be arbitrary. Yes, psychoanalysis is science; no, it does not meet experimental and mathematical standards of the physical sciences. To include psychoanalysis among the human sciences, it is necessary to seek basic changes in both philosophy of science and psychoanalysis. If the present psychoanalytic structure meets modified requirements of both disciplines, this is not the only factor in judging its worth since its success also depends on the psychological possibilities it innovates. But if this structure fails to meet the requirements, this too is not the only factor in judging its worth since both disciplines may now be too narrow empirically and too abstract systematically. Just as any future psychoanalytic inquiry must realize certain philosophical refinements of (1) observation, (2) definition, (3) transformation, (4) explanation, and (5) interpretation, so must every philosophy of science come to terms with the hard empiricism of actual psychoanalytic experience.

Recall, here, the generic meaning of science, namely, knowledge. All fields are subject to inquiry, it is clear, without having to duplicate the structure of any single one, not even of mathematical physics and molecular biology, the most idolized and idealized in this century. It is, rather, the limits and possibilities of a specific field that set the terms of its specific structure, and no one needs to justify inquiry and knowledge for all. This is no less true for psychoanalysis than for physics and biology. To put this another way, reverse the situation for a moment and try to imagine forcing the experimental and mathematical sciences to fit structures of inquiry into the qualitative study of problems in living. Whether a unified structure can ever be so formulated as to cover all fields of inquiry, from mathematical physics and molecular biology to psychoanalytic experience and systems of beliefs, values, and ideals, remains a crucial issue in philosophy. But no such structure can arbitrarily eliminate the inquiry and knowledge of any one field and, then, make its claim stick on a priori grounds.

From early roots in hypnosis and cathartic therapy, psychoanalysis has moved the development of this structure forward. It did this by stating and restating its definitions to simplify observation of deeply experienced problems in living, expanding and modifying postulates to guide transformation of defined observation, clarifying and refining its theory to explain both the defined and the transformed observations as unconscious impinging on conscious processes and patterns, all this taking place under the umbrella of various metapsychologies. Today, psychoanalysts agree most about two sets of definition, transference, resistance, anxiety and counteranxiety, counterresistance, countertransference; about three pairs of postulates, genesis and function, structure and dynamism, immediacy and reflection; and about the controlling theory of unconscious experience. They disagree most, as already noted, about perspectives on metapsychology that, depending on their individual commitments, color their statements of psychoanalytic psychology with all shades of beliefs, values, and ideals. In the heat of controversy and in the strife for innovation, some even lose sight of psychoanalysis as structure of inquiry and experience of therapy, and use it instead to defend such extrapsychoanalytic ends as religious visions of man and utopian theories of society, acceptable styles of living, and preferable codes of acting, existentialist irrationalisms, and mystical quests for transcendence.

IV

Hence the new significance of psychoanalytic structure. Psychoanalysis is here conceived as organized therapeutic inquiry into experiential fields of relatedness and communication. The structure of this inquiry, made up of orders (1) through (5), is that special field of psychology designed to clarify the operation of unconscious processes and patterns in personal experience. This new psychoanalytic structure, essentially I propose, outlines the limits and possibilities of a special type of psychological therapy. Structure of inquiry is not the same, clearly, as experience of therapy. It guides inquiry into selected aspects of gross experience, explaining psychological problems in living by defining and transforming them into conscious processes and patterns. Its (1) observations, (2)definitions, (3) transformations, and (4) explanations are not stated apart from a complex of (5) interpretations and speculations—intrapersonal, interpersonal, transpersonal, and nonpersonal—that both psychoanalyst and patient bring to their common effort at psychoanalytic inquiry and experience. In other words, as already noted, they apply the structure to a complex range of experience with the chief aim of expanding the shared scope of awareness. They try, that is, not to shrink but to expand awareness.

Potentially, everything either participant ever experiences of self and intimates, family and culture, society and world may be encountered in the therapeutic field, but insofar as their common effort is psychoanalytic, everything encountered is explored by application of the structure. For example, organic symptoms and disease are observed in some psychoanalytic inquiries, yet they are directly studied by biochemistry and neurophysiology; definition and enactment of social roles are observed, yet they are directly studied by sociology and social psychology; judgments of value are observed, yet they are directly studied by ethics and theory of value; cultural attitudes and philosophies of experience are observed, yet they are directly studied by anthropology and metaphysics. The present structure of inquiry guides the conduct of a therapy that is psychoanalytic, and distinctly so I believe, by virtue of its special empirical observations and definitions and by virtue of its special systematic postulates and theory.

NOTES

1. See, for example, Hook (1959).
2. For a clear review of them, see Mullahy (1948).

REFERENCES

Bion, W. *Elements of Psychoanalysis.* New York: Basic Books, 1963.
Hook, Sidney, ed. *Psychoanalysis, Scientific Method and Philosophy.* New York: New York University Press, 1959.

The New Significance of Psychoanalytic Structure

Mullahy, Patrick. *Oedipus*. New York: Hermitage House, 1948.

Rapaport, David. *The Structure of Psychoanalytic Theory*. New York: International Universities Press, 1960.

Thompson, Clara. *Psychoanalysis*. New York: Hermitage House, 1950.

Wolstein, Benjamin. *Theory of Psychoanalytic Therapy*. New York: Grune & Stratton, 1967.

The Interpersonal and the Intrapsychic
in Severe Psychopathology

The two and a half decades that have passed since Sullivan's major contributions have seen an increasing recognition of how much of the self originates from other persons. The roles of the family, society, culture, or any particular type of human environment have been steadily clarified by the numerous authors who have followed Sullivan's lead. After two and a half decades of exploration of the interpersonal, one of the main tasks that remains ahead of us is, in my opinion, the integration of the interpersonal with the intrapsychic. Though it is true that the self is built by virtue of relations with other human beings, it is also true that the sequence of the external influences is mediated and integrated by intrapsychic mechanisms. It is generally tacitly accepted that between the psychological input and output there are intervening processes. However, these processes must not be taken for granted and ignored, but studied in detail in their various and specific modalities. This internal processing does not consist only of a selection of response patterns but of an autonomous and in some respects creative organization of durable inner objects. These inner objects in their turn affect the output that is involved predominantly in interpersonal relations.

The study of the integration of the interpersonal with the intrapsychic is extremely difficult and will require decades of work by many investigators. In various writings I have reported some of my preliminary efforts in this field (Arieti, 1948, 1955, 1956, 1962a, 1965, 1967a, 1967b, 1967c, 1968). When interpersonal experiences cannot be put into a syntonic relationship with the self, special psychological states that may lead to severe pathology develop. In this chapter I shall try to illustrate how some flaws in this integrative function may be causally connected with several important aspects of such conditions as psychopathic personality, schizophrenia, and psychotic depression.

The Psychopathic Personality (Simple Type)

The first condition I shall take into consideration, and the least complicated of those I shall discuss in this chapter, is the psychopathic personality. I shall discuss only that variety that I have called the simple type (Arieti, 1967a).

The simple psychopath is an individual who periodically experiences strong wishes or needs that urge him toward immediate gratification. The gratification requires actions incompatible with the structure of the society in which the patient lives. Moreover, this gratification involves a type of object relationship in which no delay is possible. The desired object is not an object of contemplation but has to be possessed immediately. The nongratification of the need builds up tension, which is experienced by the patient as an unbearable discomfort. Whereas the psychotic realizes his wishes by changing his thinking processes, the psychopath realizes them by putting into effect actions that lead to a quick gratification. It does not matter how much in contrast with the norms of society these actions are. The patient resorts to an intrapsychic short-circuited mechanism which promptly leads to a feeling of gratification. By short-circuited mechanisms I mean the use of a quick or not adequately elaborated mental process, when the age, social situation, and usual mental condition would require a better-integrated response. When the simple psychopath acts in a psychopathic way he lives in accordance with what Freud called the pleasure principle. Difficulties are bypassed. For instance, when a feeling of hostility develops it is easier for him to discharge it than to try to change it, repress it, postpone it, or neutralize it.

In many instances, the psychopath could satisfy some of his needs in a more or less distant future, if he resorted to complicated series of actions which are necessary for a mature and socially acceptable attainment of goals. But he cannot wait. It is true that in many cases the immediate gratification is a substitute for something else he cannot hope to achieve or get. The problem, however, is more complicated. When the patient acts psychopathically he reverts to a type of intrapsychic organization that needs quick responses. Future satisfaction of needs is something that he cannot understand very well and that has no emotional impact on him. He lives emotionally in the pres-

121

ent and completely disregards tomorrow. Intellectually, of course, the psychopath *knows* that the future exists and that he could obtain his aims in ways acceptable to society. He also knows that by resorting to his quick methods he will get into trouble. But this knowledge has for him only a theoretical reality, and he experiences it only in a vague, faint way, without any emotional impact.

At first impression, thus, one could think that the simple psychopath is the victim of the so-called irresistible impulse, and, as a matter of fact, during legal prosecutions psychopathic patients have defended themselves by declaring that such was the case. However, we all know that if a policeman is nearby the psychopath will not indulge in the antisocial act; he will control himself until a more opportune moment. Thus the doctrine of the irresistible impulse is shattered to pieces. The psychopathic impulse seems indeed at least theoretically resistible.

The presence of the policeman, as a preventive measure, can give us, however, some clues about the interplay of the interpersonal and the intrapsychic in the symptomatology of the simple psychopath. This type of patient is in some respects similar to a little child, who wants immediate gratification; the breast now, the rattle now, the toy now, being on mother's lap right now. He cannot postpone his pleasure. Mother repeatedly teaches her child what not to do. Many mothers have noticed that between the age of two and four the child will not do the forbidden thing only if mother is present. If she is absent, the child will follow the urge. Only at age four has the maternal sanction become well internalized. The "no," originated interpersonally, has become intrapsychic. One could thus be inclined to conclude that the simple psychopath has reverted to a type of intrapsychic organization, which corresponds to that of the child between two and four. This interpretation however is not complete. First, we must study how this internalization takes place in normal children; second, we must see why this mechanism is defective in the psychopath.

Normal children learn gradually to postpone gratification. They learn to do so if they are consistently trained to expect substitute gratification at progressively lengthening intervals. For instance, little George wants a second ice cream. He wants it at all cost; he says he needs it. But if the mother keeps the child on her lap, caresses him, and says, "No, George, you can't have it now," little George will be able to accept this deprivation, because it is immediately compensated by the tenderness of mother. Later, in similar cases, he will get the approval of mother as a compensation for the deprivation, instead of direct tenderness. Still later he will get only a promise, that is, the hope that something good will happen to him as a reward for not responding immediately to impulsive urges. Promises and hopes, though abstract visualizations of things that have not yet materialized, retain the flavor or an echo of mother's approval and tenderness. The mother who used to be only the giver, the helper, the assuager of hunger, thirst, cold, loneliness, immobility, and any other present discomfort from now on becomes also the giver of hopes and promises. She becomes the announcer of the future; she opens the door to a mental orientation of optimism for what is yet to come.

It could be that the future simple psychopath did not go through these normal stages. What appeared to the child as deprivation held no compensations. No benevolent mother was there to help the child to make the transition from immediate gratification to postponement. He did not learn to expect approval and tenderness, to experience hope, and to anticipate the fulfillment of a promise. Frustration remained for him a very unpleasant, unbearable experience. Thus he continued to exercise his neuronal patterns in circuits that referred to the present and led to quick responses.

This explanation is in my opinion correct, but not yet a complete one. Inability to modify, suppress, or postpone the need for gratification does not constitute the whole pathology. Wanting two ice creams right now may be immature, but not necessarily psychopathic; to reveal psychopathic tendencies, the child must steal the second ice cream.

A person may be desirous of quick gratification, but if he has the ability to experience a sufficient degree of anxiety or of guilt feeling he will not become a psychopath. In this particular context, anxiety means anxiety about future punishment; guilt feeling means the unpleasant feeling of deserving punishment, irrespective of whether the punishment is actualized or not.

Again, the interpersonal parent-child relationship has a great deal to do with this intrapsychic lack of anxiety or guilt of the psychopath. If at a certain stage of his development, the parents impress the misbehaving child with the possibility of future consequences of his behavior, if they present to the child the possibility not only of present but also of future punishment, and carry out the punishment at a certain interval after the misbehavior, the child is not likely to become a psychopath. Present punishment is experienced immediately and is immediately related to the external world. Future punishment is not yet in actualization, and therefore exists only intrapsychically, that is, as a mental representation. These words may sound strange and harsh. For many years, in fact, opposite points of view have prevailed in psychiatry. Parents have been told how harmful it is to provoke anxiety in children, and how excessive anxiety, once it has been engendered, may lead to severe psychoneuroses and to schizophrenia. These statements are substantially correct. However, it may be equally true that the attitude of permissiveness, which parents have recently assumed, is excessive and is a contributing factor to the recent increase in juvenile delinquency all over the world. There is nothing wrong in eliciting some anxiety and guilt in children, provided, of course, these feelings are moderate and provided the mother has been able to orient the child toward a general state of optimistic expectation, by making it possible for him to live in an atmosphere of hope and promise.

Schizophrenia (Paranoid Type)

In the paranoid type of schizophrenia we have a markedly different interplay of interpersonal and intrapsychic mechanisms. Whereas in the psychopath some mechanisms fail to become intrapsychic, in the paranoid type of schizophrenia an attempt, though a fallacious one, is made to make interpersonal or external what is intrapsychic and cannot be syntonically integrated with the rest of the self.

I shall start by making some comments on concepts recently expressed by a distinguished guest of the William Alanson White Institute, the British psychiatrist, Ronald Laing. It seems to me that though there can be no doubt about the profundity and originality of some of Laing's observations, he does not draw any line of demarcation between schizophrenia and some possible antecedents of schizophrenia. For Laing the disorder is a brokendown relationship. The environment of the patient is so bad that he has to invent special strategies in order "to live in this unlivable situation." According to Laing the drama of the schizophrenic is a social drama or a family drama. Now it seems to me that the drama is even more tragic than

Severe Psychopathology

Laing portrays. As a matter of fact, we may even state that as long as the drama remains an interpersonal one and is not internalized in abnormal ways we do not have schizophrenia. In order to lead to schizophrenia the drama must injure the self very much and become a drama of the self by virtue of high symbolic processes and of special intrapsychic mechanisms. It is too simple to visualize the patient merely as a person who struggles in the midst of an unlivable situation, seen in cross section. People often deal with so-called unlivable situations with nonschizophrenic mechanisms. They rise to the occasion, tap their resources, rebel, escape, lead others, have new insights. The drama of the schizophrenic is that he cannot resort to these or other nonpsychotic strategies because his intrapsychic self is vulnerable and less apt to cope with the situation. He is not only the victim of others; he is also the victim of his self.

What I am trying to say is the following:

1. Even more than the normal person, the schizophrenic is not a replica of how the world saw him in childhood or adult life. His self-image is also the result of his own beliefs and feelings about the world and himself.

2. The early interpersonal relations have a definite impact on the way the patient experiences himself and the world and on how he builds his self-image. However, this impact is not one of direct causality. Intrapsychic mechanisms are at play; these transform experience into self.

What follows is an extremely simplified outline of the way I visualize the psychodynamic course that leads to schizophrenia.

In early childhood the young child finds himself in a family that for various reasons cannot offer him a modicum of security or basic trust. Early interpersonal relations are characterized by intense anxiety, hostility, or false detachment. The child raised in this condition has to contend with a delay or blocking in some areas of his development. More than the average child, he has to interpret the world, life, and himself in accordance with immature cognitive processes.

The self and self-image at this stage are already abnormal. The self-esteem is not low just becaue it reproduces a negative appraisal from others. The young child does not respond equally to all appraisals and roles attributed to him. Those elements that hurt him more, and, in some cases, please him more, stand out and are integrated disproportionally. Thus the self, though related to the external appraisals, is not a reproduction but a grotesque representation of them. Moreover, the self is constituted of all the defenses that are built to cope with these appraisals and their distortions. The more disturbed the environment, the more prominent is the role and lingering of that type of cognition I have described elsewhere and called primary cognition (Arieti, 1965, 1967a, 1967b, 1967c). Some other factors, biological or environmental, play a role in making the self-image different from reflected appraisals.

The grotesque representation of the self the patient retains would stupefy the parents, if they were aware of it. According to my own observations, it would stupefy a large number of them, who never, consciously or unconsciously, wanted to inflict it on the children. This grotesque self-image is very painful, and would become even more painful if the patient would continue to be aware of it and would continue to connect it with an increasing number of ramifications and implications. Fortunately, to a large extent, this image is repressed from awareness. The individual would not be able to bear it.

In various writings I have described how this inadequate self and self-image bring about a series of events, defenses, unsuccessful dealings with the world, and other complications (Arieti, 1955, 1967b, 1968). The time comes when the patient, adolescent, young adult, or adult will believe that his future has no hope, the promise of life will not be fulfilled. Not only does the patient come to feel that the segment of the world that is important to him finds him unacceptable but he also believes that as long as he lives he will be unacceptable to others. He is excluded from the busy, relentless ways of the world. He does not fit; he is alone. It is at this point that he experiences the state of panic so well described by Sullivan (1953a). The panic is an intrapsychic, experiential phenomenon. According to my clinical observation, it is at first experienced as a sort of strange emotional resonance between something that is very clear (as the devastating self-image the patient has acquired recently with mature forms of cognition and in relation to the conceptual world) and something that is unclear, and yet gloomy, horrifying. These obscure forces, generally silent, but now reemerging with destructive clamor, are the repressed early experiences of childhood and the original self-image. In other words, the ineluctable conceptual conclusions reached recently and their emotional accompaniment reactivate the early inner experiences of childhood, not just because of their strength but also because of their fundamental similarity. These resurging experiences reinforce the recent ones as they are in agreement with them, and the result is of dire proportions and consequences. It is this concordance, or unification, of early and late experiences that first reawakens the early experiences and second completes and magnifies in terrifying ways the horrendous vision of the self. In the totality of his human existence, and through the depth of all his feelings, the individual now sees himself as totally defeated, without any worth and possibility of redemption. Though in the past he had undergone similar experiences that were faint, now these experiences are vivid. They are vivid even though they are not verbalized and occurring in a nonrepresentational, almost abstract, form.

The patient cannot accept this vision of the self. This is the drama of the schizophrenic, the unbearable and unlivable drama. The psyche thus undergoes an inner metamorphosis. By adopting new intrapsychic mechanisms, that is, by using new forms of cognition, the patient partially removes the influence of the conceptual interpersonal world that has afflicted the recent injuries. He also transforms the intrapsychic danger into an external or interpersonal one. Whereas during the period of panic everything inside the patient appeared in a state of turbulent change, now the external reality seems different and strange.

During the prepsychotic stages, the patient had, so to say, protected the world from blame and had to a large extent considered himself responsible for his defeat. Now he externalizes again this feeling. No longer does he accuse himself. The accusation comes from the external world. The voices accuse him of being a spy, a murderer, a traitor, a homosexual. These developments are defensive, though they do not seem so. As painful as it is to be accused by others, it is not so unpleasant as to accuse oneself. Moreover, the patient feels falsely accused. Thus, the projected accusation is not injurious to the self-esteem. On the contrary, in comparison with his prepsychotic state, the patient experiences a rise in self-esteem, often accompanied by a feeling of martyrdom. The really accused person now is not the patient but the persecutor, who is accused of persecuting the patient.

The unbearable tension of the inner conflict is now somewhat decreased in intensity by being turned into an interpersonal one. The patient blames, blames, blames. In the words of Mullahy (1968), according to Sullivan "the essence of the paranoid dynamism can be said to be the wholesale transference of blame." Contrary to Laing, who encourages the patient to blame, and in agreement with Sullivan, who taught us that we must help the paranoid to assume responsibility for his own attitude toward the world, I firmly believe we must guide the patient to recognize his own contribution to his predicament.

Psychotic Depression

In a paper published in 1962 I expressed the opinion that we must distinguish two prevailing types of psychotic depression (Arieti, 1962b). The first type corresponds to the one described in the classic textbooks of psychiatry. In addition to a general feeling of intense melancholia the patient presents strong guilt feelings. He feels he has committed crimes or actions equivalent to crimes. He expresses the idea that he should be left alone, allowed to die; he deserves death or harsh punishment. I have called this syndrome the self-blaming depression. Until approximately fifteen years ago we used to see quite frequently very pronounced forms of this type of depression: pictures of immobilizing stupor, or of women who would say they had consumed all their tears, would pull their hair, would say that they had lost all their internal organs. Though cases as pronounced as these are rare today, milder cases of self-blaming depression continue to occur in decreasing number. What seems to increase is the frequency of the other type, which I have called claiming depression. In this condition all the symptoms seem to have a message: "Help me; pity me. It is in your power to relieve me. If I suffer it is because you don't relieve me of my suffering. If I sustained a loss, it is because you did not give me and still don't give me what I need."

Even the suicidal attempt or prospect is an appeal: "You have the power to prevent my death. I want you to know it." The symptomatology is not just characterized by an everlasting and generalized depression but also by a gigantic claim. Now it is the picture of depression that looms in the foreground with the claim lurking behind; now it is the claim that looms with the depression apparently receding. Self-accusation and guilt feelings play a secondary role or no role at all in this type of depression.

The common denominator in the manifest symptomatology of these two clinical pictures is the state of depression. However, there is an important factor in common also in the psychodynamics. As I have mentioned elsewhere (Arieti, 1962b), the depressed patient undergoes a feeling of failure, which even if apparently the result of a nonpersonal event, is experienced mainly or exclusively in relation to one person in his immediate environment. Because of the importance in the life of the patient, I have called this person the dominant other.

The dominant other is represented most often by the spouse. Far less often in order of frequency follow the mother, a person to whom the patient was romantically attached, a grownup child, a sister, the father. Also frequently the dominant other is represented, through anthropomorphization, by the firm where the patient works, or a social institution to which he belongs, such as the church, the political party, or the army. In some cases the dominant other is a composite of two important persons in the life of the patient, such as the mother and the husband. The dominant other is generally symbolic of the mother, as she appeared to the patient in very early childhood. The patient (who in approximately two thirds of the cases is a female and therefore I will refer to as she) is in a relation of dependency on the dominant other. She wants a great deal from him and is always afraid of losing or of having already lost what she needs from this dominant figure: love, affection, praise, admiration, approval, a precious supply of intangible things that only he can give. On other major points the two types of depression differ. In the self-blaming type some attitudes of the mother, as she originally appeared in childhood, and later of the dominant other, are internalized. They become intrapsychic objects. As Bemporad (1970) has classified, we do not mean that the patient models after her parents or wants to imitate them, or identify with them, but only that she wants to live up to their ideal. The attainment of the parental ideal would ensure parental love, affection, and praise. The depression occurs after the realization by the patient that she has not lived up to what the dominant other expected of her. The patient feels responsible and guilty for not having met these expectations. Inasmuch as some real or assumed aspects of the dominant other are introjected, the patient feels deprived of love, affection, admiration, and so on even if the dominant other is absent or dead or in actuality shows an attitude that is different from the assumed one. A profound feeling of guilt confers to the depression the particular self-blaming aspect.

In the claiming type of depression we have a different prepsychotic picture. The patient did not necessarily try to obtain gratification or fulfillment through her own efforts but by receiving support, praise, admiration from others, especially from the dominant other. In some cases, there is an apparent variation in the symptomatology, inasmuch as the patient tries desperately to submerge herself into work and activities, hoping that eventually she will find something to do that will make her worthy of recognition from other people. The patient may hate and depreciate herself, but not with a real attitude of self-blame. Her sorrow derives predominantly from the fact that she cannot obtain gratification from others. As Bemporad (1970) wrote, the patient is not able to obtain autonomous gratification. To quote Bemporad (1970), "The need for approval and love from a dominant other, requiring constant replenishing, creates a cliff hanging existence in which the expectancy of pleasure or meaning is wholly unreliable." Like the psychopath discussed in the first part of the chapter, the patient suffering from the claiming type of depression is not able to transform an important part of the interpersonal into the intrapsychic. She must depend on interpersonal contacts for gratification. It is true that she may eventually praise herself, but only after she has been admired by others. However, whereas the psychopath needed the external agent to control him, the depressed patient of the claiming type needs an external agent from whom to extract praise and approval.

REFERENCES

Arieti, Silvano. "Special Logic of Schizophrenia and Other Types of Autistic Thought." *Psychiatry* 11(1948):325–338.
———. *Interpretation of Schizophrenia.* New York: Brunner, 1955.
———. "Some Basic Problems Common to Anthropology and Modern Psychiatry." *American Anthropologist* 58(1956):26.
———. "The Microgeny of Thought and Perception." *Archives of General Psychiatry* 6(1962):454.(a)
———. "The Psychotherapeutic Approach to Depression." *American Journal of Psychotherapy* 16(1962):397–406. (b)
———. "Contribution to Cognition from Psychoanalytic Theory." In Jules H. Masserman, ed., *Science and Psychoanalysis*, vol. 8. New York: Grune & Stratton, 1965.

——. *The Intrapsychic Self: Feeling, Cognition and Creativity in Health and Mental Illness.* New York: Basic Books, 1967. (a)

——. "New Views on the Psychodynamics of Schizophrenia." *American Journal of Psychiatry* 124(1967):4. (b)

——. "Some Elements of Cognitive Psychiatry." *American Journal of Psychotherapy* 21(1967):723–736. (c)

——. "The Psychodynamics of Schizophrenia: A Reconsideration. *American Journal of Psychotherapy* 22(1968):366–381.

Bemporad, J. R. "Some Reconsiderations of the Mechanisms of Depression." In Silvano Arieti, ed., *The World Biennial of Psychiatry and Psychotherapy,* vol. 1. New York: Basic Books, 1970.

Laing, R. Schizophrenia: Sickness or Strategy? Lectures under the auspices of the William Alanson White Institute in New York City, January 1967.

Mullahy, P. *Psychoanalysis and Interpersonal Psychiatry.* New York: Science House, 1968.

Sullivan, Harry Stack. *Conceptions of Modern Psychiatry.* New York: Norton, 1953. (a)

——. *The Interpersonal Theory of Psychiatry.* New York: Norton, 1953. (b)

Implications of Interpersonal Theory

The purpose of this essay is to review some basic tenets of interpersonal theory with particular reference to their clinical applicability. More than thirty years have elapsed since Sullivan presented his *Conceptions of Modern Psychiatry* (1940), and the time is ripe to evaluate their therapeutic usefulness, their potential limitations and their place in modern psychoanalysis.

Today Sullivan's (1953) interpersonal theory is widely known. His psychiatric formulations constitute a significant restatement about the nature of observable human relations and disturbed patterns of living. The postulate of interpersonal processes provided an open-ended, interdisciplinary frame of reference for the exploration of personal encounters in a therapeutic setting. Furthermore, Sullivan's ideas stimulated the social sciences, the field of psychology, and the discipline of psychiatry and gave impetus to the development of group and family therapy.

My aim is not merely to repeat what is already common knowledge. I wish to focus attention on a few of the more controversial issues in regard to identity, anxiety, the notion of an illusory self, and the realm of intrapsychic phenomena in a clinical frame of reference. I also wish to correct occasional misunderstandings and misinterpretations, which extend even to friendly critics of his work. At the risk of repeating some familiar conceptions, I will reiterate here a few basic notions pertaining to the theory of interpersonal relations.

The Framework of Interpersonal Theory

I would like to suggest that interpersonal theory justifies its inclusion in the framework of an ego psychology in view of its genuine appreciation of the human organism's adaptational capacity. It stresses the active reaching out, or intentionality, of the growing child in his particular interpersonal setting. Under favorable circumstances, the unfolding of maturing capacities takes place at the appropriate time, aided by environmental affirmation. Timing is an essential factor in leading to valuable experience. In addition, we find an adherence to structural concepts without reliance on a topographic point of view.

I might also add that Sullivan's conceptualization of personality, dynamism, and self-system, in particular, is closely in tune with the principles of general system theory (von Bertalanffy). Furthermore, Sullivan evidently had some appreciation of a feedback principle as indicated by his observation that people tend to give information in order to get information. Finally, it may be stated that he was one of the first psychiatrists who expressed greater concern with the mode of transmitting information than with inherent or intrapsychic conflicts.

In highly abbreviated form interpersonal theory may be outlined as developmental, field-oriented, and adhering to an operational point of view. Human personality and specific identity are conceptualized as predominantly action-bound manifestations with flexible boundaries. People have to engage in interpersonal activities in order to bring their personal characteristics into focus.

The Artifact of an Immutable Self

Interpersonal theory distinguishes between two different conceptions of a self. One pertains to a process related to an elementary goal of human striving; the other, to a self as a self-contained unit. Individuation is often confused with the concept of an atomistic self, one of mankind's most cherished illusions. The immutable self may be viewed as an artificial verbal construct similar to that of the ether, which was falsely thought to have been an element of the heavenly bodies. This is not to deny anyone his private inner world, his native endowment, his one of a kind fingerprints, or other more or less durable aspects of identity. It merely emphasizes the observable, relational phenomena pertaining to the self as an experiential matrix rather than as the core of human existence. The self is perceived as the content of consciousness within the framework of a person's socialization, acculturation, and his formative relational patterning. Another way of defining the self is that part of the personality central in the experience of anxiety. The above outlined definition of the self has an affinity to modern information theory, since the self is postulated to be more or less coterminous with the information directly available to the individual; in turn we find that self-regulation and control are involved in the informational process.

Interpersonal theory postulates that each individual has a variety of personal responses to others which are directly related to his developmental encounters with significant people. A major part of therapy consists in expanding the observational and communicative field when multiple facets in the patient's personality become engaged with the psychiatrist as a real and distorted person. Treatment per se is an ongoing interpersonal process in which the therapist participates. His method of observation and his expectation of a legitimate therapeutic goal tend to modify attitudinal and emotional roots of current behavior and have an impact on the immediate future. Clinical data, as they evolve in the therapeutic process, are categorized and evaluated on the basis of certain hypothetical constructs. They pertain to a formulation of psychiatric ecology, the nature of anxiety, the significance of similarity, and the principle of tenderness.

The Ecological Principle

Let us consider Sullivan's attempt to approach psychiatry as the study of interpersonal relations from an ecological point of view. His thoughts on the subject are outlined in "The Illusion of Individual Personality" (1950). Ecology deals with the relations between organisms and their environment in a biological sense and concerns itself with the process of interpenetration or interdependency in that respect. It also deals with man's relatedness to his social institutions, with an appreciation that the individual and his overall environment are intertwined. Sullivan uses the example of the oxygen—carbon dioxide interchange in the process of inhaling and exhaling. He points out that the human organism has extremely limited storage capacity for oxygen. Accordingly, human life is dependent on an almost uninterrupted flow between oxygen and carbon dioxide in the body and atmosphere, respectively. Sullivan transposes the ecology principle to the field of psychiatry by postulating the necessity of a more or less continuous contact on a person to person basis in a humanly compatible environment. He contends that the specifically human qualities are highly labile and require an open-ended channel for their potential growth and enduring survival. Insulation and isolation from the human mainstream of life is tantamount to mental illness. The concept is related to the phenomenon of sensory deprivation, which may also be viewed in terms of entropy, whereby the organism must import negative entropy in order to maintain a relatively stable state to prevent a total equilibrium or cessation of function. The current requirement for meaningful contact with others is considered to be an elementary biological need; the felt component of this need is loneliness.

Many questions pertaining to theory and practice need to be considered once we view psychiatry within an ecological framework. For instance, the problem of an unalterable core, conceptualized as an individual self, becomes rather meaningless when we apply the concept of a fluid, interpenetrating system with reciprocal channels of interchange. The question of what is inside or outside, intrapsychic or extrapsychic, then becomes predominantly timebound and cannot be answered on an either/or basis. It also modifies our thinking about what is internalized or introjected.

One may interpolate the notion of a nexus where coding, encoding, symbolization, and related processes take place in a hypothetical borderline territory between inner and outer world. There is merit, however, in the concept of a complementary frame of reference in which internal and external phenomena are closely intertwined with somewhat indefinite and adaptable boundaries. In many instances the distinction between core phenomena and field phenomena depends largely on the viewer's platform and the element of time. We may observe the same process at different times when the activities at the core level appear to be more prominent than the transactional aspects. Accordingly, I consider the distinction between intrapsychic and interpersonal in great part to be a phantom problem. (Max Planck illustrates a phantom problem by facing an audience and indicating the obvious arrangement of left and right side from his particular position; he then points out that the opposite is true from the audience's point of view since the order of left and right is reversed in their seating arrangement. The phantom problem consists of the attempt to determine the "real" left and the "real" right side.)

Another application of the ecological principle is to be found in the way in which Sullivan postulates the perpetuation of more or less durable interpersonal patterns. Such an assumption changes the concept of transference by viewing it as a two-way phenomenon in a field, rather than as an intrapsychic, self-generated form of behavior. Stated differently, transference is not merely a carryover from the past; it incorporates in its manifestation the other person's response to the distortion.

In this frame of reference, the here and now dyadic encounter is appreciated as a dimension in its own right against the background of early object relations. The past, present, and immediate future are interrelated, and transferential distortions pertain more to the adult person than to the predominantly regressive, infantile aspects of the personality, as theorized in classical conceptions. It is most doubtful that we can ever make contact with the pristine child once a person has reached the adult phase of life (see Schachtel's concept of childhood memories). Furthermore, the ecological point of view focuses a great deal of attention on the personality of the analyst as a therapeutic instrument that is constantly monitored by a detailed self-observation of his security operations.

Generally speaking, the ecological model calls for an altered conceptualization of the therapeutic process. It makes it mandatory to focus on the interpersonal process above and beyond the patient's individual difficulties. What matters most is the evolution of a communicative network in which there is a relatively uncomplicated feedback to complex messages in a field of expanding personal rapport. Thus the way is paved for an open-ended system of interchange, which is not dissimilar to the concept of modern information theory. (The reader is referred to the work of Roy Grinker, Sr., Harley Shands, Juergen Ruesch, et al.)

Shortcomings of Sullivan's Ecological Model

Sullivan was far ahead of his time in his ecological construct, despite the fact that he had not fully emancipated himself from the restrictive doctrine of an economic ideation derived from libido theory. He maintained a remnant of his point of view in his preoccupation with energy transformation. Today, however, it is quite clear that the exchange of information is an interchange without the expenditure of significant energy. Furthermore, Sullivan did not sufficiently appreciate the organism's necessity to draw negative entropy from the environment in order to survive. Every living organism continually increases in entropy, which means that it has to organize itself in a fashion designed to control the state of a decaying equilibrium.

Another important limitation in the interpersonal ecological model is the overemphasis of one to one relationships in the formative patterning of neurotic and psychotic disturbances. The model advocated here calls for a greater appreciation of the overall familial interplay in its impact on the individual person as well as in the shift from dyadic to triadic relational patterns; it stresses family ecology, or family dynamics, as the setting in which dyadic and triadic relationships take place. The small-group phenomena in the nuclear family affect the nature of alliances and negative integrations within the network of the overall unit. Interpersonal theory stands to gain much by including family dynamics in its conceptual frame of reference.

In this connection, we may also come to explore in greater detail the ecology pertaining to the family unit and society at large. There is still a great deal to be learned about appropriate, familial distance from encroaching societal pressures, as compared to isolating tendencies that artificially separate a family from the mainstream.

Finally, one more limitation exists in Sullivan's psychiatric ecology; this pertains to the relative neglect of cognitive processes. Thought disorders exist to some degree in all mental disorders. Yet interpersonal theory has not given adequate attention to those disorders found in obsessional, hysterical, and various characterological disturbances. It is not sufficient to postulate general categories of cognitive patterns, such as proto-, para-, and syntaxic modes, useful as such generic terms may be. There is a need to correlate pathological thought processes to personal experiences and their genetic origin. We usually find indications that a disturbed network of familial communications has created faulty cognitive patterns, which, at least partially, have penetrated the patient's way of thinking. Aside from outright misinformation as a distorted cognitive frame of reference, there is the emotionally warped manner in which basically legitimate information has been processed and transmitted. We are dealing with a prevailing thought pathology in the familial communicative system, rather than predominantly a thinking disorder in one particular family member. Much detailed work remains to be done in this direction. It highlights a somewhat belated recognition that the field of cognition and nonsymbolic behavior looms large as one of the poorly charted frontier areas of modern psychiatry.

The Anxiety Principle

The interpersonal concept of anxiety is the only significant formulation of anxiety on a purely psychological basis with the assumption that it has no neuroanatomic underpinning of its own. Anxiety usurps every available physiological pathway and is highly indiscriminate in its choice. The experience of anxiety is empathically acquired from anxious people who have direct contact with the growing child. (Again, it is preferable to think of an anxious familial atmosphere than just one anxious person.)

Disruptive and destructive in every respect, anxiety interferes with meaningful communication, precludes intimacy, hinders creative thought processes, and leads to profound human malintegrations. Sullivan's postulation leaves no room for existential, humanistic, or potentially constructive aspects of anxiety. To him, anxiety in all its manifestations is harmful and antithetical to human progress.

From a clinical point of view, there is merit in viewing all aspects of anxiety as pathological. This leads to confusion, however, when a dichotomy between constructive and destructive anxiety is introduced. Legitimate guilt, questions of conscience, morality, loyalty, and related reality problems induce distresses of varying degrees; these are better grouped with fear reactions than anxiety. We stand to lose a great deal clinically by placing universal human conflicts in the realm of psychopathology. In my opinion, interpersonal theory makes a genuine contribution by reserving the concept of anxiety for those interpersonal experiences that have irrationally lowered the person's self-esteem. The resulting security operations are valid data for psychiatry and are best treated apart from issues arising on a primarily realistic basis. It may be argued that all human conflicts are real, and indeed they are. However, a major question is raised: Does a here and now problem stem from an unavoidable external situation, or does it trigger off distress related to past experiences, with the concomitant distortions and exaggerations?

The aim of therapy is not necessarily to diminish a person's anxiety. Actually, there is some legitimate doubt that this can ever be done. Rather, the goal is to educate the patient about the great variety of disguises and irrational attitudes that indicate the unnoticed presence of anxiety, and to loosen the rigidity of the self-system, which has the function of avoiding anxiety. People can learn to function in the presence of moderate anxiety without immediately taking refuge in self-defeating security operations.

The Similarity Principle

The similarity principle in the interpersonal frame of reference implies that the basic characteristics of the human species are dominant over the multitude of deviations in people's behavior, whether the people are mentally ill or well. What matters most is what people have in common, not the extent of their foibles, peculiarities, and malfunctioning. It also means that repetitive patterning takes precedence over individual isolated acts, thoughts, or events, regardless of how dramatic or unique an individual performance may be. The behavior of every person occurs within the spectrum of basically human attitudes. Mental illness, then, is viewed as an integral part of the human situation, as an unfortunate aspect of human existence. It is considered to be a miscarriage of human relations or, more specifically, an end state of anxiety-fraught experiences with significant people in the process of acculturation. The major problem in malfunctioning is to be sought in failures pertaining to quantity and timing of responses in interpersonal situations.

The similarity principle has considerable significance in the therapeutic situation. It treats mental disorders as inadequate and inappropriate modes of living with and among other people. The deviation is not considered to be an illness but rather a valid though deviant mode of existence. It is the result of prolonged exposure to warped relational experiences with people who have had a major impact on one's life.

Therapy is a form of participant observation in regard to the relatively intact part of the patient's personality. The primary encounter between patient and doctor takes place on the level of their common humanity, while stressing the similarities of their respective experiences on the arduous road to becoming a person. It is essential that the psychiatrist not participate directly in the patient's pathology lest he enter the disturbed system, thus depriving himself of a functional, therapeutic platform. Similarity, as outlined here, does not mean an adaptational process. It implies the constant search for a mutually meaningful pathway of communication.

Expanding the Similarity Concept

I believe there is still another way of utilizing the similarity concept, and this is the exploration of what the patient has in common with his familial background. We are not merely interested in the multitude of mishaps pertaining to the family's influence. One of our major therapeutic concerns is to bring to the fore past positive experiences, constructive encounters, and the here and now freedom to incorporate worthwhile familial attitudes. Therapeutically rewarding work frequently depends on our ability to elicit favorable similarities between the patient and his family in a personally selective manner. It is often more difficult to clearly demonstrate the positive experiences of the past than to point to obvious destructive influences. A persistent genuine effort along these lines guards the therapist against assuming the unwanted role of the savior, or the idealized parental substitute. The road to self-differentiation and individuation usually means some affirmation of the past, regardless of how limited and infrequent its favorable impact may have been.

The Tenderness Principle

The tenderness principle constitutes a conceptualization of collaborative human integration. It is generally known that Sullivan felt that psychiatry required an appropriate language of its own, capable of transcending the conventional meaning of everyday terminology. For instance, he considered the word "love," as used in the conventional way, to be practically useless for interprofessional communication.

The tenderness principle is an noninstinctual postulate which constitutes a foundation for relatively anxiety-free experiences. This is not to doubt a predisposition for tenderness in human beings. However, tender behavior on the infant's part requires a relatively anxiety-low atmosphere between mother and child which facilitates mutual satisfaction. We are dealing here with a transactional model in which the respective needs of mother and child reinforce each other while setting up a workable system of communication. A favorable chain reaction develops if all goes reasonably well. The infant's expressed needs evoke an appropriate response in the mothering person who in turn experiences tenderness in her ability to satisfy the infant's requirements. A corresponding feeling of relaxation and well-being on the part of the infant furthers collaboration in regard to the task at hand. It stands to reason that the nature of this earliest person to person encounter has a powerful impact on future interpersonal patternings.

The principle of tenderness has a wide area of clinical applicability. For once, it focuses our attention on the mother-child relationship taking place in a field, rather than thinking in terms of two potentially separate units. Furthermore, it does not unduly concern itself with value judgments about motherly love, the infant's appreciation of the love, and so forth. The concept of tenderness and collaboration places a different emphasis on conventional concepts of early child-rearing.

In the therapeutic situation, the postulate of tenderness suggests a transactional model that concerns itself with the needs of both patient and doctor. It is customary in the analytic process to speak in terms of "the analysis taking." Our thinking has undergone many changes in this direction since Freud laid the foundation for his initial concept of an analytic situation. The notion of finding a key to unlock the patient's unconscious and to transform unbridled, instinctual forces into meaningful interpersonal alliances still has some clinical meaning in a sophisticated way. But the concept of bringing light into darkness and of liberating the inner core of a person has distinct limitations. In the above-mentioned frame of reference, we are still bound to a biological therapeutic model. It implies that, in one form or another, attempts are made to deal with the patient's internal "sickness," whether it is considered to be moral, social, or biological. The picture changes significantly, however, once we conceive of mental disorders as difficulties of living that result predominantly from faulty human integrations. The principle of tenderness, then, aims for a collaborative endeavor as a therapeutic goal in its own right. Hopefully, it implies an evolution of intimacy in a relationship of growing equality. Tenderness is conceptualized as an intricate interplay of attitudes and behavior. On the one hand, it evokes the freedom to communicate basic and often unrecognized needs; on the other, it facilitates the capacity to respond adequately and appropriately to those needs that are compatible with the nature of the therapeutic relationship. In other words, "an analysis taking" may now be illustrated in the old saying, "manus manum lavat" ("one hand washes the other"). When applied to therapy, this concept transcends the conventional role relationship between patient and doctor by fusing it into a cohesive unit. It liberates us from the stereotyped tyranny of such concepts as love, warmth, kindness, gratitude, and related global terms and attenuates the impact of everyday polarities, such as love-hate and hostility-friendliness.

A Brief Reference
to Other Therapeutically Valid Conceptions

In addition to the basic tenets outlined above, there are numerous other interpersonal conceptions that are highly relevant to the therapeutic process. I will allude briefly to only a few of the clinically relevant ones.

The formulation of elementary biological and sociocultural needs is one of the more important theoretical constructs. This concept avoids the pitfall of biological causality inherent in classical theory. Instead, it stresses the interdependence of human nature and nurture in a transactional frame of reference. The human animal (the id in classical theory) and the human being (the ego and superego) are conceived of as an inseparable intricate blend. Accordingly, we deal with the pursuit of satisfactions and security as basic motivating forces in all interpersonal situations, rather than with underlying structural entities. There is a delicate balance between these elementary requirements. A major difficulty in living consists of the excessive pursuit of personal approval at the expense of complementary requirements in the realm of satisfaction. The recurrent intervention of anxiety compels the person to approach life on a one-dimensional level. It may also be argued that a conspicuous indifference to other people's approbation constitutes a disorder in itself. Our clinical thinking is frequently geared to the observation of security operations that tend to truncate or inhibit the achievement of satisfactions rather than lead to humanly insensitive behavior.

Comments on the Self-system

In Sullivan's scheme, the conceptualization of a self-system plays an important part. He sees it as a vigilant guardian against the experience of crippling anxiety, resembling in many respects the classical conceptualization of the ego, and its defenses (Sullivan, 1953, p. 167 n.). Its purpose is to organize educative experiences even under highly unfavorable circumstances. The self-system is an explanatory conception rather than a specific entity. Among other things, it explains the personification of the self, which may be said to be a way of seeing oneself. In other words, one's image is controlled by the self-system, since it manipulates the content of consciousness depending on the prevailing level of anxiety. On a theoretical level, it places the ego and its character defenses directly within the field of interpersonal relations. Sullivan's formulation of the self-system is unsatisfactory in several respects. It does not fit too well into the conceptual scheme of interpersonal theory. The concept of an automatic control mechanism, which tends to distort the nature of a particular interpersonal situation by vigilantly avoiding the awareness of anxiety, has a mechanistic quality to it.

However, viewed in the context of information theory the picture changes considerably. It permits us to conceptualize the self-system as a relatively stable process involved in the transmission of information. The notion of a self-regulating device connected with a negative feedback places the self-system in a different clinical light. It places the process more clearly in a transactional or interpersonal frame of reference more in keeping with other interpersonal formulations.

In addition, I believe that a thoughtful application of familial dynamics can enlarge the clinical applicability of the concept of self-system. We may also think in terms of the principle of imprinting or of posthypnotic suggestion (Rioch, 1949) which has a less mechanistic flavor and presents a therapeutically more workable platform.

An interesting by-product of Sullivan's formulation of the self-system is his conceptualization of secondary anxiety which has been pointed out by Clara Thompson (1952). In classical theory, secondary anxiety is an automatic defense reaction to an old danger. Freud (1936, p. 901) thought that the neurotic person "remains under the spell of all the old causes of anxiety."

Interpersonal theory has a basically different point of view. Sullivan's concept of secondary anxiety emphasizes the independent resistance of the self-system to change, even if the change is for the better. Many patients who are clinically improved fear a major setback at the point of favorable change. They suffer profound anxiety when their defenses are in danger of yielding. The clarification between primary and secondary anxiety, which frequently evoke the same feeling tone, is a most important area of therapeutic intervention. Patients need to learn the difference between being in the grips of an old danger, or reacting as if they were totally helpless to a situation that they are now strong enough to cope with.

There are still other conceptualizations I would like to mention in passing. Checking and verification, as formulated in the term "consensual validation," has distinct clinical merit, as long as it does not become a folie à deux. Considerable therapeutic significance may also be found in the formulation of integrating tendencies pertaining to interpersonal situations. The notion is that human relations do not ever stand still; they have a dynamic quality and tend to fuse attitudes along the polar constructs of intimacy and hostile integration.

Another clinically useful conception is that of malevolent transformation that converts tender impulses into hostile operations and constitutes a large therapeutic field in the area of resistance. The origin of malevolent transformation is attributed to the initial inappropriate response from parental figures to expressed needs for tenderness. A close link between this concept and Erikson's lack of basic trust is evident. Be that as it may, we encounter clinically a reaction formation whereby the overt behavior is in distinct contrast to the underlying need. On a behavioral plane, we often observe an ugly attitude that obscures a constructive unrecognized desire. I alluded to this principle previously in my discussion of secondary anxiety.

Summary

I have endeavored to reexamine some basic tenets of interpersonal theory in regard to their clinical applicability. The main purpose of this chapter is to present a condensed theoretical frame of reference, since in the psychoanalytic situation, the theory constitutes one important aspect of the remedial expectation.

It is my contention that interpersonal theory is a valid contribution which deserves to be expanded in its ecological formulation, its attitude toward cognitive processes, and its familial considerations. Among its major assets is the pathological conceptualization of anxiety, its formulation of the principles of similarity and tenderness. Some suggestions were made as to how to transcend the scope of pre-

Implications of Interpersonal Theory

vailing postulates within the framework of interpersonal thinking. A brief reference was made to the precursory nature of interpersonal theory in regard to information theory.

I believe that the basic framework of interpersonal theory is sufficiently flexible and open-ended to lend itself to an adaptation to the zeitgeist of the 1970's and far beyond it. In the final evaluation, all systems and theories must supersede the persons whose creations they were. Eventually, psychoanalysis must rise above the narrow factionalism of competing schools of thought. It must emancipate itself from its stranglehold as a political movement.

Furthermore, it must also aim for an egalitarian discourse with the behavioral sciences and provide a new platform for cumulative knowledge in the overall field of psychiatry. We are still in search of a broad, interdisciplinary theory of therapy. In the meantime, interpersonal theory as an open-ended discipline deserves to be studied, modified, expanded, and clinically applied until more workable formulations are available.

REFERENCES

Blitsten, Dorothy R. *The Social Theories of Harry Stack Sullivan.* New York: William-Frederick Press, 1953.

Chrzanowski, G. "What is Psychotherapy? The Viewpoint of the Sullivanian School." *Annals of Psychotherapy* 1(1959):31–36.

———. "A Presentation of the Basic Practical Features in the Application of the Psychoanalytic Method." In P. H. Hoch and J. Zubin, eds., *Current Approaches to Psychoanalysis.* New York: Grune & Stratton, 1960. (a)

———. "Termination in Psychoanalysis: Goals and Technical Principles Evolving from Sullivanian Conceptions." *American Journal of Psychotherapy* 14, no. 1(1960). (b)

———. "The Impact of Interpersonal Conceptions on Psychoanalytic Technique in Progress of Psychoanalysis." In C. J. Hogrefe, ed., *Verlag für Psychologie.* Vol. 1. Göttingen: 1964.

———. "Discussion of the Concept of Stress." In A. Duehrssen, A. Jores, and W. Schwidder, eds., *Zeitschrift für Psycho-somatische Medizin.* Vol. 4 Göttingen: 1965.

———. "The Independent Roots of Ego Psychology and Their Therapeutic Implications." In Jules H. Masserman, ed., *Science and Psychoanalysis.* Vol. 11. New York: Grune & Stratton, 1967.

———. "Einige Grundpositionen der Interpersonellen Theoric." *Zeitschrift für Psycho-somatische Medizin.* Göttingen: 1968.

Cohen, Mabel Blake, ed. *Advances in Psychiatry.* New York: Norton, 1959.

Freud, Sigmund. "The Problem of Anxiety." *Psychoanalytic Quarterly* (1936).

Green, Maurice R., ed. *Interpersonal Psychoanalysis: The Selected Papers of Clara Thompson*. New York: Basic Books, 1964.

Mullahy, Patrick, ed. *Oedipus Myth and Complex*. New York: Hermitage Press, 1948.

——, ed. *A Study of Interpersonal Relations*. New York: Hermitage Press, 1949.

——, ed. *The Contributions of Harry Stack Sullivan*. New York: Hermitage House, 1952.

Rioch, Janet. "A Study of Interpersonal Relations." In Patrick Mullahy, ed., *A Study of Interpersonal Relations*. New York: Hermitage Press, 1949.

Salzman, Leo. "Harry Stack Sullivan." In A. M. Friedman and H. I. Kaplan, eds., *Comprehensive Textbook of Psychiatry*. Baltimore: Williams & Wilkins, 1967.

Sullivan, Harry Stack. "The Common Field of Research and Clinical Psychiatry." *Psychiatric Quarterly* 1(1927):276–291.

——. "Psychiatric Training as a Pre-requisite to Psychoanalytic Practice." *American Journal of Psychiatry* 91(1935):1117–1126.

——. "Psychiatry: Introduction to the Study of Interpersonal Relations." *Psychiatry* 1(1938):121–134.

——. *Conceptions of Modern Psychiatry*. New York: Norton, 1940.

——. "The Meaning of Anxiety in Psychiatry and in Life." *Psychiatry* 11(1948):1–13.

——. "The Study of Psychiatry: Orienting Lectures." *Psychiatry* 12 (1949):325–337. (a)

——. "The Theory of Anxiety and the Nature of Psychotherapy." *Psychiatry* 12(1949):3–12. (b)

——. "The Illusion of Individual Personality." *Psychiatry* 13(1950):317–332.

——. *The Interpersonal Theory of Anxiety*. New York: Norton, 1953.

——. *The Psychiatric Interview*. New York: Norton, 1954.

——. *Clinical Studies in Psychiatry*. New York: Norton, 1956.

Thompson, Clara. "Sullivan and Psychoanalysis." In Patrick Mullahy, ed., *The Contributions of Harry Stack Sullivan*. New York: Hermitage Press, 1952. Pp. 101–116.

von Bertalanffy, Ludwig, "General System Theory and Psychiatry." In Silvano Arieti, ed., *The American Handbook of Psychiatry*. Vol. III. New York: Basic Books, 1966. Pp. 705–721.

E. Witenberg, J. Rioch, & M. Mazer. "The Interpersonal and Cultural Approaches." In Silvano Arieti, ed., *The American Handbook of Psychiatry*. Vol. II. New York: Basic Books, 1959. Pp. 1417–1431.

PART THREE
Clinical Studies

THE CHAPTERS IN THIS, the clinical section, illustrate different approaches to the crucial task of the analyst—to help the patient. Edgar A. Levenson states that to treat young adults one has to attend particularly to form and style of their communications rather than to content and meaning. His interest is in increasing the information of the patient about his experience. He avoids the substitution of one metaphor for another, the explaining in a "nothing-but" way. His approach is derived from those of McLuhan and von Bertalanffy, particularly the latter's concepts of perspectiveness and isomorphism. John L. Schimel focuses on the ability of the gifted adolescent to use higher order abstractive thinking as a distinguishing characteristic. The metaphor of the patient must be noticed by the therapist. He should admire this ability when it is a positive attribute. When it is used as a defense this should be pointed out. The goal of therapy for Schimel is to point out the interrelationship between internal and external perceptions and this intellectual activity.

For Joseph Barnett the sexual life of an obsessional mirrors his characterological template, which results from the implosion of affects interfering with his ability to draw correct inferences. He avoids the shame resulting from drawing correct inferences (namely that he was unloved) by substituting performance for expressiveness, noninvolvement for freedom, being loved with being served. He uses ambiguous referential systems. And the various sexual symptoms of premature ejaculation, retarded ejaculation, impotence, and compulsive sexual activity show varying degrees of influence of the above factors.

Ruth Moulton spells out the problems of contemporary woman. In a rapidly changing society, there is an emphasis on modification of behavior or of role for women. The time lag between learned developmental responses and role modification results in uncertainty and unsureness. Since there are no models to be followed, the increasing freedom of choice increases anxiety. Rapid social change elicits and obscures deep personality conflicts, particularly for women. Among today's issues the mechanization and depersonalization of sex result in loss and viability of intimacy. Premature pressure to have sexual experience destroys faith and constancy. Indiscriminate sexual pleasure results in its loss as an important human bond. Inhibition is replaced by ennui.

In his chapter, Otto Will describes the work in detail with Sarah, a young schizophrenic person. Much time and effort were spent in establishing a strong, lasting, and understandable relationship. This is viewed as the biological component of the psychotherapeutic procedure. This tie, while vital, may be destructive as well as profitable. How it develops depends upon the therapist's personality characteristics as well as on his technical skills.

Leopold Caligor and Miltiades Zaphiropoulos report on their seven years of treating union blue-collar workers. They find that (1) treatment facilities will be used if the membership of the union is properly educated; (2) time limits set by insurance benefits are not abused; (3) modified analytic techniques—analysis of dreams, resistance, and transference—may be used with selected blue-collar workers as they are with selected middle-class patients.

Psychotherapy of the Young Adult:
The Fallacy of Understanding

Oscar Wilde once said that it was only shallow people who did not judge by appearances. The mystery of the world, he added, is the visible, not the invisible. This essay is just about that, the visible and observable. It is, in essence, a claim that the core of psychotherapy lies in the recognition of pattern, the formal structure of events that constitutes what might be called the aesthetics of experience, aesthetics not in the vulgate sense of beauty and light but more precisely, sensitivity and perception, that is, that concerned with the forms and organization of sensory experience rather than content and meaning.

The younger generation lives in a world oriented aesthetically whereas we are still concerned with understanding and insight. Moreover, the famous generation gap looms between us and the entire contemporary culture of which these youngsters are part: arts, values, technology, and even science. So, inquiring into young adult behavior is intended not only to help a specific group of patients but also to orient ourselves in a rapidly changing society where the dangers of "old fogeyism" are as real for psychotherapists as for parents.

Professionals reading papers on youth are much given to quoting cranky inscriptions from Ur of the Chaldees or ancient Egypt attesting to the churlishness and ingratitude of the younger generation. "I see no hope for the future of our people if they are dependent on the frivolous youth of today, for certainly all youth are reckless beyond words. . . . When I was a boy we were taught to be discreet and respectful of elders, but the present youth are exceedingly wise and impatient of restraint." Except for the rhetorical style, that could be Johnny's dad, or Ronald Reagan, but it is Hesiod, "rapping" in the eighth century B.C.

We have one critical advantage denied the ancients. Cultural and technological change have accelerated so remarkably that, for the first time within a person's lifetime, it is possible to achieve perspective. The Taoists say you cannot speak of ice to the summer insect. To recognize change, one must either live long enough or things must move fast enough. We are, hopefully, at that latter point for, as the anthropologist Weston LaBarre (1954) pointed out, man has shifted his evolutionary development from his own body to his environmental extensions; in so doing he has tremendously accelerated the evolutionary process. Biological evolution has been supplanted by technological evolution. Man's uniquely human propensity for molding and changing his environment rather than himself has resulted in an entirely new dimension. He has become the animal that creates his own environment, indeed his own biotype.

Unlike other animals, whose evolutionary developments eventually box them into environmental rigidity, man can, unless he blows himself up, extend indefinitely, not adjusting to an ultimately limiting environment, but making his own environment. The bird perfects the wing, the porpoise the low-frictional surface, and they must then live within their limits. Man does not perfect, he invents, and each technological advance thrusts outward, widening his range and changing his world. He has extended language through the technologies of writing (papyrus, stylus, paper, block printing, Guttenberg press, photocopying). He has extended his musculoskeletal system thru the lever, wheel, and machine (manual, hydraulic, gasoline, electric). He is now in the process of extending his central nervous system, again by technological means, into the outside world using vacuum tube and transistor (that is, electronic devices) and, the latest technology, the laser (that is, pure light).

You may recognize the concepts of Marshall McLuhan (1964), that stormy petrel of the new sensibility. One might balk at his apparent oversimplifications, but unquestionably there has been a continuous extension of man's technological skills, each of which works a radical change on his environment and his ways of thinking, feeling, and valuing. To quote McLuhan (1964, p. 3), "During the three thousand years of the mechanical age we extended our bodies in space; today, after nearly a century of electric technology we have extended our nervous system itself in a global embrace, abolishing both time and space as far as this planet is concerned. Rapidly we approach the final stage of the extension of man—the technological simulation of consciousness." Absurd? The work on rapid eye movement sleep is an early step, an electronic technology bringing, for the first time, dreams outside the dreamer's head. It is not beyond the realm of technological possibility that we shall, some day, be able to project the dreamer's dream on a screen or with the newer laser technology project a three-dimensional picture, a hologram.

Changing technology, then, may be considered as an evolutionary environmental extension that creates its own world. The prevalent technology will pervade every aspect of the culture: its science, literature, arts, even its concepts of social and psychiatric aberrancy. Thus, even apparently disparate aspects of any culture will be found to share what Kuhn (1962) called the paradigm of the epoch. It has been said that we do not know who discovered water, but we do know it was not a fish: The paradigmatic consistency is so pervasive and encompassing that we are largely unaware of our immersion in it.

Freud was as much part of the mechanical paradigm of his time as was Newton or Marx. The prevalent technology was an extension of the musculoskeletal system, the work machine. Its social consequence was the first industrial revolution. It will be noted that in the mechanical paradigm, from muscle to automobile, energy is processed, transformed from one form to another. Scientific theory of that paradigm reflects the concern with energy transfers, the mechanics of transformation, and the clockwork dependability of process. In Newtonian physics, as in Freudian psychodynamics, processes are reducible to basic, precisely interlocking mechanisms that are reversible, that is, they run either forward or backward. Thus, in Freud, his metaphors are of drive, energy transformation, force and counterforce, the hydraulics of depth, pressure, and repression. Since processes are reversible, regression and fixation become points in the machinery cycle. Most important, therapeutic cure is a reversing of the pathological machinery (Levenson, 1958). Since there is purpose and motivation in human behavior, teleology had to be established (a driver must be found). The Cartesian ghost in the machine is invoked; thus, resistance, transference, unconscious motivation.

We are, at present, immersed in the electronic paradigm. Its technology is an extension of the central nervous system, and its machines process not work but information. Even such contemporary work machines as jet aircraft, rockets, and complex industrial machinery are dependent on electronic servomechanisms. Its social consequence is what Anatol Rapoport (1968, p. xix) called the second industrial revolution, namely, automation. We are now living with its consequences. From brain to computer energy exchanges are infinitesimal in the electronic world. Processes are statistical, contingent, irreversible, singular. Cybernetics, for example, does not examine transformations of energy. It examines patterns of signals by means of which information is transferred within a system. Quantity of information is central, and unrelated to its meaning, truth, or significance.

Concern, then, is not with mechanics but with the organization of information, namely, pattern. This contemporary model underlies modern statistical physics; general systems theory and its implications for psychiatric theory have been examined by Shands (1968), Grinker (1968), Ruesch and Bateson (1951), and Buckley (1968). There has been a very considerable effort in psychiatry to replace the mechanical language with a more contemporary lexicon; thus we find concepts of feedback, transaction system, double bind, mystification. However, more often than not the metaphor is changed but not the paradigm. The imagery is different, but the larger cultural assumptions remain the same. The therapist's view of the symptomatology of the patient, his "diagnosis," the goals of therapy, may reflect the old paradigm. It is a bit like teaching a Solomon Islander to drive a jeep: The old world learns to master the new by rote.

The new is often dealt with by incorporating the language without changing the concepts. We need a view of the patient and our relationship to him which is rooted in the new paradigm. Young adults are a particularly felicitous group for this kind of inquiry, since they are children of the brave new world and particularly irritating and incomprehensible to those of us, paradigmatic anachronisms, who try to see them and their world (dress, hair, music, values) in our terms.

Now, the cultural manifestation of the electronic paradigm is aesthetics, aesthetics, as I defined it previously, being concerned literally with perceiving, sensation, and the patterns and forms in which this sensory experience is cast by the observer. The traditional distinction between form and content is abolished. Form becomes, in Susan Sontag's terms (1961, p. 35), an epistemological decision, an interpretation of how and what we perceive and content becomes a variety of form.

We are no longer as interested in the machinery as we are its patterns of consequence. If insight, Freud's primacy of the intellect ("put the driver in the driver's seat"), is the therapeutic goal in the mechanical paradigm, then expansion of sensory awareness (turn on, tune in, experience) is the goal in the electronic paradigm.

We have, in a sense, rediscovered the tribalism of the primitive who goes into ecstasies over the polyrhythms of an automobile backfiring without the slightest interest in its mechanics. Contemporary art manifests the same interest in the aesthetics of an object apart from its internal machinery or function; thus, a crushed automobile can become a work of art.

Much of the exasperation engendered in us by young adults can be traced to this change in paradigm. We tend to think of their language as incoherent, stereotyped with endless repetitions of "uhs, ahs, like you know man. . . ." It has about as much content as the beeping of dolphins. But it is a highly formalistic, structured communication system in which the pattern is more important than the content. After all, one could build a computer language around "uhs"; we send telephoto pictures from one end of the world to the other, using only a dot. Young adult humor is equally alien: "What is purple and hums?" Answer: "an electric grape." "Why does it hum?" "Because it does not know the words." If you do not think this joke is funny, you will never make a computer programmer. You are content oriented, uncool.

The electronic-aesthetic paradigm is evident in their lexicon: "Turn on," "turn off," "blow your cool" (even "beautiful," as the highest accolade.) As C. D. B. Bryan (1968) pointed out, their morality is based on aesthetic rather than social values: "If it's beautiful, do it." When informed that high decibel levels of noise cause permanent deafness, one discotheque owner said that he would list the daily decibel level outside along with the temperature and humidity. In horror, we assign that hoariest of old-fogey epithets, "amoral." Yet, it is nothing more than respect for idiosyncrasity, the privacy of pattern, "doing your own thing." Perhaps our Protestant ethic of work is too machinery oriented. Work is, after all, an energic definition. We may need a new ethic of role, one's place in the pattern of things. Oddly enough, the Protestant ethic led to the sweatshop and contempt for the shiftless. The new amorality seems to have led to social consciousness and the Peace Corps.

I might add that when I talk of youth culture, I do not mean to imply that this is a general manifestation. The great majority of young people, in statistical terms, live quite comfortably in the old environment. I am limiting myself to those young adults who, for a variety of complex determinants, are tuned into the new sensibility. They are not all successful in it; some of them, like the canaries miners carried into coal shafts, are destroyed by their prescience.

There is, then, a greater concern with formal structure than content in the youthful ethos. And, when one is concerned with idiosyncratic patterns rather than basic, commonly held machinery, a high premium is put on uniqueness. "Doing your own thing" is a paen to uniqueness, or style. In the movie *The Graduate* the hero looks like Kafka's cockroach, but wins the girl away from the handsome medical student, who is a cliché of everything desirable in American youth. Banality, not ugliness, is the cardinal sin of aesthetics.

We, on the other hand, content-oriented vestiges of the mechanical age, want to know, to understand, what it really means. We are hopefully too sophisticated to ask of an abstract painting or Theatre of the Absurd, "Yes, but what does it mean? What did the author try to say? What is his message?" But we ask the self-same questions in therapy. Sympathetic adults who want to understand get the same short shrift from these kids as the white liberal who wants to understand the Negro militant. Understanding is, in these cases, a dissection. It fails to respect the separateness and inaccessibility of human experience. It boils the person down to a set of commonly held universal mechanisms. If happiness is a warm puppy, then love may be the capacity to enjoy it without taking it apart to see what makes it tick.

One must understand clearly that these are not simply metaphors but paradigms, all-pervasive models, imbedded in a concrete technology and that this technology is in rapid evolutionary flux. Otherwise, one can easily fall heir to the horseless carriage fallacy, the nothing but fallacy, namely, the automobile is nothing but a mechanical horse, the new technology is nothing but an extension of the old. Rather, the automobile is a radical extension of human control of space and movement, which has created an entirely new environment; one need only visit California, the most highly realized automotive society in the world, to appreciate that. To say that Sullivan's parataxic distortion is a nothing but restatement of Freud's transference distortion is to miss the point. The paradigms are entirely different. To criticize a particular concept as shallow, lacking in depth, or not dealing with basic drives may be simply a matter of one's paradigm showing.

I suspect that this was a continuous burden for the great innovators in psychiatry. Freud and Sullivan were essentially great artists, what Rilke and McLuhan (Sontag, 1961, p. 35) called, in slightly different words, experts in sensory awareness (I presume this is an aesthetic definition). They were also, by virtue of their profession, teachers, since they, perforce, had to translate their immense clinical sensibilities (which is what initially attracted proselytes to them) into message. The language of the expert is often one cultural epoch behind the sensibilities of the artist. With both authors, one has very much the sense of brilliant innovators struggling to keep their intuitions viable within the nothing but language of their particular science. Freud attempted to surmount the problem by great literary style and classic analogy; Sullivan virtually invented a new language. In the end, both men despaired of being understood, and rightly so. It is only when the paradigms change that the message seems perfectly evident and the heresy becomes a commonplace. No man is a prophet to the next generation and his followers, alas, become the apostles of the obvious.

If you will entertain my premise that young adults reflect a new paradigm, and that aesthetic considerations are the social homolog of the electronic environment, what does this position offer the clinician? Models of exact science, Newtonian physics, or general systems theory are of great value to the theoretician, but for the grass-roots therapist they are about as consoling as reading Kierkegaard on one's deathbed. The aesthetic homolog is simpler and, I think, more human. What if we eschew understanding and ask instead what is the patterning, how is it structured, what relationship does one event have to another in this person's life?

First, you will note, that we are asking how people are different rather than alike. Metaphorically we are more interested in their appearance, fingerprints, voice patterns (anything unique) than in their common biological heritage (one heart, two lungs, the parts depot on nineteenth-century taxonomy). Second, we are interested in the particular patterning of the person's life, necessarily the recurring patterns. Interestingly enough, and consistent with my thesis, Ludwig von Bertalanffy in his general systems theory (1968) has equivalent terms—perspectivism and isomorphism. I am, of course, using these aesthetically rather than scientifically, but the congruence of concepts, the common paradigm, is apparent. In von Bertalanffy's (1968, p. 55) words, perspectivism implies that

it is arrogant and parochial to consider our own form of experience as a singular point, a facsimile of the real world, while relegating other—for example, the mythical, the Aristotelian, the artistic, the mystical universe—to the realm of fancy and delusions. Rather, we should recognize—in line with psychological research, critical philosophy and modern physics—that each world view is a certain perspective of unknown reality, seen through the spectacles of human, cultural and linguistic categories.

Smiling at monkeys, as any visitor to an Indian temple can attest, is a serious matter. One is very likely to be bitten. For, in the simian world, baring one's teeth is a statement of aggression. The monkey and the aesthetician agree: Form is, indeed, content. Is the monkey paranoid? Not at all. He simply has a different experience, a different vocabulary of behavior. That my intent is benign is entirely irrelevant. The meaning of my message lies in your response. If the monkey could talk, being Indian, he could refer to the Vedanta: Cause and effect, it says, are the same event observed from different vantage points. Too often, we tend to confuse intent with effect, meaning with consequence.

We show the monkey more charity than we often show our families, friends, and patients. If I notice that every time I show warmth toward you, you beat a hasty retreat, I am merely observing a pattern of transaction. I may note that it recurs consistently under certain circumstances, or that variations of this pattern occur or have occurred in different aspects of your life. But I cannot say with any conviction that you are a person who retreats from intimacy. Can I be sure that I am offering intimacy, or that it is appropriate to your needs? What is your experience of my warmth? Another therapist, treating the husband of my patient, said, "I think he really loves his wife, but she is such a cold, paranoid person." If she is really cold, then he only wants the experience of being loving. If he really loved her, would she be cold and paranoid? In the old paradigm there is his machinery/her machinery, stimulus/response; the husband is Mohammed trying to move the mountain. In the new paradigm, they make a pattern. It is not our job to know who is "truly loving, truly related, truly rejecting." This kind of understanding is a reification of experience, as Laing puts it, a destruction of the other person's experience. Sartre, in *St. Genet* (1964), a study of the aesthetics of perversion, said that "Evil is the systematic substitution of the abstract for the concrete," in my terms, the substitution of understanding for awareness, of insight for sensitivity.

Parenthetically, Sullivan's and Fromm-Reichmann's effectiveness with schizophrenic patients hinged on this awareness. Perspectivistically, one could wonder at the structure of the hallucinatory experience. Under what conditions did it occur, what form did it take, what feeling accompanied it? If it occurred with the therapist, under what circumstances. The schizophrenic experience is regarded as real for the patient and relevant to his life. They made no effort to understand hallucinations in terms of an internal machinery, nor did they attempt to understand the experience of anxiety that accompanied the hallucination. They knew that to be the ineluctable domain of the schizophrenic person.

If the first step in the assessment of structure is perspectivism, the second is isomorphism. As we attempt to elaborate the patterns of behavior and the consistent relationships of these patterns to different aspects of the patient's life, we see that there are not only enduring patterns but a remarkable homology of pattern, over and over in every aspect of the patient's life. The same structure runs through language, past history, present behavior, fantasies, dreams, and behavior in the therapy room. Recognition of this isomorphism was at the core of Freud's clinical perceptions. Indeed, the ability to detect and elaborate isomorphic patterns, regardless of the metaphor, may well be at the core of therapy or, for that matter, any creative process.

It is possible, very much as Lévi-Strauss (1963) did with primitive cultures, to delineate very consistent structural relationships between dreams, fantasies and behavior. Jones (1962), for example, did exactly this with patients' dreams, relating the structure (not content) of the dream directly to Erikson's epigenetic levels. Erikson suggested that a dream should be studied not only in terms of its figurative content but also in terms of its configurative forms. Jones was able to demonstrate a consistent structure in patients' dreams and a shift in the relationship of epigenetic residuals as the patient improved in treatment. One does much the same in connecting a patient's anal imagery in a dream, his characterological stubbornness, and his fastidiousness. In other words, all therapists look for isomorphic patterns. And, when these patterns occur in the therapy room, we capitalize on the opportunity to demonstrate to the patient the machinery of his "distortions." Isomorphism is considered classically a machinery of replication, to wit, the repetition compulsion. The patient is presumably unaware of this machinery or at least of its pervasiveness.

I would go three steps further. (1) There is a continuous ongoing isomorphic recurrence of the patient's patterns in the therapy room not just under conditions of anxiety. (2) The structure of the relationship between the patient and therapist in any given session is a homolog of the content of the session. A supervisor given the content of a session could predict the direction and affect of the therapist-patient relationship. I am talking now of form not content. (3) The isomorphic experience is real; it is not the patient's distortion or, for that matter, the therapist's.

Man, it will be recalled, is the animal that creates his own environment. Indeed, Sullivan (1956) defined the self-system as "a series of linguistic tricks by which we keep our world satisfying." Assuming a certain passivity on the part of the therapist (guaranteed by his relative anonymity, the fee arrangements, and psychoanalytic technique) he will become part of the patient's psychological surroundings, his environment. The patient will create the therapist in his own image. As Tauber (1954) pointed out, one can utilize this curious experience of being the patient's invention. By noting one's participation (in fantasy or action) one can learn not what is wrong with you but who the patient is and who you have become. It is very much as the tourist in a foreign land expects to be cheated, becomes increasingly hostile and insulting, and is in reality finally badly gulled. Is he imagining the abuse? Is he then justified in saying the foreigners are cheats? Perspectivistically, the issue is not whether the patient's experience is real or imagined but rather the structure of his world and the particular form he impresses on events. The question for the therapist, then, is not "Why do you see me that way?" but "How did we get into this real and familiar fix?"

There is an old psychiatric joke that goes: "What is a sadist?" "Someone who is kind to a masochist." To a masochist any behavior is sadistic. What is more, any therapist working with a practicing masochist will become sadistic. This is not countertransference, a failure of analysis or moral fiber, but a realistic consequence of entering the other person's world. Now, within any given session, there will be a similar formal integrity; that is, all the events of the session, reported and observed (dreams, experiences, fantasies, transactions of therapist and patient) will share the same form, will be part of a whole. Thus, regardless of the therapist's system of hermeneutics (his content) the patient will hear only what is consistent with the session. Let me give a familiar example: During the session the patient complains about his inability to defend his own interests, his victimization by others, his dependency and passivity. His ingratiating behavior is followed by, let us say, a partially dissociated rage and self-destructive acting out. The session ends, the patient heads for the door, turns, and says, "Oh by the way, Doctor, I can't come in next week. I have to study for a series of exams," or, "It's the only time my wife and I can go on vacation." The inexperienced therapist smiles lamely and says, "Well, O.K. Have a good time." The seasoned campaigner might insist he come back to discuss it, refuse to let him off, casually inform him he must pay, and so on. He will be outraged or hurt. Or, perhaps, relieved that the therapist is not malleable, he may learn by example that one can dare to court rejection. He becomes a reformed masochist. God knows, there is no prig like a reformed masochist, but we hope he works it through and levels out. Supposing, instead, we point out to him that the pattern of his exchange, the form, regardless of the content, is to complain bitterly about some disability, engage the other person's support or at least sympathy, then hoist them on exactly the same petard. But, could not the patient then say, "Look, you encourage me to be assertive, but see what happens when I try. You jump down my throat." Ask him why he waited till the end of the session. He may say that he was too timid to ask before.

The therapist, depending on his metaphor, will interpret this exchange variously. The patient's behavior can be seen as testing, acting out, or a first timid assertion. One therapist would say that the content of the session is followed by an acting out of the conflict. Another might say that he brought up that content only because he was preparing to ask for a vacation and did not dare without first preparing the therapist, binding him to a sympathetic position or whatever. Perhaps he is asking for a sadistic attack, or a show of strength. This scatter of interpretive postures will be familiar to anyone who has attended a clinical case seminar or had supervision.

The therapist then has defined his own structure and has required that the patient become part of his environment. He has told the patient who he is in the therapist's world: pathetic, tricky, ruthless, exploitative, lovable, unlovable. Even if he maintains absolute silence, that refuge of the very good and very bad therapist alike, he has invented the patient. It is a psychiatric aphorism that Freudian patients dream of penises, Jungian patients dream of castles, Frommian patients dream of love. Getting well can be becoming what the therapist makes of you, what Fromm called "reform."

The patient learns the therapist's metaphor. He does not hear the content because it is irrelevant. Being more contemporary than his therapist, the patient may learn the therapist's patterning, whereas the therapist learns only the content of the patient's communication. Your behavior really means that if both therapist and patient were aware of the recurrent patterning of the patient's experience with authority, requests, or indulgence, they would note that whatever the therapist says or the patient says, they will be reenacting that same pattern.

This Gordian knot can only be unraveled by an exchange of experiences. The patient must become aware of what he was feeling at every step of the exchange. The therapist must be equally aware of his responses, though whether he informs the patient will depend on his own rules of therapy. An expansion of sensory awareness is then the first step. Having delineated the pattern of their experience, therapist and patient can begin to look for the homologies in other aspects of the patient's life: dreams, social behavior, fantasies, history. In other words, one accumulates as much sensory experience as possible and then patterns it. Ideally, one could do the latter without any other knowledge of the patient. Perhaps that is how really brilliant intuitive therapists work. The rest of us try to resonate to the rhythms of the other's experience. Sensory awareness and pattern-making may be the heart of therapy: you will note these two dimensions have also been defined as the process of creativity. Perhaps, in an aesthetic paradigm, cure is an aesthetic experience. Edel (1959, p. 133) said that it is the novelists and poets who have a feel for "the sensibility with which the outer world is appreciated and felt." Freud, by his own admission (Roazen, 1968, p. 53), was more an artist than a scientist, though he considered it a regrettable shortcoming.

This is the dream of a woman in her twenties. She is watching a brightly lighted stage. There is a play in progress. The audience is sitting in the dark. She, herself, is not in the audience. There is an aristocratic lady sitting at stage right. There seems to be a play within a play being performed to entertain her. A series of richly decorated possessions are being paraded before her. The lady does not seem gratified. She sits impassively. At the front of the stage there is a team of caparisoned horses of the sort used in weight-pulling contests. They are prancing about, and the patient thinks they are too close to the edge. She feels that she should do something, perhaps call out, but she does not move. The horses go over into the orchestra pit, pulling the groom with them. She thinks, my God, he will be killed. Oddly, there is no sound, as though the fall were somehow not completed. The expected carnage does not materialize. The dream ends. There are many possible interpretations of this dream, depending on one's predilections. But, suppose one examines the form of the dream. First, the dreamer is at a great distance, doubly removed, that is, not in the audience, which is itself in the dark; there is a play within a play. There is an effort to involve a detached queenly woman, who can be neither gratified nor really distressed. The collapse of the work horses, the overthrow of the groom, have no consequence. The dream ends with nothing really happening. Now, this form will surely be repeated in her family history, her behavior outside the therapy room; in the traditional sense it reflects her characterological style. But within the session in which the dream is reported it will predict the course of the session, the form (not the content) of the therapist's efforts, and her reaction.

We can predict that she will remain at a distance from her own dream. The therapist will be provoked into an elaborate effort at interpretation which will be received politely, his effort will be sabotaged, and quite likely, neither he nor the patient will be aware of any annoyance or distress. If he becomes aware of her resistance and points it out to her, it will become only another futile effort in the play within the play. The dream being reported and the session have the same isomorphic structure. The therapist is doomed to play out this role of the unsuccessful entertainer; the patient plays out her part as disdainful lady.

In actuality, the therapist made such an interpretation, the patient rejected it by showing polite interest. The therapist responded by pointing out that she was behaving as the dream predicted. She became irritated. The therapist stopped to examine his feelings. He was feeling really rather hurt, insulted. He felt that the patient encouraged his performance and then never seemed impressed or grateful. These feelings were stated, not as fact but simply experience. She responded by her feeling that she was supposed to admire the therapist's cleverness, applaud him. From her point of view, it developed that the panoply, the artificial display on the stage was more to the point than the lady's disdain. Her life experience had been with virtuoso intellectual performers (men) toward whom she was expected to behave with admiration and approval. The therapist now under-

stands that to be clever with this woman is a fatal flaw. Had he mis-
interpreted the dream? Was it a statement of his countertransference,
her resentment of his need to demonstrate prowess? Yet, the therapist
feels something withholding in her silence. It is not as though she
feels what she is being given is worthless; rather she will not admit
that it is of value. This is checked against her perceptions. When the
patient learns that the therapist is not interested in fitting her to his
metaphor, but rather "brain-storming," freely exploring sensory responses, she is rather likely to help out.

When one has extended the limits of sensory awareness, one attempts to pattern the mutual experience. If the patterning is correct,
the isomorphic replication of past and present will become evident,
and both patient and therapist will have a sense of completion, of
aesthetic wholeness in the design. This does not cure the patient. It
does educate her in a method for extending awareness and gives her
a sense of the idiosyncratic structure of her life. She hopefully will be
able to see how she creates her own environment. The experience
with the therapist was a homolog of the patient's experience with her
father. But he had never been able to tell her what it felt like to be
on the other end of the exchange. She did not have sufficient data to
structure her experience. In this perspectivistic framework, it is not
important to know whether the therapist's response to her was rational, neurotic, or appropriate. All that is necessary is that one person know what the other feels and acknowledge that the response is
relevant. The goal of the analyst's own training should be not to
make him free of distortion but free to use his perceptions on the
premise that any response is useful as long as it is authentic. Let us
take a last clinical example using a rather classical dream. A woman
struggling with her relationship to her husband dreams that she has
bought a summer cottage. It is in terrible shape, but particularly the
kitchen is very poor. The floor is covered with filthy worn linoleum;
the sink is rusty, dirty; the stove is ancient and encrusted. She thinks,
if only I could scrub it up, it would not be so bad. She goes outside;
all the trees are dead, stunted. She walks over to one forked tree, sees
that cement had been poured in the crotch of the tree and one half is
still alive. She thinks someone has repaired the tree, things cannot be
so bad. She feels cheered. The metaphor of the mutilated tree with
cement in its crotch would delight the heart of a first-year resident in
psychiatry. It makes one feel there must be something to the castration complex and penis envy!

There is no doubt that that is how she sees the female condition. But the structure of the dream also suggests her behavior in the face of this feeling. She accepts the condition, tries to tidy up, settles for small signs of life, accepts the radical castrating surgery of the tree as benign. One could predict that in her present life and in her therapy she experiences herself as driven into a role that is degrading, but which she must accept in good grace. Now this woman and her husband are both in private treatment. The four participants meet for a once-weekly session. It was evident to both therapists (she had been discussed before her dream) that in the joint session that preceded the dream, she had in fact been excluded and that a quasihomosexual community of the men had been set up to cut her out. She had no conscious awareness of that exchange. To interpret her feeling of penis envy or exclusion would be worthless, without her awareness of the actual events in the joint session. But even that will be greeted with resentment at the exclusion, now acknowledged, and humiliation that she was not able to see it without male help. It would be the boys letting the little girl play because her feelings were hurt. She was able to identify a number of marginal cues she had experienced in that session that could have alerted her to her feelings. She must learn to listen to her own promptings, develop awareness, and contribute her own sense of structure to the sessions. The therapists and her husband treat her with contempt because she does act stupid. She acts stupid because everyone is too guilty to accuse her of acting stupid. When she is responded to authentically, she responds differently. The event is like a pebble dropped into a pond of awareness. The circles spread endlessly. If one stops at any point and says this is the truth, here is the real motive or understanding, one reifies the patient and automatically falls into the trap of playing out the very material under examination. How can a therapist with contempt for a woman talk to a woman about her penis envy? How can one not have contempt for someone who treats herself stupidly? Will one's own analysis solve that problem? To think that one will never again feel contempt for a contemptible person confuses beatification and analysis.

To the therapist schooled in the mechanical paradigm this will seem overly simple, or perhaps "nothing but." In the machine model, breakdown occurs when the machine fails to work, clunks, or leaks oil. The mechanic repairs it, returns it to its previous level of function, perhaps a bit more finely tuned. In the electronic paradigm, nothing really happens. Information is exchanged, possible patterns of the information are tested for isomorphic recurrence. The therapist functions only as an expert in sensory awareness. Sullivan (1954) cautioned the therapist to limit his performance to being an expert. It is enough. It is not required that one cure the patient. Change results not from fixing something but simply from feeding more information into the system, acting as a consensual validator of the patient's experience and aiding in the delineation of homologous patterns of experience in the patient's life, including his experience with the therapist. One might say that the patient improves because of a new experience, an authentic exchange with a therapist who responds honestly and openly. But the openness and authenticity can be experienced by the patient as a seduction, an exploitation of the patient's wish to trust. With young adults, this is particularly true, since the therapist is often tempted to signal, "Look, trust me, I am honest and open and not like your parents." Thus, the therapist's vaunted authenticity can become nothing more than an isomorphic repetition of the parents' "We will do anything to show we love you."

The correctness of interpretations ceases to be relevant. There are many different formulations possible for any observable event in therapy. But primarily one tries to enrich the aesthetic banality of neurosis. If a patient understands himself with great clarity, but cannot entertain another perspective, another possible way of patterning his life, then he is like the philistine who has learned to like opera or abstract painting. Neurosis requires a very low level of sensory awareness.[1] Great sensory awareness without patterning or with simplistic patterning runs the risk of paranoia. To be aware is to be endangered. Henry James (1951, p. 402) said, "the power to guess the unseen from the seen, to trace the implications of things, to judge the whole piece by the pattern, the condition of feeling life in general so completely that you are well on your way to knowing any particular corner of it—this cluster of gifts may almost be said to constitute experience."

Accordingly, the difference between a good therapist and a duffer may be not how he formulates things, but whether he sees them at all. To put it more succinctly, the experienced therapist enriches information, the beginner enriches metaphor. We have always referred to exceptional therapists as "talented," for we have intuitively recognized that the core of therapy is artistic. Great sensitivity and pattern-making are talents, not taught skills. We should in our selection

Psychotherapy of the Young Adult

and training of therapists look for those abilities and develop techniques for nurturing them. Unfortunately, out of our need to be scientific we have developed elaborate systems of hermeneutics. In our present society, science and aesthetics appear to be undergoing an unexpected confluence. Perhaps we can at long last use an unscientific language without being unscientific.

According to my young patients, we are already untrustworthy and approaching senescence. Let us try to keep our concepts uncalcified and our language young.

NOTES

1. Singer (1951 and Ch. 14, this book) has done some quite novel and pioneering work on the relationship between neurosis and perceptual insensitivity.

REFERENCES

Bryan, C. D. B. "The Same Day: Heeeeeewack!!!" *The New York Times Book Review,* August 18, 1968, sect. 7.

Buckley, Walter. *Modern Systems Research for the Behavioral Scientist.* Chicago: Aldine, 1968.

Edel, Leon. *The Modern Psychological Novel.* New York: Doubleday, 1959.

Grinker, Roy R. "Conceptual Progress in Psychoanalysis." In Judd Marmor, ed., *Modern Psychoanalysis.* New York: Basic Books, 1968, pp. 1–43.

Jones, Richard. *Ego Synthesis in Dreams.* Cambridge, Mass: Schenkman, 1962.

Kuhn, Thomas S. *The Structure of Scientific Revolutions.* Chicago: University of Chicago Press, 1962.

LaBarre, Weston. *The Human Animal.* Chicago: University of Chicago Press, 1954.

Levenson, Edgar. "Changing Time Concepts in Psychoanalysis." *American Journal of Psychotherapy* 12(1958).

Lévi-Strauss, Claude. *Structural Anthropology.* New York: Basic Books, 1963.

McLuhan, Marshall. *Understanding Media.* New York: McGraw-Hill, 1964.

Rapoport, Anatol. Foreword to Walter Buckley, ed., *Modern Systems Research for the Behavioral Scientist.* Chicago: Aldine, 1968.

Roazen, Paul. *Freud: Political and Social Thought.* New York: Knopf, 1968.

Ruesch, Jurgen; and Bateson, George. *Communication: The Social Matrix of Psychiatry.* New York: Norton, 1951.

Sartre, Jean-Paul. *Saint Genet.* New York: Mentor Book, 1964.

Shands, Harley C. "The Revolution in Communication." In Judd Marmor, ed., *Modern Psychoanalysis.* New York: Basic Books, 1968, pp. 82–110.

Singer, Erwin. "An Investigation of Some Aspects of Empathic Behavior." *American Psychologist* 6(1951):309–310.

Sontag, Susan. *Against Interpretation*. New York: Noonday Press, 1961.

——. "The Basic Unit of Contemporary Art Is Not the Idea But the Analysis of and Extension of Sensations." In Gerald Stern, ed., *McLuhan, Hot and Cool*. New York: Dial Press, 1967.

Sullivan, Harry Stack. *The Psychiatric Interview*. New York: Norton, 1954.

——. *Clinical Studies in Psychiatry*. New York: Norton, 1956.

Tauber, Edward S. "Exploring the Therapeutic Use of Counter-transference Data." *Psychiatry* 17(1954):332–336.

von Bertalanffy, Ludwig. *Organismic Psychology and Systems Theory*. Worchester, Mass.: Clark University Press, 1968.

Zabel, M. D. *The Portable Henry James*. New York: Viking, 1951.

Dilemmas of the Gifted Adolescent

The gifted adolescent who presents himself for therapy is distinguished from other adolescents in at least two ways: (1) His view of
himself and the world reflects his greater aptitude for and tendency
toward the use of the higher, more abstractive operations of the mind.
(2) He has a special identification problem in finding his place in the
social continuum in a society that does not regard differences between people with equanimity.

The gifted adolescent shares much with other adolescents, psychodynamics as well as the variations from the undefined and undefina-
ble norms to which we defer by the use of our various diagnostic
labels. In common with other adolescents he reveals himself to be in
a state of flux, with the repressed not so securely bound as it will most
likely be later on. His unconscious processes are, by and large, more
readily available than with the adult. Regression and growth have a
more fluid relation to each other and are frequently expressed in the
same behavior or in successive bits of behavior, closely proximating
one another in chronological as well as developmental time. He is
not, therefore, distinguishable from his fellows according to our usual
psychiatric criteria.

The gifted adolescent may be distinguishable, however, by the clinician, as he may be by the teacher and some others. To some extent
his differences are ineffable, as indeed some aspects of the clinician's
response to the gifted may be. To the extent that existence itself and
the occasional occurrence of an exceptional mind are mysteries, a
clinical response that is admiring is appropriate, as it may be to a
marvel of nature or a work of art. Since idolatry is not the function of
the clinician, however, we will pass on to a brief consideration of
those functions of the mind, the cognitive, in which there are de-
monstrable differences between the gifted adolescent and his fellows.

Psychoanalysis has provided valuable insights into the effects of the
emotional life of the individual on the workings of the mind. These
latter, the so-called logical processes or cognitive faculties of the

mind, have been the subject of study for millennia. Adler (Ansbacher and Ansbacher, 1956), Piaget (Inhelder and Piaget, 1958), Sullivan (1940), and latter-day learning theorists (Hall and Lindzey, 1957; Johnson, 1955) have worked to correlate and integrate our understanding of these two aspects of mental life. The view that one aspect is deep and the other superficial is reductionistic and may deflect the attention of psychiatrists from important areas of clinical investigation.

The capacity for the logical processes is innate. Its stages emerge serially as the individual matures. The extent of the possible development of skill in the cognitive processes is genetically determined but may be facilitated or diminished by the vicissitudes of individual experiences. A schema representing logical processes begins with an initial experience, sensory in nature, with the stimulus or referent either internal or external, or both. This must be accompanied or followed by an act of recognition to become part of the logical processes and can occur either within awareness or not. In the latter case there may be interference by the dissociating processes of the self-system or by selective inattention. A special, important, and not well-understood situation is the fate of a sensory experience which does not fall within an already established frame of reference (see Tauber and Green, 1959). This is the mystery of the fate of prelogical or preverbal experience and may be related to certain adult phenomena which arouse uncanny feelings in the individual, such as déjà vu. The act of recognition becomes closely related to the thought-processes, particularly language. To become part of the logical processes, emotions and other inner experiences, as well as objects and events in the external world, have to be learned in the sense of either correctly or incorrectly identifying them and placing them within a frame of reference. At the proper stage naming becomes important. Recognition and the possibility of description follow the initial experience.

Hilde Bruch (1961, 1963) pointed out that misidentifications of internal events on the recognition level can lead to serious psychopathology. The obese patient labels a variety of internal events, even fullness, as hunger. In therapy, the obese and the anorexic must learn certain matters on a level of recognition and description. The confusion caused by the double binding leads to similar phenomena. The mother may label expressions of rejection and hostility as love. The problem here is not so simple as one of repressed hostility but a more

Dilemmas of the Gifted Adolescent

serious one of mislabeled and repressed hostility. You will recognize the foregoing considerations as not new but as a particular dimension of the same data that led to Freud's original formulations of the operations of suppression and repression. Sullivan's notion of the prototaxic and of the uncanny can fit into this schema as examples of reverberating sensory experiences without an act of recognition. It follows that Sullivan's concept of the parataxic distortion relates to misidentifications on the level of recognition, which necessarily involve the next cognitive stage, the process of categorization.

"This warm furry thing is Kitty" is a statement of recognition. Warm little Kitty is moreover a cat, a term that also includes a cold flat picture in a book. That the word "cat" also includes a tiger roaring in his cage not only indicates the nature of categorization, but that this everyday phenomenon is a monumental achievement (Sullivan, 1940). Without categorization there can be no true learning, insight or psychological therapy. Insight can be seen to be the patient's new categorization of previously unrelated data. "I see it now" can be an expression of categorization. It may be a recognition, a new categorization, that "I fear all women." This is not, however, very far from the child's mastery of the category of cats, namely, all women are cats; all cats have claws; cats can scratch and maim; they can hurt; women hurt; all women hurt, castrate, and so on.

Categorization may serve psychopathology in many respects. The "lightening" (lessening of anxiety) described by some paranoids occurs when they "realize" (a new categorization) that everyone is joined in a conspiracy against them. The formerly disquieting and disparate experiences are now seen to fall into one category with a concomitant feeling of relief. Even though from some points of view the patient is now sicker, from his own point of view he experiences a cognitive mastery of his environment, even though in error.

One begins to see striking differences between the adolescents. In their abilities to gain insight they are independent of, though influenced by, the level of anxiety and the type and seriousness of the psychopathology that is present. This can be discerned on the level of category formation. The more gifted adolescent often delights with his far-ranging and profound insights, which may include many and diverse aspects of his existence by penetrating to the core of their essential sameness, their common denominator, which is the key operation of categorization. Others plod along, slowly building up this category or that, unable to make the flight that illuminates the sameness in diversity, which serves to make life more comprehensible and hence more manageable. Certain dynamisms, such as the obsessive, serve to dampen the above aspects of giftedness. The negativistic and the argumentative and other prideful experts of insignificant differences have lost a precious birthright.

The observation of differences is a more primitive capacity than the correlation of similarities and is probably related to survival mechanisms. Primitive man, the hunter, and creatures in the wild are necessarily excellent observers of differences since they may indicate peril. A slight variation in the pattern of light filtering through the leaves of a tree provides a clue to the lurking puma or boa. This is a far cry from Newton's falling apple and the comprehension of the movements of heavenly bodies.

Psychiatrists have long observed (and lamented) the fact that insight is not the same sharp tool for every person and that in some instances insight does not seem to help matters much, if at all. The beginning psychiatrist, often a gifted young man, who may have been impressed by the meaningfulness and usefulness of insight in his own analysis, is often dismayed to find insight much less than a sharp tool in the hands of certain patients. Defense mechanisms are known to play a role as well as the need for working through. Nevertheless other factors are involved. Insight can be conceptualized, as a paradigm, to be a situation in which a is seen to vary with b ($\bar{a}b$). "I see that because father is still the most wonderful man in the world to me, I cannot seriously consider marrying John" is an example. Patient and analyst may be pleased. The latter however may become dismayed if the insight does not illuminate and influence behavior, if it does not clarify the patient's awareness of self, her relationship to John, father, teacher, employer, and others. The failure may be considered from a number of points of view. From the standpoint of category formation, there is a failure to identify the fact that no man, including father, is to be taken seriously. The condition for constructive insight would then be established: a, our young woman varies with b, all men, including father, in the same manner. The category a (all men as insignificant) has not been clarified or restructured. And the attitude, the enduring feeling or mood in relation to a category, does not change. A comparison of her unexamined attitude toward father, characterized as "the most wonderful man in the world" and toward

John, whom she "cannot seriously consider marrying," reveals only insignificant differences. The patient's linking of the two in a pseudo-causal relation can lead, predictably, to an obscuring rather than a clarification of the issues.

"When I came to see you I avoided all social activities. I was withdrawn, frightened, and anxious. I'm not afraid anymore. I do everything. Now I see that I'm simply obnoxious." These were the statements of a gifted young woman who had seen in a flash that her withdrawn and frightened, self-defeating behavior had been an appropriate reaction to hostile and demeaning parents. Now she was free to be like them, to live out shared attitudes toward categories shared with her parents. This is a regular finding in the psychoanalysis of withdrawn patients. Increasing freedom reveals category-based behavior shared with parents and significant others, no matter how lamentable the patient may consider these activities to be.

Theorization and prediction follow close on the heels of categorization in the logical processes. Theorization goes beyond categorization by including unobserved data. A simple example would be that "all cats have claws." It is a theory because the child will not have seen "all cats." Theories are, for this reason, not facts. Theorization is, even at this simple level, subject to error, i.e., my house cat has been declawed. A child (and some adults) may literally believe that "all cats are friendly—or unfriendly." This fundamental type of error is epitomized in the saying: "If one man kicks one dog, that dog knows that all men kick all dogs."

Prediction follows theorization, that is, "the next cat I meet will have claws" or "the next man I meet will kick me." A theory can variously be defined as a statement that serves to explain, correlate, or link in some way all the observable and available data and which can serve a predictive function. As one pursues the logical processes he gets further from the observable data; he is abstracting from many bits of data, forming categories, and extending his abstractions to include unobserved data.

In the foregoing we have been doing what we have been describing and have been arriving at abstractions concerning one aspect of mental functioning. We theorize that these abstractions are pertinent to all manifestations of the mind. We theorize further that differences in the quality, quantity, facility, and dexterity of these mental operations between one individual and another are observable.

There are other theories of mental functioning, such as psychodynamic theory, which can be utilized to explain and correlate psychological data and which can be used for prediction. In the category, which we may call "theories of mental functioning," we can place psychodynamic and cognitive theories along with other theories of human behavior derived by sociologists, anthropologists, theologians, and others. We can make the error (that we try to correct in our patients) of throwing out one or the other since they may not quite fit. On the other hand we can work toward what some refer to as a "unified theory of human behavior" (Grinker, 1956).

The logical processes go on whether or not the initial experience is correctly recognized, described, and categorized, as in the "paranoid solution." The higher abstractive processes continue and may even occupy more, and in some instances, almost the entire attention of the individual. It is marked in the hysteric. The frigid and disappointed woman, for example, may nevertheless insist on offering transcendental theories on ideal sex or on the nature of love; she may even write a best-selling guide to love.

The schizophrenic's ability to recognize internal and external sensory experiences has been grossly impaired. The logical processes have gone on however. He lives and speaks within the metaphor. His solemn universals may be beautiful, cogent, and true but not securely tied to his sensory experience. Internal inconsistencies regularly appear and represent failures in the logical process. His abstractive operations may be likened to a large balloon attached to earth by a slender thread or floating free and not attached at all. Much of the working through in psychotherapy is achieved by following the thread back to the source and by illuminating the relation of the balloon to perception and vice versa.

There may be interferences at the higher levels of abstraction as well as at the primary ones. There are individuals whose perceptions are sharp and accurate but who are not facile in going on to the higher abstractive levels. These are the people who stay close to the data. They do not jump to conclusions. They do not speculate. They play it safe. Categories and theories can be challenged, and they regularly report fear of ridicule and humiliation in this regard. These patients frustrate therapists who experience unpleasant countertransferences with them. They are seemingly forever on the verge of a great discovery (insight) but do not go on to the necessary processes of categorization and theory formation. Daydreams, fantasies, and night dreams—and extrapolations from them—all exercises in the higher abstractive functions, are encountered but may fail to be fruitful with this kind of patient. The obsessive tends to stop with the process of description, though his unconscious is loaded with hardened categories. The hysteric's categories are rigidly aligned to the subjective.

The gifted are capable of more developed and skillful manipulations of the higher abstractive functions. There is a push in this direction which may be particularly marked in the gifted adolescent. As with the computer, the mind's ability to handle and abstract from bits of information depends on the complexity of the mechanism. It has been suggested that creativity is the expression of an ability to synthesize aspects of experience in a way that reveals hitherto unrecognized relationships. In these terms, creativity is a product of the higher abstractive (cognitive) functions of the mind. It is not absolutely related to giftedness, but is related in a statistical manner, that is, it is more likely to occur in the gifted. The parallel to the capacity for achieving effective insight is a close one.

Creativity is not a common occurrence. Educators cannot create creative writers in a course labeled (or mislabeled) "Creative Writing." Though we do not know how to produce creative people, the analyst can help the patient deal with those interferences with the higher abstractive processes that lead to creativity. We are assuming, of course, that the organism tends to express its highest and most complex capacities and will do so if facilitated and fail if there are significant interferences.

Gifted adolescents tend to report in terms of high-level abstractions. They express many theories that are on a high level of complexity and internal consistency. It may take a special effort to get experiential data from such adolescents so that psychiatrist and patient can build new categories and theories (develop insight) together. Some adolescents have retained a playful and relaxed attitude toward the complex interrelations of experiences. Others are desperate in their attempts to arrive at a simplistic comprehension of all the phenomena of their lives.

It may be difficult at first to distinguish the gifted adolescent who is schizophrenic from the one who is not. The distinction lies in how clear a line exists between the formulations of the higher faculties and the initial experiences. Success in therapy depends on this clarification process whether with the schizophrenic or nonschizophrenic.

The therapist who would deal successfully with the gifted must himself be familiar with and free to enter the realms of abstract thought, to operate and interpret "within the metaphor," as Ekstein and Caruth (1963) put it. Once there he must know his way, be able to resist the intoxication of the experience, to separate his own from his patient's flights and be able to find his way back (and to lead his patient) to terra firma. Psychotherapy itself is, among other things, an exercise in the communication of abstract thought (Ruesch, 1961). It is unfortunate that intellectualization is generally looked at as a defense mechanism, leading to a dichotomy of intellect and emotion. One might note in passing that intellectualization by the patient is called a defense and by the analyst, an interpretation. There can be an excitement, even a passion associated with ideas. The world moves for the gifted with each new view of the universe and his place in it. An emotional contagion may subtend the exploration and the communication of ideas and be fused or confused with the sexual.

The therapist of the gifted must be in touch with the foregoing circumstances, aware of their ego expressive functions as well as their defensive functions, and prepared to utilize them as an asset in therapy. Indeed many gifted adolescents appropriately tend toward the more abstract disciplines. An approach that regards certain emotions —love, hate, and sex—as deep and real, and the zest and curiosity that may be connected with the intellectual life, the higher abstractive functions, as superficial and defensive, is reductionistic. It may result in or confirm a state of hopelessness and resignation in the patient, which may be appropriate to such a situation.

The therapist must be prepared to meet the patient on his own ground, in his own language. In child psychiatry the therapist must learn such esoteric skills as the ability to communicate the notion of transference to a five-year-old in terms the latter can understand. It is equally true with the gifted adolescent, whose productions tend to be in terms of theories concerning universals. The therapeutic goal is not to cure the gifted adolescent of the exercise of his higher faculties but to help him appreciate them more and to see the connection between them and his inner and outer perceptions (Watts, 1962). When the latter goals of the therapist are apprehended by the patient, the result is generally a firm, lasting, and facilitating transference.

Dilemmas of the Gifted Adolescent

Rapid transitions occur in some gifted adolescents from under-achiever in school to achiever under such circumstances with a concurrent shift from a spirit of hopelessness to one of optimism. One need not apologize for such transference cures. They set the stage for further therapy, aided by the augmented self-esteem experienced by the patient. Such rapid change is the rule rather than the exception in those cases in which therapy has been successful.

Other Related Considerations

Social categories tend to perplex the gifted adolescent and complicate the essential identification processes crucial to this period of development. The cliches that provide the categories and theories that men live by do not fit him: Success is not the fruit of hard work. Mother does not know best. All men are not created equal. (The "completely committed" to this credo or that are stupid or sick.) Teachers have little to teach. His superiors are inferior. He has been given reading readiness tests when he was already capable of higher mathematics. He is capable of solving his father's business problems, though the latter may be giving him lessons on the meaning of a dollar (Schimel, 1961).

The gifted adolescent, however, often cannot know what he knows. He cannot until it is consensually validated, which is the great opportunity in therapy. He necessarily finds school work easy but feels he is a fraud since an easy success violates the cliche, the accepted categorization. Often enough he does little or nothing and comes to the psychiatrist as an underachiever.

Validation of the soundness of his conceptual capacities plays an important part in the overall treatment plan. The therapist is in a position to help the patient correct the pendulum swing from self-abnegation to omnipotence commonly found in this group. A matter of fact recognition that he is superior, that father is not and that peers or teachers are not, may take some of the heat out of these everyday observations which enter the awareness of the gifted but are opposed by so much and so many.

The gifted adolescent may have to learn the art of dissembling when dealing with his intellectual inferiors, especially if the latter are in high places. More than other adolescents he may need to arm himself with some degree of cynicism in dealing with the adult or the youth establishment. The sigh of relief is audible in some when it is validated that they are superior and that most people are not and that there is no great issue involved in such recognitions and categorizations. Often they settle down and do their school or other work that is genuinely easy for them. Time opens up for other productive activities. Relations with parents and peers improve. Gratifications become available to them on the various levels of which they are capable (Galdston, 1969).

Summary

The gifted adolescent is one who has a greater conceptual capacity, which is reflected in his IQ score but is not identical with it. Difficulties arise out of interferences with any stage of the logical processes. A knowledge of these latter, as well as psychodynamics and personality development, are important in the therapy of the gifted. Cultural expectations may lead to an alienation of the gifted adolescent from self and others and lead to a loss of his rightful place in the social continuum.

REFERENCES

Ansbacher, Heinz; and Ansbacher, Lawrence. *The Individual Psychology of Alfred Adler.* New York: Basic Books, 1956.

Bruch, Hilde. "Transformation of Oral Impulses in Eating Disorders." *Bulletin of the Association for Psychoanalytic Medicine* 1, no. 1(1961):7–12.

———. "Effectiveness in Psychotherapy, or the Constructive Use of Ignorance." *Psychiatric Quarterly* 37(1963):322–339.

Ekstein, Rudolf; and Caruth, Elaine. Interpretation Within the Metaphor: Further Considerations. Paper presented to the Sixth Western Divisional Meeting, American Psychiatric Association, San Francisco, September 27, 1963.

Galdston, Iago. "Psychiatry and the Maverick." In Jules H. Masserman, ed., *Science and Psychoanalysis.* Vol. 13. New York: Grune & Stratton, 1969.

Grinker, Roy R., Sr., ed. *Toward a Unified Theory of Human Behavior.* New York: Basic Books, 1956.

Hall, Calvin S.; and Lindzey, Gardner. *Theories of Personality.* New York: Wiley, 1957.

Inhelder, Barbel; and Piaget, Jean. *The Growth of Logical Thinking: From Childhood to Adolescence.* New York: Basic Books, 1958.

Dilemmas of the Gifted Adolescent

Johnson, Donald M. *The Psychology of Thought and Judgement.* New York: Harper, 1955.

Rokeach, Milton. *The Open and Closed Mind.* New York: Basic Books, 1960.

Ruesch, Jurgen. *Therapeutic Communication.* New York: Norton, 1961.

Schimel, John L. *How To Be an Adolescent and Survive.* New York: Richards Rosen Press, 1961.

Sullivan, Harry Stack. *Conceptions of Modern Psychiatry.* Washington, D.C.: William Alanson White Foundation, 1940.

Tauber, Edward S.; and Green, Maurice M. *Prelogical Experience.* New York: Basic Books, 1959.

Watts, Virginia N. "Effect of Therapy on the Creativity of a Writer." *American Journal of Orthopsychiatry* 32, no. 1(1962).

Sexuality in the Obsessional Neuroses

The sexual life and difficulties of the obsessional patient embrace a range of behaviors including mechanization of sex, impotence, premature ejaculation, retarded orgasm, and the compulsive genital activities. These difficulties are functions of the obsessional character structure and of the cognitive disorders which are their dynamic core. This essay will explore these major symptomatic expressions of obsessional sexuality and relate them to the dynamics of the cognitive disorders. The importance of shame and the special nature of obsessional dependency will be examined.

In previous papers (Barnett, 1966a, 1966b, 1968) I developed the thesis that the basic fault of obsessional living is a cognitive disorder in which interpersonal inference-making is disturbed in order to prevent comprehension of specific cognitive configurations that threaten self-esteem. I have observed that cognition may be regarded as a system of experiential knowing that integrates apprehended modes of knowing organized in sensate, affective states, and the comprehended mode of knowing organized in syntactic, linguistic terms as thought. Cognition, in this view, is considered as encompassing both affect and thought in a constantly interacting system. Interference of any kind with the balanced interchange between affect and thought creates defects in understanding of experience. In the obsessional neuroses, this interference results from the use of a mechanism I call "implosion of affects." In this mechanism there is an internal eruption of primitive, undifferentiated affects that flood the cognitive system, jamming and disintegrating the inferential processes that are necessary to organize the implications of ongoing interpersonal experience. This occurs especially in historically determined areas where such comprehension would be threatening to self-esteem. Implosion helps the obsessional patient maintain innocence in specific areas by using primitive affects to restrict inference-making and comprehension of experience.

These characteristic disturbances of knowing are central to an understanding of the obsessional patient's sexual life. Stylistically and symptomatically, his sexual life mirrors this characterological template. Since sex involves intimacy, it is often an area of especially poignant conflict for the obsessional person. I shall attempt to show why this is so and to relate the sexual developments in the life of the obsessional to this character organization.

The obsessional way of life is largely organized to meet the historical dilemma created by the hypocrisy and ambiguity characteristic of the obsessional's early family situation. The self-system of the obsessional develops in a climate of hostility, rejection, and power struggle hidden beneath a façade of loving care and concern (Sullivan, 1956). In lieu of warmth and acceptance, he has been the object of overprotective and restrictive demands. Parental approval was predicated on the degree of the child's conformity to parental needs and expectations, which disregarded or exploited the needs, feelings, and capabilities of the child. He is caught, therefore, in the paradox that he is most approved when he is least himself or for himself. Faced with this deceptive definition of love, he can maintain the illusion of being loved, accepted, and therefore worthwhile as a person only if he accepts the parents' explicit behavior and avowed concern. Were he to draw inferences, that is, to examine what is implicit in the parental behavior, he would be threatened with the knowledge that he is unloved and rejected, and with the conclusion that he must be insignificant, worthless, and bad.

The explicit and the literal thus become the guidelines to what appears to him to be self-esteem, whereas the implicit and inferred come to represent the self-contempt and self-loathing that constantly lurk beneath his façade of perfection and achievement. This dilemma leads to the pervasive unwillingness to know about himself and the impact he makes on others or they on him that I feel characterizes the obsessional's cognitive system, and which I call "systems of innocence." By creating disturbances in inference-making which might organize the implicit meaning of interpersonal events, he avoids comprehension of events that threaten self-esteem and maintains the childhood systems of innocence that accept the infallibility of the parents. He maintains this innocence by the mechanism of implosion of affects.

The maintenance of these systems of innocence and the avoidance of the implications of interpersonal transactions result in the development of pervasive feelings of shame and concomitant fears of exposure. Shame, in my clinical experience, is an affective tone of considerable significance to the obsessional way of life. It is the specter of his own self-loathing, always present to confine him to the known and the literal and to restrict his behavior to the narrow boundaries created originally by his family's limited and conditional acceptance of him, and perpetuated by his development of a self-system organized around these private conceptions of good and bad, right and wrong. Convinced, as he is, that he is bad, insignificant, and unworthy of love, he cannot face those needs and feelings that were exploited or frustrated in his early life experience and that came to be elaborated as defenses against his underlying lack of self-esteem. His dependent cravings, his infantile narcissism, his anger and power needs, all verify his fears of his unacceptability, exemplify his emotional vulnerability, and intensify his sense of shame and his fears of exposure, of being revealed to himself and others. Worst of all, he feels disgraced by his own capitulation to the demands that compromised him and avoids knowledge of the shameful exposure of his craven surrender of himself, and of the needs that drove him to it.

For the obsessional, the more intimate the interpersonal experience, the more pronounced is the sense of shame and the more severe are the fears of exposure. Intimacy, by its very nature, presupposes knowledge and demands exposure. But in the experience of the obsessional, the closer the relationship, the more he feels his needs and the more vulnerable he is to censure and exploitation of these needs, and to shame for his self-compromising efforts at satisfaction. Intimacy thus poses a special problem for the obsessional. The area of sex is particularly dangerous, especially when it is not casual and when it is related to a meaningful and intimate interpersonal situation. The sexual situation is highly revealing of needs, impulses, and attitudes about self and others. It is largely dependent on the ability to assert one's wants directly. Ideally, sex evokes spontaneous behavior, thoughts, and feelings that are expressive and abandoned. In that it demands self-exposure and self-expressiveness, which are restricted by the dynamics of the obsessional's need to maintain innocence, sex is threatening. In that a rehearsed performance may not dependably suffice for an interpersonal situation which, as Ruesch (1951) pointed out, by definition demands responsiveness to the partner's response, sex is doubly threatening. A solution often utilized by the obsessional is to separate sexual and emotional needs and to employ massive guarding techniques in regard to his emotional needs, while he pursues a narrow spectrum of largely ritualized and stereotyped sexual responses that can safely be adapted to an intimate interpersonal situation.

Stylistically, therefore, he presents the picture of a mechanized sexual performance that is competent, stereotyped, unspontaneous, and unimaginative. This mechanized performance derives, on the one hand, from the inhibition and restriction of action to minimize the risks of shame and self-exposure and, on the other, from the concretization and literalization of experience created by the mechanism of implosion. The mechanized solution is unsatisfactory because the obsessional's comprehension of himself and his partner is seriously impaired by the mechanism of affective implosion, which prevents inference-making. He remains unaware of his impact on his partner and substitutes stereotyped transference assumptions in the place of active, ongoing inferences that might help him to understand her. He is even in the dark concerning his own intentions, for, failing to infer the operational premises of his own behavior, he is separated from his intentionality and forever bemused about the apparent gulf between his stated intent and the effect he seems to have on others.

Simultaneously, he creates what I call the "secret life" of the obsessional. Isolating those aspects of his affective life that are strongly connected with shame, such as aggressive impulses or the need for nurturance, he organizes them into a secret life of fantasy, thought, and feeling, which is kept divorced from his intimate interpersonal field. This becomes an encapsulated system, existing in varying degrees of dissociation, depending on the extent of pathology present. Clinically, I find it present to some degree in all obsessional patients, reflecting and reinforcing the experience of shame and its determinants. It varies from completely organized fantasy lives to the presence of occasional thoughts and feelings. It may exist as conscious obsessional ruminations or in the form of dissociated systems reflected only by the "brown study" states described by Sullivan (1956). It may exist entirely as a cognitive enclave isolated from behavior, or it may erupt into the field of action, either as discrete compulsive acts or as an organized other life.

More commonly, the experience of shame is associated with avoidance and inhibition, both of action and commitment to action. Shame most frequently, therefore, remains largely encapsulated in the secret life, far from the sphere of interpersonal intimacy. Occasionally, however, it may enter the sphere of action, either through acting out or by externalization of shame. Acting out of shame, in the form of compulsive outbursts of behavior directly expressing part or all of the patient's secret life, may occur when the anxiety attendant on inhibition of action is great. Even when acted out and conscious, the behavior is felt to be alien, that is, it continues to be isolated from the cognitive system of the patient and is not integrated through inference-making into the patient's comprehension of himself. This is accomplished by massive implosion of affects, with a resulting increase of turbulent and chaotic feelings after such compulsive acting out.

Externalization of shame may occur. Especially as experiences evoking shame are accentuated, and the feelings threaten to enter awareness, some patients involve themselves in behavior in the environment that justifies their inner sense of shame. Actually, their behavior and exposure to experiences of shame and humiliation serve to maintain dissociation of even more threatening aspects of self. The felt experience reported with such behavior is that of shame, humiliation, and degradation. I have found that externalization of shame in certain extremely obsessional patients accounts for a great deal of compulsive behavior that we designate as perverse. I have treated extremely obsessional patients whose compulsive homosexual, exhibitionistic, fetishistic, or transvestite activities were expressions of this mechanism. I view this mechanism as being analogous to counterphobic phenomena in the hysteric where anxiety dominates the picture and the patient defiantly flies into the face of what she fears. In behavior that we may call "counterobsessional," the patient, dominated by his sense of shame, is impelled to behavior evoking that very experience. Just as the anxious patient may develop counterphobic attitudes and behavior to deny and rationalize anxiety, the obsessional patient may develop counterobsessional attitudes and behavior to deny and rationalize shame.

The dependency problems typical of the obsessional neuroses also result in characteristic sexual difficulties. The obsessional's marked infantile dependency cravings are acted out in his sexual relations in a variety of ways that may best be understood if we examine further his early life experience. Historically, the role the obsessional has played in his family has been a paradoxical one, in which he has been infantilized in regard to interpersonal skills and instrumental competence within the home, while considerable demands have been made for him to achieve outside the home in such areas as school and intellectual achievement or sports and athletic achievement. His insignificance to family life, coupled with the low premium put on him as a person in relation to his own needs and development, leads him to seek to verify his significance by performances of ever-increasing perfection. However, within the family, his dependent role fosters his feelings of insignificance and incompetence, even in the face of successes in the larger world. This historical picture is a most frequent paradigm of the obsessional's role in intimate heterosexual relationships. He doubts his competence and withdraws from performance or competence in tasks related to the simple business of living with others, even as he develops high degrees of skill and competence in outside areas that do not involve his intimate relationships, such as business or intellectual pursuits.

A cultural example of an extreme of such situations has been drawn by Zborowski and Herzog (1952) in their description of the cultural attitudes and family structure of the middle European Jewish *shtetl.* Men and boys were free of the responsibilities for the tasks of daily life, even to the extent of earning a living, so that they might devote themselves to the study of the Bible and the Talmud. Their area of greatest significance was outside of the family, while the women managed the family life. It is to this dynamic constellation that I attribute the fact that the Talmudic scholar has become almost the extreme model of intellectualized obsessionalism, and the reason why the term "talmudic" is so readily applied to any rather obsessional, overintellectualized, scholarly pursuit.

This peculiar contrast in the experience of the obsessional reflects itself in several ways in the dynamics of his sexual conflicts and their resolution. In intimate relations, his tendency to feel incompetent and insignificant, and his dependence on others both for care and for verification of his significance, places him in a bind in which he feels insignificant if no sexual demands are made on him, but anxious, inadequate, and resentful if they are made. His fear of being exploited, should he expose his vulnerability and need, leads him to maintain emotional distance from his sexual partner, and not infrequently to cloak his affectional needs as simply erotic demands. His dependent orientation in intimate situations is further seen by his passive wishes and fantasies about sex. Since being loved means to him being cared for and served, his wishes are for activity and even aggressiveness on the part of the sexual partner. Fantasies of passive acquiescence to aggressively sexual women and fantasies concerning fellatio are common. His dependency, and the feelings of insignificance and of rage that constantly accompany it, add to the burden of shame and fears of exposure which make intimacy so difficult for him.

Also related to this dependency is the fact that the obsessional substitutes performance for expressiveness. Adequacy and competence of performance guarantee more safety than the uncertainty of spontaneous expression. Stereotyped performance can channel the response of the interpersonal environment and create relative safety from the possibility of evoking a feared response from the environment. It is also seen as the ultimate denial of dependency, ineptness, and insignificance. Because of this preoccupation with performance, and the ability to play to an audience for a planned effect, the obsessional is often able to perform competently as a lover, given the appropriate interpersonal climate. Where intimacy does not exist, where the partner's narcissistic preoccupations bar her attempts to explore and interpenetrate the other, where there is no curiosity on the part of his partner as to who he is and what he is like, where there is no capacity on the part of the partner to react to the impact he makes on her, the obsessional can usually function or perform fairly well. His performance may also be enhanced if the audience, that is his partner, accepts the limited conditions of the performance and does not demand that needs other than those he defines be met.

However, the high premium placed on his achievement and performance, arising from his dependency, makes him particularly vulnerable to anxiety about sexual performance. Sex is often an agonizing test of his prowess, robbing it of pleasure or play. Relying heavily on intellectualized and mechanical competence, prone to ritualized and stereotyped performances, he is constantly threatened by the expressive ability required in successful sexual activity. Anxiety about performance, when added to the already large burden of shame and fears of exposure, may trigger symptom formation, such as withdrawal from sex or impotence, and may add to the dynamics of such conditions as premature ejaculation or retarded ejaculation.

The obsessional's difficulties with sexuality are further compounded by the existence of what I call the "ambiguous referential systems" that are derived from the duplicity of his early experience and from the characteristic patterns of family structure and interaction. As we have seen, in the obsessional's early life experience, he has been the object of overcontrol and overprotection, which has been equated with and rationalized as the loving warmth and support of which he has been deprived. His early autonomous moves have met with disapproval when they were made outside the narrow confines of his parents' expectations and needs. Experimental and exploratory activity have been stifled, spontaneity and responsivity restricted as undesirable and dangerous. His experience has served to define masculinity as weakness and impotence and femininity as aggressiveness and effectiveness. In the area of intimacy, noncommitment is seen as freedom, being loved is equated with being served, exposure is associated with vulnerability, passivity and inertia connected with power, and tenderness identified with control. It is as though the obsessional has a private lexicon, derived from his experience, which defines important concepts concerning interpersonal relations in terms that often contradict common usage and his own explicit definitions. The resulting clash between these implicit and privately held referents with more explicit and syntactically shared meanings may create uncertainty or even paralysis. Without clear and unambiguous referential premises, the interpersonal world becomes a morass of poorly grasped and inadequately understood occurrences. The obsessional patient, more than any other, often finds it embarrassingly difficult to understand the meaning even of relatively simple interpersonal events. Much of the obsessional's ambivalence, uncertainty, vagueness, obscurity, indecisiveness, and problems of commitment are based on the confusion of meaning that results from these ambiguous referential systems.

The typical gender and role confusions and reversals of the obsessional are more correctly assigned to these ambiguous referential systems than to factors of bisexuality or unconscious homosexuality, concepts that, unfortunately, have served to confuse some of our thinking about sexuality. The gender identifications of the obsessional are related to his wishes for the power, strength, activity, and effectiveness he asociates with the woman, as well as to avoid the weakness, impotence, and exploitability that he associates with the man. In his role identifications, he similarly yearns for the passivity he connects with power and the service that he equates with love; he flees the control he identifies with tenderness, the vulnerability he associates with openness and commitment, and the exploitation he expects from active giving.

It has been noted that obsessional patients often show a markedly diminished sexual interest. Apparently impressed by the clinical facts of this diminished interest and withdrawal from sex, and by the reduced passion and excitement in the sexual act, Rado (1959) suggested that obsessionals have a congenital deficiency in the capacity for orgastic pleasure. My own clinical experience does not agree with this hypothesis. Diminished sexual interest in the obsessional seems related to several dynamic factors. Perhaps most important of these factors is that of depression. As I have indicated elsewhere (Barnett, 1968) I find that some degree of depression is almost a constant finding in the obsessional. I would say that I have never seen an obsessional patient in whom either overt or covert depression is not a prominent feature. This can be attributed to the prominent use of the mechanism of implosion of affects. Phenomenally, depression is the felt or apprehended experience involved in implosion. The more massive and inclusive the areas of interpersonal living involved in implosion, the more extensive the depression. Dynamically, conflicts between giving and withholding, anger and tenderness, power drives and dependency, and narcissism and love are central to the omnipresent depression of the obsessional. The characteristic withdrawal of interest from the environment in depression is responsible for much of the obsessional's diminished sexual interest. Therapeutic intervention and alleviation of the depression, which is constantly in the background, is usually accompanied by a marked upswing in sexual interest.

The obsessional's need for control and the pervasive effect of that need on his interpersonal relationships and on sexual behavior has often been noted. Salzman (1968) used this need for control as a central explanation for most obsessional behavior. In my opinion, this need for control, of his environment and of himself, is not a central phenomenon but rather derivative of the need to maintain innocence so central to obsessional dynamics. In the interpersonal situation, control functions to minimize the threats inherent in intimacy, essentially the dangers of self-exposure and exposure to shame and humiliation. Historically, its most common root lies in the identification with a controlling parent with whom the patient had a symbiotic relationship. The dependency and suppressed rage inherent in this type of relationship, in which needs for tenderness are equated with a control-submission hierarchy, become the paradigm for interpersonal intimacy. When the high cost, for even counterfeit tenderness, is submission, to be the one in control is to avoid the dependency and rage that accompany the submission. At the same time, being in control allows one to design the conditions of intimacy and avoid areas threatening to self-esteem. Control, from this perspective, may be seen as an attitudinal and behavioral analog to denial. It is basically organized around the obsessional's extreme dependency problems and their denial, serving to maintain innocence and avoid the shame and humiliation that would be inevitable if these aspects of the self-system were comprehended.

All these factors, evolving from the characterological structure of the obsessional, affect his sexual life. The need to maintain innocence, the inferential disturbances, the mechanism of implosion, the ambiguous referential systems, the nature and structure of his dependency needs, as well as the derivative issues of performance, control, his sense of shame, and the organization of a secret life—all contribute to the stylistic difficulties with sexuality that characterize obsessional living. They are also responsible for the major symptomatic expressions of sexuality prominent in obsessional patients.

Let us now examine briefly some major symptomatic expressions of obsessional sexuality and relate them to the dynamic factors of the personality.

Premature ejaculation is a common symptom of obsessional sexuality. It tends to occur in rather severely obsessional men who show particular rigidity and an almost martinet-like exterior, combined with severe underlying infantile dependent attitudes. They tend to be rather paranoid toward women, with fear, suspicion, and projection dominating their attitudes in heterosexual relationships. Still caught in an unresolved symbiotic relationship with a controlling parent, their excitement is overdetermined both by the appeal and by the threat of total absorption by the partner should their brittle shell crack. Sexual excitement is potentiated by this ambivalent anxiety and by the shame and fears of exposure connected with their dependency and rage. Ejaculation occurs as an almost undifferentiated physiological response to this summation of affective overload. The intensely ambivalent, dependent, and paranoid attitudes to women create severe tension and uncertainty that precipitate the premature ejaculation. Fromm (1959) contrasted the anxieties of men and women in regard to the sexual act, attributing the man's anxiety to his role of performer, and the woman's anxiety to her dependence on the man's performance. He considers a man's confidence in his performance essential to adequate male sexual functioning and a woman's ability to trust essential to adequate female sexual functioning. In cases of premature ejaculation, in my experience, these distinctions are far from clearcut. The man in such cases, deeply distrustful of women, labors under a constant apprehension of rejection and is unable to depend on the continuity and stability of the woman's presence for the duration of the sexual act. He cannot bear, either, even the short time interval of exposure and vulnerability that normal orgasm requires, convinced as he is of his partner's essential malevolence, and of his own worthlessness. The pressure and meaning of time and its condensation in the dynamics of premature ejaculation are related to this profound distrust and fear that pervades his relationship to women.

The infantile nature of the conflicts, and the diffuse nature of the excitement and discharge, causes some of these patients to equate the premature ejaculation with urination, adding to the burden of shame and humiliation. The implosion of affects and inferential defects that occur to prevent comprehension of these phenomena are augmented by the development of obsessional thoughts concerning control. These thoughts are, in my opinion, secondary to the dynamics that cause the symptom and serve mostly to reinforce innocence.

Retarded ejaculation, in which orgasm is delayed or cannot be achieved despite the presence of erectile potency, is a fairly common aspect of male obsessional sexuality. Its equivalent in the female obsessional patient is the presence of retarded orgasm despite the presence of sexual pleasure and excitability during coitus. This symptom, in its simplest and most benign form, is related to the detachment and restraint of passion, which results from the obsessional's implosion of affects and represents the sexual analog to the overintellectualized and unemotional presentation of the obsessional patient in all of his interpersonal activities. In this form, it is stylistic rather than symptomatic, especially in the case of the male obsessional, who frequently views his capacity to delay orgasm with some pride as evidence of his competence and adequacy as a lover. In more extreme form, however, it is clearly seen as pathological and often is connected with considerable mental and even physical discomfort, especially in those cases where the patient is totally unable to reach orgasm.

Close investigation of the more severe symptomatic expressions of retarded ejaculation and retarded orgasm reveals an almost constantly occurring intrusion into the sexual act of obsessional ruminations triggered by the conflicts engendered by intimacy. In some cases, the patient rationalizes his use of these fantasies as deliberate attempts to increase his potency or his competence as a lover, without acknowledging the fears of failure that necessitate them.

The form that this symptom takes in the female obsessional, that of retarded orgasm, must be differentiated from other forms of frigidity. The contrast with the hysterical form of frigidity is especially apparent, as the latter is characterized by sexual anesthesia through part or all of the sexual act. Different also are the underlying causes of these seemingly similar phenomena, for, though hysterical frigidity arises from the fear of sex, retarded orgasm stems from the typical mechanisms of the obessional disorder, and these women rarely suffer from anesthetic forms of frigidity. The obsessional woman most usually experiences sexual pleasure and excitement despite the delay or absence of climax. As with the male, this symptom may progress to a point where considerable discomfort is experienced during coitus in desperate and frantic efforts to achieve orgasm.

The symptom complex of retarded orgasm in both male and female obsessional patients is determined dynamically by several factors: (1) The detachment and loss of expressive affect resulting from the need to maintain innocence and the mechanism of affective implosion; (2) The shame and fears of exposure, especially of dependency and rage, implicit in the obsessional's interpersonal transactions; (3) The preoccupation with performance with its narcissistic and defensive implications; (4) The intrusion of obsessional ruminations into the sexual act.

On both clinical and dynamic grounds, I disagree with Ovesey and Meyers (1968), who link the symptom of retarded ejaculation to paranoid rather than obsessional difficulties and who explain the dynamics as a displacement into the sexual area of a nuclear paranoid conflict of hostile rivalry toward men. My own experience is that, in all its degrees, retarded orgasm is a relatively common obsessional symptom, which occurs in either sex and is present even when paranoid symptoms are absent. Furthermore, in a previous communication (Barnett, 1968), I pointed out that paranoid and depressive tendencies are frequent developments in the obsessional character and may be readily understood on the basis of the cognitive organization of these conditions.

Impotence, in which there is a failure of erection at some point in the sexual act, is a common symptomatic manifestation of obsessional sexuality. It represents the extreme of effective withdrawal and diminution of excitement which so characterizes the stylistic approach of the obsessional to sex and intimacy. The individual dynamics vary considerably with the details of the early experiences of the patients, but certain generalizations may be outlined.

Impotence reflects the genuine underlying sense of inadequacy and incompetence in interpersonal relations, which I have described above as characterizing the obsessional's early family experience. At the same time, it is a disowned statement of his dependency needs in which he manifests his helplessness and wishes to be given to rather than to give, without the necessity for cognitive awareness. It is a defense against anticipated exploitation by the woman, and a hostile retaliation by withholding and frustrating her. The frequency with which it occurs in men whose relations with women are characterized by competitiveness suggests, additionally, that the symptom may express conflict related to dominance and submission as much as conflict about sex. Finally, the paralysis results from the ambiguous referential systems derived from his background, which create increasingly confusing binds in intimate relationships. The bind tightens as the obsessional finds that, though weakness may be a potent weapon by which the female opponent is defeated, his triumph is clouded by further lowered self-esteem.

The vicious cycle that often occurs with impotence is exacerbated by the obsessional's absorption with performance as well as by his fears of exposure and self-revelation. His needs for sex then become confused with his needs to prove himself by performing, and this becomes a typical obsessional system, divorced even further from any reasonable approximation of the excited, need-oriented, even playful orientation to sex which is ideal.

Compulsive genital activity includes a group of symptoms characterized by the eruption of repetitive, compulsive, and often stereotyped behavior into the field of sexual activity. Compulsive masturbation and compulsive promiscuity, either heterosexual or homosexual, all fall within this category. Symptomatically, they appear to be rather typical compulsive activities. The patient, often without much sexual interest or excitement, feels compelled to perform the sexual activity. There may or may not be an accompanying fantasy, and the act is followed by temporary relief of tension. There is a cyclic tendency with return of tension and repetition of the act. Unlike other compulsive acts, however, compulsive genital activity rarely occurs in well-compensated obsessionals whose obsessional defenses appear to be working reasonably well. When they occur in the obsessional (and compulsive genital activity occurs also in covert and agitated depressions, schizophrenic reactions, and psychopathic conditions), they have a long history. Compulsive genitality usually signals that the obsessional dynamism is working particularly poorly or that it has never worked well, and that the patient is in considerable trouble. Paranoid or depressive decompensations are the most common root of the problem. Still other patients prove to be schizophrenics whose obsessional defenses prevent psychotic deterioration.

Dynamically, compulsive genitality is triggered by an intensification of anxiety which occurs in relationship to increasing interpersonal isolation. Despite the limited repertoire of interpersonal operations that are available to the obessional, he is, nevertheless, able to function fairly adequately within the confines of his defenses. With the advent of severe anxiety and the failure of his obsessional defenses, even these limited avenues of interpersonal relations are closed to him, and he is threatened with total isolation. The intense anxiety attendant on isolation or its threat causes the eruption of the compulsive sexual activity in an attempt to resolve the isolation, either in fantasy or in desperate attempts at pseudointimacy.

In patients who are markedly dependent and infantile, and whose past experience has structured considerable resignation to isolation, this threat may be handled by compulsive masturbation and fantasy resolution. They are generally found to be covertly depressed, but the anger and helplessness are not openly felt but are entirely diverted into the behavioral symptom and its associated fantasies.

Those patients who resort to compulsive heterosexual promiscuity to meet the threat of isolation are usually those who are more defiant and less intimidated by authority. They are, at the same time, more prone to isolate their feelings of tenderness from their sexual needs and to manifest their dependency conflicts in open needs for approval from women, and in covert exploitation of them. More prominent in these patients is the grandiosity and perfectionistic performance orientation that results from their dependency conflicts and their denial.

An interesting group of homosexual patients who show a markedly obsessional character formation and compulsive promiscuity can be mentioned here. Their homosexuality seems organized largely around severe obsessional role and gender confusion, and their compulsive promiscuity around essentially counterobsessional mechanisms, which are detonated by the anxiety of isolation. In other words, their promiscuous behavior is largely an externalization of shame in an attempt to deny and rationalize the shame. Despite the seeming severity of their symptomatology, I have found these patients more amenable to psychoanalytic treatment and resolution of their homosexual problems than other types of homosexuals.

In summary, then, we find that the phenomena of obsessional sexuality are varied and range in severity from the stylistic to the symptomatic. The common roots of these sexual difficulties lie in the cognitive disturbances characteristic of the obsessional way of life. At the core of these difficulties are the obsessional's need to maintain innocence, his inferential disturbances and the mechanism of implosion that maintains them, the ambiguous referential systems that define his roles and expectations, and the nature and structure of his dependency needs. Derived from central cognitive difficulties, the obsessional patient develops a pervasive sense of shame and a secret life of fantasy or action which strongly influence his sexual life. Counterobsessional phenomena, excessive performance orientation, and needs for control are derivative issues that complicate the dynamics of his sexuality and prevent the intimacy and spontaneity that would be ideal.

The obsessional way of life is a poignant mixture of isolation, shame, tortured ambivalence and indecision, impotent yearning, and frantic attempts at restitution and substitute gratification. At the same time, the obsessional is absorbed in his aggression, power needs, narcissism, omnipotence, and grandiosity. The sexual life of the obsessional patient is often the battleground on which much of this conflict is waged; it is often the area in which major battles may be won in the patient's efforts toward intimacy, spontaneity, and freedom from the rigid confines of his cognitive prison.

Sexuality in the Obsessional Neuroses

REFERENCES

Barnett, Joseph. "On Cognitive Disorders in the Obsessional." *Contemporary Psychoanalysis* 2, no. 2(1966):122–134. (a)

———. "Cognitive Repair in the Treatment of the Obsessional Neuroses." In *Proceedings of the Fourth World Congress of Psychiatry*, Madrid 1966. Excerpta Medica International, Congress Series, no. 150, pp. 752–757. (b)

———. "Cognition, Thought and Affect in the Organization of Experience." In Jules H. Masserman, ed., *Science and Psychoanalysis*. Vol. 12. New York: Grune & Stratton, 1968. Pp. 237–247.

Fromm, Erich. "Sex and Character." In Ruth N. Anshan, ed., *The Family: Its Function and Destiny*. New York: Harper, 1959. Pp. 399–419.

Ovesey, L., and Meyers, H. "Retarded Ejaculation: Psychodynamics and Psychotherapy." *American Journal of Psychotherapy* 22, no. 2(1968):185–201.

Rado, Sandor. "Obsessive Behavior." In Silvano Arieti, ed., *The American Handbook of Psychiatry*. Vol. 1. New York: Basic Books, 1959. Pp. 324–344.

Ruesch, Jurgen. "Values, Communication, and Culture." In Jurgen Ruesch and Bateson *Communication*. New York: Norton, 1951. Pp. 3–20.

Salzman, L. *The Obsessive Personality*. New York: Science House, 1968.

Sullivan, Harry Stack: *Clinical Studies in Psychiatry*. New York: Norton, 1956.

Zborowski, M.; and Herzog, E. *Life Is with People: The Culture of the Shtetl*. New York: International Universities Press, 1952.

Sexual Conflicts of Contemporary Women

Rapid social change is an outstanding characteristic of our times.
Man has been able to alter traditional institutions, modify laws,
gather and disseminate new information that offers to free him from
superstition and irrational fear, and yet, anxiety and personal insecurity seem to be at a new high. This is partly that changes are often superficial, more apparent than real. It takes generations for rapid
changes to be absorbed into the culture. The unconscious tends to lag
behind, reflecting the past as well as the present. Intellectually, man
recognizes outdated concepts and rationally accepts new ones, but
the hidden influence of childhood impressions, reflecting the childhood of the parent, continues to affect behavior. Their persistence in
the unconscious cannot be erased by reason or will. Thus the unconscious of modern woman contains many remnants of the conscious
misconceptions of her grandmother. Man's adaptive powers are remarkable for their ultimate versatility, but rarely for their speed. A
culture in flux offers an apparent breadth of choices, but effects are unpredictable, traditional guidelines are absent, and confusion prevails.
Man becomes uncertain about his role, cannot conceive of his place
in the larger order of things, feels alienated from his world and his
fellow man, and experiences multiple identity crises. This affects all
people, but changes in the social and sexual functions of women have
been particularly dramatic during the last twenty-five years. This
chapter is concerned with the reflections of these widespread cultural
changes on the lives of women as seen in the nature of the problems
they bring to the analyst for treatment.

Since intrapsychic structures are not innately predetermined but
develop in the process of an individual's interaction with his environment, it follows that social changes influence the manifestations of
conflict characteristic of a given decade. Battlegrounds and weapons
shift to meet new pressures, though basic drives remain essentially
the same. The social scientist (see Bernard, 1968) notices the enormous stability of social forms; the modal or typical segments of the

population show great inertia; they change slowly. What does change rapidly is the form the nontypical takes; this fluctuates greatly and characterizes a given time. Therefore, to say that the characteristic issues for young women during the 1960's are rights to privacy, contraception, and greater sexual freedom does not necessarily mean that the average or typical young woman actively espouses these issues. The 1960's may be known later as the decade of the hippies, which does not mean that the latter are a numerical majority. Thus, there is an overt sexual revolution which dramatically affects the external form of complaints brought to the psychiatrist or physician but has little impact on their internal sources. At the core the basic problems of women are age-old, and deeper change evolves slowly.

Recently, a woman psychiatrist (Robinson, 1959, pp. 9–10) writing about women starts with the statement that

women have today, beyond the shadow of any doubt, achieved complete equality with men. . . . We now know that woman has the same need for passion, the same capacity for sexual response that man has. . . . The image of Victorian woman, that sexually frozen, emotionally withdrawn vestal virgin, has faded quickly from our minds. . . . Perhaps for the first time in the history of man the two sexes find themselves in a position to explore the rich potentialities of real love [with full sexual expression].

This seems to me overly optimistic and misleading. It is obvious that women have been emancipated from most overt restrictions on their activities. Conspicuous patriarchal domination has been replaced by apparent equality in most manifest areas. They can vote, hold their own property, and participate in almost any area along with men. They have profited more from the so-called sexual revolution than men because restrictions on their sexual activities were so much more stringent and incapacitating. However, this revolution is more of a promise than a present reality. It reflects external rather than internal changes. Victorian inhibitions do not fade so quickly from the minds of those who come for treatment. There are fewer external pressures for sexual restraint, less danger of unwanted pregnancy, crippling infection, death in childbirth, or social ostracism for nonconformity, but there has not been the expected increase in sexual satisfaction. Nor has there been the rapid rise in promiscuity that many predicted, though there has been a mild increase in the frequency of premarital sex. The nature of sexual problems has changed more than their frequency. Relaxation of the cultural tyranny of Freud's day has not brought the relief he might have expected. Instead, new problems have arisen.

I would like to contrast the social forms that reflected woman's struggle to change her sexual role during the nineteenth century with the shape this continuing struggle assumes in the twentieth century. The battle for women's rights began in America, partly because many settlers were rebelling against traditional restraints in the Old World and partly because frontier life required women to be strong and independent. Vast dichotomies existed in attitudes toward sex as rigid puritanical taboos on any sensual pleasure coexisted with demands for complete sexual freedom. Rebellion against all restraint was reflected in the radical movements for free love that characterized the midnineteenth century. Marked contrasts can be seen among the various kinds of women who spent their lives fighting for the emancipation of their sex. Elizabeth Blackwell (Hays, 1967), who fought against tremendous institutional and personal odds to become the first woman physician in 1849, belonged to a group of idealistic reformers who were also concerned with abolishing slavery and making other legislative reforms. She was so shy and inhibited with men that she avoided marriage and pursued a dedicated but asexual life. Most of the early group of militant women refused marriage as it symbolized giving up one's identity, one's legal existence, one's name, to become a "thing" owned by man. One ceased to be a person in one's own right. There seemed to be an irreconcilable antagonism between love and work, and most of those who had children found their dual role almost impossible to maintain. Elizabeth, alone among her sisters and coworkers, had no doubts of her career. The lives of many other such women were full of hardship, heartache, and nagging self-doubt. Lucy Stone, for example, retained her maiden name even after marrying a Blackwell brother, but later gave up public life after the death of a child, which caused her to feel unbearably guilty about being away from home too much.

It is interesting to contrast this dedicated group of reformers with another incredible but very different type of woman, Victoria Woodhull (nicknamed Mrs. Satan) 1838–1927 (see Johnston, 1967), who challenged male supremacy in a most outrageous way, using her beauty and sex appeal as well as her brains. Her parents had little education, no money, few morals or convictions, and led a peripatetic existence. She became an ardent defender of free love, preaching that marriage was not sacred but a bondage, that women should be free to do anything men did, from being promiscuous to being stockbrokers. She was the first woman stockbroker, ran for the Presidency of the United States, lectured to national conventions such as that of the spiritualists in 1873. There she insisted that "the veil of secrecy and shame be dropped from sexual activity and that the truth about sexual intercourse be explored and discussed publicly." She claimed "nothing was so destructive as intercourse carried on habitually without reciprocal consummation. Every man should have thundered in his ears the need for female orgasm." How astonishing to find a woman taking this stand one hundred years ago while Freud was still an adolescent. It could have happened only in America, and it is not surprising to discover that this came from an eccentric woman of great strength and conviction but who was very unmotherly toward her children, rather opportunistic with men, and whose zeal was narcissistic and often unscrupulous.

A militant aggressive pattern was later characteristic of the Suffragettes, who tended to deny rather than use their femininity and often imitated men by dressing and acting like them. This tendency for women to see femininity as a sign of weakness and inferiority culminated during the 1920's when the flapper went to the extreme of trying to conceal even her breasts, becoming a caricature of a woman. Direct imitation of men and hostile competition with them may have served a purpose in breaking old patterns, but it involved such a rejection of the positive values of womanhood that both sexes found it unappealing and unsatisfying.

Overt rebellion against being a woman has declined since then, and most women of the midtwentieth century are trying to find a way to preserve and enhance the positive aspects of femininity while still being active individuals in their own right. The difficulties with this phase in the evolution of her social and sexual role are much more subtle and obscure rather than overt prejudice and discriminatory rules. As with other reform movements, the battle for women's rights has changed from the original concern with legislative and administrative norms to rights denied or made elusive by cresive norms, that is, those involving mores, convention, and tradition. Few privileges are impossible for her to obtain, but the price and the consequence are often hidden. A recent example of the subtle pressures that still undermine women can be found in a letter by Mary Calderone (1968). She reports a conversation with a man who admired her work in directing SIECUS. He said, "You are the greatest! You think just like a man." She asked how he would feel if she said he thought just like a woman. He was infuriated but could not say why. The prejudice that women are irrational and cannot think clearly makes it difficult for them to use their minds well without self-consciousness and embarrassment. Some inadvertently side with those men who dislike the woman who thinks. Others are sharp and moralistic, as though they too believed that only hard women can think.

The wall of Victorian mores, which cut women off from many male prerogatives, also protected her from some kinds of exploitation and pressure and relieved her of the burden of individual choice, guilt, and blame. Confronted with these new anxieties, modern woman often finds herself fleeing from the new freedom, immersing herself in frantic domesticity, competing in gourmet cooking, and evincing a strenuous, overinvolved preoccupation with child-rearing. The pendulum has swung back to large families, with a spectacular upsurge in the birth rate from 1940–1957 (Bernard, 1968). Among the causative factors suggested (other than the war) is the role of the feminine mystique in capturing the minds of women who had begun to fear, partly because of Freudian psychoanalytic concepts, that women who sought fulfillment outside the home were a lost sex. This mania for maternity was accompanied by a decrease in graduate study and career aspirations of women. Assertive women, such as Margaret Mead, Pearl Buck, Marya Mannes have deplored this regression into maternity and failure of women to use the new opportunities. Women seem so unsure of their role that they have a deep need to justify themselves, whether in the home or outside. They often look outside to see what is expected of them or what will please, since many lack an inner sense of their own intrinsic value. The men in their lives frequently add to their confusion, alternating between wanting them for comfort and nourishment while pressuring them to work outside the home to add to income and family prestige. Women are not really free to choose whether or not to have children or how many to have as long as they are subject to irrational pressures from within (guilt, identification with mother, competition with other women) or from without (by husband or culture.) They would probably be less possessive and less resentful as mothers if the choice were more voluntary, arising from a genuine interest. In spite of the apparent relaxation of role expectations for women, conflict continues in characteristic present-day patterns.

Among the first analysts to study this problem was Clara Thompson who, twenty-five years ago, wrote an illuminating series of papers (Green, 1964, pp. 201–273) on the changing role of women in this culture. She felt their restlessness was owing to the newness of their situation, the lack of precedents to follow, the fact that parents and/or husbands had their own traditional expectations so that there were many compromises and inconsistencies that produced conflict. To make a cult of home and child left the intelligent, capable woman discontented; to put career first might leave her unmarried and lonely or in danger of threatening the virility of her man. Both extremes of sexual behavior may occur. Promiscuity can be a result of either an effort to imitate male freedom or it may reflect rage at men, a need to castrate, to collect scalps, to compete with and diminish male virility. On the other hand, sexual inhibition and frigidity may result because of guilt about accepting the new freedom, a woman being unable to get her own inner consent. Clara Thompson (Green, 1964, p. 238) felt that many apparently emancipated women were still afraid that adequate sexual fulfillment, including children, could not be reconciled with adequate self-development. Thus, penis envy was not to be taken literally but as a symbolic expression of woman's envy of the greater freedom of man and his relative clarity about his basic drives. She emphasized that the central problem of a woman's sexual life is not in becoming reconciled to having no penis but in accepting her sexuality in its own right, with its full strength and dignity (Green, 1964, p. 255).

Contemporary writers are still debating this issue amid even more radical shifts in attitudes toward sexual roles as well as new knowledge of sexual physiology. The latter helps us to discard old theories, such as the vaginal-clitoral dichotomy, the limited libido of women, and the assumed domination by endocrine states (Masters and Johnson, 1966). Changing attitudes toward sexual role clarifies other issues. With submissiveness less in style, inordinate dependency needs are more exposed; previously they could be hidden or even rewarded and then rationalized as a healthy part of femininity. Masochism can now be seen as a neurotic adaptation to controlling or sadistic parents and later husband rather than as an essential part of woman's psychology.

It can then be separated from a healthy ability to bear realistic pain, such as that in childbirth.

Discarding superstitions seems easier than building new, constructive hypotheses. Among current writers, the person who has formulated the most convincing positive concepts about the nature of women, seems to me to be, Erik Erikson (1968). He felt that most men have tried to understand the female psyche with male means of empathy, overemphasizing the missing external organ and overlooking the inescapable significance of a productive inner bodily space. From earliest childhood, this suggests creative, as well as dangerous, potentials to the little girl. Her knowledge of her genitals, menstruation, and child-bearing capacities forms the rudiments of female identity. Female anatomy suggests fullness, warmth, generosity, a capacity to protect and nourish rather than merely the negative connotations of a dirty, bleeding wound that are too often stressed by mother or others in the environment. A woman may misuse these basic modalities to be overprotective and intrusive, or she may renounce her role and refuse to participate, hiding her fears in a passive-masochistic role so often assigned to her in the past. Erikson noted that it is woman's unique job to create a home, to nourish, and to have children but that in this modern world she need not, and should not, restrict herself only to this, as the world needs her contribution to social evolution to help preserve and restore, to keep peace and to build, rather than to leave human affairs in the hands of gifted but competitive and driven men who seem more able to make war than to make peace. He feels women often waste their new freedom in limited career competition or else are apt to quickly "go back to their place" whenever they feel out of place.

These comments of Erikson lead directly to some of my observations about the special problems of contemporary women. I am talking about a particular group of women, aged approximately twenty-five to fifty, who are struggling to combine professional and domestic roles and who thus illustrate the conflicts of function and identity typical of educated women in a metropolitan area, faced with a multiplicity of choices. It is hard for them to work out a stable life style that allows the growth of their own interests or careers while still satisfying their needs to create a comfortable home atmosphere, be good mothers and loving wives. Since there is no universally accepted time-honored recipe for this mixture, it takes more than average self-esteem, ego strength, and a clear sense of sexual idenity to settle on a unique but workable pattern. There are conflicting environmental attitudes, and consensual validation is hard to get. Young children are bound to want mother with them as much as possible, and both children and husband are apt to blame her when things do not run well. Other women may envy her or genuinely disagree with her arrangement, so that she often finds herself facing her dilemma alone. The husband who encouraged her originally to work outside may find himself later becoming unexpectedly demanding and resents her turning her attention elsewhere. This may occur because she really is too preoccupied and unavailable and has a neurotic need to flee from the house. He is much more apt to accept her outside activity if she handles it effectively and is therefore free to share their marital life together fully. On the other hand, the husband may be deeply ambivalent, more dependent on women than he knows, or threatened by her competence. He may want her to outshine other women but not him, needing her to be dependent on him in ways that make him feel masculine and paternal.

Any two people living together have problems in adjusting to each other's needs, but with husband and wife these are often projected on to sexual roles, and the knife cuts deeper. Old childhood fears and expectations are reawakened, bringing strong guilt and rage, which make it even more difficult to work out practical, realistic solutions. The woman who feels guilty because she wants more of life than she or her mother felt was her lot fears both the envy of less fortunate women as well as her husband's jealousy, imagined or real. She may be quite competitive, or she may simply have more drive and energy than she has been led to feel is appropriate for a woman. This can lead her to ask for undue reassurance from her husband that he does not mind her work, in which case she puts a double burden on him. He not only has to go without some of the comforts other men have, but he needs to encourage her that it is all right. Both may be uneasy about their equilibrium, so that when she forgets to place a grocery order or to call the cleaner, her guilt makes her overreact to his irritability. Then both can interpret the episode as a sign of deep hostility rather than a transient mishap.

Since the dual role is more difficult, the woman who chooses it needs to be able to get real satisfaction from the variety and stimulation it offers, rather than feeling that special allowances should be made for her. If she got professional training to please an ambitious mother or to be the son her father wanted, she may resent rather than enjoy it, expecting her husband to reward her for working so hard and earning her own money. He may enjoy having her do so providing she enjoys it also and does not take it out on him. This requires a degree of self-assurance and competence, a firm belief in one's ability to do well in both aspects of the dual role, which is hard for women to achieve. Like many other types of rebels, women work against an entrenched system but simultaneously want partial approval from the old authorities (parents) and from their less convinced coworkers (men). Neither of these groups feels it has as much to gain from change, so they are obviously not likely to back it consistently.

Efforts to implement the belief in equal right for the two sexes is fraught with problems even if it is recognized that "equal" does not necessarily mean "identically the same as." Without stereotyped guidelines, the way is wide open for difference of opinion as to who is responsible for taking care of what. Strenuous competition results from conflict of interests, individual preferences, and overlapping of dependency or narcissistic needs. The battle may be essentially reduced to whose dependency needs come first, who needs reassurance most, who gets the most attention, who does the dirty work when no one wants to, and so on. As one male physician, married to a female physician, said, "What every professional woman needs is a wife!" The word "wife" here refers to one who can be expected to do menial chores uncomplainingly as part of her role; when a woman finds that these can be delegated or done mechanically, she is less willing to spend time in a fashion that is dull, unrewarding, and seems no longer either necessary or worthy. With less clearly defined roles and tasks, it is easy for battles to develop over whose job it is. Many of these recall sibling situations where the mother assigned jobs, but now there is no accepted authority and each couple must work out its own division of labor; this requires much good will and cooperation.

Cultural change precipitates conflict by removing old guidelines and opening the way for new untried solutions. This arouses anxiety in many people which is connected with childhood conflicts and deep-seated insecurity, but the resultant problems may be rationalized in terms of the external changes as though the latter were the sole cause. Resentment of men may be blamed on their chauvinism and prejudice in a disproportionate degree. The husband or lover inherits the internal turmoil engendered in the woman's childhood. The mother may have failed her daughter by being an inadequate or unhappy model for identification. If the mother was poorly educated or housebound, she may simultaneously resent her own way of life while still overtly defending it. She becomes envious of her daughter's aspiring to more freedom; the daughter senses this envy and is afraid to go ahead to be successful in a new way of her own, as it means giving up all hope of maternal approval. Such a mother may even have warned her daughter that a career would make it impossible to be either a good wife or a good mother; though the evil prediction can be consciously rejected, it can still hang on like a curse. A creative, assertive woman, who has fought all her life to be unlike her submissive, long-suffering, dependent mother, may find herself slipping into her mother's masochistic role after she herself becomes a mother (Erikson, 1968). Old identifications are awakened, unsolved dependency needs are aroused, and she has no healthy pattern of womanhood to fall back on. She can be a new kind of woman until an anxiety-provoking situation occurs, such as marriage, childbirth, or giving herself to a man in orgasm. Some professional women then lose their hard-earned conviction and sense of an independent self and fear losing their new identity. They may then avoid marriage and/or motherhood, seeing it as a trap rather than a refuge, as their grandmothers did in an earlier generation, or they may try to vindicate themselves by having an exceptionally large family.

An example of conflict between having a profession or a large family was seen in a young woman whose mother used Orthodox Jewish restrictions as well as Old World superstitions to justify her agoraphobia and to keep her daughter close. The daughter was told she would be sterile if she ever touched her genitals and that any strong physical exertion would injure her. In her rebellion, she became an energetic worker, went into dangerous slum areas on house calls, married a Gentile, had several abortions, then a divorce and a more appropriate marriage. Fears of having ruined herself sexually made her fear she could not conceive or carry a healthy baby to delivery. When all went well with her first child she was temporarily reassured about her capacity for feminine function, and a year later went back to get a graduate degree that would enable her to use her skills to better advantage. She was very torn about being away from home part time, both wanting freedom and feeling guilty. When the graduate work became difficult and somewhat disappointing, she developed a desperate need to have another child immediately. Only this could justify stopping work. She also insisted on her husband's wholehearted approval. He was skeptical, unsure of the stability of her motivations, and afraid that an impulsive pregnancy would not solve the problem. He was busy completing his own professional training, had little time at home, and was not too anxious to share her with another child at this point. Instead of seeing his wish to have her more to himself as being at least partly complimentary, she twisted it into "he only wants me for sexual release." This thought combined with her resentment at the lack of his enthusiastic endorsement of immediate pregnancy, made her nonorgastic and sexually reluctant. He then felt "She only wants me for my sperm, not for myself. She prefers having babies to being with me." She did not conceive immediately, became panicky about being barren, as though her mother's warning would come true. When some of the deeper, personal sources of this conflict were analyzed, her orgastic ability promptly returned, and she conceived after five months of futile effort to do so.

This is not the final solution to her conflict about how to distinguish herself from her mother. If she plays it in her mother's direction, she feels she wants three or four children as compared to her mother's two. Otherwise, she wants to arrive at a high professional level to validate the time spent in training and to justify her rebellion against her mother. She is still too involved in self-vindication and competition with women to make a truly autonomous choice, independent of her mother's influence.

The father also plays a role in laying the groundwork for future conflict about femininity. He may encourage competence, physical activity, even scientific interests in his young daughter, and be able to enjoy her curiosity and zest. Later, he becomes afraid of the strength of her adolescent passions, cuts off the companionship that nourished her, and shows a preference for a more demure, passive kind of woman. She then feels abandoned or spurned, assumes that she is unattractive as a woman, whereas she may actually be too attractive to him as well as too threatening. The creative, energetic girl senses she is too much for such a father, too big, too bright, too tempestuous. Competence in school and other outside activities may make other girls jealous and tease her, while awkward adolescent boys are too unsure of themselves to approach her. This further confirms her fears about being unfeminine. One father was able to help such a daughter immeasurably by reassuring her that she would be attractive to men later on, which she was, and also saying he thought most men were jealous of a woman's ability to bear children. This opened the way for her to enjoy motherhood. Parental support is very important at such a point in a girl's development as it is rare for a person to have sufficient ego strength to fight successfully against both cultural norms and parental disapproval.

In addition to the roles of both mother and father as specific people, the growing girl is also influenced by the cultural milieu in which she is raised. Maximum strain is felt when there is a wide discrepancy between childhood culture and the present one or when man and wife grew up under totally different cultural assumptions. The man whose mother overfed and overcontrolled him may flee to the arms of an opposite kind of woman, only to find that he feels underfed and deprived. An example of the difficulties one woman had in bridging an enormous cultural gap is seen in the following:

A thirty-year-old successful artist had been raised in a rigid, culturally primitive, Germanic family in a very small town, where women were uneducated and literally lived as domestic slaves. She vowed to leave this stifling environment, became highly skilled, and arrived at a quite sophisticated level of urban living in a large metropolitan university. She became a gourmet cook, did efficient modern housekeeping while maintaining a strenuous work schedule, and had emancipated herself without therapy in a remarkable way. It was as though she had jumped 200 years ahead of her mother. Her husband had come from a Calvinistic, mountain village in the south, and they had helped each other escape. However, she sought treatment because of a deep-seated phobia of body penetration, which caused her to avoid full intercourse with penetration during eight years of an otherwise happy marriage, despite great sexual excitement. Psychotherapy disclosed enormous fears of impregnation, as she felt child-bearing and child-rearing to be a repugnant burden that enslaved women. She also had inordinate fears of male aggression, based on early experiences with sadistic males, which she could not free herself from despite the help of a nonagressive, considerate husband. All the anxieties, rigidities, and obsessive defenses resulting from bizarre prohibitions and ascetic restrictions of her background seemed focused on the vaginal opening; it was the last line of defense, the hidden closed door. After many interrelated aspects of her character structure were clarified, there was improvement in many areas of living, but she still was sexually impenetrable. Then, an external event, namely the mother's breaking her hip, suddenly hastened her growth. She discovered that her father had never seen her mother unclothed or touched her sexually since the patient's birth. The mother had been so adamant in her refusal of sex that she was also impenetrable. Rather than accepting abstinence, the father had had a long-standing but discreet affair with a woman in a neighboring town. This new data dramatically released the patient. Seeing the extent of her mother's neurosis finally broke the negative identification with mother while the fact of her father's partial access to sexual satisfaction gave her permission to go ahead and find some of her own. The patient was finally able to change, to permit penetration, and to conceive of enjoying a child in the future.

Another young woman, who withdrew from feminine function, came from an opposite type of family structure, in that it was dominated by a tyrannical grandmother. The growing girl saw a childish, dependent mother, who joined the grandmother in ridiculing the weakness of men. Her solution was to avoid marriage, as she could only see it as a power struggle; sharing did not seem possible except in intellectual matters, where she worked well with men. She avoided marriage as a trap, had no great yearnings for children but was able to have sexual pleasure in an unpressured situation. Thus, one woman who sees marriage in a submission-domination context may avoid marriage; another may avoid orgasm and/or pregnancy. There are many styles of avoiding full commitment when it is seen as irrevocable loss of freedom, autonomy, and independence.

In contrast, a second typical conflict is the inordinate fear of never getting a man or of losing one's man, if one dares to be successful and expresses oneself fully. This syndrome can occur in attractive, sexually exciting, and passionate women, who feel they must pretend to be weaker than the men they admire or keep their abilities undeveloped for fear of "scaring a man away." This was found to be a problem in several women who developed a work block on their way to getting graduate degrees. One had lost a husband because her obsessional preoccupation with collecting research data had left him wifeless for months. Under her narcissism was a deep wish that he be the good mother, while she was the precocious student. There was also a great deal of unrecognized hostility toward men that had to be worked through. This was what prevented remarriage, rather than her erudition. The fact that she was brilliant was attractive initially to men; what was unattractive was how she used it against them and for her own inordinate ambition. She needed to learn to use her strength and intelligence constructively rather than hiding it under a charming façade, waiting to use it as a weapon. She had antagonized several men by her clinging hostility, which she saw as valid self-assertion. In therapy, she was forced to recognize the inordinate dependency under her façade of omnipotence and pseudoindependence. Panic replaced her former arrogance with men, and she became sexually greedy. Thus, the sexual reflections of her particular conflict were excessive demands on men and resulted in inappropriate sexual activity rather than in the restriction and inhibition more commonly seen.

Another example was a young married woman afraid to finish her training in spite of her husband's encouragement, because she felt he really did not want her to. This could be traced back to an emotionally remote father who said, "no woman needs a Ph.D." Her mother had stayed home and raised a large family but had basically been unmotherly and lacked tenderness. This patient also feared that if she left her child even part time, the latter would resent her as she had resented her mother. This fear persisted even though she had given her child much more than her mother had ever been capable of, and adequate help was available for child care. She feared that exercising her professional competence would unduly threaten her husband in spite of the fact that he had always admired that aspect of her and enjoyed sharing their mutual interests. She felt she should be weaker than he was, and kept inferring signs of his unconscious resentment of her work. Therapy was necessary to help her experience him as being quite different from her father. She withheld herself from participation in outside activities with her husband and also in lovemaking, where she was nonorgastic. In putting aside her own interests, unconsciously hoping to gain the parental approval that was not forthcoming, she became frustrated and depressed, losing much of the vitality and strength that originally attracted her husband. When this marital stalemate was broken by analyzing many aspects of it, both were more active in their own right as well as together and infinitely more alive in their marriage. Had the analyst had a stereotyped concept of what a woman should be, a satisfying solution would have been impossible. Developing her talents appropriately gave her more self-assurance and charm, making her more rather than less lovable.

There is a different dilemma for the woman who has no profession or major outside activity. Though this may have been her own choice and she genuinely prefers to be primarily domestic, she may be looked down on by husband and friends and find it difficult to gain their respect. She may find herself jealous of her husband's profession or job, which may seem more exciting, usually pays better, and lends itself more readily for general conversational and social uses than her own work. Her inner sense of her value and purpose seems elusive or gone. This may lead to neurotic clinging, living vicariously through him, or being too dependent on him for stimulation. A more resentful, bitter wife may use her energies to battle with, or undermine, her husband or to tie him down and dampen his freedom by her constant complaints and dissatisfactions. This type of competition between the sexes may not be new, but it has a special flavor in contemporary metropolitan and suburban areas.

Turning from problems involving sexual role to those of specific sexual problems in lovemaking, the most common problem to be found here is inhibition of orgasm. This symptom is often of deep intrapsychic origin related either to early preoedipal dependency needs or unresolved oedipal conflicts. It may be associated with massive sexual repression and, therefore, very difficult to treat. Such specific sexual conflicts of an individual genetic origin are not the central focus of this chapter, but should be mentioned before going on to discuss more superficial sexual problems that are influenced by environmental factors. For instance, inhibition of orgasm can occur in the seemingly uninhibited, emancipated woman, who is apparently free of the old misconceptions and expects a high level of sexual pleasure. She feels she has a right to have as much fun in bed as a man and usually has a partner who agrees with her. Both or either may feel cheated, mystified, and as though they had failed if orgasm is not predictable and mutual. They may share a false application of the new egalitarianism (Schimel, 1962), assuming that women's sexual response should be the same as a man's. There are significant differences; women's physiological mechanism is much more complicated than that of men, involving a wider area of the body, taking longer to arouse, and being more subject to variation not only with endocrine

Sexual Conflicts of Contemporary Women

tides but also with general well-being and psychological mood. Difficulties arise if her response is measured solely in terms of his, without appreciating the unique qualities of each. They may believe that her orgasm should always be acute and explosive as is more typical of men, and probably typical of clitoral sensitivity (the greatest concentration of neural receptors lie in this area). The widespread, voluptuous sensation, which may be added with uninhibited response to inner vaginal stimulation, has a different quality. It often allows satisfaction in a more total but less dramatic way. This may be elusive to the woman who still feels that previous, clitoral stimulation is infantile in spite of recent proof that both areas are involved in any response, no matter what the method of stimulation (Masters and Johnson, 1966).

A deadening of response can also occur when a woman is trying to react in a hurry to please male expectations, when she is too anxious because of doubts about her femininity, or when she is resentful of the man consciously or unconsciously. Full orgasm may still unconsciously mean submission to male dominance, a "giving in to" his more open sexual needs, a loss of control, allowing oneself to be possessed, invaded, taken over by another. This may coexist with restraint and withholding in other areas, or it may be a lone vestige of resenting and fearing male sexual prowess and his apparent invulnerability. The male sexual urge tends to be more acute; the demand is focused on a specific area (the penis). Concomitant wishes for affection, tenderness, and intimacy may be considered weak or unmasculine. Then they are so telescoped into genitality that their existence can easily be overlooked. Woman's sexual urge is not only less focused and more vague, but she is encouraged or permitted by the culture to show tenderness and warmth directly. If the man fails to express tenderness openly, it is easy for her to jump to the conclusion that he merely uses her for the satisfaction of his needs; she may then feel that he forces sex on her without asking her permission or taking her mood into account. This results in falling into old stereotypes and failing to notice and respect individual modes of expression.

A milder, less frequent, female sexual response was taken for granted in the past, but the new preoccupation with mutual orgasm as a badge of success has given mankind a new weapon. The woman's withholding or delaying orgasm may not be inhibition but a subtle way to castrate the man, to make him feel ineffectual. This allows the man to blame the woman, as though she did it to him purposely, when actually she may be feeling quite receptive and vicariously enjoying his pleasure but unable to be fully with him for a variety of reasons not necessarily related to him. An example of this was seen in a girl in treatment who had just emerged from a depressed, withdrawn state. She had been working on early childhood conflicts about her parents, which had been further stirred up on a particular day by her mother's being hospitalized for an acute abdomen. She was in love with a boy and quite happy to be physically close to him that night, not only for solace but to give him pleasure. She did not expect herself to be responsive, but he did. When she failed to, she did not feel cheated but he was upset, saying, "What's wrong. Don't you love me anymore? So I can't satisfy you." (Then, with increasing sarcasm and blame:) "You don't think I'm any good anymore. All you ever think of is yourself; guess you don't think I'm good enough for you." Anxiety about his own masculinity made him experience her being less excited than usual as a narcissistic would, and a malevolent transformation with accusations set in. This also illustrates how a man can seem to be concerned about the woman's satisfaction when actually he is insisting that she have an orgasm for him not for herself.

Victorian mores prevented the outcropping of many such conflicts, as submission was expected of women in marriage but orgasm was not. If she was unable to have full pleasure, there was less chance of disappointment on either side, less guilt, blame, and recrimination. If she was able to give her man pleasure, she could feel successful as a woman without having to worry about being submissive or failing to have orgasm. The man felt a right to enjoy her without the burden of always needing to transport her into ecstasy. Narrow definitions of sexual roles were restricting, but they had the advantage of simplifying performance demands.

Now, there is much confusion as to how much and what kind of activity is accepted as feminine. A woman who accepts cultural permission to be active elsewhere may still feel she should be passive in lovemaking, not ever take the initiative, never be on top, as though that would be interpreted as masculine. A woman who is proud of being equal in other areas, may expect the man to take all responsibilities in matters of sex, as he was more apt to do in Victorian times. She may even refuse to take contraceptive precautions even though it is more pleasant for both of them, or refuse to actively stimulate him in any way feeling that is unladylike. Again a discrepancy between old and new concepts of sexual roles.

Masters and Johnson (1966) did a great service in showing the extent, nature, and degree of the full sexual response of the human female. No one can now say that she has limited capacity for passion, or that there is no proof she even has an orgasm. Some women are obviously responsive during pregnancy and long after the menopause. Some have multiple orgasms and can wear out a man, though this can certainly be of dubious value if used hostilely. However, the fact that these potentialities exist does not mean they are always available to every woman at any time.

The new sexual freedom can be a burden as well as a release. Women have no culturally acceptable way to hide their inhibitions, fears of exploitation, or dependency needs. The constant expectation of sexual performance even during menstruation, pregnancy, and menopausal irregularities leaves them no excuse, no respite from male demands. Those women who embrace, rather than try to escape from, the new freedom may demand orgasm almost as a civil right. If man accepts this as his sole responsibility, sex becomes a demand performance, a hurdle not a pleasure. This is particularly apt to be a problem in middle age when male prowess and frequency of performance may decrease, whereas women can remain receptive and have physiological capacities for prolonged excitement into old age (Masters and Johnson, 1966). This can undermine established male virility and is reflected in the growing literature on masculinity crises in modern man. The increased sexual expectations of women have a depressing effect on some men.

In one sense pressure on the male is more consistent, more unidirectional; he needs to be assertive, to take initiative, to thrust out in most if not all areas of his life. His difficulties arise when he is not temperamentally or characterologically suited or willing to do this, but if he can be appropriately active, he gets constant tangible reaffirmation, a visible product with each sexual act (Fromm, 1943). Women, on the other hand, must be able to alternate between being active, giving, nourishing, and being passive receivers, capable of lying back, taking in, and waiting long periods of time (nine months for gestation or for weeks each month) for concrete proof of their productivity or normal function. They need to be able to shift pace dra-

213

matically from being passionate mistress to understanding wife, from full-time work outside the home to periods of full-time work within the home. This allows a wider variety of satisfaction than is often available to man, but it requires maximum flexibility and ability to maintain long-range perspectives.

In conclusion, let us examine the role sex plays in today's culture. It has been said that we have a neurotic, unhealthy preoccupation with sex compared to Victorian silence and the pretense of its unimportance—at least to women. Now it is either too important or too much talked about. Instead of duplicity or inhibition, there is a self-defeating self-consciousness which prevents spontaneity, deadens imagination, and brings about a secondary inhibition comparable to "bashful bladder" or to "a watched kettle never boils." Concentration on sexual techniques and physiology leads to a mechanization that deprives man of much of the interpersonal meaning that sexual activity may have as a uniquely meaningful expression of intimacy. The success-driven modern man or woman often uses a high level of sexual performance as another badge of success, so that frequency or variety becomes more important than the expression of tenderness and deep affection. Instead there is a tendency for pseudointimacy to develop between people, more fashionable and competitive than authentic. Leslie Farber (1966) commented that sex has lost much of its viability as a human experience and has undergone a degradation owing to its increasing bondage to will. Sex offers man a chance to regain his body by knowing the body of his loved one. Instead he tends to become separated from his body and his real feelings by trying to make his body do what he tells it to. This mechanical approach is even more difficult for women to cope with than for men, whose sexual lives have often been more competitive and impersonal, whereas women tend to have a greater stake in theirs, a deeper involvement, and a more long-term investment. Possibly because of this, they are more apt to lose sight of the importance of sexual satisfaction than are men. They may fall into the trap, laid by earlier generations of men, that sex exists primarily for the pleasure of the man. Sometimes women forget that in cheating man of his excitement and relaxation they also equally cheat themselves.

It is hard to anticipate the nature of clinical symptoms that will be most prevalent in the future. I would expect sexual inhibition to be much less important among those currently coming of age, those who passed through puberty after the coming of the "pill" and who are growing up during the current youth rebellion. Their mothers were less Victorian and their peer group less inhibited. If anything, they have felt pressure for premature sexuality, which may destroy faith in the meaning of intimacy and lead to depression or apathy, but in any event the external form of conflict is apt to be different. For instance, it has been said that the hippies, with their emphasis on group love, are fleeing from preoccupation with the orgasm and the emphasis on the intimate one to one relation. Many young girls feel frigidity among their peers is rare; maybe this will become an unusual rather than a frequent complaint. However, if sexual pleasure is indiscriminate, much of its importance as a human bond may be lost. The old problem of unsatisfied desire may be replaced by sexual ennui.

As of this time it is important to pursue sexual symptoms as a particularly valid wedge into the intricacies of character structure and its genetic origins. Problems with intimacy are often hidden here that do not interfere with function in other areas. The most valid reason for being concerned with sexual behavior is that it has such special meaning to man. Sex is unique among man's biological functions in that it is the only one that requires the involvement of another person for its fullest expression. Man is the only animal whose physical constitution allows full ventral face-to-face contact with possibility of maximal skin stimulation. Thus, prolonged intimacy and tenderness are encouraged. Sex is also the only biological function that can be postponed for long periods of time or abandoned totally (Salzman, 1967). Though man may not be able to will himself into a state of frequent and complete sexual satisfaction, he is able to will himself into abstinence or renunciation of pleasure. He has used this fact to build religions, ethical and moral systems, in a way that has often been quite crippling, causing sexual behavior to be subject to more guilt, inhibition, and superstition than probably any other area of human behavior. Sex can, therefore, be either among the most invigorating or most stultifying aspects of man's life.

Though orgasm may have been falsely emphasized as an end in itself, it is important to study and reinstate it in its appropriate place, since lack of it makes such a large contribution to marital unhappiness. Failure to have orgasm does not make mental illness by damming up the libido; this is now seen as a mechanistic nineteenth-century concept, which treated libido as a finite, measurable energic quantity that was dangerous unless released. The current concept is that sexual drive atrophies rather than accumulates with disuse. Sex is now conceived of not as an instinct with a life of its own but as one of many interrelated physiological functions and one where the biological significance is only a small part of its total importance. Learning and the development of interpersonal ties based on experience play a larger role than with any other physical function. Orgasm does not necessarily bring about intimacy, but lack of it can cause such disappointment, withdrawal, and increased sense of isolation that it may gravely limit interpersonal contact and contribute significantly to hostility and misunderstanding. This is particularly apt to happen when two people are unable to talk about their sexual fears and frustrations.

One of the goals of writing on this topic is to improve communication between men and women as well as between therapist and patient. When sex goes well one of its delights can be peaceful respite from verbiage where emotions can be expressed simply and directly without the need of symbols, but if there is difficulty, silence or avoidance allows misconceptions to continue and words become temporarily necessary in order to work toward solutions. This is especially true during periods of rapid change, when one cannot rely on old assumptions but must be open to the wide range of possibilities in the mind of the other, whom one loves and with whom one wishes to make love.

With the loss of many moral and religious standards for judging appropriate sexual activity, it is useful to weigh it from a new angle. Is sex used for a constructive purpose, such as intimacy, love, pleasure, affirmation of oneself, and/or the other, or is it used destructively for creating mischief, making distance, dominating, getting revenge, demonstrating success or failure? (Schulman, 1968). In this day, it can be studied in terms of the motive of the person, the effect on the partner, and on the total life pattern they share. The amount of cooperation required for satisfying and meaningful sex is probably greater than that required in most other human relationships and reflects the ability of a couple to cooperate in other aspects of living. Women must actively participate in determining their role in this mutual venture, neither waiting for it to be assigned to them by men nor imposing it on men, but working it out with men.

REFERENCES

Bernard, Jessie. "The Status of Women in Modern Patterns of Culture." *Annals of the American Academy of Political and Social Sciences* 375(1968):3–14.

Calderone, Mary. *The New York Times*, drama sect., October 13, 1968.

Erikson, Erik H. *Identity: Youth and Crises*. New York: Norton, 1968.

Farber, Leslie. "I'm Sorry Dear." In *Ways of the Will*. New York: Basic Books, 1966. Pp. 51–76.

Fromm, Erich. "Sex and Character." *Psychiatry* 6, no. 1(1943):21–31.

Green, Maurice R. *Interpersonal Analysis: Selected Papers of Clara Thompson*. New York: Basic Books, 1964.

Hays, Elinor Rice. *Those Extraordinary Blackwells*. New York: Harcourt, Brace & World, 1967.

Johnston, Johanna. *Mrs. Satan*. New York: Putnam, 1967.

Masters, William H.; and Johnson, Virginia E. *Human Sexual Response*. New York: Little, Brown, 1966.

Moulton, Ruth. "Multiple Factors in Frigidity." In Jules H. Masserman, ed., *Science and Psychoanalysis*. Vol. 10. New York: Grune & Stratton, 1966. Pp. 75–93.

Robinson, Marie N. *The Power of Sexual Surrender*. New York: Signet Books, 1959.

Salzman, Leon. "Recently Exploded Sexual Myths." *Human Sexuality* (1967).

Schimel, John. "The Psychopathology of Egalitarianism in Sexual Relations." *Psychiatry* 25(1962):182.

Schulman, Bernard H. "The Uses and Abuses of Sex." *Human Sexuality* 2(1968):48–51.

Blue-Collar Psychotherapy:
Stereotype and Myth

General Background

During 1963 the William Alanson White Institute entered into a relationship with a United Mine Workers Local whereby it agreed to furnish diagnostic and psychotherapeutic services to members of the local.

The prospect of working with blue-collar patients offered a fascinating challenge to an analytic institute. The literature-reported failures resulted from traditional psychotherapy (with its middle-class orientation) being used with this population. Too, the prospect of working with blue-collar workers represented an important step in the clinical implementation of the institute's basic theoretical orientation—recognition of the fact that the cultural milieu is an important consideration in all psychiatric problems. Grey (1956) stressed this need for a cross-fertilization between psychoanalysis and community psychology. Implicit in this need is a clarification of the principles underlying suitability of various types of therapy.

The clinical services of the institute had long noticed that practically none of the lower socioeconomic groups utilized these facilities. We also were aware of the many reported failures in working with this population, more because of the therapist than the patient.

Miller and Swanson (1960, p. 397) stated:

In clinics which serve patients of both classes (blue-collar and middle), a disproportionate number of blue-collar workers drop out of therapy very early because of dissatisfaction with the therapeutic procedures. It is important that psychotherapists learn more about the characteristics of manual laborers and about conditions under which these people mature . . . our results indicated the desirability of exploring a variety of new psychotherapeutic techniques, particularly those in which words and concepts are subordinated to non-verbal and even motoric activities.

Blue-Collar Psychotherapy

Further, the literature has clearly indicated that the blue-collar patient has been too infrequently seen and too infrequently helped by psychotherapy. In explaining this fact, every major study has noted a socioeconomic factor operative, with those of lower socioeconomic status receiving different diagnosis and treatment from those in the middle and upper classes, even when, presumably, the illness is the same.

When the industrial worker becomes mentally ill, he is usually institutionalized, in contrast to the outpatient treatment for the middle and upper classes. For example, Srole, Langner, Michael, Opler, and Rennie (1962) observed that considering psychotic patients only, it was found that 50 percent of upper-class patients were treated in the community on an outpatient basis, whereas only 10 percent of the lower-class patients remained in the community (90 percent were institutionalized). Grey (1956, p. 115) noted that "middle class personnel of a psychiatric hospital were found to regard and treat middle class (male) patients more favorably than lower class (male). They judged the outcome of treatment to be more favorable for middle class patients." Hollingshead and Redlich (1958) reported that one third of the neurotic patients in the lowest socioeconomic group receiving treatment for the first time were in a state, military, or veteran's hospital. They concluded (1958, p. 264), "The state hospital is utilized in sharply increasing percentage as the class structure is descended."

Their study clearly indicated the relationship between class and the type of therapy rendered. The lower-class patient, in contrast to the middle- and upper-class patient, was given shock or drugs more frequently and tended to get the less-trained therapist assigned to him.

To complicate matters further, the lower-class patient has many misconceptions about mental illness and tends to think in terms of "psycho" and "Bellevue." He does not present himself as a patient until his condition can no longer be avoided, thus nullifying the possibility of early detection and treatment as well as reducing the possibility of success in psychotherapy.

The Union Therapy Project

Thirteen William Alanson White graduates planned the project, with Leopold Caligor and Miltiades Zaphiropoulos as codirectors.

Mr. Sam Meyers, president of United Auto Workers Local 259, was invaluable to the planners. It was decided that the project would be run as an autonomous clinic within the clinical services.

A contract was signed in the fall of 1963. The project initially agreed to render ten evenings or Saturday sessions of therapy a week, at a nominal fee. In addition, three hours a week of social work were to be made available for the intake of new cases, referral of the patient to more appropriate sources, such as to group health insurance for necessary medical service or to a family or child guidance agency for a relative's problems. The worker alone was seen rather than family members, on the assumption that ten therapy sessions would do the most good that way. We found, however, much to our surprise, that we usually ended up doing family therapy anyway, the patient frequently bringing wife and children to his sessions. We were pleased when the union, in 1965, saw fit to increase the number of therapy hours to fifteen a week and to include services to all family members.

The project's first concern has been the education of union members, especially officers, trustees, and stewards, to have an understanding of the concept of mental health. The education program has included attendance at union meetings where open discussions have been initially greeted with humor, tolerance, and occasional guffaw. Memoranda were written for distribution to every member by the union's health and welfare plan. Articles were written for the local's newspaper. This education program was of great importance since early detection and early referral is most helpful. For example, if a steward, who commands respect as the elected representative of his fellow workers, recognizes the worker's difficulties in an early stage and suggests therapy, he will be listened to. Mr. Meyers, highly experienced in the area of mental health, has been most effective in communicating the criteria for therapy to his men. A system was instituted where a worker, recognizing the need in himself, could call Mr. Meyers directly or arrange to see him; then Mr. Meyers would get in touch with the clinic. The project is geared to see the patient almost at once for intake evaluation and immediate referral to an analyst who can see the patient in his office during evening or Saturday hours. The entire project is kept within the union framework. The worker pays nothing. The union pays the entire fee. The worker feels that the union and the analyst take a personal interest in him. There is no clinic, no waiting list, no feelings of receiving "charity"; treatment is the worker's due as a member of the union.

Blue-Collar Psychotherapy

The project's second concern has been the exploration of new ways of using psychoanalytic insights and techniques. Aware of the relation between illness and its sociocultural matrix, we have tried to determine methods of therapy which would be most helpful for these blue-collar patients, and, by extension, for a large segment of the American population. As we have experimented with these new procedures, they have been carefully examined in peer-group seminars. Cases have been discussed in great detail; techniques used by the therapist have been described and their effects have been evaluated.

The third concern, the outgrowth of the peer-group seminars, has been the integration of clinical observation with clinical research, that is, clincial experimentation with new therapy modalities to scientifically test their efficacy.

The initial program was with Local 259 in New York City. In September 1966, the United Auto Workers International inaugurated a national prepaid insurance program which made short-term psychotherapy available to 3.5 million members and their families. Our institute undertook to service two additional locals within a thirty-mile radius of New York City, including 50,000 eligible union members and their families. Thus, the total eligible population to be served for all three locals has been 63,000. The project is now five years old. More than 3,600 hours of therapy have been rendered to more than 360 patients. There are presently forty-five participating analysts rendering fifty therapy sessions per week. There have been eighty peer-group seminars.

For a more detailed discussion of the history, scope, and goals of the union therapy project, see Caligor and Zaphiropoulos (1971). For a discussion of the problems and possibilities in providing mental health care to organized low-income groups, see Zaphiropoulos and Caligor (1967).

The Stereotypes of Blue-Collar Personality and Psychotherapy

At inception we were not clear as to who the blue-collar patient was and what the best ways were to treat him. We consulted with authorities and combed the literature. According to Frank Riessman (1964; Riessman and Goldfarb, 1964), it is clear that there are real differences in attitudes, values, goals, and life styles between the lower and upper classes. Riessman explained the blue-collar worker as action oriented, rather than verbal, extrospective rather than introspective, poorly educated, relatively unimaginative, and little given to fantasy compared with the middle-class individual. In a therapeutic relationship, the lower-class patient is oriented toward problems and symptoms rather than personality change. He expects quick and direct results, for example, a specific behavior change in his marriage or job. Riessman concluded that psychoanalytic procedures and psychodynamically oriented psychotherapy in which great weight is placed on the use of introspection, fantasy, and dream material, as well as on strong motivation for long-range personality changes, is of little value for the blue-collar worker. Since psychoanalysts and depth therapists base their therapies on psychoanalytic procedures they are unequipped to cope with the blue-collar patient. For Riessman and others, the new blue-collar techniques of psychotherapy should rely on the following: direct advice, benevolent authority of the therapist, pills, role-playing, hypnosis, catharsis, physical therapy, suggestion, conditioning, environmental manipulation, and so on.

Thus there has emerged a picture of the blue-collar patient and a picture of the therapy of choice for him which is a stereotype. We too went along with this trend in the field. Gould (1967), an analyst with the project, wrote a paper one year after its inception, which was strongly influenced by Riessman.

Since then we have been examining this stereotype. In peer-group seminars, cases have been discussed in detail, with the focus on the picture of the blue-collar patient and the therapy and technique of choice for him. Meanwhile our skilled analysts have been free to use a range of techniques drawing on the Riessman orientation as well as from analytic and depth therapy.

A global picture of the blue-collar patient, derived from our peer-group seminars and research, indicates that blue-collar characteristics have been accurately identified and described by Riessman and others. Frankiel and Wassell, in a study comparing the characteristics at intake of blue-collar and middle-class patients applying to the clinical services of our institute, made the following observations:

ATTITUDE TOWARD SEEKING HELP
The union patient often felt that treatment was a way to get justification for his behavior and feelings. The interviewer was seen as an authority dispensing praise and blame in this connection, where difficulties were acknowledged as self-derived, treatment tended to be seen as a chance to overcome

Blue-Collar Psychotherapy

"bad" traits. Problems were often seen as arising from circumstance rather than from inner sources. However, where there were symptoms, relief from them was always a clearly articulated motivating factor.

The [middle-class] clinic applicants sought treatment actively. They had to find out about the Institute, obtain an application, and make contact on their own. The union patient was invited to apply through his union. . . . The [middle-class] Institute clinic patient shares this [articulated relief from symptoms as a motivating factor] in that he tends to see treatment as a way of getting relief from symptoms, but also as a way of expanding his capacity for pleasure and achievement.

STYLE OF SELF-PRESENTATION

The union patient tends to be unpredictable. He might be extremely passive or hyperactive, waving arms and raising voice, standing up, etc. When hostile, he is usually openly so, challenging and blustering. Subtlety, mildness, polish were absent in the union patient's self-presentation. . . . Words were de-emphasized, action is what counts. Vocabulary tends to be impoverished and stereotyped.

The Institute clinic patient tends to come in, sit down, start describing his problems. Confiding to an expert, introspecting, articulating his inner experience to someone else, are all more familiar to the Institute clinic patient than to the union patient.

RELATIONSHIP TO SELF AND HISTORY

What makes for the impulsivity and primitiveness of the blue-collar patient's approach? The less middle class the patient, the less able he seems to turn his attention toward experiencing his inner life. Further, there is a stereotype of behavior and values and self-expression. Impulsivity replaces introspection.

One possible explanation of these observations is in the differences in the early life experience of the union patient as contrasted with the middle class Institute clinic patient. Brutality in the early life experience is found in [most of the] blue collar patients. In the more middle class Institute group, emotional neglect or lack of involvement was found [in most], and physical brutality was absent.

In all instances but one, at initial interview, the union patient ignores past experience as a significant source of present difficulty. One might speculate that the ubiquity of trauma and tragedy in the lower socio-economic class leads to a social climate in which tragedy is not novel, a marked contrast with the middle class sense of outrage and injustice at the "raw deal" one is getting if things do not conform with middle class expectations.

Further speculation could lead us to wonder if there is not a relationship between early experience with brutality and the dependence on activity, avoidance, shutting out, or projecting as defenses. The common element being that the brutality, since it always involves an assault on integrity of the self, calls out a bodily response—fight or flee.

ATTITUDE TOWARDS WORK

The union patients in this study showed a high degree of work satisfaction, but low aspiration, whereas, the Institute clinic applicants reflected a large degree of dissatisfaction with what they were doing, had high aspirations and considered that they were under-achieving and not mobilizing their resources effectively.

SEXUAL ADJUSTMENT

The union patient appears to follow, on the surface, the more "regular" pattern of sexual adjustment. All the blue-collar workers in this study are, with the exception of one, living at present with their wives and children. The real picture, however, is that they have had numerous separations and some live in brutally destructive circumstances emotionally and physically. There seems to be a pattern of ongoing hostility between the sexes; an antipathy between male and female that is accepted as a way of life.

In our attempt to obtain another view of our patients, ten rating scales were designed, covering: Ties to Natural Family, Aggression, Impulse Control, Delinquency, Social Awareness and Responsibility, Sexual Adjustment, Vocational Life, Marital Adjustment, and Total Adjustment. Firstly, the Institute clinic applicants have less exclusive ties to family, more involvement with issues and causes of more impersonal, more widely social nature. Verbal aggression is about equally distributed in the two groups, physical aggression is more pronounced in the union group, and most strikingly, appears in delinquent behavior both past and present. In general, more passivity and avoidance characterizes sexuality in the middle class, Institute applicants; aggression characterizes the union patients. As would be expected by virtue of their superior education, the Institute clinic applicants had a closer correspondence between their functioning and their aspirations, but the union patients experienced somewhat more satisfaction. When married, the amount of disruption seems about the same in the two groups; however, Institute patients are more often single. In general, the union patients have more problems, their lives are more disrupted and have a higher incidence of serious pathology, if total life situation is taken into account.

Though the above is a valid identification of many personality characteristics of the blue-collar worker, his global profile will probably be modified as we study such variables as ethnic group, level of work skill, level of income, social upper mobility, social-rootedness geographically versus migrant or newly arrived, and level of education. From this study, several discrete blue-collar profiles will probably emerge.

Though the stereotype of the blue-collar worker is acceptable, with modifications, the stereotype of blue-collar psychotherapy is open to serious contention. Our analysts, because of their initial lack of self-

Blue-Collar Psychotherapy

confidence with a new population as well as their familiarity with the literature, started off attempting to use the recommended nonanalytic techniques. With time, skilled analysts have found themselves swinging back to analytic and depth therapy, though with modifications because of the short-term nature of the therapy. It would seem then that the stereotype of blue-collar psychotherapy has been based on a lack of knowledge of alternatives.

Statistical Data

The total number of therapy sessions was 1,244; the mean number of therapy sessions for one year was sixteen. Roughly 80 percent of the patients were seen for twenty or fewer sessions; roughly 10 percent were seen for twenty-one to thirty-five sessions; roughly 10 percent for thirty-six or more sessions.

Table 12–1 indicates the distribution of cases carried for one year and the breakdown of the number of treatment sessions.

TABLE 12–1
Number of Treatment Sessions
per Patient for One Year from
June 1, 1967 to May 30, 1968

NUMBER OF SESSIONS	NUMBER OF PATIENTS
1–5 sessions	23
6–10 sessions	26
11–15 sessions	16
16–20 sessions	12
21–25 sessions	6
26–30 sessions	1
31–35 sessions	1
36–40 sessions	3
41–45 sessions	0
46–50 sessions	2
51–55 sessions	2
56–60 sessions	2
89 sessions	1
160 sessions	1
TOTAL	96 patients

Duration and Kinds of Treatment

As of the last tabulation made in March 1968, 266 patients were seen for a total of 2,801 therapy sessions. The number of sessions comprising treatment has continued to be low, most patients terminating in twenty or fewer sessions with a mean of sixteen, which is in accord with the yearly distribution already mentioned. The number of therapy sessions has not been limited by finances in the greatest portion of cases since more than two thirds of patients are from Local 259, where the number of sessions is unlimited. Too, none of the patients has been paying for his own therapy since union insurance coverage has permitted more sessions than have been used. The tabulation of duration of treatment and the kinds of therapy rendered is presented in Table 12–2.

TABLE 12–2

Number of Treatment Sessions and Kinds of Therapy Used for the 266 Project Patient Population from November 1963 to March 1968

NUMBER OF SESSIONS	INDIVIDUAL THERAPY ONLY	INDIVIDUAL THERAPY PLUS INTERVIEWS WITH MARITAL PARTNER	INDIVIDUAL THERAPY PLUS FAMILY INTERVIEWS
1–3	63[a]		
4–29	63[b]	16	96[c]
30 plus[d]	12	4	12
TOTAL	138	20	108

[a] After one interview, fifteen in this group were referred to other agencies for help with medical problems, alcoholism. Patients living far from the clinic were referred to child or family guidance agencies. Two patients in this group were seen for consultation and then hospitalized.
[b] Five of these patients resumed treatment after some time had elapsed following termination.
[c] Eight patients in this group were seen in multiple-therapist family therapy.
[d] One patient out of nine had thirty or more sessions.

Patient Categories

Patients seemed to fall into several categories about which certain generalizations can be made. However, these observations are clinical and will be subject to further systematic research investigation.

Blue-Collar Psychotherapy

Category 1

This category consists of patients who are severely schizoid, alcoholic, sociopathic, and psychotic. These patients include many who are very sick chronically, as well as those who are decompensating. Patients in this category frequently require medication and environmental manipulation, as they can no longer function on the job and at home. Some need hospitalization or more hospitalization. These patients sometimes stay in therapy but are difficult to make contact with, are undermotivated or unevenly motivated, and frequently have magical expectations of therapy. They have a high rate of broken appointments and more often than not come to therapy because the union or employer sends them.

Many of the sixty-three patients (approximately 24 percent of the total) seen individually for one to three sessions belong here.

Category 2

This second category includes those patients who are having difficulty functioning in the environment, that is, family or job. Because of malfunction in or loss of support from the environment, the patient experiences little gratification from it. Patients in this category occasionally exhibit symptoms, but usually the emphasis is on the character and behavior disorders. The men tend to act out; the women, if they come to treatment for themselves, tend to show more depression than anxiety. They complain about their husbands' drinking, sexual running around, irresponsibility, absenteeism on the job, foolish spending, neglect of the children, and so forth. Essentially, they report feeling trapped with the children and getting too little emotionally from their husbands. Often the wife of a schizoid passive-aggressive patient in desperation pushes him and then the family into therapy and ends up becoming a patient in her own right.

Children in this category are usually referred because of school problems such as learning difficulties, unacceptable behavior, and truancy. The common family picture of such children is the father yelling and beating the child, or completely uninvolved, the mother depressed and overwhelmed.

Most of the 128 patients (approximately 48 percent of the total) seen for four or more sessions in individual therapy plus interviews with marital partner and in individual therapy plus family interview were in category 2.

Category 3

This third category is comprised of the symptom neurotics. Obsessive-compulsives and hysterics are found here, with an emphasis on hysteria-anxiety and somatic symptomatology. Depressive and phobic reactions are also quite common. As would be expected, there are frequently some manifestations of character and behavior disorders, but the major emphasis is on the symptom picture and internalization of difficulties rather than conflicts with the environment.

Most of the seventy-five patients (approximately 28 percent of the total) seen individually for four to thirty plus sessions fall in this category.

The Therapy of Choice
For Each Category of Patients

Category 1

The severely schizoid, alcoholic, sociopathic, and psychotic are included here. Many in this group border on economic and social dissolution and may deteriorate into the unemployed poor.

With this group our analysts have tended to use much of what Riessman (1964) suggested: environmental manipulation, medication, direct advice; the analyst assumes the role of magic helper and benevolent authority. However, the techniques Riessman recommended have been used with these patients, not because of any commitment to blue-collar therapy but because these techniques seem most appropriate given the sickness of the patient, be he blue-collar worker or middle-class businessman. But the techniques Riessman recommended are not suitable with blue-collar workers who are viable economically and socially unlike those in category 1.

Category 2

This category includes patients with character and behavior disorders. The prevalent picture is of an unhappy wife initiating therapy for her mate and then ending up as a patient in her own right.

Here, our major focus is on family and couple therapy combined with individual therapy for the index patient. The style of therapy with patients in this group—individual combined with family or couple therapy—is essentially the same as with middle-class short-term psychotherapy patients with similar disorders.

Category 3

This category includes the symptom neurotics, for example, obsessive-compulsives and hysterics, with a prevalence of hysteria-anxiety and somatic symptomatology with the considerable presence, too, of the depressive and phobic reactions. A variety of modified psychoanalytic therapy techniques are used.

Discussion of Blue-Collar Psychotherapy

I would like to make some observations on individual psychotherapy with patients from categories 2 and 3. (They include all the patients in category 3, seventy-five; at least one person in each couple, ten; and probably one fourth of family members seen, twenty-seven.) This adds up to 112 patients, roughly 42 percent of all cases seen and includes nearly all the potentially treatable cases seen for four or more sessions.

My impression from the peer-group seminars is that analysts, gaining experience with the blue-collar patients, have increasingly used modified analytic techniques. These techniques include the use of dreams, free association and introspection, transference and resistance, as well as the exploration of etiology and so on.

A pilot study bears this out. This project by Caligor, Grey, and Ortmeyer is an attempt at determining which therapy techniques are associated with considerably improved blue-collar patients and which with unimproved blue-collar patients.

As part of the project, analysts have been asked to rate each case at the end of treatment in terms of their satisfaction with the outcome of treatment. The ratings are (1) yes, (2) qualified yes, improved, and (3) no or little improvement. The first cases fell into qualified yes, improved and no or little improvement groups in a ratio of two to one. Not one analyst thus far has answered yes. This is not surprising. We do not expect miracles when it comes to the efficacy of any form of psychotherapy, especially brief psychotherapy. However, it is interesting to note that preliminary findings indicate that many patients who terminated therapy voluntarily would have answered yes. The discrepancy between the analyst's satisfaction with treatment as compared with the patient's might reflect the discrepancy between the blue-collar patient's expectations of therapy as compared with the middle-class analyst's expectations.

Analysts have also been given a list of seventeen therapeutic techniques ranging from the stereotyped blue-collar approach through some typical analytic procedures, presented in the following random order: direct advice about actions; role-playing techniques; investigation of childhood experience; investigation of analysts' own experience; analysis of dreams; open warmth and support; evaluation of patient-analyst interaction; analysis of patient's interaction with others; examination of patient's feelings; free association of introspective data; use of medication or placebos; separate interviews with other family members; conjoint interviews with several family members; group therapy (with members not in the family); direct intervention, such as contact with outside agencies; confrontation of the patient with resistance re time, money, and so on; and explanation about psychological processes. The analysts have been asked to rate each of these techniques for the following: seldom or never used; used occasionally but was of little use; used occasionally but useful; or used often or regularly. The therapeutic techniques that were significantly more used with the qualified yes, improved group than with the no or little improvement group were investigation of childhood experience; analysis of dreams; free association of introspective data; and confrontation of the patient with resistance re time, money, and so on.

Two questions emerge at this point: (1) Were these therapeutic techniques used only with patients who were more amenable to their use? (2) Were these same patients the ones most capable of change? These questions have been explored, but, as yet, answers have not been found. We plan to make a correction in the experimental design that will permit us to differentiate between the use of a particular technique and the selection of patients amenable to that technique. Essentially, we will be testing the hypothesis that most effective changes with blue-collar patients were made by using modified psychoanalytic techniques.

Middle-Class Analysts and Blue-Collar Patients

Initially, the different value sets of patient and analyst create strain for both. To diminish the strain caused by these differences, the analyst must have a realistic awareness of them, rather than attempt to deny or ignore them. Too, the analyst must keep in mind that the goal in blue-collar therapy is that the patient be improved or changed intrapsychically or interpersonally within the context of his own system of needs and social structure. Ortmeyer (1971) illustrated this with a case he carried over four years on a once a week basis. The patient benefited considerably from therapy; however, his values, modes of perception, thinking, behavior, and class identification remained blue collar throughout.

Blue-Collar Patients and Middle-Class Patients

Why do blue-collar patients frequently achieve some measure of success in a limited number of sessions in contrast with the prolonged number of sessions with middle-class patients? I would like to suggest several possibilities: The blue-collar patient sets limited goals for himself. Once symptoms are removed and he feels better able to cope with his work or family problems, he feels satisfied and frequently initiates termination. He is relatively free of the middle-class patient's probing of his imperfections and endless striving.

The analysts in our project are geared to do brief psychotherapy. This is often a difficult mental set to effect. Analytic psychotherapy looks down on symptom removal as a flight into health and as an unworthy goal for a patient to set for himself. Most training centers emphasize that long intensive cases are somehow better than briefer ones. For example, Riess (1969) noted that many middle-class patients have their symptoms removed in fifteen to twenty sessions and then the analyst goes on to define deeper and long-range goals for the patient. Despite this generally negative attitude toward short-term psychotherapy, we have found that the majority of patients in the project achieved the goals they set for themselves and voluntarily terminated with an average of sixteen sessions even when the number of hours available was unlimited, as with Local 259 patients.

The Impact of Education on the Utilization of Therapy

We know that utilization has been directly related to education of the local's trustees, officers, stewards, and members via open discussion at meetings, memoranda to members, and articles in the local's newspapers. Our utilization rates for the first four years of our program with Local 259 were 0.60 percent, 0.90 percent, 1.32 percent and 1.10 percent of the eligible population. After each educational effort, there would be an increase in the number of patients referred, and then a gradual falling off until the next educational campaign. We diminished our educational efforts somewhat during the fourth year because of the demands on our time made in initiating therapy programs with two other locals.

Our education stresses the definition of psychological problems to include: work, marital, and family difficulties (for example, an emotionally upset child); anxiety attacks, severe headaches, and stomach pains owing to emotional origins; feeling angry at work and at home for no known reason; feeling lonely, miserable, and unhappy for no known reason; drug addiction and alcoholism. Once this education reaches the family level and the wife becomes aware of the availability of therapy, she usually becomes an active instigator of family or child therapy. This is especially true where there is a direct mailing by the union to the home. Too, since many of the men tend to disregard written material, we have found a word-of-mouth campaign, which educates and uses shop stewards as referrants, quite helpful.

It is my conviction that with appropriate education, the total patient sampling will have higher percentages of categories 2 and 3 patients. Where there is no educational program, the blue-collar worker has little concept of what mental health is or how he can get help if he is experiencing difficulties. Thus, the severely and chronically ill who can barely cope on the job and interpersonally, that is, category 1 patients, tend to be referred by an irate employer or desperate union official whereas the less severely ill continue to superficially cope on the job and interpersonally.

Since we want to reach those patients who can best utilize therapy as well as those who most need help, we need basic data on the total union population as well as on our patients. We need to know the social and psychological characteristics, demographic data, values, attitudes toward mental health, indices of mental health, and so on for both. Only then can we answer the question: Are we reaching those patients who can best utilize therapy as well as those who most need help?

Tentative Conclusions about Blue-Collar Psychotherapy

1. There is no global blue-collar psychotherapy. The concept comes more from sociology than from experience with patients.

2. It is important to define the blue-collar patient's severity and style of illness, that is, diagnosis, as with any patient of any class. The therapy of choice stems from this rather than from class origins. "We are all much more simply human than otherwise," said Harry Stack Sullivan (1953). It is the person who must be treated, not the class.

3. What is needed with blue-collar patients is not primarily new therapy modalities but education, that is, awareness of emotional difficulties, thus permitting early detection and referral through well-delineated channels. With education, he more nearly approximates the middle-class patient who comes to a family or community clinic.

4. There is an abundance of the following characteristics, which leads us to believe that they are amenable to the use of modified analytic techniques: intelligence, hysteric-liability, free-floating anxiety, phobias, somatic condition, nonintellectualization, naïveté, suggestibility, available affect, excessive reliance on repression in coping with impulses and the demands of the world about them, resiliency, the capacity for acting out but also acting. We suspect that Freud's upper-middle–class Viennese hysterics, who showed many of the above qualities and with whom quick cures were frequently obtained via hypnosis, suggestion, and catharsis (Freud, 1894), have many similarities to the blue-collar psychologically unsophisticated population, which tends to show much less of the middle-class obsessive-compulsiveness, overintellectualization, constriction of affect, lack of spontaneity, and inhibition.

REFERENCES

Caligor, Leopold; and Zaphiropoulos, Miltiades. "History and Scope of the Union Therapy Project." In G. D. Goldman and D. S. Milman, eds., *Psychoanalytic Contributions to Community Psychiatry.* Springfield, Ill.: Charles C Thomas, 1971.

Frankiel, R.; and Wassell, R. "Initial Interviews: A Comparison of Trade Union Members and Psychoanalytic Clinic Applicants." Unpublished study.

Freud, Sigmund. "Studies in Hysteria" (1894). *Standard Edition. Vol. 2.* London: Hogarth, 1894.

Gould, R. "Dr. Strangeclass or: How I stopped Worrying about the Theory and Began Treating the Blue Collar Patient." *Journal of the American Orthopsychiatric Association* 37(1967):78–86.

Grey, A. "A Cross-Fertilization Between Psychoanalysis and Community Psychology." In G. D. Goldman and D. S. Milman, eds., *Psychoanalytic Contributions to Community Psychology.* Springfield, Ill.: Charles C Thomas, 1971.

———. "Social Class and the Psychiatric Patient: A Study in Composite Character." *Contemporary Psychoanalysis.* 2(1956):87–121.

Hollingshead, A. B.; and Redlich, Fredrick C. *Social Class and Mental Illness: A Community Study.* New York: Wiley, 1958.

Miller, D.; and Swanson, G. *Inner Conflict and Defense.* New York: Holt, 1960.

Ortmeyer, D. H. "Clininical Illustration of Psychotherapy with the Blue Collar Worker." In G. D. Goldman and D. S. Milman, eds., *Psychoanalytic Contributions to Community Psychology.* Springfield, Ill.: Charles C Thomas, 1971.

Riess, Bernard F. New York, Post-Graduate Center for Mental Health. Personal communication on research in progress, 1969.

Riessman, Frank. *New Approaches to Mental Health: Treatment for Labor and Low Income Groups.* New York: National Institute of Labor Education, 1964.

———; and Goldfarb, J. "Role Playing and the Lower Socio-Economic Group." *Group Psychotherapy* 17, no. 1(1964).

Srole, Leo; Langner, Thomas S.; Michael, Stanley T.; Opler, Marvin K.; and Rennie, Thomas A. C. *Mental Health in the Metropolis: The Midtown Study.* New York: McGraw-Hill, 1962.

Sullivan, Harry Stack. *The Interpersonal Theory of Psychiatry.* New York: Norton, 1953.

Zaphiropoulos, Militiades; and Caligor, Leopold. "Providing Organized Limited Income Groups with Mental Health Resources: Problems and Possibilities." Psychiatric Outpatient Centers of America Proceedings, 1967.

The Psychotherapeutic Encounter:
Relatedness and Schizophrenia

Either you believe that mental disorders are acts of God, predestined, inexorably fixed, arising from a constitutional or some other irremediable substratum, the victims of which are to be helped through an innocuous life to a more or less euthanasic exit—perhaps contributing along the way as laboratory animals for the inquiries of medicine, pathology, constitution study, or whatever—*or* you believe that mental disorder is largely preventable and somewhat remediable by control of psychosociological factors. In the first case, I have no message for you, being deluded in believing that I have shown the possibility of profoundly modifying the processes called schizophrenic by the use of personality factors. In the other case, it must be evident that your subscription to a psycho-sociogenetic point of view *entails inevitably* a new scrutiny of your custodianship of the mentally ill, and the evolution of a program of study and technique-development in the utilization of persons working under you [Harry Stack Sullivan, 1962e, p. 270.]

It is the hope that a number of those fortunately located for such research (in the field of schizophrenia) may escape the restraint of neurological explanations, dualist bugbears, and anthropomorphic reifications, to the end that they engage in that intimate personal observation of schizophrenic content and behavior which may eventuate in views which do not expend the universe, and do offer at least a promise in the preventive field. . . . It is hoped that many others will return to this field of work; for even if the individual patient is not deemed worth the effort, the profit in the field of mental hygiene which will result from the comprehensive understanding of this mental disorder is of unparalleled importance; and the prophylaxis it would make possible justifies a wealth of intensive work [Harry Stack Sullivan, 1962d, p. 22].

In this chapter I am concerned with an aspect of psychotherapy, and, in a broader sense, human relatedness, namely, the basic elements in the formation of a tie or bond of attachment between the participants; being a product of my inheritance, my past, my experience, and anticipations of my future I am not detached from but immersed in the minutiae of my daily living. I make no pretense of reporting in some clearly objective fashion my recollections of clinical experience; nor do I insist on the rightness of views, or seek to defend conclusions. I shall only give my impressions of certain events in which I have participated and speculations as to their significances. Again I turn to Sullivan (1962a, p. 148):

May I take the liberty of discussing a pitfall in this understanding of the patient? That it is one of my own difficulties will perhaps negative an appearance of preaching. The personality of the observer must either be exterior to the scientific observations which he secures or be represented explicitly in their context when it enters into them. . . . How curiously opaque we are to our own observational scotomata. How easy it is to overlook things which do not fit into our tentative explanation. How more than difficult it is to see evidence of an unpleasant theory. It is sad indeed that medical men are so human as to find theories pleasant and unpleasant. There is no scientist but should blush at an accusation that he liked or disliked an hypothesis, on the basis of ethics or aesthetics, or—and this is the important ground —on the basis of his own early training. Convicted of such an accusation, he is adjudged no scientist; he is but a bigoted layman thrusting his likes and dislikes into the serious business of observation, the method of knowledge.

With that cautionary note in mind, and recognizing that I, for one, subscribe to its imperative and too frequently fail in its practice, we shall now turn our attention to a search for the fundamentals of the human relationship that may (with skill, care, and good fortune) develop into a profitable and useful psychotherapeutic encounter.

The Patient

In an account of this nature it is useful to begin with a brief look at the person who has become a patient, usually as the result of a series of misadventures cumulative from infancy, uncorrected throughout the years, and leading in adolescence or later to behavior so deviant from the requirements of society that attention is attracted to it and regulatory action required. The account of such a course is so commonplace that only its outline need be presented for our purposes. Though the manifestations of disorder are in this instance those of schizophrenia, the issue of relatedness is central in psychotherapy irrespective of the behavioral patterns being dealt with. Schizophrenia is a paradigm of human living, demonstrating in stark simplicity the need for, and the fear of, involvement in intimate, revealing, and enduring relationships.

The Psychotherapeutic Encounter

Sarah was twenty years old when we first met. She was the oldest of three sisters in a family of comfortable economic circumstances and considered to be outstandingly successful until the end of her first college year, at the age of eighteen. Her earlier years were said to have been happy; she was active socially, was well liked in the community, and had an excellent scholastic record. In college she was restless, had difficulty in adjusting to dormitory life, withdrew to herself, began to do poorly in her studies, and appeared to be depressed. Later she told of her feeling that she was becoming estranged from all that had once seemed familiar to her, that she was essentially evil and destructive, and that she was undergoing a change in her body and personality that was becoming embarrassingly evident to all who had contact with her. Sleep was interrupted by frightening dreams, which extended into and continued during times of wakefulness until the figures and voices of the night threatened to intrude and control all her life. In a state of terror she drove her car off the road, incurring only minor injuries but being so obviously preoccupied and odd in her manner thereafter that she was brought to a psychiatrist by her parents at the recommendation of the family physician. Sarah, however, would not speak with the therapist, refused to go to his office, left school, and made a suicide attempt with barbiturates. There followed hospitalization, treatment with insulin coma and electroshock, the use of various ataractic drugs, and interviews with several therapists who were rejected by her one after the other. On occasion she was assaultive; for long periods she was mute and kept to herself, allowing no one to come near her. She denied that she was troubled or had a need for anyone, insisting that she be left to her own devices despite her failure to eat adequately or give herself the most elementary care. She rejected the role of patient, and those who dealt with her soon came to feel ineffective as well as unwanted, and for the most part were willing to leave her alone except for such contacts as were necessary to maintain her life. Some pitied her and said that she was hopelessly ill; others more openly resented or hated her and would have been delighted had she gone elsewhere or disappeared. In brief, Sarah was troublesome to all who knew her, and her feelings of being wicked and destructive were confirmed by the growing resentment and hostility of those associated with her. Despair increased with isolation, and the behavior of all participants in this unhappy system seemed strangely designed to produce what no one allegedly

237

desired. If Sarah sought freedom—from anxiety and a hospital—her actions led only to greater restriction. Members of her family felt guilty for whatever they might have done in contributing to her difficulties; they were also angry at being disappointed in their expectations for their oldest child and would now have little to do with her or with hospital personnel. The latter spoke of wanting to help, but as they were repeatedly rebuffed their own feelings of hurt and anger were not easily tolerated, and they avoided Sarah as much as they could, or they treated her as an object, as a "case" of schizophrenia.

Sarah's successes during earlier years had been accomplished in spite of her persisting sense of estrangement, and her feeling of isolation was increased when she was praised for what she did. Those who spoke well of her seemed to her to be hypocritical, ignorant of the true state of affairs, or afraid to accept the fact that she was desperate and afraid that she was mad. She was unable to deal with the requirements of growing up, though outwardly she appeared to be an adult. Failing to obtain the needed balance between desire and satisfaction, she recoiled from the world, first physically by flight and attempted suicide, and finally, using Sullivan's (1962b) phrase, "by the route of symbols, schizophrenia."

Psychotherapy

When we consider the possibility of psychotherapy being useful to someone living as Sarah did it is necessary to give a definition of the proposed enterprise. In the simplest terms, psychotherapy may be thought of as a process whereby a troubled person discusses his difficulties in living with someone who by experience, training, and personal characteristics has been accepted as an expert in such matters. The numbers of people involved in these encounters vary, as do the techniques used. Essential to all forms of this therapy, however, is the concept of the one who seeks help and the one who has certain qualifications that enable him to provide it, albeit not always successfully.

In this instance we are describing aspects of the one to one treatment situation. There are many definitions of this form of therapy. It is described as a social relationship developed between two people to bring about desired changes in the behavior of one, the client or patient. Some speak of it as treatment in the traditional medical sense; others, as a form of relearning and education. It has been referred to as a dialectical process in which the personalities of both participants are revealed, permitting a mutuality of growth. No matter how described, psychotherapy is an interpersonal process, though in some of its forms the therapist seeks to be unobtrusive as he studies phenomena of transference and pursues insight; in others he participates more freely in what he may hope will become a corrective emotional experience; and in still others he seeks to shape behavior without clearly identifying himself as the author of that which he proposes.

Despite current interests in the possible beneficial effects of bodily contact, emphasis in the majority of definitions is on the verbal exchange, whereby the patient's conception of himself and his world is elaborated, gross misperceptions corrected, and autistic modes of reference rendered unnecessary except when resorted to by choice, as in literary productions.

The Patient in the Role of Patient

In keeping with these definitions of psychotherapy is the concept of the patient as someone who fits into their requirements, however awkwardly. He is expected to have a complaint, that is, he is aware of something going awry in his living and is able to protest about it, even though in doing so he must resort to such vague terms as depression, emptiness, ennui, and so on. It is important that he can forsee the possibility of favorable change; despite feelings of discouragement, distrust, and frustration he can at least envisage life as being different—worse if not better. To some extent such a person is motivated to seek help from other people; his experience has been such that he can still place confidence in others, trusting not only in their abilities and good intentions but in his own competence to make use of these. He may question and oppose parents and authority figures, but not to the extent that he rejects them in their entirety. He is often miserable, seemingly uncompromising and unapproachable, and he may act as if his main concern was to defeat those who try to aid him, but there is hope in him and he will continue the struggle to make some sense of his life with his fellows. This person can recognize and cooperate with the major requirements of the therapeutic situation and the personal needs of the therapist; to some extent he can put himself in the other person's shoes and can even dare an occasional sharp look at himself, hopefully with a touch of humor.

Sarah as Patient

Except for the fact that she was in a hospital Sarah did not conform to the role of patient or as one suitable for psychotherapy in the more conventional use of the term. Though she had been in serious difficulties and had attempted to kill herself, she said that there was nothing wrong with her life that she could not herself correct, and she would have nothing to do with being labeled a patient. She said that she had been forced into the hands of psychiatrists against her will and that she had not benefited from their ministrations, which latter opinion might seem to be evident in view of her present confinement. She wanted to see no therapist and correctly said that she had taken no part in selecting me as one. This was a poor way to begin, but no other was currently available. Though I was interested in this form of human dilemma I was not particularly attracted to Sarah, and at times felt like following her own suggestion, namely, leaving her alone and going elsewhere to find greater appreciation and use for whatever skills I had.

Sarah did not subscribe to the simplest rules related to our meeting. She refused to come to my office or to meet with me anywhere else; to do so might seem that she gave approval to the possibility of forming a relationship that was to her threatening, coercive, and humiliating. In retrospect, I think that I might have chosen another course, but what I did is of interest now.

I told Sarah that I wanted to meet with her daily even though we might both experience much discomfort in so doing. Many days I sat in a chair on the hospital ward without making any apparent impression on Sarah, who walked by me without looking at me or simply stayed out of my sight, leaving any area in which I was present. Eventually I insisted that she stay in her room with me, the door being locked if necessary. Because of her destructiveness the room was bare of furniture, and I often sat on the floor in a corner. On these occasions Sarah's fear was intense. She paced around the room, taking care not to come close to me; she hit the walls with her fists, shook the door, and frequently called out for help, saying that she was about to be murdered by me. At times she rushed at me in attack, and then ran away as if frightened; at other times she spit at me or suddenly came near to hit my arms held up in defense. I continued my visits, and there came long silences, the muteness extending over weeks, during which the young woman huddled in a corner or lay on a pallet with a blanket pulled over her head.

In this situation I did not feel comfortable or effective. In attempting to hold to my concept of the role of therapist I acted in a variety of ways, some of which are outlined in what follows:

1. I made an effort to listen and to make some sense of what was said. For the most part Sarah's comments were sparse and repetitive; the major theme being: "Let me alone. Let me out of here. I'm being killed. They are cruel to me. No one is any good." Some of her speech was fragmentary and so low in volume that I could hear little of what was said. I was unable to piece together from her remarks anything that gave me any detailed or precise picture of Sarah's life.

2. Attempts to engage Sarah in conversation failed. I talked to her, I read to her when she was silent, I suggested topics for discussion, and so on. But there was no true verbal interchange that could be continued.

3. I observed Sarah's behavior and commented on its possible significance. Such interpretations often were not based on sound data and were ignored or contemptuously rejected by the recipient. Thus I came to eschew their use.

4. For extended periods I sat for the most part in silence. Often my mind wandered, and I thought with relief of matters and people other than Sarah. Then I would feel guilty and attempt to pursue my therapeutic task, the result often being that I would say something that would appear as completely irrelevant to the current situation, if not simply banal or nonsensical. I did learn that my efforts to do something, to be therapeutic at any cost, reflected more my own discomfort and my training as a physician who is supposed to take action than the actual needs of the patient or the nature of our relationship.

5. Though it often seemed to me that I was inactive I discovered after some meetings that I had presented Sarah with a dozen or so notions of human growth and development and my ideas about their relevance to her own behavior. It occurred to me that my doing this might lead her to have doubts about my belief in my own theories and might well increase her evident confusion.

6. As the months passed by I experienced a variety of sentiments

among which were boredom, anger, discouragement, frustration, pity, and despair. As a psychiatrist and psychoanalyst I felt useless; the technical devices on which I relied to some extent were apparently of no great value in this situation. I thought of Fromm-Reichmann, Sullivan, and other teachers and colleagues known for their understanding and useful ways with disturbed people, but was unable to emulate what I thought they did, and could only admire, if not painfully envy, their accomplishments, which now seemed to be more magical than real.

The work in which I was engaged with Sarah did not fit into a clearcut, established frame of reference, and in a conventional sense I did not find myself to be acting as a physician, a psychiatrist, or a psychoanalyst. I should have felt more at ease had I been able to behave in accordance with one of these roles, but Sarah seemed to prevent this. I noted that we often seemed to be engaged in a struggle of identities; she fought against being a patient, and I wanted her to be one, not necessarily for her own advantage, but out of my need to be confirmed in a familiar professional position. As I thought myself unable to be of value professionally I hoped that I could rely on my worth as a human being, but even this was denied by Sarah. It was at this juncture that I experienced considerable anxiety, threatened by a loss of my professional and personal identities, and having to alter the concept of myself or face the frightening alternative of finding that there was no longer a dependable self. Thus, in a mild way, I may have experienced a reflection of Sarah's terror at the breaking apart of her previously poorly organized view of herself when confronted by certain interpersonal demands during her first college year.

7. There were other thoughts that preoccupied my attention as the apparently therapeutically unproductive time passed by. Perhaps, I thought, Sarah suffers from a strange organic defect of the central nervous system producing somehow an inability to enter into a meaningful human relationship. Though I knew better, I should have liked to have been able to subscribe to the view that such organicity would relieve me of all responsibility for relating to the patient; the trouble would be "in" her and would thus not be so distressingly interpersonal.

Often I resented spending time uselessly, and easily recalled other tasks that possibly would lead to more tangible results and be more clearly profitable. Day after day I went to visit someone (Sarah) who sought to escape from me, who denied my worth, and who told others that she did not recognize me even after many months. Then, thinking of all this, I would feel the fool and picture myself as publicly exposed to the ridicule of any observer. Spending so much time with a single person seemed improvident if not actually wicked. I was well aware of the conflicting views regarding the nature of schizophrenia and its treatment, and it would suddenly occur to me that I was at best a romantic dilettante or, much worse, someone driven on a course destructive to both the patient and himself in response to hidden, unanalyzed, and hurtful motivations.

8. With all the above, however, there was also pleasure in what I was doing. The silences no longer disturbed me, and were often a relief from the many noises of the world of sanity. Sarah grew quieter, and the door was no longer locked. We then went for walks (not exactly together, as she usually kept a few yards ahead of me), and though she seldom spoke she did not run away. Any attempt to question her, to seek information, to come too close, brought with it a recurrence of fear and its accompaniments of attack, flight, withdrawal, and perceptual disturbances, such as hallucinations. Slowly I came to be more content with my humble position, realizing that I need not be so preoccupied with doing something in the way I had conceived of my professional life and that being in itself was a kind of activity to which I had given small credit and about which I knew very little. The remainder of the work with Sarah is of no moment to us now.

Of particular interest to me was my growing attachment to Sarah despite her rejection and denunciation of me and the unpleasant personal experiences that I encountered with her. I discovered that I frequently thought of her when away from her and that my emotions regarding her were often intense, ranging from murderous rage to feelings of great tenderness. At times I felt as if she were a dependent child, and during some of the long silences in her room I felt strangely enough as if I myself were a child once more sitting peacefully at home in my mother's bedroom, comforted by her quiet manner, and protected by her from the world outside. I would speak of stopping the work with Sarah, and yet found that this would be easier said than done.

In my own analysis I sought for an understanding of my responses, and it was evident that my interest in such encounters did indeed reflect early life experiences with an interesting but difficult mother, as well as later contacts with able teachers and challenging clinical circumstances. All of what transpired, however, was not to be dismissed as character structure, countertransference, or professional concern.

There was no doubt that in this strange encounter Sarah and I had become attached to each other. If this tie was not simply a reflection of planned and skillful psychotherapy (and there was little evidence of that being the case) I might think that there was some essential ingredient of humanity in me that could in some subtle ways alter the schizophrenic state. I do not question the value of skillful rather than careless and inept therapy, or the need for kindliness, respect, and serious concern on the part of the therapist. Nonetheless, there did seem to be more to this matter than was made clear in my psychiatric studies, and I was not content to rely on some oversimplified humanistic explanation or semimystical interpretation. Furthermore, there was another factor in this situation well worth the observation. Sarah was also strongly attached to her mother and often tried to seek her out, despite saying that she hated mother and wanted to kill her, all in the face of her mother's now open dislike and fear of the daughter.

What was the nature of this attachment? Was Sarah bound to me (and I to her) because of my psychiatric approach, my good qualities and understanding, the time we spent together, or even as the result of our many rude and unkind exchanges? Was there an essential ingredient in our encounters that would help to clarify this issue?

Psychotherapy: A Basic Quality

It is of interest here to consider qualities that may be common in all definitions of the psychotherapeutic process. That is, what is it in this process that its practitioners consider to be fundamentally important? Only a few sources will be consulted, though a more complete review would be of interest. During 1960, Strupp (1960, pp. 288–289) summarized his survey of the subject as follows:

In more recent years, partly as the work of Sullivan, Horney, and other exponents of the "cultural" school, some of whose ideas were anticipated by Rank and Ferenczi, the totality of the therapist's personality and the reality aspects of the therapeutic situation have received increasing attention. In keeping with these newer formulations I shall elaborate on the notion that the therapist's personality, attitudes, and values are very much in the picture at all times, and that they color and influence the direction and quality of his therapeutic operations. . . . The therapist's contribution is both a *personal* and a *technical* one.

During 1964 he wrote (Strupp, Wallach, and Wogan, 1967) as follows:

The emergence of a large general "warmth" factor in all forms of psychotherapy deserves particular emphasis. A solid working relationship in which the participants develop a sense of mutual trust is unquestionably a *sine qua non* for all forms of psychotherapy. In its absence there can be no successful psychotherapy . . . overshadowing this attitudinal-emotional factor is the patient's conviction that he has the therapist's respect. This faith in the integrity of the therapist as a person may be called the capstone of a successful therapeutic relationship subsuming all other characteristics. . . . Technical skill on the part of the therapist may go a long way to capitalize on such a relationship, and the data do not specifically inform us how such a relationship comes into being, is deepened, or turned to maximum therapeutic advantage.

The following comment by Snyder (1961, p. 2) is also of interest:

We have become convinced that the persons who most need psychotherapy are those who are starved for affection; they have not developed satisfactory interpersonal relationships, largely because their learned interpersonal behavior prevents them from doing the appropriate things to cause other people to like them. . . . We have been impressed by how deeply and positively clients have felt toward their therapists, and how much the therapists have reciprocated these feelings. It is evident that therapy is often a major human experience, one of life's high spots, especially for the clients, but also many times for the therapists. . . . Only a person's mate, and often his children, hold positions involving a comparable amount of significance.

Another example of attempts to evaluate the therapeutic atmosphere is from the writing of Rogers (1967, p. 11):

Regardless of what method or technique the therapist uses, regardless of the theoretical orientation he might hold, it was hypothesized that effective therapy would take place if the therapist fulfilled the following three "conditions": a) The therapist responds as the real person he actually is in this relationship at this moment. He employs no artificial front and does not have to hide or fear his real reactions. This condition was termed "congruence" (congruence between the therapist's experiencing and his thoughts and behavior). b) The therapist senses and expresses the client's felt meaning, catching what the client communicates as it seems to the client. This condition was termed "empathy." c) The therapist experiences a warm and positive acceptance toward the client, a prizing of the client as a person whether the feelings and behavior he is now exhibiting are regarded as valuable or as deplorable. This condition was termed "unconditional positive regard."

An important trend in many current studies of the psychotherapeutic process is the moving away from a strict adherence to the classical medical model in which the disease is to be found within the patient and removed through the good offices of the physician, actually a caricature of more modern and sophisticated medical practice. Psychiatric disorder is seen to be multiply determined, reflecting vicissitudes of human inheritance, growth, and development, allied to econosociocultural conditions and intimately involved with the symbol-creating character of man.

What has all this to do with Sarah and her therapist? It is difficult for me to evaluate within myself what Strupp (Strupp et al., 1967) referred to as a "warmth factor." The facts are, if I recall them rightly, that the term "cold" has been applied to my performances at least as frequently as has the word "warm." Certainly with Sarah I was at times withdrawn, self-preoccupied, and anything but approachable. I was also on occasion (and I take no pride in this) downright unpleasant with her. "Integrity" is a term more difficult for me to evaluate. Sarah often questioned my integrity, and I think she was referring to her fear that I should prove to be devious, less than open, and perhaps dishonest. In time she came to see me as honest; but she had to work hard (as I did) to bring me to this state consistently in my dealings with her.

Snyder's (1961) comments are meaningful to me because the experience with Sarah was eventually one of closeness and constituted for both of us a "major human experience," as he phrased it. But why should this occur when it began so badly, progressed so slowly, and was one in which (as Sarah often said) I was a kind of hired hand or paid companion?

Roger's (1967) remarks are of particular interest to me; in general I agree with what he said but I have been unable to live up to such ideals as those he listed. I did try increasingly to attain what Rogers called congruence, seeking thereby to save Sarah from the confusion that can arise from attempting to organize and synthesize conflicting messages presented by a therapist, perhaps disconcertingly reminiscent of similar complex stimuli received on earlier occasions from a parent. Thus I might say something like: "Here I am today. I wear a different suit than I wore yesterday. I think I look rather down in the mouth, because I feel so. That's partly because of other events at the office that have nothing to do with you—and partly because I do get discouraged at times with your infernal obstinacy and your pushing me away." This is an attempt to decrease differences in my appearance, the tone of my voice, the content of my speech, and my emotional state—all in an effort to help the patient integrate into a single, recognizable, dependable concept the various and changing aspects of the object, in this instance the therapist. I often failed, however, to do this, did not recognize lack of congruence, and was frequently accused by Sarah of being inconstant, hypocritical, and devious. "You are so many things, so many people," she would say. "I can't make anything of you."

As for the empathy described by Rogers (1967), I did not possess it as it has seemed to me that others did; Fromm-Reichmann and Sullivan were particularly impressive to me in this regard, perhaps because I knew each of them as my therapist. As a substitute for some lack here I attempted to pay close attention to what went on, and patients often made valiant efforts to make things clear to me.

Lastly Rogers referred to a prizing of the patient as a person no matter what form his behavior might take, and the demonstration of warmth and acceptance. It is true that I came to prize Sarah, in the main to accept her and to feel warm toward her. (Incidentally, I wish we could get away—to some extent at least—from these thermal and linear descriptions of relationship, such as cold, warm, close, distant, and so on. On second thought, however, perhaps they are more objective than they may at first appear to be.) It should also be recorded that I thoroughly disliked certain of her behaviors, and I often did not attempt to distinguish between herself and what she did. Frequently I was angry and distant, and on some occasions she seemed less than human to me.

Perhaps the work would have gone better had my actions been closer to the standards I have been discussing. It may be worth noting that in the course of this intervention I learned from Sarah, and to some extent I grew with her. I taught her but she was also my teacher, and this reciprocal quality is, I think, an important aspect of the therapeutic relationship.

There was more to the tie, however, between Sarah and myself than has been accounted for here. With her the tie was a factor in leading to her improvement and greater freedom. In contrast ties can develop that lead to disaster; witness the invidious attachment that forms in the delusional involvement of a paranoid person with a therapist. We must, then, look further.

A Condensed Summary of the Work with Sarah

It is not possible to separate into meaningful segments the several years that I spent as the therapist of Sarah. Any attempt to do so is to some extent artificial; events overlap each other, experience exists on a continuum, and life is not lived in terms of segregated events. Nonetheless, an artificial separation can be made and there may be value in making the attempt. There follows a crude approximation of what occurred in our meetings.

1. Fear. This was a time of confrontation in which Sarah and I were forced—by her difficulties, by chance, and by my duties and interests—to be together. She attempted to run from me, to ignore me, and to destroy me, realistically through physical attack, or magically through word and gesture. Anything that I did or said was perceived as an affront or an attack; the tone of my voice was experienced as the cutting edge of a whip, no remark was innocuous or without covert and destructive significance, and each word and movement bore with it expectation of hurt and disaster. With some patients this period has lasted a matter of minutes, days, or weeks; for Sarah it endured for months; unnecessary contributions of mine to its continuance are important but not my concern at the moment.

2. Exploration. With the decline of anxiety and suspicion, through familiarity, the patient can begin an exploration of the object that has rudely, and seemingly thoughtlessly or destructively, intruded itself into a life already troubled beyond tolerance. There is now more direct looking at the therapist and a more open testing of his responses. Sarah would walk out of her room, ignore me on the ward, run ahead of me on walks, and speak of jumping out of the car when we drove together. Would I fail to notice her absence, would I pursue her, would I restrain her attempts to hurt herself—and indirectly me? She attacked me verbally and was keen in observing my being hurt, or

angry, or unmoved. If I curtailed her movements she complained of restriction, and if I let her go, of neglect. This was a time of approach and retreat, of promise and disappointment, of frustration and confirmation. Each advance seemed to be followed by relapse, and there was a testing of belief and hope and confidence.

3. Acceptance. The increased acceptance of the therapist—and by him of the patient—may for a time go unrecognized by each. The meetings go on, but so does the quarreling which, bit by bit, becomes less intense, more stereotyped, and more a form of the getting together. Sarah was scornful of much that I did, contemptuously referred to me as an interfering "shrink," and imperiously treated me as a possession that had no value when present and yet could not be permitted to be out of sight for long or in the hands of someone other than herself. She denied any value in our relationship, and I often agreed with her views; nevertheless, we rarely failed to seek each other out to express our discouragement and our distaste for each other. We claimed freedom and independence and acted out our dependency on the bond that had formed between us.

4. Attachment. In the earlier stages Sarah had attempted to escape from me, to drive me away, or to change me into something less threatening to her existence. To a somewhat lesser extent I had attempted to do the same with her. Later the attachment that had developed was recognized and accepted. Sarah was openly dependent on me, and for a time I enjoyed and to some extent was dependent on her dependency. But this form of relationship was not enough, and in our discussions of her historical past and her observable present we recognized more clearly the interdependency that contrasts with the feared dominance and crippling of unduly prolonged dependence, and with the isolation of an independence in which the need for others goes unrecognized. In this period object and self are identified and each learns to accept the deficiencies and virtues of the other as perceptual illusions are decreased.

5. Separation. In some form or another separation will occur, even though this may mean no more than a change in the nature of the relationship. Sarah was invited to dare, to put her trust in someone and to love. At first she wanted no part of such adventuring and later said that she would extend her confidence only if the permanence of the attachment was guaranteed. Long past she had learned that human relatedness is a necessity of life, but that it was too expensive and

painful for her unless distorted by a variety of behavioral performances eventually labeled as psychotic. Now she learned that the only guarantee of a relationship is its impermanence, and that love includes the loss of the object loved. With this lesson learned Sarah was free to go, not with happiness or sorrow but with an increase of wisdom.

The Basic and Essential Task

As I review the work with Sarah it seems to me that the essential and basic task was the development of a social bond, a tie, an attachment on which the therapeutic relationship itself could be elaborated.

It is noteworthy that the tie between Sarah and myself was formed before its existence was recognized by either of us and before there was any feeling of comfort to be gained from it. Such an unrecognized and apparently unrewarding bond is not in itself necessarily beneficial and must acquire additional elements for its structure. Among these elements are the following:

1. The relationship must be marked increasingly by a quality of security, which will exist before the relationship itself is accepted.

2. In time the attachment will be admitted as viable, and eventually as a personal as well as a more general human need. That is, the need for relatedness is accepted, its formation with the therapist is observed, and ways are found to generalize the need so that fulfillment of it can be experienced with others.

3. An aspect of the improving relationship is the accompanying facilitation of communication, both verbal and nonverbal exchanges being recognized and harmful misperceptions corrected through consensual validation.

4. On the basis of the above is constructed the formal aspect of psychotherapy. The following comments by Sullivan (1962e, p. 268) are of interest at this juncture:

Personality reorganization . . . is a psychobiological procedure more in keeping with the behavior of a husbandman who removes from the organization of a growing plant, mechanical, physico-chemical, and biological obstacles, and by providing optimum circumstances, encourages a superior growth and fruition. In our sense, the superior growth and fruition of this plant is the analogue of personality reorganization. It is *not* pampering and petting into living—this does not produce good results with plants or animals. . . . Useful personality reorganization is manifested as a broadening, a deepening, or both, of interest in interpersonal relations—not by dependence on a "strong" personality, the adoption of fantastic rituals, or the development of paranoid situations.

The Interpersonal Bond

Of particular interest in any study of the formation of a therapeutic relationship are the following questions: (1) Why is there a need for the seeking of such a relationship, which in a number of ways is artificial and contrived? (2) Once sought (by the patient himself or others acting for him) why is it then feared as well as desired, held suspect, dealt with in complicated and indirect ways, and repeatedly rejected?

We have looked for the answers to such questions in the experiences of infancy and early childhood, both by inference from the contacts in the treatment itself and more recently through the direct observation of youthful development. Emphasis has been placed on the existence of social bonds first formed between infant and mother on the basis of tension reduction in nursing, through the physical contact in handling, and through the object-seeking tendency of the infant. The interpersonal aspect of this early bond was described by Sullivan (1953, p. 40) as follows: "The tension called out in the mothering one by the manifest needs of the infant we call *tenderness,* and a generic group of tensions in the infant, the relief of which requires cooperation by the person who acts in the mothering role, can be called *need for tenderness.*"

I have assumed that schizophrenic behavior has its social origins in infancy, prior to the development of dependable object identities and the acquisition of verbal skills. Experience at that time (and this statement is based largely on inference from work with adolescent and older people) may have been so marked by anxiety and motivational obscurities that the maintenance of the degree of security required for survival could be provided only through perceptual distortions and the dissociation of systems of sentiments vital to satisfactory later development. It is my impression that many such unfortunate beginnings are, at least in part, corrected by later experience with parents, siblings, friends, and other associates in intimacy. When

251

there is a gross failure in the appropriate matching of unfolding individual potential with sociocultural interpersonal experience, and there is an accompanying dissociation of major motivational systems, the chances for success in meeting the demands of adolescent and early adult living are diminished and schizophrenic behavior may be evidenced.

The grossly oversimplified replies (not necessarily answers) to the questions asked above are as follows:

1. The need [1] for human relatedness is a fundamental aspect of our lives, and were it not developed to some extent through maternal responsiveness the infant would not have survived. Autistic children and those labeled childhood schizophrenic seem to have formed an attachment to living that is maintained only by the greatest of personal and developmental sacrifices. Someone like Sarah has a stronger tie to her fellows, its defects being clearly revealed in the stresses of adolescence.

2. The attachment that is developed has been accompanied by insecurity and pain and has been somewhat covertly maintained by subterfuge and the elaborate patterns of behavior called "symptoms." The reconstitution of a bond that is both needed and threatening involves the experiencing of anxiety and uncertainty; hence the complications of the process.

The Process of Primary Socialization

Though there are risks in any attempt to relate human behavior to that of other animals, it is useful to remember that man is himself an animal and his actions very probably can be illuminated through the study of other forms of life.

Scott studied the process of early socialization in various animals, primarily man and dog, and what he reports is of interest in our efforts to comprehend the tie that develops in the psychotherapeutic encounter.

[T]he general phenomenon which we are describing is the way in which the young animal of any species becomes attached to other members of the same species. . . . A [social] relationship could theoretically be established entirely on the basis of the hereditary nature of the two animals, but all evidence indicates that more is involved, that such relationships are set up by mutual adaptation and adjustment. . . . [Socialization] is a mutual process affecting both adults and young. . . . The basic process involved is not a behavioral one but some sort of internal reaction which consists of forming an attachment for another individual. [Scott, 1963, pp. 2, 4].

[I]n attempting to analyze the development of affection and social words objectively, scientists have often tried to simplify the problem by postulating various unitary, unromantic, and sometimes unesthetic explanations. . . . [E]vidence is accumulating that there is a . . . general mechanism involved—that given any kind of emotional arousal a young animal will become attached to any individual or object with which it is in contact for a sufficiently long time. . . .

It should not be surprising that many kinds of emotional reactions contribute to a social relationship. The surprising thing is that emotions which we normally consider aversive should produce the same effect as those which appear to be rewarding. This apparent paradox is partially resolved by evidence that the positive effect of unpleasant emotions is normally limited to early infancy by the development of escape reactions.

Nevertheless, the concept leads to the somewhat alarming conclusion that an animal (and perhaps a person) of any age, exposed to certain individual or physical surroundings for any length of time, will inevitably become attached to them, the rapidity of the process being governed by the degree of emotional arousal associated with them. . . . [I]f this conclusion should apply to our species as well as to other animals . . . it provides an explanation of certain well-known clinical observations such as the development by neglected children of strong affection for cruel and abusive parents, and the various peculiar affectional relationships that develop between prisoners and jailors, slaves and masters, and so on. Perhaps the general adaptive nature of this mechanism is that since the survival of any member of a highly social species depends upon the rapid development of social relationships, a mechanism has evolved which makes it almost impossible to inhibit the formation of social bonds [Scott, 1962].

The development of social bonds is facilitated by experience that occurs during a critical period of the individual's life. Scott and Fuller defined (1965, pp. 117, 147) this term as follows:

By a critical period, we mean a special time in life when a small amount of experience will produce a great effect on later behavior. . . . The period of primary socialization in human infants extends from approximately six weeks to six months. . . . This means that the baby can form its primary relationships only with those persons who take care of it, as it is unable to make contacts of its own; and it also means that the first and probably the deepest relationship will be formed with the mother rather than with the father or siblings.

The implications of the above in terms of our psychiatric interests include the following:

1. In man critical periods are not so clearly delimited as in other animals, such as the dog, and in the imprinting processes of birds. We have assumed that infancy resembles a critical period in human development, and that events of that era have far-reaching consequences in terms of personality structure. Each era—childhood, juvenile, preadolescence, and so on—is critical in the sense that skills appropriate to that stage of development are learned best at that time and are developed incompletely or in a distorted fashion if learning is put off to another period. Sullivan emphasized the importance of pre- and early adolescence as a time in which earlier misadventures in the acquiring of social interpersonal skills might be corrected. So far we know little of learning in the prenatal period.

2. The capacity to form meaningful attachments is not limited in the human being to particular eras, though the nature of the bond developed in one era will differ from that formed in another. I am of the opinion that the failure to develop in infancy some semblance of what Erikson calls "basic trust" leads to such defects that their correction in later life is, for all practical purposes, unlikely. In the main, however, social bonds can be developed at any period of human life, though the process may be slow and difficult during later years as the result of earlier experiences that color the necessary learning activities with anxiety and fear.

3. Social bonds will be formed between two people, such as therapist and patient, if the following requirements are met: (a) recurrent meetings occur; (b) the meetings are accompanied by emotional arousal; [2] (c) there exists a factor of the unpleasant which may serve to intensify the tie.

Review of the Elements of the Work with Sarah

In brief summary the work with Sarah was characterized by the following:

1. Sarah had developed interpersonal ties in early life that enabled her to make a superficially adequate adjustment to the demands (sociocultural) through chronological adolescence.

2. The demands for intimacy and the clarification of personal identity in adolescence required the activation of hitherto dissociated motivational systems, leading to the experience of intense anxiety and psychotic behavior as previously reliable patterns of action failed.

3. Sarah expected little but anxiety and disaster in human contacts and withdrew from them or distorted their perception through the behavior that came to be labeled "symptoms."

4. The meetings with the therapist were required, limits were set to seriously destructive behavior, there was an intense display of feeling, and, despite discouragement and protests, the contacts were continued.

5. With this procedure a strong, lasting, and eventually understandable relationship was formed.

6. The development of such a bond or tie is the beginning. The course of its development involves much of what we know as psychotherapy.

7. Of importance, but not to be considered here are such matters as (a) the how of the meetings, namely how they are to be accomplished in the face of objections and resistance; (b) the when, namely, matters of frequency, duration, time of day, and so on; (c) the where, that is, the places in which meetings are held; (d) the form of contact in terms of sight, smell, touch, sound, space, and the overall influence of time; (e) the technique of listening, responding, and so on.

8. The tie itself, though vital, may be destructive as well as profitable. How it is developed will depend not only on the patient but on such matters as the therapist's skill and what was earlier referred to as warmth, respect, and regard for his associate in the enterprise.

9. The formation of the social bond as briefly described here may be looked on as a biological component of the psychotherapeutic process. Basic to psychotherapy are the following human characteristics: (a) a need for relatedness; (b) development through the sequential matching of potential with appropriate experience; (c) the flexibility of so-called critical periods in growth; (d) the ability to form relational bonds; and (e) the creation and use of symbols.

10. The two other major components of the psychotherapeutic procedure are (a) the sociocultural creations of man and his ability to deal with these in a historical perspective and (b) the symbolic universe that man creates and that has no existence outside of himself.

Conclusion

I shall conclude with remarks made by Sullivan (1962c, pp. 201–202) forty years ago but still relevant to our concerns today.

It must suffice that I add a statement pleading the urgent necessity for much broader investigation as to adolescence and as to schizophrenia than has been anywhere so far recorded. Our perspectives must include far-reaching and intensive study of the whole subject of interpersonal relations. . . . What we will come upon in such a really scientific attack upon this major mental disorder will in all likelihood exceed any returns that we can obtain from any other field of study. I say this because I am convinced that in the schizophrenic processes and in the preliminaries of schizophrenic illness—so common among adolescents who are having trouble in their social adjustments—can be seen, in almost laboratory simplicity, glimpses which will combine as a mosaic that explains many more than half of the personalities that one encounters.

NOTES

1. The word "need" is not used to suggest the operation of an instinct but to refer to forms of behavior arising from states of tension and developing through interpersonal experience.

2. For another study of relational bonds in animals other than human see Woolpy (1968) and Cairns (1966).

REFERENCES

Cairns, R. B. "Attachment Behavior of Mammals." *Psychological Review* 73, no.5(1966):409–426.

Rogers, Carl, ed. *The Therapeutic Relationship and Its Impact: A Study of Psychotherapy with Schizophrenics.* Madison: University of Wisconsin Press, 1967.

Scott, J. P. "Critical Periods in Behavioral Development." *Science* 138, no. 3544(1962):949–958.

———. "The Process of Primary Socialization in Canine and Human Infants." *Monographs of the Society for Research in Child Development* 28, serial no. 85, no. 1(1963).

———; and Fuller, J. L. *Genetics and the Social Behavior of the Dog.* Chicago: University of Chicago Press, 1965.

Snyder, William. *The Psychotherapy Relationship.* New York: Macmillan, 1961.

Strupp, Hans. *Psychotherapists in Action.* New York: Grune & Stratton, 1960.

———; Wallach, M. S.; and Wogan, M. "The Psychotherapy Experience in Retrospect: A Questionnaire Survey of Former Patients and Their Therapists." (1964). *Psychological Monographs* (1967).

Sullivan, Harry Stack. *The Interpersonal Theory of Psychiatry.* Helen Swick Perry and Mary Lade Garvel, eds. New York: Norton, 1953.

———. "The Common Field of Research and Clinical Psychiatry" (1927). In H. S. Perry, ed., *Schizophrenia as a Human Process.* New York: Norton, 1962. (a)

———. "Peculiarity of Thought in Schizophrenia" (1925–1926). In H. S. Perry, ed., *Schizophrenia as a Human Process.* New York: Norton, 1962. (b)

——. "Research in Schizophrenia" (1929–1930). In H. S. Perry, ed., *Schizophrenia as a Human Process*. New York: Norton, 1962. (c)

——. "Schizophrenia: Its Conservative and Malignant Features: A Preliminary Communication" (1924–1925). In H. S. Perry, ed., *Schizophrenia as a Human Process*. New York: Norton, 1962. (d)

——. "Socio-Psychiatric Research: Its Implications for the Schizophrenia Problem and for Mental Hygiene" (1930–1931). In H. S. Perry, ed., *Schizophrenia as a Human Process*. New York: Norton, 1962. (e)

Woolpy, Jerome H. "Socialization of Wolves." In Jules H. Masserman, ed., *Science and Psychoanalysis*. Vol. 12. New York: Grune & Stratton, 1968. Pp. 82–94.

PART FOUR

Research
on Psychoanalytic
Hypotheses

T
HE FOLLOWING THREE CHAPTERS illustrate the application of methods from other fields to test some psychoanalytic hypotheses.

Erwin Singer has tested the hypothesis that hysterical symptoms develop in an atmosphere of hypocritical and special concern. Reading disability is used as an example of an hysterical symptom. People with reading disabilities were able to identify absurdities to a greater extent than were those in the control group. The latter performed better with proverbs. Black nonreaders had a higher sense of the absurd than white nonreaders, whose reading disability was less.

Raymond Sobel has tested the influence of highly traumatic childhood on adult performance. In the course of a three-generational study of high-risk behavior in children in a rural population of 91,000, Sobel identified a group of women whose early lives are indistinguishable from those who later on developed severe psychoses or neuroses. Evaluated by various mental health scales and by psychiatric interviews, these women showed fewer psychosomatic difficulties, sexual and social problems. The reasons that these women were able to overcome the traumata of childhood are unknown.

In Chapter 16, Charles Clay Dahlberg, Stanley Feldstein, and Ruth Mechaneck test the hypothesis that experimental procedures may be carried out without invalidating the therapeutic process. It is one of a series demonstrating relationships among administration of LSD, language patterns, and therapeutic procedures. There is a rigorous demonstration of language style varying with different states of personality integration. It is suggested that analysts may be able to use language style to tell in what stage treatment is.

Hypocrisy and Learning Disability

One of the most persistent themes throughout the history of psychoanalytic theory development is its effort to construct a genetic-dy-
namic model of human behavior. It was an expression of Freud's genius that he succeeded in evolving a subtle and unified system
defining the mainsprings and the psychogenetic progression of behavior, irrespective of disagreements voiced by some about certain of his
conclusions. And probably one of the more important reasons for
Freud's enjoying greater acceptance than other psychological system
builders has been the latters' failure to propose a comparably unified
and universal theory of behavior origins (see, for instance, Munroe,
1955). Among later analytic theorists Sullivan (1947) alone advanced
a developmental model comparable to Freud's in its detailed exposi-
tion of constructs and propositions leading to viable formulations
about human interaction.

Aside from its importance as a contribution to man's knowledge,
the main value of a developmental paradigm is its pertinence for a
theory of psychopathology. Using the roots of motivation advanced
by him as his point of departure, Freud (1953b) suggested that the
social and cultural forces and conventions of his time were inappropriate reactions to biological and instinctual drives thereby adversely
molding the then prevailing educative approach to the child. Stated
simply, Freud observed that hypocritical disregard of elementary biological truths led to pathological developments. In this insistence that
hypocrisy was a significant precursor of neurotic phenomena, we find
an important bridge to the ideas advanced by Sullivan. For Sullivan
(1947), too, believed that certain forms and expressions of hypocrisy
encountered by the child during formative periods were fundamental
to the development of selective inattention, thereby cancelling the
maturation of perceptual-cognitive processes; unless resolved, he
thought, this self-restricting development could eventuate in ominous
dissociative security operations. Thus Freud and Sullivan agreed on
the disabling effects of hypocrisy though they were worlds apart in

delineating their respective metapsychologies (despite Sullivan's disclaiming any intention of writing a theory of ultimate motivational causation, there is an implicit Sullivanian metapsychological system), and they were worlds apart in defining the nature of the pathogenic structure of the child's environment.

This twin emphasis on the evolution of the child's personality and on cultural forces facilitating and/or interfering with the fulfillment of man's potentialities made it inevitable that psychoanalytic theorists and practitioners would become concerned with formal educational problems. Indeed, throughout the history of psychoanalytic theory we encounter a significant body of literature addressing itself to issues related to educational development and progress. Adler, Redl, Aichhorn, Zulliger, Anna Freud, Pearson, Blanchard, and more recently Levenson and his associates are but a few of the names that come immediately to mind. Their thoughtful contributions established several often contradictory and yet at times interlocking frames of reference for the understanding of a glaring developmental failure, the inability of youngsters to fulfill the basic task of certain developmental stages, their baffling failure to acquire fundamental skills and to absorb in meaningful fashion subject matter presented to them in formal schooling. Yet more or less hard-nosed research findings in this area have been meager. This is not too surprising if one keeps in mind the history of scientific progress, that is, the sequence in the interplay and cross-fertilization of a priori and a posteriori thinking. Naturalistic observation leading to tentative theory construction must precede the design of studies that will serve to appraise the substantiveness of extant hypotheses.

The data I am about to present were collected and interpreted in the hope of contributing to the investigation of the proposition that the climate of hypocrisy and an at least erstwhile awareness thereof are significantly associated with important developmental failures. But since this issue is too broad to lend itself to the collection of readily quantifiable data, my focus is on a particular psychological developmental failure more amenable to quantification and rigorous investigation: the failure of children to acquire the essential and fundamental communicative skill of reading, despite exposure to opportunities to acquire this basic tool for contemporary living.

A few years ago one of my students and I (Singer and Pittman, 1968) published a study using one of Sullivan's observations as our point of departure in examining the problem of reading disability. We suggested that the inability or the apparent reluctance of youngsters to learn a basic skill such as reading, barring organic malfunction, could be understood as being comparable to hysterical phenomena, and we found certain comments by Sullivan concerning some psychogenetic aspects of hysteria highly provocative and germane to our concerns. Specifically, Sullivan (1956, p. 211) remarked:

In the case of the hysteric, one usually finds . . . a self-absorbed parent or some other highly significant figure who regards the child as something of a plaything—a decoration of the parent's personality—rather than a growing personality. The parent with this lack of respect and appreciation for the child is . . . an instance of the relatively self-centered personality. . . .

Implicit in this comment and similar remarks made by Sullivan is the suggestion that the hysteric is a person who developed with the growing conviction that insincerity accompanied by specious concern constituted the attitude of significant figures in his environment.

If this inability to learn how to read in fact represented a hysteric-like phenomenon and if Sullivan's notions concerning the psychogenesis of hysteria had validity, we reasoned, then the outlook and the orientation of youngsters who did not learn this skill should be dominated by a pervasive sense that their surroundings were characterized by insincerity, phony interest, and feigned concern. In addition, it occurred to us that Sullivan's focus on the parent as the source of this insincerity, though well taken, represented a theoretically unnecessary restriction because such powerful forces as broad cultural attitudes and such institutions as the educational complex, in loco parentis, may equally well serve as an impetus for the development of a sense that insincerity is rampant all around.

We thought that this conviction concerning the insincerity surrounding them might well reflect itself in the youngsters' heightened, though not necessarily conscious, sensitivity to what is unreal, to what is unauthentic, to what is pretended, and to what is feigned around them. With this idea in mind we set out to design an instrument to measure the degree to which an individual is capable of noticing what is hypocritical around him and to what extent this ability to sense what is unauthentic differs from his capacity to perceive that which happens to be genuine, authentic, and meaningful. If Sullivan's suggestions about hysterical psychogenetic factors and our thought that reading disability was hysterical in nature had validity, then youngsters displaying inability to learn how to read should selectively do quite well in fathoming the hypocritical and conversely do selectively relatively poorly in grasping that which is genuine or at least not hypocritical.

The method of assessment we developed was relatively simple. From available tests we culled items designed to measure a person's ability to detect absurd incongruities. In such items some silly, feigned, hypocritical statement or a situation in which a person behaves in a hypocritical manner is presented and the individual is asked to explain what is silly about the statement or the situation. To illustrate, one of the items coming from the well-known Stanford-Binet test ran somewhat like this: "The judge said to the prisoner: 'You will be hanged tomorrow and let it be a lesson to you never to do it again.'" As stated, some of the items were borrowed from existing tests, though the language was occasionally modified, and we constructed others until we had a total of ten. In addition we selected from the available test literature (once again occasionally modifying the language employed) ten proverbs such as "One swallow does not make a summer," and individuals examined were asked what the broader meaning of the statement embodied in the proverb might be. Finally, we made up some ten simple statements describing a situation neither hypocritical in content nor amenable to broader interpretation, and here the child was asked to comment on what he had heard. These items were developed and incorporated into our test to mask the intent and objectives of our inquiry. This total of thirty test questions was then presented in random order and became a scale designed to measure an individual's sensitivity to hypocrisy, for each person examined on this scale achieves a score reflecting his adequacy in perceiving hypocritical statements or situations and another score describing his ability to understand certain precepts of his culture as reflected in his adequacy in understanding the broader meaning of proverbs. Employing the usual procedures for assessment of reliability, it may be stated that our test was found highly adequate in terms of generally accepted statistical criteria.[1]

To repeat the hypothesis advanced earlier, we thought Sullivan's conceptions concerning the psychogenesis of hysteria and our inference that reading disability represents a hysteric-like phenomenon would be supported (1) if youngsters displaying learning difficulties were to show on our scale a relatively higher adequacy in solving items describing hypocrisy than in their understanding of the meaning of proverbs and (2) if control subjects, that is, youngsters comparable on all other relevant variables but making adequate progress were to do better in their understanding of the meaning of proverbs than in their grasp of the silly, hypocritical, and unauthentic. Under such circumstances, we reasoned, selective attentiveness and attunedness to hypocrisy in our reading-disability subjects would be demonstrated. Our findings supported our reasoning and hypotheses well beyond chance expectancy. They are summarized in Figure 14–1.

Though these findings were highly significant and gratifying,[2] they also raised important questions. First, the data were obtained from Negro children. It could be said that such findings supported by repeat investigations were to be expected when Negro children were examined because the black child raised in a ghetto atmosphere was likely to be more sensitive to the dishonesty, being exposed to its poi-

FIGURE 14–1

Comparison between Disability Group and Control Group (Negro)

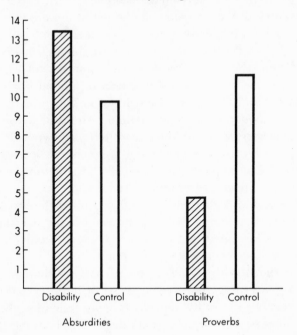

sonous manifestations and effects constantly. Furthermore, it could be argued that those Negro children who tried to make the best of a bad bargain and tried to survive and perhaps even thrive to some extent, despite being surrounded and dominated by a piously hypocritical culture, would have to shut their eyes selectively, would have to keep out of awareness that which is unreal, unauthentic, and hypocritical around them. Consequently, one of my students set out to study comparable white populations, groups of white youngsters who did not learn how to read, and their peers who did progress satisfactorily.[3]

Immediate and to be expected difficulties were encountered in locating a comparable white nonreading group of children. The criterion for reading retardation had been a functioning of at least two years below age expectancy. Though such retardation is not uncommon in ghetto schools, predominantly white school systems simply do not allow the development of gross malfunction. Children exhibiting pronounced retardation are either not promoted or are exposed quickly to tutorial help making for a relative dearth of comparably severe educational failures. Consequently, we were unable to secure a group of equal debility. Therefore, one had to predict that the findings obtained in examining the original populations—reading-disability versus control group—would not be duplicated. All one could anticipate was an approximation of previously obtained results, that is, findings similar in trend but lacking the magnitude of differences observed earlier, for after all the relatively slight retardation can be thought of as comparatively mild hysteria associated with comparably mild selective attention to the absurd. By and large the data obtained bore out these predictions, and they are summarized in Figure 14–2.

The selective attentiveness and sensitivity to the absurd and hypocritical items found among Negro nonreaders were evidently also present among white nonreaders, albeit in less dramatic form, paralleling the less dramatic retardation among the whites. And since the disability was relatively small, it is not surprising to find the pattern in the control group similar to, though less accentuated than, that noted in the disability grouping. What is dramatic and striking is the difference in response pattern between the Negro control group and the white control group. It will be recalled that the ghetto youngsters who progressed satisfactorily exhibited a selective adequacy in under-

FIGURE 14–2

Comparison between Disability Group and Control Group (White)

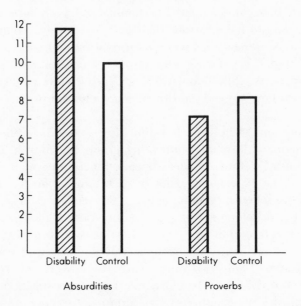

standing proverbs and a relative inadequacy in perceiving the absurd and dishonest; a comparable white group reveals about equal ability on both types of tasks. In Figure 14–3 the differences between the two control groups are depicted.

Once again these differences are readily explainable: White children eager to progress in their world need not shut out hypocrisy selectively as they encounter it for its extent is not so oppressively overwhelming as it is in the black child's world, forcing those among the latter who want to adjust to their setting to studiously avoid its existence. Certainly I do not want to imply that the social realities of the white child are devoid of hypocrisy and dishonesty. I am merely suggesting that, by and large, these destructive social phenomena are prominently associated for the black child with the process of elementary education. Though the data do not and cannot suggest explanations for this heightened sense of the absurd in the black child, a speculative rationale may be advanced: The whites' pious protestations to the contrary notwithstanding, the sad truth is that the education of the black child has been badly neglected and that this neglect

Hypocrisy and Learning Disability

may be deliberate rather than accidental because the perpetuation of the social and economic order demands a reservoir of readily exploitable and socially inferior citizens. This consequently insincere and pretended interest in the early educational progress of the Negro child, our findings suggest, may well be associated with the disproportionate amount of failures noticeable in the elementary educational development of black children.

In addition to the racial issue raised by our original study, another important theoretical question suggested itself. Sullivan (1956) maintained that the old saw concerning the apple not falling far from the tree was more applicable to hysteria than to any other psychiatric entity. He insisted that the hysteric, who, he maintained, was essentially a self-absorbed character, was the progeny of equally self-absorbed hysterical characters. His focus on and interest in the unreal, Sullivan wrote, paralleled his background's focus on the unreal, leading the parent to treat the child with feigned and pretended rather than with genuine interest. If this is true, then by extension it would be reasonable to expect that the parents of children manifesting hysteric-like

FIGURE 14–3

Comparison between the Two Control Groups
(White and Negro)

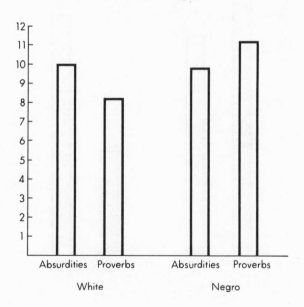

reading disabilities should reveal a test pattern similar to that of their offspring; furthermore, their pattern of performance should in instances of severe reading retardation differ markedly from that achieved by a control group of parents, that is, parents whose offspring progressed satisfactorily in their ability to acquire this fundamental reading skill. One of my students spent considerable time and effort in securing the cooperation of two parent groups comparable in all the relevant aspects except the circumstance that the children of one parent group were rather severe reading retardates whereas the offspring of the other group progressed at least adequately. In Figure 14–4 his findings are presented.

The evidence is rather conclusive. The patterns observed and the relationships depicted are strikingly similar to those found among children with severe reading retardation and comparisons with con-

FIGURE 14–4

Comparison between Parents of Disability Group
and Parents of Control Group (Negro and White)

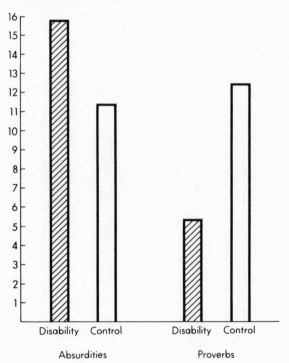

FIGURE 14–5

Comparison between Disability Group and Parents of Disability Group (Negro and White)

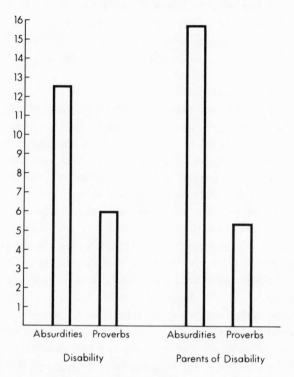

trol groups reveal the anticipated results. In Figure 14–5 these comparisons are depicted.

Thus the data speak for themselves: youngsters who exhibit marked decrements in their ability to absorb formal instruction in this basic tool for living show a remarkable sensitivity and selective attunedness to what is feigned rather than genuine, to what is pretended rather than authentic, and to that which is hypocritical rather than sincere. Though these findings hold true for all groups studied, they are more marked for Negro youngsters than for their white peers. In this, their reactive pattern, our subjects revealed features in striking harmony with what one might expect on the basis of Sullivan's (1956) theories concerning hysteria. It is as though the troubled students and their parents were selectively absorbed in catching the unreal components of the world around them. In the black community this is not too surprising; it might well be expected and to some extent it might be deemed realistically adaptive even though tendencies are ultimately self-defeating to the person in whom they operate. In the white group the same trend was observed and seems to represent the heightened sensitivity of some youngsters to hypocritical forces around them, though these forces express themselves in the white world in different ways and with less direct and with less immediate impact than in the ghetto.

In their general trend these data, however, not only support Sullivan's line of thought but also dovetail with some observations reported by Freud (1953a), though not with the specifics of his conclusions. The most famous of all hysterics discussed in the psychoanalytic literature, his case of Dora, was clearly a young woman enormously concerned with and sensitive to the hypocrisy all around her. The very basis of her father's referring her to Freud was a pretense of concern for her physical welfare when all he really wanted was to have the doctor dissuade her from what she sensed was true. There was the pretense of intact family life while Dora, as can be seen most strikingly from her first dream, knew all too well that dissatisfaction permeated the home. And in her second dream her realization of deadly hypocrisy is all too apparent. Of course Freud saw the dishonest pretending in Dora's surroundings, but his particular bent for a reductionist libidinal theory made him focus on the sexual arena in which the hypocrisy of Dora's family revealed itself most strikingly rather than on the broader issue of the dishonesty itself. Obviously dishonesty can express itself in areas other than sexual matters, but its effects on those surrounded by it are debilitating and conducive to preoccupation with the dangers of deceit all around.

One final comment may be in order. Our data are also in harmony with the clinical material reported and interpreted by Levenson and his associates (Levenson, 1965, 1966; Levenson and Kohn, 1964, 1965; Akeret and Stockhamer, 1965). These investigators have shown skillfully and cogently how the college dropouts with whom they worked (a type of learning disability of later years) are frequently young people remarkably attuned to certain truths around them despite efforts on the part of authorities, be they parents or school officials, to dissemble the nature of reality. Their findings have pointed out how frequently parental efforts to help the youngster grow personally and academically are insincere and actually represent attempts to sabotage the growth of independence. Similarly, the general unrest on the campuses from Berkeley to Morningside Heights is only all too clearly a response to a dishonest, hypocritical, and unauthentic setting pretending to be a community of scholars when it is more often than not simply a diploma mill, even though some individuals will of course join the demonstrating students for less mature reasons. Significantly, Kohn and Levenson (1966) in their work and Bay (1967) in his provocative report on the campus activists have shown that their subjects come from among the most perceptive and sensitive of college students. Furthermore, Levenson, Stockhamer, and Feiner (1967) have discussed a frequently observed but rarely mentioned phenomenon: how often the dropout who simply cannot study comes from a liberal family in which at least one member had harbored at one time ambitions of defying existing orders and of becoming a social reformer, ambitions abandoned with sadness somewhere along the road by the parent for a variety of reasons. Many of his young patients were remarkably attuned to what the real attitudes of people important to them were (Bay [1967] incidentally reports similar findings in examining campus activists) and apparently acted in response to these attitudes rather than in accordance with their parents' pretenses. Data collected by me in studying the sensory acuity of one of Levenson's groups, data that I am not yet prepared to discuss in detail, lead me to a related observation: We have noticed their remarkable sensitivity to nuances in external stimuli but simultaneously we observed their much less successful efforts to grasp the nature of their own inner cues, sensations, and reactions.

In summary, I am suggesting that learning difficulties in the absence of organic causes or gross psychological pathology occur with striking frequency in young people keenly sensitive to hypocrisy around them, youngsters who also seem for whatever reason incapable of dealing with the assault of deceit in any other but self-restricting and ultimately self-defeating ways.

NOTES

1. Detailed information specifying the items incorporated in the scale, scoring criteria, reliability coefficients, and so on can be found in the contributions of Singer and Pittman (1968) and Tuschman (1968).

2. A study employing an essentially similar design and rendering comparable results is Banks (1964).

3. See Kramer (1965). For a related study by the same author see Kramer (1966).

REFERENCES

Akeret, Robert U.; and Stockhamer, Nathan. "Contertransference Reactions to College Drop-Outs." *American Journal of Psychotherapy* 19(1965):622–632.

Banks, R. Sensitivity to Hypocrisy and Its Relationship to Openmindedness. Unpublished research paper, The City College of the City University of New York, School of Education, 1964.

Bay, Christian. "Political and Apolitical Students: Facts in Search of a Theory." *Journal of Social Issues* 23(1967):76–91.

Freud, Sigmund. "Fragments of an Analysis of a Case of Hysteria." *Standard Edition*. Vol. 7. London: Hogarth, 1953. Pp. 3–122. (a)

———. "Three Essays on the Theory of Sexuality." *Standard Edition*. Vol. 7. London: Hogarth, 1953. Pp. 125–245. (b)

Kohn, Martin; and Levenson, Edgar A. "Differences Between Accepted and Rejected Patients in a Treatment Project of College Dropouts." *Journal of Psychology* 63(1966):144–156.

Kramer, Lore S. Sensitivity to Hypocrisy and Its Relation to Reading Disability. Unpublished research paper, The City College of the City University of New York, School of Education, 1965.

———. Persuasibility and Its Relation to Reading Disability. Unpublished Master's thesis, The City College of the City University of New York, School of Education, 1966.

Levenson, Edgar A. "Why Do They Drop Out?" *Teaching and Learning* (1965):1–8.

———. "Some Socio-Cultural Issues in the Etiology and Treatment of College Dropouts." In Lawrence A. Pervin, Louis E. Reik, and Willard Dalrymple, eds., *The College Dropout and the Utilization of Talent*. Princeton: Princeton University Press, 1966. Pp. 189–206.

———; and Kohn, Martin. "A Demonstration Clinic for College Dropouts." *College Health* 12(1964):382–391.

———; and Kohn, Martin. "A Treatment Facility for College Dropouts." *Mental Hygiene* 49(1965):413–424.

———; Stockhamer, Nathan; and Feiner, Arthur H. "Family Transaction in the Etiology of Dropping Out of College." *Contemporary Psychoanalysis* 3(1967):134–157.

Munroe, Ruth L. *Schools of Psychoanalytic Thought*. New York: Dryden Press, 1955.

Singer, Erwin; and Pittman, Marion E. "A Sullivanian Approach to the Problem of Reading Disability: Theoretical Considerations and Empirical Data" (1965). In Gladys Natchez, ed., *Children with Reading Problems*. New York: Basic Books, 1968. Pp. 55–65.

Sullivan, Harry Stack. *Conceptions of Modern Psychiatry*. Washington, D.C.: William Alanson White Psychiatric Foundation, 1947.

———. *Clinical Studies in Psychiatry*. New York: Norton, 1956.

Tuschman, George. Historical Antecedents in Hysterical Reading Disability. Unpublished Master's thesis, The City College of the City University of New York, School of Education, 1968.

"What Went Right?"
The Natural History of
the Early Traumatized

There is hardly a psychoanalyst or psychotherapist who has not encountered a patient about whom he has wondered, "How in the
world did this person manage to stay as healthy as he is?" Usually
these reflections follow on the patient's disclosure of early life events
associated with the development of later mental illness. Equally dis-
concerting is the discovery that a friend or acquaintance whom one
has admired for his maturity and good judgment turns out to have
had a horrendous childhood blighted by emotional deprivation and
parental neglect. Or occasionally, one chances to meet the mother
and father of a person whom one has considered to be a paradigm of
mental health only to discover that they are the kind of parents described as schizophrenogenic. I could continue this list of surprises,
but the essential features would remain the same: Here are people
who seem to have surmounted adversity and, moreover, who appear
to have few if any residual disturbances of their mental health. Goertzel and Goertzel (1962) described many such individuals in their
survey of the emotional and intellectual climate in which eminent
people of the twentieth century were reared.

This chapter is the result of my own concerns with these issues of
why some persons survive trauma and stress and others succumb.
Like most psychoanalysts, I have always been interested in how my
patients developed their difficulties in living, why they failed to cope
when they did, and why they succumbed in their own particular fashion. Our large body of psychoanalytic theory is derived from such observations, and we turn to it for explanation of adult mental illness
since a good portion of our training is devoted to learning to look for
and to identify those factors in the life history of patients that lead to

This study was supported by U.S. Public Health Service research grant UI
00058-04 from the National Center for Urban and Industrial Health.

later disturbances of interpersonal relationships. These theories and the therapies derived from them have stood the test of time—they work. However, I believe that the nature of psychoanalytic practice often leads the analyst, particularly the private practitioner, to conclude that exposure to inordinate stress and strain during the earlier years will almost inevitably lead to later maladjustment. The tendency to arrive at such a conclusion is the result of the sampling error inevitably encountered in clinical practice where practically every patient seen is a sick person who has a traumatic life history. The psychoanalyst does not see the healthy people with the same histories since they have no reason to enter his consultation room or clinic. This is neither good nor bad, but a fact that we clinicians tend to ignore in determining the etiology of mental illness. It constitutes a serious limitation since we often do not have adequate control groups of healthy persons with whom we can compare the sick ones we treat. As a result, it becomes difficult on methodological grounds to transfer the conclusions drawn from our patient samples to the behavior of the larger universe of nonpatients in the world outside the consultation room. There is a surprising dearth of in-depth and in-breadth studies of healthy individuals, let alone studies of success in overcoming a bad early start. This essay is a preliminary effort to overcome these methodological shortcomings by using the large-scale methods of the epidemiologist. It reports the life histories and current psychosocial functioning of twenty-five women who have surmounted childhood adversity and psychological trauma. Since they were chosen from a sample representative of the local population at large, it is possible to compare them with this population as a control. Hopefully, this chapter will shed light on a seldom studied group, since we know very little about the life histories of mentally healthy individuals and particularly of persons who are not cast in the role of psychiatric patient. Such persons have no reason to go to the mental health specialist and when they consult the physician for organically determined illness there is little likelihood of detailed psychiatric history taking. I am sure there are vast numbers of people whose life histories are identical with the sick persons who have sought psychiatric treatment but who are not functionally incapacitated. What sort of data do we have about them? We have very little since they are very rarely seen, and then only in the course of infrequent large-scale epidemiological research into the prevalence of mental disorder (see

"What Went Right?"

Srole, Langner, Michael, Opler, and Rennie, 1962). Unfortunately, these latter studies have always focused on people who have failed to adjust rather than on those who have overcome psychological trauma. Psychiatry and psychoanalysis are not alone in their tendency to concentrate on pathology rather than on health. The same situation exists in general medicine. Normal, healthy people with old histories of illness are just not very interesting to the gastroenterologist or cardiologist since he is understandably more concerned with active disease than with active health. It is only within the past decade that studies of healthy adaption have captured the interest of the medical researcher, quite possibly because there has been so much to learn about the causation of disease up until now. However, as we continue to increase our knowledge and as epidemiological research has become more refined and its methodologies available to clinicians, we can now study the life histories and adjustment of the nonpatients, whose early lives are comparable to those of the patient population. In this study we are concerned with women whose early lives are indistinguishable from those of patients who broke down with schizophrenic illness, neurotic maladjustment, or just depression and despair. The respondents in this population are mentally healthy today, as defined by the instruments used to assess mental health: interview, questionnaire, and clinical evaluation (Grinker, Grinker, and Timberlake, 1962; Jahoda, 1958; Nunnally, 1961; Offer and Offer, 1968; Offer and Sabshin, 1966).

Research Methods

The research approach I used is not at all original. Though it is not my intent to be autobiographical, it reflects the three major influences to which I have been exposed in my career: psychoanalysis, child psychiatry, and research investigation. It is psychoanalytic, which is to say that it is developmental and considers the unconscious dynamics of behavior. It stems from child psychiatry in that the individual's disorder of living is taken to be a resultant of forces within the family. Lastly, the research approach has been shaped (and my use of that term with its behavioristic implications is not inadvertent) by the influence on my thinking of the theories and methods of the psychologist, sociologist, and the epidemiologist.

The original research project was a four-year study of the psychosocial antecedents of accidental poisoning in childhood. It consisted of a three-generational examination of the lives of 400 families, each of which had a child from two to five years of age. Thirteen women were trained to conduct detailed interviews in which they asked a series of 600 questions. Their respondents were seen in their own homes and in most cases the interviewer was accompanied by a babysitter. The interview lasted from one and a half to three hours, and the home contact was purposely unannounced. Each family was visited twice, once for the original questionnaire and twelve to eighteen months later for a followup. Different interviewers were used in more than half the cases to provide both a reliability and a validity check. Significantly different descriptions and accounts were negligible when the reports of the different interviews were examined. I did not see any of the respondents, but did debrief the interviewer on each case and helped her to write a descriptive and qualitative account of the family. This report is based on the data thus collected.

The Sample

In order to obtain a sample that would cut across all the major demographic variables, a universe of convenience was chosen that included the families of all live births occurring during 1962–1965 in two predominantly rural counties comprising a population of 91,000. One of these counties was in New Hampshire, and the other in Vermont. From this universe of 6,000 families, every fourth case was drawn, giving a sample of 1,250 families having a child aged two to five years. These were contacted by mail and 75 percent responded. The 25 percent nonrespondents were found to be of somewhat lower socioeconomic status when a random sample of thirty of them were tracked down for an interview. Therefore the sample reported may be of a slightly higher socioeconomic status than it would have been if all cases had responded. From these responding cases 400 were drawn for study. Ninety-seven percent of the sample originally selected for contact were successfully interviewed, a tribute to the tenacity of the trainees.

The Method

The questionnaire mentioned above was administered orally and in person to all respondents. Pertinent to this report are those questions relating to the life cycle of the mother in her childhood, adolescence, courtship, and marriage. Specific data were obtained about each major epoch of growth and development, and questions were asked that would shed light on the way in which the respondent's self-system had developed in relation to the significant others. The work of Srole and his associates(1962) served as one of the major models for the questionnaire. Many of the scales are derived wholly or in part from their studies.

The life history of the respondent, her nuclear family, and her family of orientation was recorded as a standardized anamnesis with considerable emphasis being placed on factors known to be influential in the development of adult personality and life adjustment. These included demographic and identification data on three generations: the husband and wife, their parents, and their children. Detailed life histories of husband and wife were obtained, beginning in their infancy and carried through adolescence, courtship, marriage, and the establishment of the present child-rearing nuclear family. There was also a very detailed case history of a single child selected for study.

A major methodological problem emerged at the onset of the project since the natural history approach of psychiatry and psychoanalysis leads to the accumulation of an enormous number of facts about the individual's life. The very quantity of these data is overwhelming, comprising over a million bits of information for the 400 families. Even though present-day computer techniques permit cross-correlation and comparison of each individual fact with every other one, it would be impossible to evaluate such an enormous mass of raw data. Accordingly, it became mandatory to collapse it into a workable form for analysis. To this end a series of scales were constructed to measure two major categories of variables: (1) environmental stress and (2) personal strain. These range from rather simple scales in which the number of stressful experiences were added up to give a cumulative score, to very complicated ones based mainly on the existence of pathological reactions such as psychosomatic disease or serious social maladjustment. These scales were used only if they met certain statistical criteria of internal consistency, and any that failed to measure up was discarded. The following scales were employed:

Childhood Mental Health Scale

This includes two major sorts of information: (1) Items ordinarily considered to be causally related to childhood emotional disorder. These are stress items, such as broken home, parental mental illness, socioeconomic deprivation; (2) Items ordinarily considered to be descriptive of childhood emotional disorder. These are strain items such as psychosomatic disorders, phobias, conflict with parents. It is a cumulative measure of mental health in childhood. (See Tables 15–1 through 15–5.)

TABLE 15–1

Childhood Mental Health Scale:
Broken Home Factors

Death, separation, divorce, desertion
Stressful consequences of parental substitution
Conflict with substitute parents
Loss of substitute parent
Stressful adoption

TABLE 15–2

Childhood Mental Health Scale:
Stressful Family Life Factors

Conflict between parents
Both parents negatively perceived
One parent negatively perceived
Mother or father very strict religion
Mother working very often
Mother or father often ill or bedridden
Mother or father worrying type
Poor communication with parents
Poor relation to parents in teens
Unhappy home during teens
Parents felt to be behind the times
At home people got in one another's way
Parents not proud of children
Parents did not practice what they preached
Parents excessively demanding
Unhappiness when at home
Punishment through guilt or silence
Poor relations with siblings

TABLE 15–3
Childhood Mental Health Scale:
Self-Presentation Factors in Childhood

Congenital physical defect
Speech disorder
Psychosomatic and health factors (under ten years)
    Poor health 1–6 years
    Frequent colds
    Trouble sleeping
    Frequent upset stomach
    Arthritis or rheumatism
    Asthma, hay fever, allergy
    Bladder trouble
    Heart condition
    Skin condition
    Nervous breakdown

TABLE 15–4
Childhood Mental Health Scale:
Phobias

Strangers
Thunderstorms
Being left alone
High places
Large animals
Being laughed at
Parental separation or divorce
Scolding
Other phobias

TABLE 15–5
Childhood Mental Health Scale:
Psychosexual Factors

Sexual ignorance
Ignorance of menstruation at onset
Social isolation
Precocious dating
No dating fifteen to eighteen years

Current Mental Health Scale

This current mental health scale is a composite index or scale based on the following subscales:

1. Psychosomatic symptom factors. For practical purposes this subscale is roughly equivalent to the Srole twenty-two-item mental health index from which it was taken. Five of the original Srole items reflecting depression were not included since they are covered elsewhere. (See Table 15–6).

2. Psychosomatic disease factors. This subscale includes illnesses ordinarily considered to have an associated psychosocial etiology, such as peptic ulcer, ulcerative colitis, hypertension, and asthma. (See Table 15–7).

3. Psychiatric diagnosis and treatment factors. This subscale measures selected items indicating the use of varying types of mental health services. (See Table 15–8).

4. Life change and stress factors. This is a rating scale developed by Holmes and Rahe (1967) to measure quantitatively the amount of life stress to which an individual is subjected over a period of time. The score is determined by the presence or absence of forty stressful life changes. These range from death of a spouse to changes of place of residence. It is highly correlated with disease onset. In this study it was calculated for each of five years.

5. Marital stress factors. This subscale includes items that either produce marital stress or are symptomatic of it. They range from signs of chronic dissatisfaction with marriage to separation and divorce. (See Table 15–9.)

6. Marital sexual maladjustment factors. This subscale includes those questionnaire items designed to tap the presence of sexual incompatibility, frigidity, impotence, and dissatisfaction. (See Table 15–10.)

7. Family interaction factors. This subscale was designed to group those items relating to family togetherness. It gives a rough estimate of the degree to which a family gets together for such communal activities as eating, trips, and so on. (See Table 15–11.)

8. Housewife role factors. This short subscale includes items describing the extent to which the respondent dislikes housework and child care. (See Table 15–12.)

9. Community interaction factors. This subscale measures the degree of social isolation or support that the respondent obtains from contacts and relationships outside her home. (See Table 15–13.)

The scores obtained on these subscales were added to give a cumulative number, which is the current mental health index. It is a mixture of items. For example, it includes behavioral descriptions, signs,

TABLE 15–6
Wife's Current Mental Health Scale:
Psychosomatic Symptom Factors

Worrying type	Nervous
Poor appetite	Weak all over
Upset stomach	Restless
Headaches	Acid, sour stomach
Trouble sleeping	Memory not all right
Hands tremble	Hot flashes
Shortness of breath	Cannot seem to get going
Heart beats hard	Pains in back interfere with work
Cold sweats	Trouble making up mind
Dizzy spells	Clogged feeling in head
Fainting spells	Generally poor health

TABLE 15–7
Wife's Current Mental Health Scale:
Psychosomatic Disease Factors

Arthritis or rheumatism
Asthma
Bladder trouble
Colitis with blood
Hay fever
High blood pressure
Neuralgia
Nervous breakdown
Epilepsy
Stomach ulcer
Skin condition
Medical treatment more than seven times in two years
Overeating

TABLE 15–8
Wife's Current Mental Health Scale:
Psychiatric Diagnosis and Treatment Factors

Consultation or treatment by mental health worker
Consultation or treatment by mental health worker in
    past five years
Advice or help from clergyman
Advice or help from lawyer
Advice or help from doctor
Advice or help from psychiatrist
Advice or help from social agency
Use of tranquilizers
Hallucinations

TABLE 15–9
Wife's Current Mental Health Scale:
Marital Stress Factors

Widowed, separated, divorced
Married three or more times
Married to escape unhappy home
Sleeps in separate room from husband
Husband and wife live with parents or have boarders
Moved three or more times in past five years
Worsening of companionship after marriage
Worsening of help in making decisions after marriage
Worsening of doing things on own after marriage
Worsening of freedom of action after marriage
Unhappy about marriage
Unhappy about husband's job

TABLE 15–10
Wife's Current Mental Health Scale:
Marital Sexual Maladjustment Factors

Worsening of sexual satisfaction after marriage
Admits unhappy sexual adjustment
Has intercourse less often than desired
Has intercourse more often than desired
Frigidity during intercourse
Conflict over frequency of intercourse
Abnormally frequent or infrequent intercourse

TABLE 15–11
Wife's Current Mental Health Scale:
Family Interaction Factors

Family gets together once or less a month
Family does not eat together
Husband away most or all evenings
Husband will not explain evening activities, or wife
    does not care
Wife quarrels frequently or never with husband
Husband never helps wife in the home

TABLE 15–12

Wife's Current Mental Health Scale:
Housewife Role Factors

Feels housebound
Resents husbands absence
Dislikes housework
Dislikes taking care of children

TABLE 15–13

Wife's Current Mental Health Scale:
Community Interaction Factors

Has very few friends in neighborhood
Has very few close friends besides neighbors and
relatives
Not active in organizations or clubs
Attended fewer than four weddings in past five years
Attended fewer than two anniversary parties in past
five years
Attended fewer than three funerals in past five years
Feels she has too few friends
Slow to make new acquaintances

symptoms, syndromes, and value judgments. However, this is a common problem in psychiatry, and the same mixture of taxonomically different items seems to characterize psychiatric diagnosis in general as well as the definitions of mental health and mental illness in particular.

The distribution of scale scores was computed for the entire population of the study. Figure 15–1 demonstrates the distribution of childhood mental health scores. Figure 15–2 is a similar histogram of adult mental health scores. The blacked out areas include the cases under discussion.

All cases with indices of high childhood pathology and with low adult pathology were chosen. High childhood pathology was determined by a score of seventeen or more units on the childhood mental health index. This is one standard deviation or more above the mean. The degree of adult pathology was similarly determined by the cumulative score on the current mental health index. Each individual under study was at least one standard deviation away from the mean for the 400 cases. A total of forty-three mothers whose scores fulfilled

FIGURE 15–1

Distribution of Mother's Childhood Mental Health Scores (400 Cases)

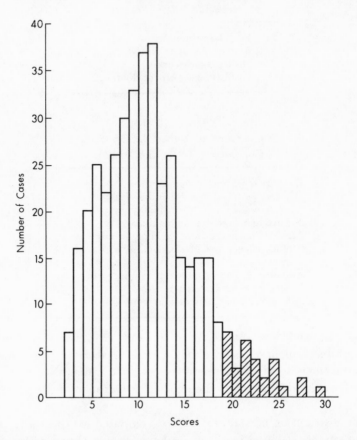

these criteria were identified, and the twenty-five with the greatest discrepancy between their childhood and adult pathology scores were chosen. It was assumed that these cases were the ones who had suffered the most in childhood and who were the healthiest in adult life.

Results

Cultural Overview

In order to understand the results of the study it is necessary to know something about northern New England. The area under study

"What Went Right?"

lies in New Hampshire and Vermont astride the Connecticut River about 100 miles below the Canadian border. The two counties encompass 3,000 square miles and a population of 91,000. The section from which the sample of 400 cases is drawn is predominantly rural, though there is a small city with local manufacturing in each county. During the last century the surrounding land and the hills were covered with pasture and grazing sheep. However, the expansion of the United States to the West and the development of mechanized farming put an end to the use of the steep-sided, hilly and rocky fields, and during recent years there has been a precipitous decline in the number of operating farms. The area remains rural, but very few of the inhabitants gain their livelihood from the land, most of them working in service fields or small local industries. However, there is Hanover, New Hampshire, 5,000 population, where the medical

FIGURE 15–2

Distribution of Mother's Current Mental Health Scores (400 Cases)

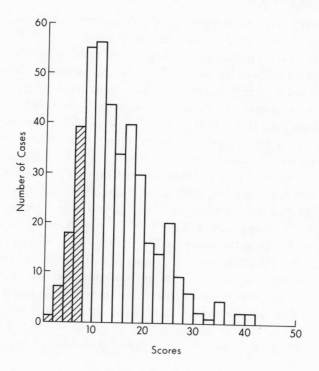

school, college and 450-bed hospital are located and which has been described as "an oasis: watered by underground streams of money, tinted Dartmouth green and hospital insurance blue."

This is a poor area with all the problems inherent to economic and social deprivation. Its population is predominantly working class with a relatively small percentage of middle-class and a very small percentage of upper-class families. In many ways it recalls Franklin Delano Roosevelt's statement during the Great Depression that "One third of our nation is ill housed, ill clothed, and ill fed." The people in Grafton and Windsor counties are not far removed from Roosevelt's description. However, what we are concerned with is whether the twenty-five women under study differ from the general population at risk, and if so, how? With this in mind let us briefly review the characteristics of the control population, the universe of the families of young children under study and note any differences that occurred in the experimental group, the twenty-five mothers who surmounted childhood adversity.

Demographic Factors

There were very few statistically significant differences between the two groups as far as demographic factors were concerned. The typical respondent in each group was thirty-one years old, most often Protestant (65 percent), less frequently Catholic (30 percent). Only 5 percent professed no religious affiliation, and there were no Jews. No differences were found in socioeconomic status, 75 percent of each group falling into the working class, 15 percent lower middle class and 10 percent into upper-middle or upper class. There were less than 5 percent of upper-class respondents in both groups, most of these being old New England families. Both the study and the control samples had large families with an average of 3.6 children. Twenty-five percent had five or more children. It was a first and only marriage for the vast majority although the "traumatized" group tended to marry earlier than the controls. Two thirds of the former had been married by the time they were nineteen, in contrast to one half of the controls. Almost all of both groups had married by the age of twenty-five. Since this is an area in which there is little female outmigration, it was not surprising to discover that 93 percent of both groups had been born in northern New England and that more than half were still living within thirty miles of their birthplace.

"What Went Right?"

Almost all these families live alone, the largest number owning their own homes. One third live under abject or poor housing, one half live modestly, and one sixth live well. Of these only a very few live extremely well, that is to say, as well as in upper-middle class suburban Scarsdale or Shaker Heights. The average family tends to remain in one place and if they move, it is usually within the area and to somewhat better housing. The only other differences in demographic factors found between the traumatized and the controls were that the former tended to marry slightly older men and to have a slightly better but not statistically significantly better income at the present time.

Family Backgrounds

As one would expect from a review of the childhood mental health index, the traumatized group suffered more privations during childhood. Three times as many came from broken homes, and of greater significance, this occurred three times more frequently at the critical periods between two and four years and between nine and eleven years. The divorce rate among their parents was 48 percent as opposed to 9 percent of the controls. They suffered maternal loss more often, 16 percent reporting the death of their mother by the age of ten in contrast to 5 percent. There was a similar but less pronounced paternal loss ratio, 12 percent of the traumatized group having lost a father through death as opposed to 6 percent of the controls. Serious conflict with substitute parents was reported ten times more frequently than in the general population from which they were selected. They were also exposed to more serious economic and social deprivations. Though not a statistically significant finding, their fathers tended to be of lower socioeconomic status than the controls. They had the same average number of siblings, but tended more often to be the oldest or next to oldest child and were more frequently given responsibility to raise younger brothers and sisters. They had a higher incidence of seriously ill and/or working mothers. Their mothers and fathers had more conflict and interpersonal difficulties than the controls, and as children their relationships with their siblings were poorer. They had fewer close friends and also tended to have poorer physical health than the overall comparable population at risk. They had more childhood colds, more trouble falling asleep, and more phobias. Of interest is the fact that the traumatized group had no socially visible physical defects or speech handicaps. Their sex education was significantly different than the controls. More learned about sex outside the family and tended to learn about it later in childhood. Twenty-eight percent knew nothing of menstruation until it happened, in contrast to 17 percent of the entire sample. Sixteen percent reported it to be a shock, whereas the controls felt this way in only 6 percent of the cases.

Looking at their later childhood and adolescence, we find significant differences in the degree of unhappiness and misery encountered at home. They got along more poorly with their parents, perceived them more negatively and were significantly more often in conflict with them.

Past Health

Some rather interesting results and significant findings emerge regarding health in adult years prior to the study. No differences between the traumatized group and the overall sample were found as far as the incidence of arthritis, bladder disease, hypertension, neuralgia, peptic ulcer, or diabetes was concerned. However, the traumatized group showed no asthma (6 percent of controls) no colitis (4.5 percent of controls), and no heart disease (5 percent of controls). Curiously, they had more hay fever (28 percent as compared to 13 percent) but fewer skin conditions (12 percent as compared to 22 percent). Only one of the 25 (4 percent) had ever consulted a psychiatrist or mental-health worker, whereas 14 percent of the overall population had had such consultation or treatment.

Present Health and Life Adjustment

As would be expected from the basis on which they were chosen, the traumatized group are currently functioning well in their everyday social roles of spouse, mother, and member of the community. They tend to enjoy their maternal and wifely activities more than their control counterparts and prove to be in better general health. There are no statistically significant differences in the two groups as far as sexual adjustment was concerned. Over 90 percent feel they have compatible and enjoyable sex lives and have no cause for complaint. There is a slight tendency for the traumatized group to report better adjustment. They tend to have intercourse more frequently than the controls, 52 percent having relations more than twice a week as contrasted to 36 percent. There are no differences in the two groups at lower rates of intercourse. In contrast to the situation I encountered among middle-class patients in private practice of psychiatry, where wives more often seemed to be frustrated, the husbands in both these groups are more interested in sexual relations than their wives. In the overall sample 31 percent of all the husbands feel that sexual relations occur less often than they would like whereas only 8 percent of their wives complain of infrequent sex. On the other hand, 25 percent of the wives feel it is too frequent, whereas only 4 percent of the husbands feel this way. The traumatized group present the same trends, but both husbands and wives report less dissatisfaction with frequency of sexual intercourse.

Turning to the use of alcohol, 80 percent of the traumatized group use alcohol regularly as opposed to 70 percent of the controls. Twenty percent of each group overindulge, but significantly fewer of the traumatized report it to be a problem in their marriage.

Family and Community Interaction

In this geographical area, considerable emphasis is placed on doing things togehter as a family. When we consider such family interaction as going to the movies, camping, and church we find the traumatized group getting together with their families slightly more often than the once a week reported by 75 percent of the controls. Their husbands tend to be home more often than in the overall population where 25 percent are away most evenings, mainly because of another job or working a night shift. The traumatized group of women complain less and are more accepting of the necessity for their husbands to be away than are the wives in the overall population. They also have fewer quarrels with their husbands and tend to enjoy their housekeeping more. However, one might consider both groups of wives severely housebound since over 50 percent never or rarely get away from their children.

Let us turn to community interaction. What light is shed here? Do the mothers who have overcome early difficulties show more support from the environment than the population from which they were drawn? Here again the answer is no. No differences are found in the number and kind of social supports they receive from neighbors, friends in the community, nearby relatives, or membership in clubs and organizations. It is interesting to note that almost 30 percent of

TABLE 15–14
Incidence of Parapsychiatric Symptoms:
Control Population

Five Years $n = 400$	
Fine, probation, or jail	9%
Juvenile delinquency	2%
Desertion, separate support, divorce	4%
Premarital pregnancy	6%
Single car auto accident	16%
Auto accident involving drunkenness	2%
Auto license withdrawal	8%
Chronic alcoholism	3%
Public intoxication with temporary jailing	1%
Suicide	1%
Homicide	0.1%
School disciplinary problem	7%
School underachievement	11%
Welfare recipiency	6%
Mental hospitalization	8%

both groups have eight or more families living nearby to whom they are related, and whom they see five or more times a year. This indicates considerable social support from the extended family as well as the neighborhood in both groups, but it is surprising that the traumatized group do not have more support than the controls. Finally we turn to what Mazer (1966) called parapsychiatric symptoms, deviant behavior that reflects underlying pathology. Table 15–14 lists their incidence in the controls over a five-year period. No differences are found in the two groups with but two exceptions: (1) auto license withdrawal and (2) premarital pregnancies, which are twice as common in the families of traumatized mothers.

Discussion

When the mean scores of the various indices of current mental health were computed for the two samples the traumatized group proved to be functioning equally as well as the overall population. When each case was reviewed qualitatively, by rereading the case history and the clinical notes made at the time of the debriefing, no differences could be found. It is difficult to find identifying characteristics that distinguish the traumatized group from the larger universe under study. At the present time, the data fail to give an adequate explanation of why these women have surmounted adversity so well. Preliminary statistical analysis has been frustrating, since there seems to be no significant correlation between the historical data and the eventual mental-health functioning of the individual, even though there is ample evidence of both early trauma and adult health. The gap is unclosed, and as Rollo May (1966) wrote "the perpetual piling of fact on fact [forces] the student to lose his immediate relation to his subject matter; the formula and testing machine intervene between the student and the human beings he purportedly seeks to understand. . . ." To avoid this, let us consider an individual case. Though this woman is one of the twenty-five from the traumatized cohort, it would be easy to find an equal number from the controls with similar childhood pathology but who, instead, had maladaption as adults.

Case History

Mrs. P is a thirty-two-year-old housewife with six children ranging in age from two to thirteen years. She left school at the eighth grade and was married at seventeen after a most unhappy childhood. Her husband has a similar background.

Both of Mrs. P's parents came from severely deprived and primitive circumstances. Her father was a logger and mill worker who was chronically ill both mentally and physically. He was frequently unemployed, and the family suffered considerable privation as a consequence. Her mother was also emotionally unstable and quarreled constantly with her husband.

At the age of seven her father was hospitalized for schizophrenia and for two years the family had a hand to mouth existence. When she was ten, her father died, and she went through a series of foster placements with relatives until her early marriage. She began dating her husband at fifteen, and both he and she had to overcome considerable parental disapproval in order to marry. Though she feels that she married too young, her current marital adjustment shows no disturbance either by qualitative life history or by quantitative scaling. She suspects that some years ago her husband may have been unfaithful, but believes he has settled down now. This has never been a cause of trouble for them, and their sexual adjustment is good.

She is a small, dark-haired woman who maintains firm gentleness in disciplining her children, and despite only six years of education she is well spoken. They live in an unpleasant neighborhood near the river and railroad tracks. Her parents-in-law live next door, but there is little visiting. She is a conscientious housekeeper and works hard before leaving for the factory at 2:00 P.M. The interviewer found the children to be well behaved, obedient, cooperative, and friendly. All in all, her current living situation, though well adjusted, is somewhat bland and uneventful. This proved to be uniformly characteristic of the present life adjustment of all respondents in both groups whose current mental health index score fell into the normal range. It recalls Tolstoi's statement, "All happy familes resemble one another; every unhappy family is unhappy in its own fashion."

None of the scales nor any of the interview material gave any clue as to how this woman had surmounted such a dismal and traumatic background, possibly because the questions were written from the therapist's point of view and were geared to an understanding of disease and illness but not to an understanding of health.

Conclusion

Explanations for the phenomena at hand are lacking. It is possible that genetic variations could account for the lack of findings but how are they measured in the population at large? It is equally possible that the methodology employed in this research is appropriate for the measurement of pathology but inappropriate for the measurement of health. As a result, I plan to individualize further study: to interview each woman in depth, to obtain typical dreams, and to carry out projective testing.

This will complete a career circle started almost twenty-five years ago when I became a candidate at the William Alanson White Institute. This circle began with the study of the individual, proceeded to the family, thence to the community, and from there to a population at large. Now I find myself back to the study of the individual, having found that quantitative methods are very useful for understanding people but in this case have not proved helpful in understanding persons. Perhaps the individual approach will provide the answer as to what went right.

"What Went Right?"

REFERENCES

Goertzel, V.; and Goertzel, M. G. *Cradles of Eminence*. Boston: Little, Brown, 1962.

Grinker, Roy R., Sr.; Grinker, Roy R. Jr.; and Timberlake, J. Jr. "Mentally Healthy Young Males (Homoclites): A Study." *Archives of General Psychiatry* 6(1962):405–453.

Holmes, Thomas H.; and Rahe, Richard H. "The Social Readjustment Rating Scale." *Journal of Psychosomatic Research* 11(1967):213–218.

Jahoda, Marie. *Current Concepts of Positive Mental Health*. New York: Basic Books, 1958.

May, Rollo. *Psychology and the Human Dilemma*. New York: Van Nostrand, 1966.

Mazer, Milton. "A Psychiatric and Parapsychiatric Register for an Island Community." *Archives of General Psychiatry* 14(1966):366–371.

Nunnally, Jum C., Jr. *Popular Conceptions of Mental Health*. New York: Holt, Reinhart & Winston, 1961.

Offer, Daniel; and Offer, Judith L. "Profiles of Normal Adolescent Girls." *Archives of General Psychiatry* 19(1968):513–522.

Offer, Daniel; and Sabshin, Marvin. *Normality: Theoretical and Clinical Concepts of Mental Health*. New York: Basic Books, 1966.

Srole, Leo; Langner, Thomas S.; Michael, Stanley T.; Opler, Marvin K.; and Rennie, Thomas A. *Mental Health in the Metropolis: The Midtown Manhattan Study*. New York: McGraw-Hill, 1962.

Systematic Research
on LSD in Psychoanalysis

This is a preliminary report of an initial portion of an investigation using small doses of LSD as a facilitating agent in psychotherapy entitled "Effects of LSD on Psychotherapeutic Communication." It is a report of one case, which had certain atypical characteristics. It should be emphasized that this case report does not describe the design of the larger project, which is more sophisticated. Nor do we attempt, on the basis of this one case, to draw any firm conclusions about the usefulness of LSD in psychotherapy. There are, however, some aspects of the case that we think are suggestive of some of the effects of LSD on which we shall comment. What we are mainly presenting is an example of the way in which clinical psychoanalysis and experimental psychology can be integrated in a systematic way to the enrichment of both disciplines (Jaffe, Dahlberg, and Feldstein, 1967).

The case history is a fortunate one for demonstration. The experiment occurred when the patient was well involved in analysis; she was neither excessively rigid nor too sick to mature, and she was well motivated. Our data are the clinical description; a paper and pencil test called the role construct sorting procedure, which takes about a half hour and which was administered after each LSD session and ir-

An enormous amount of labor went into the collection of the data reported. Most of this was not done by the authors. Credit should be given to Mercedes Barry for her labors on graphing and for her typing of the many revisions of the manuscript. Special notice should be accorded Joanna Chorosh, Aita Kallas, Mimi Sherwin, and Carol Toscano for their devotion in transcribing the thousands of words in the therapeutic sessions and for subsequently culling the word lists for data to make the graphs possible. Without their expertise and effort, none of the work here reported would have been possible.

The research reported was supported in part by PHS Grant No. MH-11670 from the National Institute of Mental Health to the William Alanson White Institute, New York.

regularly between LSD sessions; and material from the psycholinguistic analysis of the tape-recorded sessions.

The recorded sessions are the session immediately prior to the LSD session, the two-hour LSD session (which is handled in the psycholinguistic analysis as two separate hours), and the session immediately following the LSD session. Clinical notes have been made on other sessions, but only the above noted seven four-hour groups were recorded and transcribed. It was our assumption that the presessions would reflect the immediate clinical state of the patient and that there would be some carryover from the LSD session to the postsession in the psychotherapeutic interaction. This assumption appears to have been confirmed.

It is worth noting some remarks made by Harry Stack Sullivan (1934) in discussing a paper on psychopharmacology. Sullivan said in effect that if a drug could affect the interpersonal process by allaying anxiety or heightening focal attention it might enhance the interpersonal integrative process. For instance, one motive in an ambivalent relatedness (say suspiciousness) might be minimized and another (say trust) might be enhanced. Under these circumstances, conflict and blocking would decrease. As Sullivan (1934, p. 879) said, this can be done with certain drugs on some psychotic schizophrenics "with uniform predictable improvement of contact. Therefore, among other things the notion of usefully disturbing the activity of the integrating apparatus by the utilization of a pharmacodynamic agent can be demonstrated."

He went on to say (1934, p. 880), "I have no fond hopes of finding drugs specifically effective in removing defects of personality development. There should be extensive and intensive investigation of potent drugs as to their actual effects on interpersonal relations, as a parallel and mutually effective means for increasing our knowledge of personality and its inadequate and disordered functional activity." And he ended by saying (1934, p. 881), "So far, however, as practical clinical psychiatry is concerned, the utility of these drugs still waits on our having something really useful for the patient to collaborate in, once he is thus made ready to begin work."

In this chapter we shall offer some indications that point in a direction suggesting that under the specific conditions involved, LSD affected the interpersonal integrations of this patient; that her interpersonal integrations affected the response to the drug; and perhaps that

297

when there was something "really useful for the patient to collaborate in" (in this case depressive phenomena, separation, and growing autonomy) the drug can sometimes be of use and sometimes be a hindrance. Most importantly, we think we can demonstrate the usefulness of using experimental techniques to support, possibly refute, and especially, sharpen clinical observations.

Clinical Description

The patient was twenty-three when the experiment began. She was unmarried, a college student, and had started analysis three times a week about two years previously. Her symptoms included recurrent moderate depression, passivity, loneliness, overt anxiety, and highly unsatisfactory heterosexual relationships. She was the second of three children in an upper-middle–class family, bright, attractive, and aimless. The amorphousness of her symptoms and severity of her difficulties in living made the diagnosis of passive-dependent personality appropriate.

The first year and a half of treatment saw a gradual lessening of symptoms with little personality change. The therapeutic relationship was tentative. She thought of terminating and of taking a long foreign holiday during the summer. Just before this was to occur, she felt she might go on with her analysis on her return, and the analyst was agreeable to this. She made a definite commitment to analysis (her first) before leaving on a ten-week holiday, and the tentativeness of her involvement ceased.

For the next six months, analysis was central in her life, and she entered the LSD program at the analyst's suggestion, motivated by transference love. LSD was given orally in doses of fifty or sixty micrograms at roughly equal intervals seven times over a period of the next fourteen months. Analysis terminated seven weeks after the last LSD session.

Sessions were conducted as usual with the following important exceptions: (1) she had had nothing to eat for at least thirteen hours before ingesting the LSD capsule (wishing to lose weight, she took kindly to this rule); (2) she had a two-and one-half-hour waiting period after ingestion of LSD before the analytic session; (3) she usually ate a half pint of ice cream an hour and a quarter after taking the drug; (4) the session was twice as long as usual (see "The 100-Minute Hour," Dahlberg, 1967) and was tape-recorded, as were the sessions immediately before and after the drug session; and (5) she was given a brief paper and pencil test called the role construct sorting procedure (RCSP) following the session and returned home with a trained attendant of the same sex who spent the night.

The RCSP, a factor-analyzed modification of Kelley's (1955) role construct repertory test, was designed to evaluate the ways in which an individual conceptualizes people who are significant in his life. The rationale of the test is that a person deals with the world in terms of his view of it and that the more congruent an individual's constructs with the realities they represent, the more reality oriented will be his behavior. When other people are the realities, ill-fitting constructs may lead to severe interpersonal difficulties. The test has two parts, though we discuss only the second part here. For this part, the patient is asked to rate each of ten roles (among which are self, father, mother and psychotherapist) in terms of twenty adjective pairs [1] (Figure 16–1). In this essay we shall only show the patient's ratings for two of the roles in terms of three factors, which we consider to be measures of esteem (factor 1), autonomy (factor 2), and adjustment (factor 6). They represent ways in which she saw herself and her father. We shall try to show how these responses of the patient corresponded to and supported our clinical observations.

Her overall response to the LSD was dramatic and fell into three fairly distinct phases. The first we have labeled "regression, depression and working through," the second "transition," and the third, "separation and termination." The first phase included three LSD sessions and each of the other phases, two.

Phase 1. Regression, Depression, and Working Through

Session 1 may be described as regressive, with profound insights on the part of the patient into her concomitant childish and adult voices which were exaggerated by the drug. She also saw (1) how she used laughter defensively to avoid anxiety-provoking material, (2) that her sexual interests were mainly aimed at getting a response from a man (as opposed to a reciprocal relationship), and (3) that the analytic relationship was almost the only relationship with a man that meant anything to her. Toward the end of the session, she felt herself physically move toward the analyst until she got within an

FIGURE 16-1
Role Construct Sorting Procedure (RCSP)

Sample Page: "Self" Role

1. YOURSELF _____

1.	decisive	___	___	___	___	___	___	___	indecisive
2.	unintelligent	___	___	___	___	___	___	___	intelligent
3.	boring	___	___	___	___	___	___	___	interesting
4.	self-effacing	___	___	___	___	___	___	___	assertive
5.	dependent	___	___	___	___	___	___	___	independent
6.	inconsiderate	___	___	___	___	___	___	___	considerate
7.	demonstrative	___	___	___	___	___	___	___	undemonstrative
8.	mean	___	___	___	___	___	___	___	kind
9.	depressed	___	___	___	___	___	___	___	cheerful
10.	withdrawn	___	___	___	___	___	___	___	outgoing
11.	adjusted	___	___	___	___	___	___	___	maladjusted
12.	calm	___	___	___	___	___	___	___	excitable
13.	attractive	___	___	___	___	___	___	___	unattractive
14.	neat	___	___	___	___	___	___	___	slovenly
15.	poised	___	___	___	___	___	___	___	self-conscious
16.	prudish	___	___	___	___	___	___	___	promiscuous
17.	sensual	___	___	___	___	___	___	___	frigid
18.	candid	___	___	___	___	___	___	___	secretive
19.	rejecting	___	___	___	___	___	___	___	accepting
20.	selfish	___	___	___	___	___	___	___	unselfish
21.									
22.									
23.									
24.									
25.									
26.									
27.									
28.									
29.									
30.									

A page from the Role Construct Sorting Procedure (RCSP), Part 2, on which the patient rates himself ("yourself" is the role) on each of the twenty construct-contrast pairs. The scale for each pair is from 1, beginning at the left, to 7. Rows 21 to 30 are for construct-contrast pairs the patient may wish to add.

inch of him. At this point, a wall came up, which she felt was her father, and she remembered that she had always compared the men she dated unfavorably with him. The ensuing depression was heralded by the experience of a rectangular shape in her belly "which is gloom"

Systematic Research on LSD in Psychoanalysis

and "any minute could start creeping over" her. Shortly following this session she suffered a marked depression, uncharacteristic in severity, which lasted for about six months, with the first two months being the most severe. It is depicted dramatically on the self-rating of the esteem factor on the patient's RCSP and reaches its lowest point between sessions 1 and 2 (see Figure 16–2). By session 2, when her depression was lifting, there was a dramatic response—the patient bit her knuckle deeply—and there was a tremendous expressed ambivalence regarding certain male figures in her life. This was felt especially strongly in emotionally charged memories of a summer spent with her grandfather while her parents and older sister were in Europe. She compared the closeness of this relationship with the more distant one she had with her father and felt herself crying silently,

FIGURE 16–2
Role Construct Sorting Procedure: Self-Role

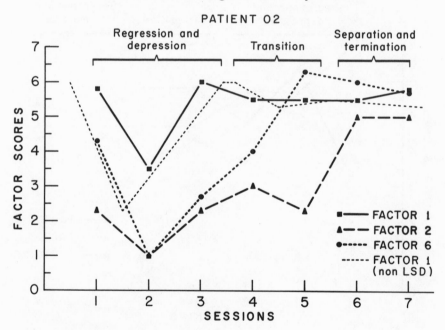

Patient 02's RCSP ratings of herself in terms of esteem (factor 1), autonomy (factor 2), and adjustment (factor 3) for seven LSD sessions. The horizontal brackets above the graph indicate the approximate durations of the clinically observed phases of the patient's progress. Her self-rating of "esteem" on non-LSD sessions is shown to indicate that the onset of her depression began shortly following the first LSD session and before the second one.

"Daddy, Daddy." She then said, "How can someone who makes you so happy make you so unhappy?" It was in this session that she first recognized the lifelong pattern of underlying depression in her makeup. The weeks following this session were marked by hostility toward her parents. She was able to keep the acting out of this hostility to a minimum and continued to work through the depression. This conflict is reflected in the RCSP by the discordance of the father rating on factors 1 and 6 (esteem and adjustment) as depicted in Figure 16–3.

Session 3 was dramatically marked by a guilt reaction, including the patient's taking a sponge bath in the therapist's bathroom because

FIGURE 16–3
Role Construct Sorting Procedure: Father Role

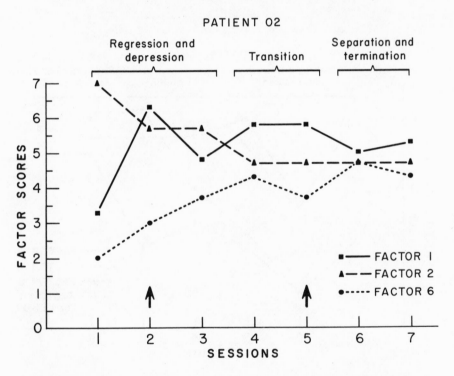

Patient 02's RCSP ratings of her father in terms of esteem (factor 1), autonomy (factor 2), and adjustment (factor 3) for seven LSD sessions. The horizontal brackets above the graph indicate the approximate durations of the clinically observed phases of the patient's progress.

she felt dirty. She also experienced pregnancy fantasies and recognized having acted these out by carelessness with contraception. She talked about her desire to expose her body, but was actually more modest than usual, felt strongly enough that her face was distorted to have to check on it in the mirror, and kept her body from the waist down in such constant motion that she complained of fatigue. All this was a dramatic representation (to her) of her sexual desires and resultant guilt.

Toward the end of this phase she experienced significant maturing in her mode of relating to men, found an accepting permanent lover, got her own apartment, and began to enjoy her work. It seems likely that the first session (in which her mood was euphoric) triggered the regressive phase, which was marked by much infantile behavior and early memories, often expressed in behavior (toilet and eating habits). The paternal rejection was reexperienced and resulted in severe depressive symptoms, which could be alleviated temporarily by enjoyable human contact but immediately returned when the contact was broken. This experience contrasted sharply with her previous depressions, which were brief and always precipitated by a present rejection. By the end of this phase, her mood had greatly lifted, and it never again fell more than temporarily.

Phase 2. Transition

The transitional nature of this phase is from a state of dependency to autonomy. Session 4 was preceded by a bombshell in her life, namely, her father's questioning the further financing of her therapy. It was a very obsessional session revolving about this sudden reality intrusion and was unlike her previous introspective explorations. She was panicky and felt she had to make important decisions about her life, but as the session ended realized that they did not all have to be made on the spot. She described herself as being in an identity crisis of the sort that most girls go through at about sixteen.

Some time after this session and before the next, the patient started thinking (but not talking) about terminating analysis, and after session 5 firmed up this decision. Her original decision was to terminate in about a year, but the time was later shortened and she actually stopped about five months after her first thoughts about it.

Session 5 introduced a change in the transference relationship combined with a constructive move toward separation. However, whereas the patient had enjoyed the LSD experience in previous sessions, she now complained of being uncomfortable with the drug, of not liking to be out of control, and of a feeling of resistance to exploration. It was also marked by a seductive sexual interaction with the therapist, confirmed by a slip of the tongue in which the word "incense" was substituted for "incest" (giving the vital clue in a dream interpretation) and also by the RCSP pattern for the father role, as was picked up once before in session 2. The sexuality experienced by the patient in the therapeutic relationship and expressed in the tongue slip is reflected in the discordant RCSP pattern for the father role (see Figure 16–3).

Phase 3. Separation and Termination

The subject matter in this phase was clearly linked to separation. Overall, she was in a good mood with short periods of anxiety and mild depression. Her relationship to her young man was developing, she had achieved orgastic potency, and she distinctly disliked LSD, as it caused a loss of her newfound and still precarious control and autonomy.

LSD sessions 6 and 7 were characterized as follows. In 6, the patient objected to racing thoughts, loss of emotional control, perceptual distortions, and so on. In session 7, she was nauseated, silent, and angry, lay on the couch with her back toward the therapist, and was initially unproductive. In both sessions 6 and 7 she became more productive with time. Furthermore, she was late for sessions 6 and 7, which was quite uncharacteristic of her throughout this whole drug administration period. She had had some lateness and a tendency to break appointments easily during the first year of treatment, but none of this behavior during her participation in the drug project or for the period of six to eight months prior to it.

She went on to work through most of her separation anxiety and terminated within a few weeks. About six months later she married the man she had been seeing. She has been seen twice for minor problems in the year and a half since termination. She has continued to mature and is relatively symptom free. On the two appointments since termination, she had largely worked out the problem she called about between the time of the call and the visit, a sign, we believe, of an ability to deal effectively with problems of living.

Systematic Research on LSD in Psychoanalysis

Summary

What we have described so far is an abbreviated clinical description of a patient in LSD-facilitated psychoanalysis with the emphasis on the more dramatic LSD productions. The RCSP provided independent, supportive evidence about how she experienced her self-esteem and aspects of her relationship to her father. This methodology, though clearly imperfect (since it does not allow for the influence of the extended session and the influence of the experimental procedure which has been allowed for in other studies), does permit analytic insight into a drug effect and into the implications of the effects of psychoanalytic therapy on pharmacological activity. By this we mean two things: (1) Clinically, an important regressive/depression episode was precipitated by the LSD and this was worked through. During this period (phase 1) the LSD was an exciting, enjoyable experience and was felt by the patient to lead to useful insights. (2) As she gained a precarious autonomy, the patient experienced LSD as a threat. In terms of transference phenomena, we think this says that in her dependent state LSD allowed her to be less defensive and to search deeper into herself and experience her early deprivation. During the third phase, however, the LSD (in its production of emotional lability, perceptual distortions, and loss of ego control) threatened her autonomy by throwing her back into a more dependent state. She therefore fought the drug effects and became uncomfortable, especially during the first hour of the two-hour session.

Experimental Findings

It should be noted that the psycholinguistic findings were obtained and analyzed independently of the clinical descriptions. The two sets of findings were integrated only at this writing. The data could be approached in at least two ways. One way is simply to compare those data drawn from the LSD sessions to those from the non-LSD sessions. The other approach is to divide the data in terms of the three phases suggested clinically and by the RCSP. We chose the latter as initially more relevant to the purposes of this paper.

A brief description of our technical procedures will help define our data. Each session is unobtrusively stereophonically recorded. All the words of the verbal interaction are then transferred to IBM punch cards.[2] The punch cards are then transferred to a computer tape, and by various programs we obtain lists of all the words used by each speaker ranked in order of their absolute and relative occurrence frequencies, a list of the words in alphabetical order (again with their frequencies), and many other things. In this chapter we shall only deal with the patient's speech. It should be noted that a statistical analysis of the relatively small number of observations with which we are here concerned would not be meaningful. However, certain trends do show up which stand out quite clearly in the graphs.

The graphs are reasonably self-explanatory. Words per minute, for instance, is a simple word count and shows the mean number of words per minute for each phase. We could show the number of words for any minute (or multiple of minutes) in any of the twenty-eight hours recorded but have not done so. Such a breakdown might give additional useful information.

The pre curve in the graphs depicts the session which immediately preceded the LSD session. Exp 1 is the first fifty minutes of the LSD session, and Exp 2 is the second fifty minutes. Clinically, Exp 1 and Exp 2 are separated by a ten-minute break. The post curve depicts the session immediately following the LSD session. The time between sessions was one or two days.

Words per minute, a measure of speech rate, has been given a considerable amount of attention in psychological studies of verbal behavior (Mahl and Schultz, 1964) and studies of drug effects (Waskow, 1967), though its use as an index of change in psychotherapy has been infrequent (Jaffe, 1961). For us, words per minute also serves as a measure of verbal productiveness in that the number of minutes per session varied little from session to session. The average number of words per minute for each of the clinical phases and each of the experimental conditions (pre, exp, post) are presented in Figure 16–4.

In phase 1 there is a fairly close cluster of all conditions at the low level that might be expected of a depressed patient. The marked increase in phase 2 began with the first drug session; note that the pre-session average remains low. Note also that this increase in average productivity was retained in the postsession. Finally, phase 3 shows a further though small decrease. The lower output of the first experimental hour in phase 3 most likely reflected the reported unpleasantness of the drug experience and consequent withdrawal by the pa-

FIGURE 16–4
Words per Minute

PATIENT 02

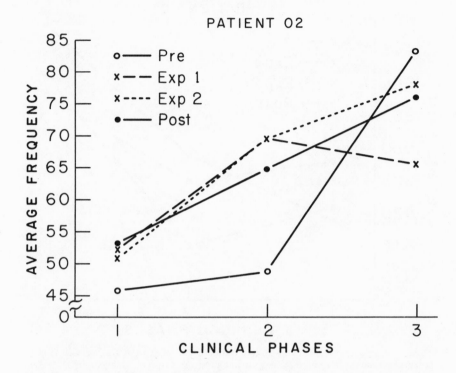

The average number of words per minute spoken by patient 02 during the three clinically observed phases of her progress in psychoanalysis. "Pre" refers to the session that occurred immediately prior to each of the LSD sessions; "Exp 1" and "Exp 2" refer to the first and second hours of the LSD sessions; "Post" refers to the session that immediately followed each of the LSD sessions.

tient. The reduction was temporary and by the second half of the drug sessions the patient's average word rate increased. There is carryover of this increase into the postsessions.

Type-Token Ratio

The type-token ratio, or TTR, is a measure of vocabulary diversity or its opposite, redundancy. It is obtained by dividing the number of different words (types) in a speech segment by the total number of words (tokens) in the segment. Originally proposed by Johnson (1944), it has been used in a variety of ways by different investiga-

307

FIGURE 16–5

Type-Token Ratio (TTR)

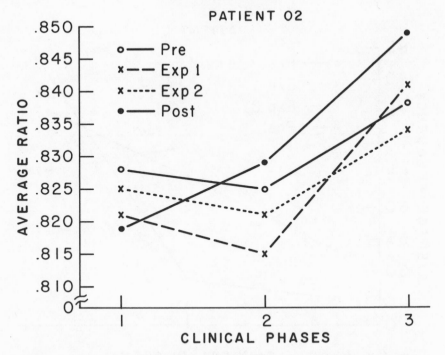

The average segmental Type-Token Ratio (TTR) of patient 02's speech during the three clinically observed phases of her progress in psychoanalysis. "Pre" refers to the session that occurred immediately prior to each of the LSD sessions; "Exp 1" and "Exp 2" refer to the first and second hours of the LSD sessions; "Post" refers to the session that immediately followed each of the LSD sessions.

tors. Mowrer (1953) reviews its history and, particularly, its use in comparing different psychodiagnostic groups. He also reports a study by Roshal (Mowrer, 1953, p. 514) which found that the TTR significantly increased from the first to the last psychotherapy sessions for a group of thirteen psychotherapy cases considered most successful, and decreased from the first to last sessions for the thirteen least successful cases. In the present study, we have used a variation of the TTR suggested by Jaffe (1961) which utilizes successive twenty-five-word segments of a speech sample. The TTRs computed for these segments are then averaged to provide a mean segmental TTR for the entire speech sample. This variation has been used in a number of previous studies (Feldstein and Jaffe, 1962a, 1962b; Jaffe, 1964).

Systematic Research on LSD in Psychoanalysis

We had expected that vocabulary diversity would be greater under LSD than in non-LSD sessions. If anything, the patient seems to have been somewhat more repetitious under the influence of LSD (Figure 16–5).

What is dramatic is the sharp increase in diversity from phase 2 to phase 3 or, in other words, during the termination phase in both LSD and non-LSD sessions. It might be conjectured that this increase represents greater creativity and less constriction than was apparent during the depressed and transition phases. Whatever its significance, it clearly replicates the trend found in the Roshal study cited by Mowrer (1953). Of interest, too, is that only during this last phase does the patient reach the level of vocabulary diversity usually utilized by a population with a higher-than-average educational level.

Mood Words

We arbitrarily took from our word lists words that seemed to represent mood. Words such as "anxiety" or "happy" gave no problem, but words such as "well" and some others were more ambiguous. The decision about which to use was made without the aid of the context (remember, we are dealing with texts totaling about 140,000 words). Obviously, ambiguous words are included. We assume that in this large sample the effects of whatever errors of inclusion and exclusion we did make are minimal.

Combined mood words. Generally, mood words in the presessions remained at an even level, indicating the relatively constant attention to feelings that would be expected of a psychoanalytic patient (Figure 16–6).

In the postsessions, their relative frequency tended to drop. Does this mean that at these times the patient talked more about problems and less about how she felt? If so, it would indicate a greater focusing on problems and perhaps on analytic work followed by the LSD sessions. We shall see that almost all of this drop is accounted for by a decrease in negative mood words.

Positive mood words. When we arbitrarily split mood words crudely into positive and negative (Figure 16–7), we see an interesting breakdown. Clearly, the patient was more euphoric in the drug sessions in phase 1 (this phase induced and covered her regression/depression). Also, both parts of the drug euphoria are above the undrugged state, though only by a small amount in phase

FIGURE 16–6
Combined Mood Words

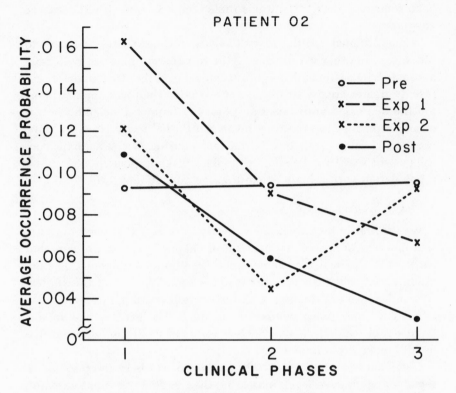

PATIENT 02

- o—— Pre
- x— — Exp 1
- x······ Exp 2
- •—— Post

AVERAGE OCCURRENCE PROBABILITY

CLINICAL PHASES

The average probability (relative frequency) with which patient 02 used mood words during the three clinically observed phases of her progress in psychoanalysis. "Pre" refers to the session that occurred immediately prior to each of the LSD sessions; "Exp 1" and "Exp 2" refer to the first and second hours of the LSD sessions; "Post" refers to the session that immediately followed each of the LSD sessions.

2. Note a slight rise in positive mood words from the transitional to the separation phase except in the first experimental hour of phase 3 where she definitely did not feel good because she disliked the loss of control brought on by the drug.

Negative mood words. Her use of negative mood words (such as "saddened," "shameful") showed even more dramatic changes. There is a tight, high cluster in phase 1 only exceeded by the even higher relative frequency emitted during the first drug hour (remember these were euphoric states when she enjoyed the drug). The presession relative frequencies remained fairly constant during the first and second phases and decreased only by phase 3. It was during the first experimental hours and postsessions that these dropped precipitiously from phases 1 to 3.

What about the second LSD hours? The sharp decrease was probably related to the abatement of the panic which, as was noted earlier, had occurred during this period of a reality crisis, the abatement having to do with the therapeutic relationship which the longer session allowed us to utilize (note "The 100-Minute Hour" effect, Dahlberg, 1967).

Note the scatter in phase 2. The confusion this seems to imply appears in Figures 16–8 and 16–9. This, we think, is a reflection of the

FIGURE 16–7

Positive Mood Words   *Negative Mood Words*

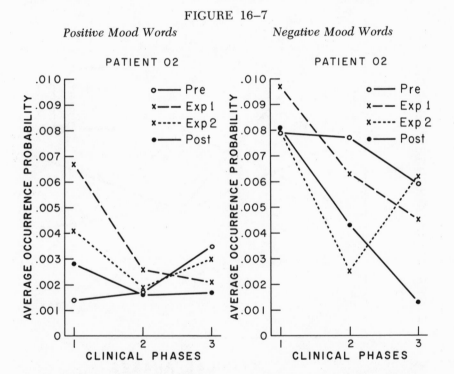

The average probabilities of patient 02's use of mood words are graphed separately for positive and negative mood words used during the three clinical phases of her progress in psychoanalysis. "Pre" refers to the session that occurred immediately prior to each of the LSD sessions; "Exp 1" and "Exp 2" refer to the first and second hours of the LSD sessions; "Post" refers to the session that immediately followed each of the LSD sessions.

transitional nature of this phase with its changing emphasis on family and the past and reflects the changing transference relationship which will also show up on the I/you ratio.

Past Tense Verbs

In a relatively crude effort to see whether references to the past were related to the use of LSD and/or to the clinical phases, we looked at the frequency of past tense verbs as they appeared in the word lists.

As can be seen in Figure 16–8, the presessions show some stability.

FIGURE 16–8
Past Tense Verbs

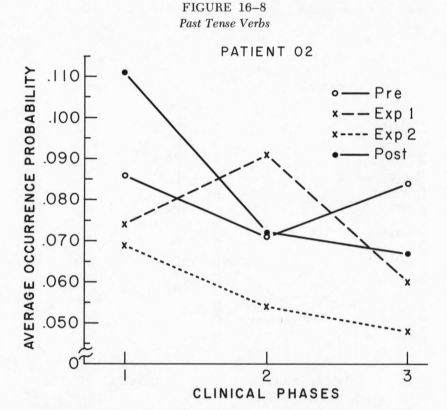

The average probability (relative frequency) with which patient 02 used past tense verbs during the three phases of her progress in psychoanalysis. "Pre" refers to the session that occurred immediately prior to each of the LSD sessions; "Exp 1" and "Exp 2" refer to the first and second hours of the LSD sessions; "Post" refers to the session that immediately followed each of the LSD sessions.

Systematic Research on LSD in Psychoanalysis

The postsessions show a decline in use of the past tense, confirming our notions about the changing focus over time following LSD. The patient spoke less about unpleasant feelings and less about the past. (Present and future verbs are extraordinarily difficult to select from word lists.) We shall see that she also talked relatively more about her analyst. The phase 2 transitional phenomenon noted for the use of negative mood words is also apparent here.

On an interpretive level, it may be that the patient's decreased use of the past tense indicates a decreased defensiveness (Jaffe, 1960). This inference is not contradicted by the clinical data. In any case, our finding is in accord with previous research reported by Mowrer (1953) which demonstrated that the completion of therapy is accompanied by decreases in the use of past tense verbs.

Family References

Another analysis we performed tabulated the relative frequency of family references. These do not include pronouns but do include family names and terms of relationship such as "mother" and "grandfather." We can see in Figure 16–9 that family references occurred frequently in presessions during phases 1 and 2 and dropped in phase 3 along with the interest in separation and growing autonomy. There is a cluster at a low level in all conditions in phase 3 when she was dealing with separation and one equally low in the drug and postdrug sessions in phase 2, where we saw she was dealing with important personal problems which apparently the drug brought into her awareness.

It is difficult to explain the scatter in the first phase, in which experimental hour 1 is the lowest and experimental hour 2 is the highest. In experimental hour 2, family references were at their highest as might be expected in a regressive/depressive phase. It may be that the low of hour 1 occurred because she was not yet used to the drug and made many comments about how she felt, tending thereby to exclude family references.

I/You Ratio

The I/you ratio (see Figure 16–10) contrasts the use of first and second person pronouns and compounds of them. It is similar to the self-referring and other-referring pronoun analysis suggested by Jaffe (1960) and to the earlier exploration of self and other references by

FIGURE 16-9
Family References

PATIENT 02

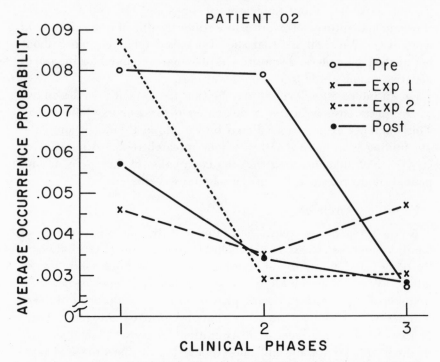

The average probability (relative frequency) with which patient 02 referred to her family during the three clinically observed phases of her progress in psychoanalysis. "Pre" refers to the session that occurred immediately prior to each of the LSD sessions; "Exp 1" and "Exp 2" refer to the first and second hours of the LSD sessions; "Post" refers to the session that immediately followed each of the LSD sessions.

Cazawick and Young reported by Mowrer (1953, p. 522). "You" is complicated by being both singular and plural and also by occurring in such expressions as "you know." Though this idiosyncratic use of "you" affects the frequency with which the word is used and may render interpretive comparisons between persons difficult, it should not affect the comparison of an individual with himself over relatively short periods of time.

First, one sees that in phase 3 (separation) the patient referred to the analyst two to three times as often as at the beginning. This was true in all conditions. In terms of drug effects, such references occurred about twice as often in phase 1 when she was on LSD as when

Systematic Research on LSD in Psychoanalysis

she was not. There was apparently no carryover in phase 1, but there was in phases 2 and 3. The transitional phase trend shows up again. Clearly as time passed she became less self-absorbed and showed a different transference interest.

The cluster in phase 3 seems to indicate that the patient achieved a stable state in which she was, in all conditions, dealing with her separation from the analyst and referred to "you" with relatively high frequency throughout. Here she was fighting the drug effect and attempting to exert her own personality and maintain a state of integration.

FIGURE 16–10

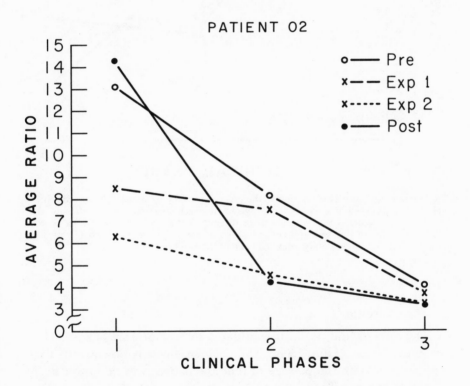

The average ratio of the "I" to "you" pronouns used by patient 02 during the three clinically observed phases of her progress in psychoanalysis. "Pre" refers to the session that occurred immediately prior to each of the LSD sessions; "Exp 1" and "Exp 2" refer to the first and second hours of the LSD sessions; "Post" refers to the session that immediately followed each of the LSD sessions.

FIGURE 16–11
The / A Ratio

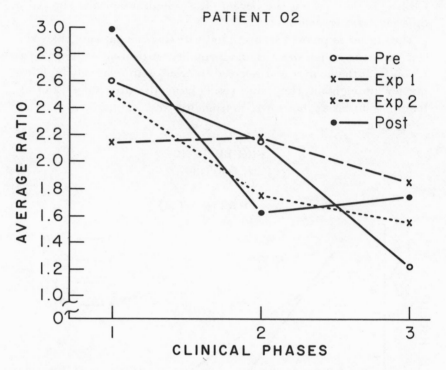

The average ratio of the articles "the" to "a" used by patient 02 during the three clinically observed phases of her progress in psychoanalysis. "Pre" refers to the session that occurred immediately prior to each of the LSD sessions; "Exp 1" and "Exp 2" refer to the first and second hours of the LSD sessions; "Post" refers to the session that immediately followed each of the LSD sessions.

The/A Ratio

The ratio of "the" to "a" is considered to be a measure of specificity, or concreteness (Jaffe, 1960). The clearcut trend is downward (Figure 16–11). With the passage of time the patient was no longer dealing with the specifics of the past but with more abstract, speculative matters about her future, and with what in a loose sense could be called philosophical questions. Her relatively greater use of the article "a" in the third phase seems to reflect these new concerns.

Summary and Conclusions

We have described the progress of a young woman during an experimentally delineated period of LSD-facilitated psychoanalysis. This progress fell rather neatly into three psychodynamic phases which appear to have been initiated by the administration of LSD. The first phase was marked by considerable insight on the part of the patient into the immaturity and barrenness of her heterosexual interests, and into her characteristic mode of avoiding anxiety. These insights precipitated a depression of unusual severity for her involving an upsurge of hostility toward her parents and of regressive sexual concerns. This was followed by feelings of guilt and, eventually, by increasingly mature interpersonal attitudes. The analysis of her language suggests that during this phase she spoke relatively little, was preoccupied with primarily negative feelings and with the specifics of her past familial relationships.

During the second, or transitional, phase the patient experienced a brief panic reaction to a reality crisis and then began moving toward greater emotional autonomy. She talked more during this period, though she used fewer references to self, to the past, to her family, and to her feelings.

Clinically, phase 3 represents the termination stage during which the patient worked through her separation anxiety. Her language revealed even greater productivity and a greater diversity in the use of vocabulary. Even more marked is what might be interpreted as her decreased concern with self, with the past, and with negative feelings. Moreover, her language revealed an increased concern with the analyst and with less immediate issues.

What might we say about the meaning of this work on one case? Our first impulse is to hide behind the cautions of experimental rigor and say nothing. Barring such an austere course, we must emphasize that the results of a single case provide little of the leverage needed for predicting the results of other cases. In other words, our conclusions must be considered tentative at best.

1. We have shown with some conviction that different clinically noticeable phases of interpersonal integration are reflected in language style. This is a matter of no little importance. At the simplest level, it suggests that the evaluations made by an analyst are based,

to a discernible degree, on the language behavior of the patient. One implication of this suggestion is that the statements made by an analyst about his patient are independently verifiable. It should be possible, in other words, to show whether an analyst was responding to what he thought and to what he said he was responding. A related implication is that some important determinants of an analyst's evaluations can be made explicit. Finally, there is the possibility that such simple indices as are derivable from word frequency lists may be indicators of analytic phenomena of major significance, such as transference shifts, empathic states, and so forth, and with greater refinement may even have predictive value in terms of the prognosis and course of therapy.

The implications stated above are independent of the correctness or incorrectness of an analyst's evaluations. Determining that a patient is healthier when an analyst says he is requires an investigation that goes well beyond the scope of our present project. We might note in passing, however, that certain of the data we have presented seem to lend some credence to the analyst's judgment that the patient was functioning more maturely at termination. We refer to the change in level and to the relatively tight clustering during phase 3 of the I/you ratio, family references, and positive mood words, which seems to us to indicate the achievement of some stability. We refer also to the fact that by phase 3 the diversity of the patient's vocabulary use approximates that generally used by a college-trained population, whereas it was distinctly below this level earlier.

2. We have at least suggestive clinical evidence at this point that the state of interpersonal integration affects and is affected by a drug such as LSD. (It may be that the state of interpersonal integration can account for the psychological phenomena in a "bad trip.")

The language analyses show no marked differences between the drug sessions and the pre- and postsessions. This may mean that there was no notable LSD effect or that the effect of the drug extended to the pre- and postsessions, or that our linguistic indices as used in this study are not sufficiently sensitive to detect the drug effect.

3. It seems to us that we have demonstrated the feasibility of achieving a very close integration of psychoanalytic and experimental procedures without impairing the validity of the therapeutic process.

Systematic Research on LSD in Psychoanalysis

NOTES

1. The patient is presented with a booklet of ten pages, each page of which has a role title at the top followed by a list of twenty adjective pairs (see Figure 16–1). The list is the same for all role titles, and each adjective pair consists of a construct and its contrast (or approximate opposite) along a seven-point scale. The patient is asked to characterize each role by every construct pair on the page. Based upon a factor analysis that was utilized in constructing the RCSP, the construct pairs are divided in seven factors. The twenty constructs are divided among the seven factors in the following way: factor 1—considerate, kind, accepting, unselfish; factor 2—decisive, independent, assertive; factor 3—demonstrative, excitable, candid; factor 4—attractive, neat, poised; factor 5—promiscuous, sensual; factor 6—cheerful, outgoing, adjusted; factor 7—intelligent, interesting. The factors are numbered in order of the amount of total variance for which they account, with factor 1 accounting for the largest portion. The score for each factor is the mean scale value of its associated construct pairs.

2. Although not utilized in this chapter, speech disruptions are also coded on the cards as is the end of each minute (Feldstein and Chorosh, unpublished).

REFERENCES

Dahlberg, C. C. "The 100-minute Hour" *Contemporary Psychoanalysis* 4, no. 1(1967):1–18.

Feldstein, Stanley; and Jaffe, Joseph. "Vocabulary Diversity of Schizophrenics and Normals." *Journal of Speech and Hearing Research* 5(1962):76–78. (a)

———; and Jaffe, Joseph. "A Note about Speech Disturbances and Vocabulary Diversity." *Journal of Communication* 12(1962):166–170. (b)

Jaffe, Joseph. "Formal Language Patterns as Defensive Operations." In D. A. Barbara, ed., *Psychological and Psychiatric Aspects of Speech and Hearing.* Springfield, Ill: Charles C Thomas, 1960. Pp. 138–152.

———. "Dyadic Analysis of Two Psychotherapeutic Interviews." In L. A. Gottschalk, ed., *Comparative Psycholinguistic Analysis of Two Psychotherapeutic Interviews.* New York: International Universities Press, 1961.

———; Dahlberg. C. C.; and Feldstein, Stanley. "Practical Aspects of Systematic Research in Psychoanalytic Office Settings: Report of the Committee on Research of the American Academy of Psychoanalysis." In Jules H. Masserman, ed., *Science and Psychoanalysis.* Vol. 11. New York: Grune & Stratton, 1967. Pp. 202–222.

Johnson, W. "Studies in Language Behavior: I. A. Program of Research." *Psychological Monographs* 56(1944):1–15.

Kelley, G. A. *The Psychology of Personal Constructs.* Vol. 1. *A Theory of Personality.* New York: Norton, 1955.

Mahl, G. F.; and Schultz, G. "Psychological Research in the Extralinguistic Area." In T. A. Sebeck, A. S. Hayes, and Mary C. Bateson, eds., *Approaches to Semi Tics.* The Hague: Mouton, 1964.

Mowrer, O. H. "Changes in Verbal Behavior During Psychotherapy." In O. H. Mowrer, ed., *Psychotherapy: Theory and Research.* New York: Ronald Press, 1953. Pp. 463–545.

Sullivan, Harry Stack. "Discussion of E. Lindemann and W. Malamud,

'Experimental Analysis of Psychopathological Effects of Intoxicant Drugs.' "
American Journal of Psychiatry 90(1934):879–881.

Waskow, Irene E. "The Effects of Drugs on Speech: A Review." In K. Salzinger
and Suzanne Salzinger, eds., *Research in Verbal Behavior and Some Neurophy-
siological Implications.* New York: Academic Press, 1967. Pp. 355–381.

PART FIVE
Applied Psychoanalysis

T HE THREE CHAPTERS in this section are devoted to information from other fields which is relevant to the goals and boundaries of psychoanalysis both in practice and theory. Joseph Jaffe introduces some of the recent neurological understanding of the biological basis for speech. This is the origin of speech which is universal and based on basic concept forming mechanisms, the anlagen of which are in the brain. Rollo May feels that the loss of myths and symbols in this culture predicts its disintegration. Leon Edel spells out the necessary requirements for an interdisciplinary approach to literary psychology. He defines the role of the analyst in this endeavor.

Joseph Jaffe points out that the essential humanity of "we are more simply human than otherwise" is close to the biological, particularly with reference to our knowledge of language mechanisms. Language develops throughout the world at the same age and in the same way. This coincides with development of the cerebral hemispheres and right- or left-handedness. It is probably genetically determined. Many symbolic functions are relatively autonomous and unrelated to speech and comprehension. Brain surgery, involving separation of the hemispheres, amply illustrates this. Theories of cognition and psychopathology must be affected profoundly by these observations. Jaffe hypothecates a universal grammar, a basic underlying concept-forming mechanism that determines all behavior, linguistic and otherwise. The common denominator is located in the human brain viewed as a great transforming machine continuously relating patterns of nerve impulses to abstract schemata both innate and learned. For transcultural communication, Jaffe calls for reliance upon the young for verbal penetration. Adults are advised to use nonverbal means if they wish to communicate across a cultural boundary.

For Rollo May the myth is the conveyor of eternal verities; it is the

323

symbol of the values and beliefs and dilemmas of man. It is the quintessence of human experience. The myth is transcultural. When a culture is flourishing—moving toward integration and unity—myths and symbols flourish. When a culture is disintegrating, there is a loss of myths and symbols. This loss is a symptom of disunity and trouble in an entire society. This is what is happening today. Myths have become objectified and have lost their meaning. The task of the psychoanalyst is to help the patient become aware of his personal myth, to experience it fully, and then to integrate it.

Leon Edel writes about the necessity for a theory and methodology so that a truly interdisciplinary literary psychology may evolve. Literary psychology deals with the story of man's imagination in making myths and creating symbols and the translation of these into words. It deals with the structure and form created by language as an illusion of reality. It is a record of the subjective life of some articulate people. Literary psychology must recognize the integrity of the literary work as a creative outcome of a personality and not as the biography of the person. It may study structure and content of literary psychology, the imagination that has given it form and pattern, the fantasy it embodies, the behavior it describes in the light of what is known of the unconscious and integrative functions of the personality. Therapeutic systems are irrelevant in literary psychology.

Structural Foundations of Linguistic Behavior

Human heart transplantations have made history. A profound implication of this achievement is the definition of life in terms of brain
function. There has been surprisingly little controversy regarding the
criterion to be used when we decide that one person may donate a
heart or a liver to another. The criterion is irreversible brain death.
This is tantamount to the statement that one's humanity consists in
the potentiality for awareness; in the ability to process information
from the internal and external environments. Since I am especially
concerned with this neural level of information-processing, I shall
comment on certain recent developments in our understanding of the
brain mechanisms that underlie the functions of speech, language, and
symbolism. But first, a bit of historical perspective.

As I review my twenty years of experience in the turbulent currents
of thought at the William Alanson White Institute, several themes,
often contradictory, seem relevant to my topic. Originally, our humanistic persuasion led us to reject certain pessimistic instinct theories, and consequently we were among the first to emphasize the role
of cultural factors in personality. We have been vindicated in this
faith by the development of the mental health movement as a social
science, apparently transcending its narrower biological tradition; yet
despite this faith, the current worldwide social upheaval has once
again dramatized the monumental barriers to communication that
exist even between subcultures, while many direct their concern to
the barriers between cultures. This institute has been a bastion
against the oversimplifications of behavioristic psychology, asserting
that what men know, fear, plan, and believe may not be simply
summed up by what they do. Here too we have been vindicated as an
increasing number of prominent behaviorists turn once again to introspection as a method of observation. Do not be misled by the eu-
phemism "verbal behavior," which has been invented to disguise this
trend or to pretend that nothing has really changed. There is a growing awareness that systems of knowledge and belief are not realized

in any direct or simple way in behavior and must be studied in their own right by appropriate methods. Yet we have curiously shared a prejudice with the most "echt" behaviorists that a complex organism can, under the most ideal conditions, learn just about anything at any time, that is, that behavioral potential is unlimited. Such ideas transcend disciplinary boundaries and create strange bedfellows. Thus we all know colleagues who would scoff at efforts to train a pigeon to dance or a chimpanzee to speak, yet who sincerely believe the equally far-fetched notion that a creative artist lurks within every child. In short, we have lived through a period in which we emphasized nurture over nature. Here, unfortunately, we have been incorrect if not downright foolish, and the point I wish to make is that the pendulum is swinging back. One can still honestly maintain that people are more simply human than otherwise, but their essential humanity (at least as far as our understanding of language mechanisms goes) is to be found somewhat closer to the biological level. This in turn imposes constraints that cannot be ignored. These biological constraints are not grounds for pessimism however, but rather for a more profound appreciation of what is realistically possible and where the challenges lie.

Let me review some current notions about the biological foundations of language in order to illustrate these points.

1. Healthy babies all over the world begin to speak at the same time and in the same way. The capacity is innate, preprogrammed, and unfolds like seeing, hearing, sitting, standing, and walking. It coincides with lateralization of the control of speech in one half of the brain and with the development of handedness. The language being spoken in the environment serves only as a model for the selection of a set of rules and distinctions that is automatically abstracted. The child gets the idea of what something means or of how to say something and suddenly can say and understand many things he has never heard. The rules are largely outside the awareness even of the adult speaker, and they impose a semantic interpretation on the spoken sounds of the environment.

Assuming normal hearing and exposure to speech there is nothing that can be done to speed up or inhibit this linguistic development; it has its own dynamic. In fact, demolition of half the brain may not stop it if the child is young enough at the time of the lesion. We may think of the particular language learned (English, French, and so on)

326

as one of many languages inherently possible; indeed, during the period of maximum language readiness, beginning at age of two, several languages may be learned side by side. The child may be bilingual, trilingual, and so on without contaminating accent. This magnificent period of symbolic plasticity comes to an end in the teens with the advent of cerebral maturity. If the child is not exposed to speech by this time, it is unlikely he will ever use it. Second language learning is still possible after the teens, but with much greater difficulty, and almost never without the telltale accent that identifies the first language. Thus, one is led to suspect that genetically controlled processes of maturation, rather than environmental influences, underlie the capacity for language.

2. Research in neurosurgery and medical psycholinguistics is revealing the relative autonomy of many symbolic functions that were previously thought to be intimately related, if not identical, for example, speech and comprehension. I remember being taught that thinking was subvocal speech. Yet, a child with complete inability to speak (congenital anarthria) was recently shown to have normal comprehension of spoken language. Thus, knowing and doing may be independent functions. Yet, in the Middle Ages a deaf mute was thought to lack a soul. And in the seventeenth century, in his division of man's functions into body and mind, Descartes attributed the soul, reason, logic, and language to the mind. This impeded the investigation of language as a biological phenomenon, and imposed philosophical distinctions that continue to hamper our freedom of inquiry.

An even more dramatic demonstration of the fact that knowing is separable from the speech mechanism is afforded by surgical disconnection of the cerebral hemispheres, a treatment that is occasionally a last resort in cases of intractable epilepsy. Recall that the speech mechanism, in a right-handed person, resides in the left hemisphere of the brain, which also controls the right half of the body. Figure 17–1 illustrates a special test apparatus which makes it possible to flash a picture so that it is received only in the right half of the brain (the left visual field is the area stimulated). The doctor monitors the visual fixation through the peephole and flashes the picture at the proper moment. The apparatus is such that the object actually seen must be selected by one hand out of an assemblage of different objects, but completely by touch and without viewing the objects. When a picture is flashed to the right hemisphere only, these pa-

FIGURE 17–1
Special Test Apparatus

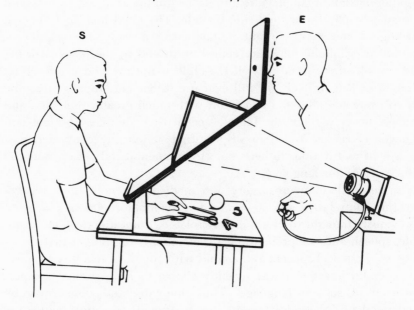

tients can select the proper object with their left hand, which of course is controlled by the knowledgeable right hemisphere. They are unable to identify the object with the right hand, however, since the left hemisphere controlling it is isolated from the right and has therefore not received the visual information. So far so good. A simple matter of electrical circuitry. Now, when the picture displayed to the right hemisphere is a word, the left hand can select the appropriate spelling from raised letters, by touch alone. Thus, in this sense, the right hemisphere can read. However, when asked, the patient cannot say what he has just read because the left hemisphere, which generates speech, does not have the information! So the patient can only guess aloud and incorrectly. But he can be observed to wince with embarrassment when he hears himself verbalize the incorrect guess. For his right hemisphere, which has the correct memory, and with its auditory inputs intact, recognizes the error in the speech coming from his left hemisphere; but being disconnected from the speech mechanism, it cannot guide the selection of the answer which is already known. One can vaguely empathize with this phenomenon by appeal to the everyday experience of forgetting a word but having it on the tip of the tongue. As we guess wildly, or even if somebody else does the guessing, we are certain when the guess is incorrect and recognize the word (or name) immediately when it is correct. The concomitant "aha!" experience when the right answer pops up has all the ingredients of an emotional insight, of a déjà vu experience, including somehow having known the answer all along. So this experiment bridges the gap between neurology, psychodynamic defense mechanisms, and the psychopathology of everyday life. Much contemporary research on memory, amnesia, and aphasia flourishes in such borderlands. It is well to remember Freud's early book on aphasia and to speculate on the connection.

There is also evidence that certain patients with surgically disconnected hemispheres are capable of being embarrassed by lurid photos shown to the right hemisphere alone, but without being able to say why. These phenomena would seem to have profound implications for theories of cognition and of psychopathology.

3. A recent formulation of great interest contends that the identical basic mechanism of concept formation is inherent in such varied tasks as perfecting a golf stroke, comprehending the grammar of a sentence, experiencing depth in a perspective drawing, or grasping the symbolism of certain paintings. It is argued that there must be some such abstract mechanism underlying language use and all organized behavior. In this view, our linguistic capability is but a specialization of this basic capacity which happens to have been linked to a speech apparatus relatively late in evolutionary history. Thus language is "a cultural product subject to laws and principles that are partially unique to it, and partially reflections of general properties of mind" (Chomsky, 1968, p. 8). Let us think of the brain as a great transforming machine, continuously relating patterns of nerve impulses to abstract schemata which may be both innate and learned. It is this wired in transformational ability that makes it unnecessary to learn about everything we may encounter. For example, my son's puppy, an Irish Setter named "Sunshine," is designed with an inherited mechanism for vigorously shaking any object small enough to pick up but too big to swallow. She really does not need to kill the bedroom slipper, which is her customary victim, but I have no doubt that she would transfer this skill instantly to the first pigeon or pheasant she lays eyes on. (This was verified eight months later with a snake.) Dalmatian coach hounds do not have to be taught to stay out

from under the wheels of moving vehicles, and Collies will herd chickens, or even rubber balls, the first time they encounter them. In the same way, it is instructive to grasp a pencil in one's teeth and write one's name. I warrant you have never used your neck muscles to execute your signature before, but the abstract schema for your signature can be instantly transformed into a pattern of instructions to these muscles. And in spite of the poor penmanship, a graphologist could identify it as your signature. Indeed, it would be more surprising if it resembled someone else's rendition of your signature, since the brain must work with the schemata available to it. A final example of a motor transformation is one that delights young children who have just learned to print their names. Give them a piece of chalk in each hand and ask them to print their names on a blackboard, in a forward direction with the right hand and backwards with the left hand, both simulataneously. It is amazing how easily this mirror-image transformation is accomplished, and fairly obvious how it is facilitated by the bilateral symmetry of the body. I find it much more difficult to perform the reverse sequence when the forward sequence is not in progress. The latter is a well learned visual-kinesthetic pattern which is easily reversed as it unfolds.

In similar fashion, current theory holds that the understanding of the meaning of the sentence "Isn't John angry?" implicitly invokes transformations such as "John is not angry" and "John is angry," since these are part and parcel of understanding the sound pattern and framing a reply which the asker of the question will understand. In fact, the set of transformations that are applicable to a sentence, those meanings which it might have but does not, is one possible measure of the amount of semantic information (depth of meaning). That there is no natural language in which we can not ask questions, give directions, make assertions, tell about past events, and so on is evidence for the universality of this linguistic transformational capacity of the brain, as is the speed with which children pick up transformational rules and apply them to an infinite number of new events. Such skills require a creative mechanism, too complex to have been learned. Thus we have the notion of a universal grammar in all races of man. And since transformation is what the brain does as long as it is alive, there is no reason for it to stop when we deprive it of incoming messages; hence the phenomena of fantasy, reverie, and dreams, the activity of the brain when attention to the external environment is suspended. The latter phenomena exhibit the ultimate creative freedom of the transformational process when it is not necessary to make another person understand.

I am suggesting a certain compulsive (compulsory) quality about this concept-forming mechanism that underlies all behavior, linguistic and otherwise. For this is how our brains interpret the world, bringing order out of chaos. This compulsory quality is easily seen when two possible interpretations, that is, conflicting schemata, are applicable to the identical sensory pattern. Stare at Figure 17–2 for 30 seconds. It is the familiar Necker cube illusion. It has two stable configurations, each three dimensional, whereas attempting to view it as flat,

FIGURE 17–2
Necker Cube Illusion

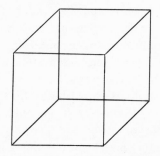

or two dimensional is less orderly and less stable. So we are forced to switch from one stable configuration to the other at intervals that are difficult to control. These intervals between reversals tend to become shorter on prolonged viewing. The overall effect is to reduce the many possible ways of viewing the pattern to just two.

Whereas the transformation just illustrated increases redundancy by reducing the number of alternatives and imposes order on contradictory patterns, others serve to introduce contradictions into previously orderly concepts. These serve to increase the depth of meaning by disruption of our familiar schemata and of our complacency. This information-generating type of transformation will be illustrated by several paintings which span the course of the surrealist style in the history of Western art.

Figure 17–3 is by the forerunner Hieronymus Bosch (1450–1516) and is a detail from his triptych of "The Last Judgment." Apart from the diabolical and macabre symbols, note the transformation of scale in the kitchen knife being straddled by a person, in the human body protruding from another person's mouth. This favorite device of the surrealists, arbitrary violation of our familiar constancies and expectancies regarding size, shape, superposition, and co-occurrence are themselves part of the message. Yet this aspect of the symbolism is much harder to discuss, is essentially nonverbal, by comparison to the obvious literary depiction of "the damned" in this painting.

Turning now to René Magritte (1898–1967) we have some very clear examples of transformations that disrupt our customary schemata. Figure 17–4 is entitled "The Fair Captive" and, in addition to the incongruous burning tuba symbol, illustrates his painting within a painting device, which abolishes the boundary between reality and rendition. This must be more than a trick since it appears in several of his works. Does it ask perhaps whether the painting is an extension of the landscape or the landscape an extension of the painting? In Figure 17–5, he offers us the choice of a rose expanding to fill a normal-sized room or a miniature room containing a normal-sized rose. The title "Tomb of the Wrestler," suggesting confinement within a small space, inclines me to the latter interpretation. If the rose symbolizes the wrestler it is indeed consistent with the whimsy and satire of many surrealist titles. Figure 17–6, entitled "Mme. Récamier," is one of Magritte's coffin paintings (in another he depicts multiple seated coffins in a theater) and is an obvious takeoff on David's portrait of this famous beauty. The incongruity yet inseparability of life and death is expressed in a single surprising symbol, which has, perhaps, universal overtones from cultures where burial postures are more active and lifelike than in our own. Figure 17–7, entitled "Castle of the Pyrenees," simply abolishes the law of gravity and perhaps allegorically questions the sturdiness and permanence of the foundations of power.

My final illustration represents contemporary abstract surrealism, and here the artist makes us work a bit harder, as in the painting entitled "Lovescape" by Nora Jaffe (1928–) shown in Figure 17–8. Here multiple transformations of the human body yield a complex series of rearrangements each of which is a new kinesthetic experience. In her own words:

Most of my work is based on human anatomy which has been distorted or displaced . . . to intensify the feeling of the human form, not to negate it

FIGURE 17-3
Detail from Triptych of "The Last Judgment" *by Hieronymus Bosch.*
Municipal Art Gallery, Bruges.

FIGURE 17-4

"The Fair Captive" *by René Magritte. Collection Brooks Jackson, New York.*

FIGURE 17-5

"Tomb of the Wrestlers" *by René Magritte. Collection Harry Torczyner, New York.*

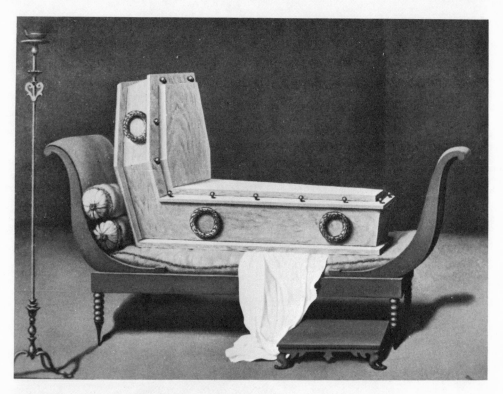

FIGURE 17-6
"Perspective: Mme. Récamier"
by René Magritte. Alexander
Iolas Gallery, New York.

FIGURE 17-7
"Castle of the Pyrenees"
by René Magritte. Collection
Harry Torczyner, New York.

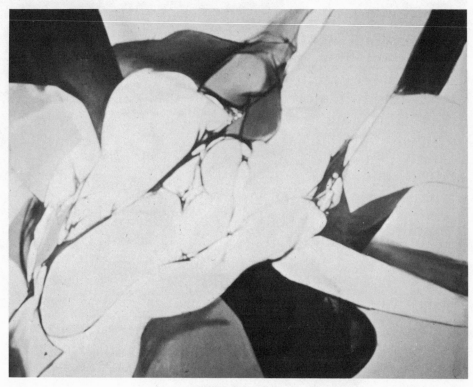

FIGURE 17-8
"Lovescape" *by Nora Jaffe. The Pennsylvania Academy of Fine Arts.*

Structural Foundations of Linguistic Behavior

. . . my attempts at distortion or displacement came from a very early interest in surrealism, where a knee can at the same time be an elbow, be any other joint of the body . . . I feel that this kind of manipulation, which is in a sense psychological in that you are using the spectator's mind as well as your own to perform the transformation, that this kind of simultaneous being several things at once is a more intense experience of the human anatomy than if a knee were simply a knee.

I should mention that most complicated of all transformations, namely, putting oneself in the place of the other person, taking the other's point of view. Topologically, this is imaginable. The person I confront is not my familiar mirror image, whose right side is on my right. Indeed, his right side is on my left. To put myself physically in his place as he confronts me is to translate my location to his, and to rotate 180° around my vertical axis when I arrive. However, attempting to assume his attitudes, his feelings, and so forth, are exceedingly complicated transformations to specify, and yet valid ones with which we must operate daily.

Notions such as collective unconscious are quite believable when rephrased in these terms. I have mentioned a universal grammar, common to all languages beneath their varying surface forms. Part of this grammar may be a universal semantic, with categories such as the actor and acted upon, animate and inanimate, subject and predicate, which presumably would be discovered by any developing organism without its being taught. If these distinctions are intrinsic functions of the brain, their origins go back much further than the history of natural languages, which are accidents of random variations, migrations, geographical isolation, and territoriality. We may be certain that all humans share a basic set of existential concerns, that is, birth, life, death, love, combat, fear of the elements, and so on which are common to the animal kingdom. So given comparable symbolic machinery adapted to interpersonal communication about these basic concerns, it would not be surprising to discover universal themes in the content of unrelated languages, handled by universal formal mechanisms. The common denominator is the human brain and its evolution, and in this respect we really are more simply human than otherwise.

Thus, innate determinants of linguistic capacity offer a point of articulation for concepts such as collective unconscious and the universality of myths. But as mental health professionals, we are certain to ask, "Do such biologic factors suggest any principles for overcoming communication barriers?" We have seen that the loss of ability for new language learning comes with brain maturation in teenagers. If this phenomenon teaches us anything, it is:

1. Rely upon the children for communication across linguistic boundaries. For true intercultural penetration, do not trust anyone more than eighteen years old.

2. For the adults, rely on all those message systems that lie closest to linguistic and biological universals; athletics (the Olympics); the visual arts such as painting, sculpture, and the film; rhythm generally and the dance and poetry in particular; music, food, sex, population control, shelter, clothing, control of the elements (for example, the weather, oceans, nuclear energy, outer space)—these are the universal biological languages and concerns of man that lose little in translation. Of course, all these have been discovered by UNESCO, but the discursive political debates in the UN indicate what UNESCO is up against. The common denominator seems to be the nonverbal modes of communication which are roughly similar throughout the human species.

But the biological approach suggests another set of languages that are culture free in that they are purely formal and abstract. These are the languages of mathematics, formal logic, and computer languages, which transcend cultural and class barriers and which can be practically implemented by scientific exchange. In short, I feel we must get both closer to and further from "the gut" in order to overcome barriers to communication which, at present, seem part of the human condition.

REFERENCE

Chomsky, Noam. *Columbia Forum*, Vol. 12, Part IV (1968). Pp. 16–23.

The Function of Myth
in Sickness and Health

There are two ways man has communicated through human history. One is by way of discursive language. This is specific, empirical, objective, tends toward mathematics in science, and eventuates in logic. The important criterion of this kind of communication is that the person who is speaking the words is irrelevant to the truth or falsehood of what he says.

The other way is myth. The myth is a story that begins in history but then takes on the special character of a way of orienting one's self to reality. The myth carries the values of the society and is the means by which the individual finds his sense of identity. The myth always moves toward totality rather than specificity. It transcends the antimonies of life, such as conscious and unconscious, historical and present, individual and social, and unites these in a drama, which is passed down from age to age. Whereas discursive language refers to an objective fact, the myth refers to the quintessence of human experience.

The myth, as Thomas Mann said, is an eternal truth in contrast to an empirical truth. It does not matter in the slightest whether a man named Adam ever actually existed; the myth about him in the book of Genesis presents a picture of the birth and development of human moral consciousness, which is true for all people of all ages and religions. Oedipus had been an archaic Greek tale, which in the hands of Homer took on the proportions of a myth, and in the pen of Sophocles became the myth of the hero who seeks his own reality. This is known in our day as the search for identity. The man who cried, "I must find out what and who I am," and then—like all of us—revolted against his own reality, stands not only for the Greeks but the everyman in his ambivalent struggle to find his identity. This myth, like most of the ancient Hebrew and Greek myths, transcends language, customs, and mores and becomes true for people of all cultures, which is the definition of a classic.[1] The great anthropologist at Yale, Malinowski, wrote, "Myth expresses, enhances, and codifies belief, safeguards and enforces morality, vouches for the efficiency of ritual, and contains practical rules for the guidance of man."

We cannot derive myth from language, or language from myth; nor can we explain one in terms of the other.[2] They develop in parallel fashion in primitive man and in man in all stages of history ever since. It was the fond hope of the nineteenth-century materialists, such as Max Muller, to explain myth away by saying "myth is but part of a more general phase through which all language has at one time or other passed." But language abandons myth only at the price of the loss of the human warmth, color, personal meaning, values. For we understand each other by identifying with the subjective meaning of the language of the other person, and experiencing what his words mean to him in his world. Without myth we listen like a race of brain-injured people, unable to go behind the word and hear the person speaking. There can be no stronger proof of the impoverishment of our culture than the popular, though profoundly mistaken, definition of myth as falsehood.

Language and myth need each other. Discursive language expresses man's perpetual need to objectify; myth expresses man's likewise perpetual need to exercise his creative imagination in giving meanings and values to experience. "Again and again," wrote Cassirer, "myth receives new life and wealth from language, as language does from myth. And this constant interaction and interpenetration attests the unity of the mental principle from which both are sprung, and of which they are simply different expressions. . . ."

The myths enable us to negotiate the crises of life—the crisis of birth in the myths underlying baptism, the crisis of puberty in the myths underlying confirmation and Bar Mitzvah, and so on through marriage, profession, up to and including death itself. Funerals and the myth of immortality may seem to be mockeries to most of us, but they are the deteriorated expression of a once sound and noble effort to give meaning to death.

Freud himself was ambivalent on the subject of myth. On one side he appreciated the value and power of myth, in addition to his using the Greek classic myths tellingly in his theory. In 1932 he wrote to Einstein, "It may perhaps seem to you as though our theories are a kind of mythology, and in the present case not even an agreeable one.

The Function of Myth in Sickness and Health

But does not every science come in the end to a kind of mythology like this? Cannot the same be said for your own physics?" But Freud also thought and spoke out of an alienated age. Wedded to nine-teenth-century Helmholtzian materialism, he struggled, though unsuc-cessfully, to formulate the motives of human behavior in physiological terms. One result of this is that he did not appreciate the positive side of myth. He saw that the myth disguises the truth, but he did not see that the myth also discloses new truth. He lacked Cassirer's insight, "Man lives with objects only in so far as he lives with these *forms;* he reveals reality to himself, and himself to reality, in that he lets himself and the environment enter into this plastic medium, in which the two do not merely make contact, but fuse with each other."

Ernest Hemingway is an example of a man whose life was given meaning by the myth of potency. He lived out the tough man in his hunting big game, in his creative writing, and in sexual potency, which was a real problem for him. When he lost these, when he could no longer write or hunt and was sexually impotent, he acted out the myth of potency in its logical conclusion in the one act left to a man, suicide, which rounded out existence like a Greek tragedy.

The process of myth-forming is essential to mental health. Since myth is man's way of constructing interpretations of reality that carry the values he sees in a way of life, and since it is through myth that he gets his sense of identity, a society that disparages myth is bound to be one in which mental disorientation is relatively widespread. I propose the following hypothesis: When a culture is moving toward integration and unity, it has a system of symbols and myths that give integration to the members of the society, and people then are rela-tively free from psychological breakdown. But when a culture is in process of disintegration, it loses first of all its myths and symbols. This loss predicts the disintegration of one culture as a whole. People then experience psychological distress and loss of identity. These are the periods when people come in large numbers to seek help by psy-chotherapy and the therapeutic-like professions.

I shall illustrate this hypothesis by referring to two cultures, the an-cient Greek and our own. In the classical phase of ancient Greek cul-ture, Aeschylus reinterpreted the myths—as is the function of men of literature—to fit the newly emerging self-conscious Greek citizen. His trilogy, the *Oresteia*, is a prime example of the myth of moral freedom and responsibility in the face of determinism. In this classical phase,

337

the myths and symbols were always susceptible to enlargement and reinterpretation but still retained their character as the carrier of the values of the society and the individual's sense of identity.

Socrates, who lived at the end of this splendid century, rationalized the myths to some extent. But he always kept their center beyond rationalization, the basis of both rational and transrational experience. Thus he could say in his *Apologia* to the court at Athens when he was sentenced to death, "I do believe in the gods, and in a sense higher than my accusers do."

In this classical period when the myths and symbols were strong, it is almost impossible to find signs of specific anxiety, alienation and lack of orienting values. Pericles, in his oration to the wives and children of the soldiers slain in the Peloponnesian war, discusses death not as a source of dread and anxiety but only as an objective fact that a man meets willingly because he is an Athenian. Indeed, it is almost impossible to find the word "anxiety" in the fifth-century literature. We cannot escape the conclusion that in this time the normal processes of drama, philosophy, science, and religion, all brought together by the myths of the day, lent the Greek citizens the integration they needed and gave them armor against inner conflict and loneliness. Psychotherapy was thus not necessary.

But in the succeeding Hellenistic period, during the third and second centuries B.C., we find anxiety, inner doubts, and psychological conflict rampant in the literature. Lucretius looked back on his master, Epicurus, in this third century and wrote a description which could almost be a description of the Great Society in our own day:

Epicurus saw that, practically speaking, all that was wanted to meet men's vital needs was already at their disposal, and . . . their livelihood was assured. He saw some men in full enjoyment of riches and reputation, dignity and authority, and happy in the fair fame of their children. Yet, for all that, he found aching hearts in every home, racked incessantly by pangs the mind was powerless to assuage and forced to vent themselves in recalcitrant repining.

He went on:

Men feel plainly enough within their minds a heavy burden, whose weight depresses them. [They] lead a life as we now see all too commonly—no one knowing what he really wants and everyone forever trying to get away from where he is, as though mere locomotion could throw off the load. . . . In so doing the individual is really running away from himself.

338

The Function of Myth in Sickness and Health

Lucretius then argued that the myths are groundless, unaware that the loss of the myths is connected with the very evil he decries. People should be free from the "unfounded fear of the gods." "There is no wretched Tantalus," he proclaimed, "as the myth relates. . . ." "Sisyphus too [is not a divine figure but] is alive for all to see, bent on winning the insignia of office. As for the Furies and the pitchy darkness and jaws of Hell belching abominable fumes, these are not and cannot be anywhere at all. . . ." There is no Prometheus anymore, for the "Agent by which fire was first brought down to earth and made available to mortal man was lightning."

Lucretius treated the myths as though his readers believed them to refer to real objects located in some part of the heavens (which it is impossible to imagine Aeschylus believing). Then he psychologized the myths: They are merely projections, that is, figurative, imaginative expressions of subjective processes from within the individual. He was here arguing what every intelligent man knows, that the myth does indeed have one pole in the subjective dynamics of the individual's experience. But this half-truth omits all the vast implications of the myth as man's way of trying to make sense of, and come to terms with, the objective world, the fact that man does live in a finite universe in which the phenomenon of Sisyphus is objectively present for the normal as well as for the morbidly anxious man. The fate of every workman who toils over and over again at the same job "is no less absurd than Sisyphus," wrote Camus. We are all engaged in eternal going and returning, laboring and resting and laboring again, growing and disintegrating and growing again. The myth of Sisyphus is present in every heartbeat, every moment of metabolism. It is only by meeting the myth on the level of meaningful fate that we escape meaningless fatalism.

Now this Hellenistic period was also the period in which every philosopher's and teacher's lecture room began to be "conceived as a dispensary for sick-souls." No longer were the philosophers interested in searching for truth and being, as had been Plato and the earlier Greeks, but rather in how a man controls his emotions, lives with some peace in an inwardly chaotic world, and finds security in times of isolation and anxiety. Now psychotherapists proliferated on all sides—good or bad as they may be—to teach the alienated Greeks how to live in an affluent but a lonely and mythless age.

I propose that our contemporary period is parallel to the Hellenistic period in ancient Greece and that we, too, suffer from the disintegration of myths and symbols. The symbols and myths that lent unity to the Renaissance and our classical seventeenth century, myths based chiefly on individualism and rationalism, have disintegrated and been replaced by various forms of collectivism and technical reason. We have our myths of the machine, but human values languish.

Our own period is always harder to see clearly, and I have to simplify greatly. Nevertheless, I cite one myth that did give values to American society for a couple of centuries, the myth of the frontier. This was a myth that emphasized individual self-reliance, individual strength, courage to draw your gun at an instant's notice, capacity for hard work and effort, honesty, and so forth. The positive side of this myth is personified in the characteristics of Abraham Lincoln; some of the trailing power of this myth rubbed off on such figures as Adlai Stevenson. This myth gave meaning and dignity to Americans' lives as they participated in the westward expansion. But during the late nineteenth century this myth spawned the Horatio Alger myth, the myth that success would attend anyone's hard effort and honesty, be he farmer in Wyoming or German worker from Bavaria or Jewish merchant from Russia landing at the Statue of Liberty.

The myth of the frontier, as well as its child, the Horatio Alger myth, has now become confused and self-contradictory. Its demise was marked by Arthur Miller's play *Death of a Salesman*. At the grave where Willie Loman is being buried in this play, Arthur Miller has the younger son, as a typical expression of the myth, say, "He had a good goal, to be number one." But the older son shakes his head and answers, "He never knew who he was." This accurately describes the situation that obtains whenever the myths by which a man has lived disintegrate.

That our age is characterized by the disintegration of myths and symbols is shown on all sides. Kenneth Kenniston concluded in *The Uncommitted* that one cause of the alienation of young people is the bankruptcy of the positive myths in our society. We now covertly believe in the "myth of a mythless society," which is a counsel of despair. Jerome Bruner, also noting this fact, wrote, "When the myths of a period are not adequate to man's predicament, the individual first takes refuge in mythoclasm, and then undertakes the lonely quest for inner identity." The other aspect of this situation is the proliferation in our day, as in the Hellenistic period, of all kinds of psychotherapy;

people come begging therapists, the carriers of the new mantle of a science of how to live, to give them help.

I do not mean to make the disintegration of symbols and myths the cause of our present predicament. They are rather the critical expression of the culture, and their demise is the surest sign of disunity and trouble in the members of the society. We do not make myths or symbols; we rather experience them, mainly unconsciously as the source of the images of the charter of the culture, such as the values, the goals, and the identity. By becoming conscious of the process we can, however, mold our myths and symbols. Marshall McLuhan sees the movement toward a new mythology: "We actually live mythically and integrally, but we continue to think in the old fragmented space and time pattern of the pre-electric age. . . . For myth is always a montage or transparency comprising several external spaces and times in a single image or situation."

A myth functions to preserve mental health. I take the following example from Hannah Green's account of her treatment by Frieda Fromm-Reichmann in *I Never Promised You a Rose Garden*. This schizophrenic young woman patient had a highly developed mythology into which she retreated whenever life was too difficult, and thus prevented further breakdown. Her mythology consisted of various gods and spirits of another world with whom she talked. The mythology made possible some health but at the price of breaking down the communication between herself and others.

In treating this young woman, Dr. Fromm-Reichmann dealt with the mythology with respect. She availed herself of it in the treatment process, making such remarks to Hannah Green as, "Tell those gods of yours that they have a worthy adversary in me." In contrast, the substitute therapist who took charge of the patient while Fromm-Reichmann was away attacked the mythology directly, with disastrous results. Fromm-Reichmann's aim was to help the patient see that (1) she herself controlled the mythologizing; (2) within limits she could form it as she chose; and (3) it was part of the richness of her imagination and her interpretation of her world.

But it would be an error to conclude that the mythology is simply a private system, what we mean when we speak of "purely imaginative." What needs to be appreciated is the endeavor in the patient's mythology to make some sense of an objective world, to live in it, and so far as possible to bridge the gap between his or her distorted self and the world. No matter how irrational the mythology may seem to us, it has within it a genuine endeavor to preserve the patient's existence in the objective world. The aim of therapy ought to be not to rationalize or dry up the mythologizing process, but to make it less compulsive, to free the patient to use it constructively, and to help him to experience the myths he molds as bridges between him and his fellowmen as well as ways of interpreting his human experience.

I have argued that the myths and symbols express the meaningful unity of society, and give the society a system of values. The myths are discovered by us as our heritage as we develop individually, but each individual must take his own stand with regard to them: attacking them, affirming them, molding them, or lamenting their absence. The social and individual factors in experience fuse at the point of myth. It is in the myths we find our intentionality or, as in our day, our lack of it. The underlying function of psychotherapy is the indirect reinterpretation and remolding of the patient's symbols and myths.

NOTES

1. There is a universal structure of the human being, as Dr. Jaffe has pointed out, and thus we have myths that are universal. These are the myths that have to do with experiences everyman goes through, such as birth and death, and are formed from universal material, such as fire, water, air and earth.

2. See *Myth and Language*, by Ernest Cassirer, for a sound demonstration of this truth.

Toward a Theory of Literary Psychology

I would like to define, insofar as I can, the scope of literary psychology (I call it that in the interest of brevity). We know that literature has been helpful in extending the knowledge of psychoanalysis; a large body of work, beginning with Freud, testifies to this. We are less sure of the extent to which psychoanalysis can extend our knowledge of literature. And we need to determine the common ground between the two disciplines. In this, we must recognize that it is always difficult to bring two disciplines together. A reading of popular books about psychoanalysis does not make a literary man into a psychoanalyst. Nor does the practice of psychoanalysis automatically bestow literary wisdom. Geoffrey Gorer (1966) put this very well:

> Psychoanalysts, by reason of their training and study, are uniquely qualified to understand, analyse, and assist the patient on the couch; but as soon as they move away from this personal confrontation . . . to comment on matters outside of their training and experience, the value of their comments would appear to depend on their knowledge and wisdom, not their qualifications.

We could adapt this to literary critics and literary biographers as well.

I

I speak of a theory of literary psychology because in the interdisciplinary process the intrusion of diagnosis and therapeutic systems into the study of literature, and the often clumsy attempts of literary men to play at psychoanalysis, in imitation of the clinical writings of members of the analytic profession, have created a great deal of confusion. The literary critics and biographers often have had no training in psychoanalytic method, and only a few of them have been exposed to psychoanalysis. They are often like the old-time candidates in your field who used to describe their analysis as didactic, as if to say:

"Make no mistake about it. There's nothing wrong with us. After all, we're doctors and we can't be neurotics as well. We're just learning a little dissection, dream dissection." Literary men, and also historians, reflect the same attitude when they read a few volumes of Freud and Jung, and some of Erikson, and announce themselves equipped to use psychology on the sensitive materials of mind and spirit. Dr. William L. Langer (1958) in his appeal to historians to use psychoanalysis, "a doctrine that strikes so close to the heart of our own discipline," urged his younger colleagues to seek special training at psychoanalytic institutes; but I suspect some of them continue to believe that an historian can bring his problems to an analyst and get his immediate answers as if he were consulting a dictionary or a gazetteer. Confusions of this sort, failures to grasp the complexity of psychoanalysis and the complexity of the literary act, have hindered our progress.

A great part of this has been the difficulty of communication between the disciplines. We know that Freud was a healer who was also a humanist, a man trained in scientific method who was not content to search his personal inner world and that of his patients, to simply record and analyze his observations. He was a literary man, who knew how to express himself with clarity and with style. His curiosity, his imagination, his ready use of example and literary allusion, make him an admirable expositor of ideas. Freud the scientist and Freud the humanist were one. We all know how he used myth to illustrate his teachings and that he wrote papers not only on literature but on the plastic arts. These studies, which came to be called "applied psychoanalysis," that is, psychological observation and the techniques Freud developed, were applied to such subjects as Michelangelo's Moses or the life of Leonardo da Vinci, subjects that could not be brought to the Freudian couch but could be studied at his desk. In all his observations and speculations, he used literature and art as adjuncts to his nonliterary process. The literary and plastic arts offered him examples, cases, illustrations. As one of his critics (Rieff, 1959, p. 121) remarked, the literary work, the work of art, was to Freud "a museum piece of the unconscious, an occasion to contemplate the unconscious frozen into one of its possible gestures."

This is not to say that Freud's writings (1950) on nonclinical subjects do not reflect insights of criticism and of biography. They contain within them however the fundamental shortcoming that they are the pronouncements of a white-coated doctor, in a laboratory or an office, on matters not requiring doctoring. This was perhaps as it should be. His writings set an example and yet imposed a limitation for those to whom a poem is a poem and not a case history, a work of literary art and not a monologue delivered in the consulting room by a patient. And then Freud tended sometimes to generalize broadly. He was often ready to see an ocean in a drop of water. We know for instance that in his essay on Leonardo (1957) there exists a fundamental error that in effect invalidates all his brilliant conjectures. James Strachey (1957) told us about this in a brief preface in the *Standard Edition*. Freud confused a vulture with a kite in Leonardo's memory of his childhood. The Italian text distinctly describes the bird Leonardo remembered as a kite. Freud, using a German translation, was provided with the bird as a vulture instead. He then related it to the Egyptian vulture-headed mother goddess Mut, so that, says Strachey, "Freud's theory that the bird of Leonardo's fantasy stood for his mother cannot claim direct support from the Egyptian myth." The essay on Leonardo may be likened to the work of a sculptor who, finding a headless statue, reimagines and reconstructs the head that might have belonged to that statue. The enterprise is courageous, but we can never know whether it is really the same head. The laws of probability are against such a coincidence. All that the new head proves, if it is well wrought, is the sculptor's skill and virtuosity. Of course artists since time immemorial have guessed the unseen from the seen. As Henry James (1956) put it, they are capable of tracing, when they are men of genius, the implication of things. They can judge "the whole piece by the pattern." Theirs is "the condition of feeling life in general so completely that you are well on the way to knowing any particular corner of it." This is true of the artist, the novelist, the poet. Sometimes it is true of those diagnosticians who recognize a disease by a remote symptom. But as a rule science is not satisfied with this kind of induction and deduction. It welcomes intuition; it recognizes the profound insight but it also always demands proof.

In his papers in applied psychology, Freud is always the great doctor looking at literature. And literature is turned by him into an interesting patient. To it he applied his new system of therapy, insofar as it could be applied. But in the process something was neglected: the simple fact that a great work of art defies definition on the strength of a few observations and the discovery of a few symptoms or character-

istics. Freud recognized this when he backed away from any suggestion that he could fathom the secret of creation. The creative process,
the literary process, the critical process, has an integrity that one violates only at grave risk. A simple lyric of a dozen lines seems a tiny
thing; sometimes it is composed of fewer than fifty words. Yet the
words have been written down not only by a hand moving a pen, or
by fingers pressing typewriter keys, but by a physical being possess-
ing nerve impulses to direct the hand and the fingers, which belong
to the body, and to the remoter mind, to an imagination and a cognitive process, which in turn belongs to an heredity and an environment. A vast body of inner learning stands behind the fifty words
emerging from that pen or typewriter. McLuhan's (1964) insistence on
man's inability to use words save in a linear fashion is a distortion of
fact; the words are linear in print, but the thought behind them has
not been linear, and the word by word, line by line record expresses
in reality a host of intricate simultaneities of experience, including
the simultaneities of the senses. Otherwise stated, the brief lyric contains within it more biography and human history than we can ever
know. It is an emanation from an extraordinary totality. Involved in
the creative act are the stages of infancy, childhood, youth, not
merely the period of the poet's toilet training or some incident of infantile libido. I am reminded of the ideas we heard expounded so lu-
cidly by Dr. Guntrip (1968) in his lectures on object relation theory: [1]
the sense he gave us of an individual whose inner world contains
within it a host of object relations and relationships, and all that such
relations mean, out of his earliest time. We must not be satisfied, as
Dr. Guntrip said, with anything less than "a philosophy of man that
takes account of his reality as an individual person." The essence of
this stands as a warning against the fragmentation of the individual
in the analytic process. So I would warn against the fragmentation of
the work of art when the analytic process is applied to it.

II

I am not suggesting that we should sweep Freud's literary essays
into the wastebasket. They are works of art in themselves. His intentions are always clear, and even when his conclusions may be faulted,
he offers us a display of the reasoning inductive side of the mind, a

mind arraying its total awareness of observed realities. There have been, however, followers who have imitated him blindly and who, as I had occasion once to remark, have spent their time snorkeling around the iceberg (in Freud's image of the unconscious) to see what was below the level of the water, forgetting the brilliant shining mass arrayed above the water line. What is more, the writings of some of these imitators, reflecting the fervor of converts but none of the imagination of their master, have nevertheless been accepted by the lay public without question because they are the words of healers. What they say acquires authority from this fact.

I think I cannot do better than to offer, in illustration of the theoretical suggestions I wish to elaborate today, an example of this kind of self-assurance in paths where angels fear to tread. As you know there exists an annual called the *Psychoanalytic Study of the Child.* It has appeared for the past twenty-five years. It has a distinguished and responsible editorial board. Over the years it has published much material by many authoritative members of the psychoanalytic movement. I suppose it was inevitable that it should sooner or later stray into the fields of literature, and into the work of Henry James, given his tales dealing with childhood and the psychology of children. In 1962 there was published in this annual what was called a causerie, a chat, on "The Turn of the Screw," James's celebrated ghost story. Its author was Dr. Maurice Katan, a psychoanalyst who had delivered the causerie to a group of pediatricians at University Hospitals in Cleveland. Then four years later, in 1966, he returned to this subject, in the same publication, in a long defensive article, which suggests that he had received much criticism in the interval. The second article was titled "The Origin of 'The Turn of the Screw.'" And he subtitled it as a study in "pathobiography." In the first paragraphs of his second article he himself tells us what his intention was, and what he thinks he accomplished. Here is how this article begins (Katan, 1966, p. 583).

Several years have elapsed since I wrote my "Causerie" (1962). I had received a request to discuss "The Turn of the Screw." Not only the book but also the author himself was unknown to me. I accepted the challenge and, with no further information to guide me, arrived at the conclusion that the story was a description of a crucial phase of James's oedipal development. The analysis did not offer much difficulty, and the result was an elaborate construction, containing James's traumatic infantile experiences and their influence upon his later development.

347

At the end of my "causerie" I promised to examine James's autobiography in order to obtain corroboration of my interpretations.

In order to delineate the extent of this task, I shall review my construction, which covers a number of successive phases. First, there were primal scene observations by the young Henry James and another sibling. The witnessing of these scenes had aroused the children to such a degree that sexual play resulted between them. Next, their mother got the notion that something very undesirable was going on between the two, and she tried to force the truth out of the children. This action had a deleterious effect upon the children as well as upon her husband.

No one reading these interpretations and then reading "The Turn of the Screw" would believe that this story was being discussed. There is no husband in the story. There is no sexual play—the boy is ten and his sister is eight—the "mother" is actually their governess; there are no primal scenes; and all this is told by the doctor as if it happened in the life of Henry James and not in the tale which he wrote. Since the analyst confesses that he had never before heard of the story or of its author it is clear that we are being offered some rather wide speculation, or what we might call "instant" analysis. His scientific method has been, by his own admission, to analyze a story without reference to any historical or other data. But he promises to do some homework. He will study James's autobiography in order to find corroboration of his assumptions.

I will for a moment ignore the literary and scientific attitude that this reveals: for I am tolerably certain (or at least I hope) that the doctor would not treat a patient in such an offhand way. To interpret a dream without associational material is at best a hypothetical exercise; yet the doctor boasts of his ignorance of the associational material. And what has he discovered when he tells us that he has unveiled a crucial phase of James's oedipal development and smoked out primal scene memories? What does "oedipal" mean in this context? What can it tell us about James that particularly characterizes him as an individual and explains the atmosphere of brooding horror he has created in his story, an atmosphere of horror that has caused many to speak of this as the greatest of all ghost stories. What relevance does "primal scene" have, especially in dealing with an artist who spent his infancy in a nursery, in a separate part of the house as was customary with well-to-do families in those days. Are we to assume that the parents displaced themselves from their bedroom to the nursery to provide primal scenes for their children? What a way, in any event, to deal with the creative spirit, with that "philosophy of man that takes account of his reality as an individual person." "The Turn of the Screw" is a story told by an immature governess of twenty, placed in charge of two children. Most persons take the governess at her word, and indeed forget that it is her story, her version of the events. They accept her word that the children are evil. She describes how the children try to communicate with ghosts and that these ghosts seek to corrupt them. James, in his uncanny grasp of the nature of paranoid fantasy, at no time commits himself. When we look back we discover that the ghosts were seen only by the governess, that the tale in reality describes a young woman frightened by her own imaginings, who in turn imposes this fright on the children. That is the extra "turn of the screw," the twist of pain given by the story. No discussion of the story can ignore the governess, her hysteria, her hallucinations, her behavior toward the children. The great question is the credibility of her narrative, and everything she tells us undermines her credibility.

From the first the analyst in his causerie reads the story as if James were his patient. The approach is diagnostic and therapeutic, but since it is just a story, he allows himself large liberties he would not otherwise take. "We find ourselves," he says, "in the same position as at the beginning of an analysis." This is a large assumption. Rare indeed the patient who offers a finished work of art at the first interview, though often he may be very artful. In his paper the analyst decides promptly that James must have had nightmares as a boy, a tolerably safe assumption from the evidence of developmental studies. He sees the governess as a mother figure; the little girl is designated a sibling; the little boy is supposed to be Henry James, presumably in latency. I will speak of this in due course. Then later the doctor switches to the hypothesis that the governess is actually playing the role of therapist to the children. If so we can record that she had little success with her young patients. In the last terrible scene between the governess and the boy, the child dies of fright, and a little earlier, in a scene with the little girl, the governess rolls on the ground and has a moment of amnesia. The little girl understandably becomes hysterical.

Surveying what the analyst has written, I would reproach him less for ignoring the historical material than for his failure to read certain other stories by James. He has been content to stay with one fantasy even while others were available. James at this moment wrote a series of tales about children. He was then in his middle fifties. The children and young adults in this significant series,[2] with the exception of the little boy in the ghost story, are all girls. Indeed the governess may have to be scrapped as mother-figure and considered as possibly belonging to one phase in James's development, and the little so-called female sibling may very well be another phase of James's development, when he was an eight-year-old, curious about the world, and defending himself against his male sibling by assuming the guise of a little girl. Finally, further research would show that three young boys, about whom James wrote stories half a dozen years before this phase, all met with the same end as the boy in the ghost story. In a word, in James's tales little boys die, whereas the little girls survive. James himself wondered about this when he reread his own work. He first offered the explanation that he had focused on young girls because they were more sensitive. Then he paused. He suddenly had to recognize a truth about his writings. The girls may have been sensitive but they were also tougher than his boys. They endured. He did not go further. But as we look closely at these data, and other abundant evidence, a picture does emerge, that masculinity had certain dangers for Henry James.

There is so much data available that one can speculate that James's return to childhood memories at this phase of his life, that is, in middle age, may have represented a significant regression in the service of his ego. But that is a subject for another essay. Suffice it to say that very rich material has been overlooked by the writer of these two essays on "The Turn of the Screw." He preferred instead to do what Freud (1957), in a paper describing an instance of a priori judgment of a given case, called "wild psychoanalysis."

"The Turn of the Screw" can be discussed by itself, simply as a story, and its inner psychology, the interpersonal relations developed within it, the behavior of the children, all this can be profitably examined. But the moment an attempt is made to read the life of the man who wrote it in the story's data, all the methodology of criticism and biography, and much of the discipline of psychoanalysis, must come into play. Otherwise we have unprofitable speculation, not to speak of fragmentation.

In his second article the doctor began by saying "I have been faced with the necessity of providing confirmation of my conclusion." He now reads the first chapter of James's (1913) autobiography, *A Small Boy and Others,* in order to obtain as he said, corroboration. Seek and ye shall find (Katan, p. 598).

This is a remarkable chapter. Superficially it might seem to be the haphazard chatter of an old man. Upon closer acquaintance with this material, however, this first impression vanishes. As we peer beneath the surface of this first chapter, we see it could very well have been the first analysis hour of a patient who is telling the analyst about his childhood. It is not an orderly summing up of a series of events, in the fashion of realistic thinking, but the rambling words of a patient who in his first hour—in conveying an important part of his life—is already letting himself be guided by free association.

The therapeutic system has again entered into play, and in this instance in a wholly fictional way. The doctor makes a large assumption, that the opening pages of James's autobiography can be read as free association because they seem to ramble. However, these pages may have been rewritten and revised any number of times before the book was published. In any event, can he be certain that James, facing him in a first interview, would bring him these data in this very order? Can he be sure that a writer of James's long practice, who thinks through his sentences down to the last comma, is not telescoping on the printed page much raw material that might be available to an analyst if he were speaking, rather than writing? And would there not be an enormous difference in the interpersonal fact: James writing for an audience is one thing; James talking to an analyst is another. I overlook for the moment the whole matter of autobiography, which is seldom as confessional as it sounds; it is usually an artful evocation of a self-concept. We can sometimes find out much more about writers in their fictions than in their autobiographical accounts of themselves. But I have said enough to suggest that the meeting of our two disciplines is not a matter for frivolous games. The doctor sensed his dangers, for he remarked at the start of his second article (Katan, 1966, pp. 584–585): "If one is sensitive to criticism one should never publish a paper of the type of my *causerie.* To conceive of a novel as a dreamlike fantasy pertaining to the personal past of the author is to risk one's reputation. When one has the audacity to continue with an analysis of the story, it is practically synonymous with sacrificing one's head." He is right. One allows for his audacity; one is quite ready to leave him his head; but one wishes he had allowed himself a little interdisciplinary theory in the margin of his Freudian guesswork.

It is palpably wrong to speak of a literary work as a dreamlike fantasy. A literary work contains within it much more than dream or fantasy. Art is not primary process; a great deal must intervene. The literary work contains many verbal voices out of the past and is itself contained in a form and a structure; between the original conception or dream and its finished state (at a hundred removes from the unconscious) have been interposed layers of language and metaphor. If the doctor had wished to use the dreamlike fantasy of James's story he should have looked for it in James's notebooks where the first idea, the initial dreaming-up, is recorded. That is closer to dream and fantasy, and mainly it describes a sense of the uncanny. James will write of the terrible things that happen to children as a result of ghosts trying to gain possession of them. The character of the governess at this first stage has not been conceived. She does not figure in the original fantasy.

I have dwelt on these two papers because they were given the authority of an authoritative publication. They offered me also illustrative material with which I happen to be familiar, and what they illustrate is a lack of method and an anarchic treatment of a work of literary art.

The two papers I have described failed wholly to recognize that "The Turn of the Screw" contained within it James's life development rather than an account of his so-called oedipal phase. It contained within it many stages and experiences of James's childhood and youth, that is, the circumstances that molded his personality and his art. This can be confirmed by studying the ways in which experiences of a similar sort appear and reappear in his other works. A philosophy of man, a science of man, cannot be arrived at within a closed system. Nor can it be studied without scrupulous observance of scientific logic.

In the interest of that logic, I will offer the following as a tentative definition of literary psychology:

1. Literary psychology is concerned with man's myth-making and symbol-creating imagination and his unremitting effort to find language and form to express these myths.

2. Literary psychology can be used in the study of the structure and content of a literary work, the imagination that has given it form

and pattern, the fantasy that it embodies, the modes of human behavior it describes—in the light of what we know of the unconscious and the integrative functions of the personality.

3. The integrity of the literary work as a creative outcome of a personality must be recognized, as distinct from the biography of the personality, though both may be studied in pursuit of creative process.

4. Therapeutic systems are largely irrelevant in literary psychology.

These points I think incorporate the essence of the matter. I would suggest that since literature is a record of the subjective and imaginative life we must always remember that the characters in a fiction or a play are not figures in real life, not subjects for case histories. They are the Rosencrantzes and Guildensterns who possess the limited dimensions with which they were endowed by their creator. They become real only in the minds of the reader or spectator, and only at the moments seen or read. Any attempt to treat them as subjects for a couch runs the risk of countertransference, or projection, on the part of reader or spectator.

Above all, let us remember that a literary work contains within it a great part of the creator's being, not stray fragments of it. Thoreau understood this when he said "Poetry is a piece of very private history, which unostentatiously lets us into the secret of a man's life." Balzac understood this when he wrote: "An artist himself does not know the secrets of his own mind. . . . He does not belong to himself. . . . On some days he does not write a line, and if he attempts to, it is not he who holds the pen but his double, his other self."

Literary psychology goes in quest of that double, and of the secrets within the work itself. Thus by the psychological study of literature, the horizons of both our disciplines are immeasurably widened; we penetrate deeply into the hidden realities of protean creation, and all this in our common pursuit of man as an entire being, his reality as an individual person.

NOTES

1. See also Guntrip (1961).

2. James's novels and tales in the series comprise *The Other House* (1896), *What Maisie Knew* (1897), "The Turn of the Screw" (1898), "In the Cage" (1898) and *The Awkward Age* (1899). The tales dealing with male children and

young male adults are "The Author of 'Beltraffio' " (1884), in *Complete Tales of Henry James* (ed. Edel) V: "The Pupil" (1891) VII, and "Owen Wingrave" (1892) IX.

REFERENCES

Edel, Leon, ed. *Complete Tales of Henry James*. Philadelphia: Lippincott, 1962.

Freud, Sigmund. *Collected Papers*. New York: Basic Books, 1950. "Wild Psychoanalysis," *Standard Edition*, Vol. 11. London: Hogarth, 1957. Pp. 221–227. "Leonardo da Vinci," *Standard Edition*, Vol. 11. London: Hogarth, 1957. Pp. 63–137.

Gorer, Geoffrey. "Psychoanalysis in the World." In Charles Rycroft, ed., *Psychoanalysis Observed*. New York: Coward-McCann, 1966. Pp. 23–50.

Guntrip, Harry. *Personality Structure and Human Interaction*. New York: International Universities Press, 1961.

———. *Psychoanalytic Theory, Therapy, and the Self*. New York: Basic Books, 1971.

James, Henry. "The Art of Fiction." In Leon Edel, ed., *The Future of the Novel*. New York: Vintage Paperbacks, 1956. Pp. 12–13.

———. *A Small Boy and Others*. New York: Scribner, 1913.

Katan, Maurice. "A Causerie on Henry James's 'The Turn of the Screw.' " *Psychoanalytic Study of the Child*, 17. New York: International Universities Press, 1962. Pp. 473–493.

———. "The Origin of 'The Turn of the Screw.' " *Psychoanalytic Study of the Child*, 21. New York: International Universities Press, 1966. Pp. 583–635.

Langer, William L. "The Next Assignment." *American Historical Review* 43, 1958. Pp. 283–304.

McLuhan, Marshall. *Understanding Media*. New York: McGraw-Hill, 1964.

Rieff, Philip. *Freud: The Mind of the Moralist*. New York: Harper, 1959.

Strachey, James. "Introduction to 'Leonardo da Vinci.' " In *Standard Edition of the Complete Psychological Works of Sigmund Freud*. Vol. 11. London: Hogarth, 1957. Pp. 59–62.

Index

Index

69; frigidity in 191; and learning disability, 264-273; logical processes in, 174, 175; origins of, 264, 269

Id, the, 64n, 81, 142; Freud's concept of, 96
Identity, 132, 133; crisis of, 303; identification process in gifted children, 177; and myths, 335
Infancy, 50, 64n; anxiety during, 29-34; congenital differences in, 3; contact comfort during, 19-20, 59, 251; dependency during, 17-18; deprivation of play during, 34; development of perceptual systems, 4, 52-54; development of relations with mother during, 17-34; experience of infant, 55-59; father's relation to infant, 25, 253; feeding experience during, 9; Freud on, 17-18; interaction between mother and infant, 3-4, 20, 22, 23, 29, 31, 32, 33, 34, 140-141, 153; and origins of attitude of attention, 16, 41, 51-59; other, development of concept of, 26; play during, 23-25, 35; sense of self, development of, 26, 32; sleep during, 71-72; smiling as infant response to stimuli, 21-23, 30, 31, 59; socialization during, 253-254
Information theory, 154; affinity to interpersonal theory, 133-134, 136; and self-system, 143
Inhelder, Bärbel, 170, 178n
Inhibition, 183, 184, 233; of women, 197, 214
Instinct, 325
Interdisciplinary work: need for, in science, 62; need for, on therapy, 145
Interpersonal relations, 6, 120, 230, 254, 275-276; ecological point of view on, 134-137; integration with intrapsychic in psychoanalytic theory, 120; and obsessive personality, 182, 185-187, 188-190, 192, 193; in origins of psychopathology, 121-131, 137; problems in, 299; in psychoanalytic process, 6, 7, 8, 9, 10, 11, 17, 26-27, 102, 109, 134, 136, 139, 141-142, 160-166, 216, 230, 235-256; and self-system, 143; and sexuality, 214-215. See also Psychoanalyst, relationship with patient; Psychoanalytic patient, relationships with analyst; Psychoanalysis, process of inter-

action between patient and analyst
Interpersonal theory, 88, 132-146; anxiety in, 138-139, 143-144; ecological principle in, 134-136; self-system in, 142; and shortcomings of ecological model, 136-137; similarity principle in, 139-140; and Sullivan, 109, 132-133, 134-137
Interpretation, 7, 102, 109; and intellectualization, 176
Introspection, 325
Isomorphism, 149, 159-166
Isaacs, Susan, 70

Jackson, Douglas N., 63n, 65n
Jacobi, Jolan, 64n, 65n
Jaffe, Joseph, 306, 308, 311, 316, 319n, 323, 325-333, 342n
Jaffe, Nora, 332
Jahoda, Marie, 277, 295n
James, Henry, 166, 345, 347, 353-354; psychoanalytic interpretation of, 347-352
James, William, 41, 65n, 70, 107
Johnson, Donald M., 170, 179n
Johnson, Virginia E., 201, 213, 217n
Johnson, W., 307, 319n
Johnston, Johanna, 198, 217n
Jones, Richard, 159, 167n
Jung, Karl, 16, 64, 65n; concept of predominance of functions, 56-57; followers of, 108; and Freud, 93, 95; patients of, 161; theories of, 108

Kafka, Franz, 156
Kagan, Jerome, 64n, 65n
Kant, Immanuel, 115
Katan, Maurice, 347, 354n
Keene, Geraldine C., 20
Kelley, G. A., 299, 319n
Keniston, Kenneth, 340
Kleeman, James A., on playful activity in infants, 35n, 38n
Klein, George S., 63n, 65n; concept of cognitive controls, 42
Klein, Melanie, 38n; on children's play, 70, 80
Koffler, F., 21, 39n
Kohler, William C., 72, 83n
Kohn, Martin, 272, 273, 274n
Korner, Annelisee, 83n
Kramer, Lore S., 274n
Kris, Ernst, 64n, 65n
Kriszat, Georg, 55, 66n
Kuhn, Thomas, 153, 167n

Index

Index

Index

THE GREAT
SCIENCE FICTION
PICTURES
II

by
JAMES ROBERT PARISH
and
MICHAEL R. PITTS

The Scarecrow Press, Inc.
Metuchen, N.J., & London
1990

Also available from Scarecrow Press:

The Great Science Fiction Pictures (1977), by James R. Parish and Michael R. Pitts

British Library Cataloguing-in-Publication data available

Library of Congress Cataloging-in-Publication Data

Parish, James Robert.
    The great science fiction pictures II / by James Robert Parish &
    Michael R. Pitts.
        p.   cm.
    ISBN 0-8108-2247-4 (alk. paper)
    1. Science fiction films—Catalogs.   I. Pitts, Michael R.
    II. Title.
PN1995.9.S26P38   1990   89-24058
016.79143′656—dc20

Dedicated to the memory of

ED CONNOR (1918-1987)

a film historian and enthusiast for all the ages

CONTENTS

v

ACKNOWLEDGMENTS

John Cocchi

Howard Davis

Film Favorites (Bob Smith, Charles Smith)

George F. Geltzer

Alvin H. Marill

Lee Mattson

Doug McClelland

Jim Meyer

Peter Miglierini

Vincent Terrace

Dr. Ray White

Special Editorial Consultant: T. Allan Taylor

INTRODUCTION

THE GREAT SCIENCE FICTION PICTURES II is our fourth volume, expanding the initial Scarecrow Press book group we did in the 1970s in our series. As noted in the other books the word "Great" in the title refers to the film genre and not to all the movies discussed in the text.

Science fiction motion pictures have probably proliferated more in recent years than any other type of film. Since our Base Volume was published in 1977 there has been a plethora of releases; in fact, the book came out prior to the great commercial acceptance of science fiction pictures with STAR WARS, E.T., CLOSE EN-COUNTERS OF THE THIRD KIND and their megabucks ilk. Thus many of the big blockbusters are here as well as many other types of genre features, including domestic and foreign releases, serials, and TV movies.

In the process of including as many relevant features as we could, we have endeavored to look at a variety of movies, with the main emphasis being on the numerous releases since the publication of our Base Volume. We have supplemented these films with vintage releases, from the early silent era through the 1940s; added films which we were unable to include in the first book, and tried to incorporate as many of the features issued in the last decade as possible. Here, however, we realize some films just simply could not be encompassed if we were to have a rounded coverage of science fiction movies from the genre's beginnings.

Perhaps we should also briefly touch on our criteria for including films and our definition of science fiction pictures. First, as with the other genres covered in our books, we have taken a broad view of science fiction movies and have included those dealing directly with futuristic events as well as those which go back in time or have prehistoric events, animals or characters involved in present day activity. Basically, if a film has something to do with science that is even a bit "beyond" what is accepted contemporary fact, we felt it could be included in the text. We realize there is a very thin line between science fiction, horror and fantasy films, and, in many cases, they overlap. For example, in our Base Volume we did just an essay on the "Frankenstein" films rather than cover them individually, but in this book we look at the films separately. Even though "Frankenstein" is a horror series, its basis is steeped in science gone awry.

In the same vein it should be registered that quite a few of the vintage films we included are no longer considered science fiction because science has caught up with, and surpassed them. We have included several such titles, however, because in their day they were futuristic and deserve to be noted as such.

Finally, a word on our use of the term "science fiction." Purists claim only the words "science fiction" should be used and not "sci-fi" or "sf" or other abbreviations. Since these terms have gained general acceptance in the last few years, however, we have utilized them at times in discussing assorted films. There are so many types of science fiction movies that we do not feel such terminology dilutes their value.

As with the other volumes in the series we welcome comments, additions and corrections. With the ongoing popularity of science fiction movies there no doubt will be plenty more to cover, plus those left out in our first volume, so we hope to be back with you in the not too distant future with THE GREAT SCIENCE FICTION PICTURES III. Until then—"May the Force be with you!"

James Robert Parish
Michael R. Pitts

GREAT SCIENCE FICTION PICTURES II

ABBOTT AND COSTELLO MEET DR. JEKYLL AND MR.
HYDE (Universal, 1953) 77 mins.
Producer, Howard Christie; director, Charles Lamont; suggested by the novel *Dr. Jekyll and Mr. Hyde* by Robert Louis Stevenson; story, Sidney Fields, Grant Garrett; screenplay, Leo Loeb, John Grant; art directors, Bernard Herzbrun, Eric Osborn; music director, Joseph Gershenson; makeup, Bud Westmore; special effects, David S. Horsley; camera, George Robinson; editor, Russell Schoengarth.

Bud Abbott (Slim); Lou Costello (Tubby); Boris Karloff (Dr. Jekyll/Mr. Hyde); Craig Stevens (Bruce Adams); Helen Westcott (Vicky Edwards); John Dierkes (Batley); Reginald Denny (Inspector); Eddie Parker (Stunts for Mr. Hyde); Patti McKaye, Lucille Lamarr (Can-Can Dancers); Carmen de Lavallade (Javanese); Henry Corden (Javanese Actor); Marjorie Bennett (Militant Woman); Harry Cording (Rough Man); Arthur Gould-Porter (Bartender); Clyde Cook, John Rogers (Drunks); Herbert Deans (Victim); Judith Brian (Woman on Bicycle); Gil Perkins (Man on Bicycle); Hilda Plowright (Nursemaid); Keith Hitchcock (Jailer); Donald Kerr (Chimney Sweep); Clive Morgan, Tony Marshe, Michael Hadlow (Bobbies).

In gaslight London, deranged Dr. Jekyll (Boris Karloff) is engaged in brain transplants on animals and he also develops a serum which turns him into murderous Mr. Hyde (Karloff) who kills the scientists who have ridiculed his work. Jekyll is in love with pretty Vicky Edwards (Helen Westcott), his ward and an advocate of women's rights. During a rally for the latter she is jailed along with reporter Bruce Adams (Craig Stevens), and bumbling American policemen Slim (Bud Abbott) and Tubby (Lou Costello) who are in London to learn British police methods. Jekyll bails out Vicky and Bruce while the police inspector (Reginald Denny) dismisses the Americans. Jekyll plans to kill Bruce but the boys capture him and put him behind bars when he is in the guise of Hyde. Thinking they will be reinstated, the American law enforcers bring the Inspector on the scene, but it is now Jekyll who is in the cell. The doctor plots to kill Tubby and hires the Yankee duo as his bodyguards, whereupon Tubby accidentally drinks a dose of the doctor's serum and turns into a huge mouse. When Vicky informs Jekyll she is going to wed Bruce, the physician transforms into Hyde and attempts to murder her. However, Bruce saves her, then Tubby sits on a syringe accidentally and becomes a monster. He chases Hyde across London

1

with the doctor falling from a high wall to his death. Slim captures Tubby, who returns to Scotland Yard only to bite the Inspector and a policeman, turning them into monsters.

Abbott and Costello had first been teamed with Boris Karloff in 1949 in ABBOTT AND COSTELLO MEET THE KILLER, BORIS KARLOFF. This new entry continued the duo's celluloid meeting with various "classical" monsters and it proved to be a solid box-office success, although cinematically it was far from one the series' best. Stuntman/actor Edwin (Eddie) Parker performed most of the action Hyde sequences, but most of the pacing and humor drags. Boris Karloff is effective as Jekyll, but the film provides none of the entertainment value of ABBOTT AND COSTELLO MEET FRANKENSTEIN (q.v.).

Reviews of this film, however, were surprisingly affirmative. *The Motion Picture Herald* stated the teaming of Abbott and Costello with Boris Karloff results in a motion picture which "provides some pleasing nonsense and horror," while the *British Kinematograph Weekly* wrote, "Excellent schizophrenic lark, dressed to kill but fundamentally innocuous." In *Classic Movie Monsters* (1978), Donald F. Glut judged it ". . . one of Abbott and Costello's funnier and more atmospheric horror film parodies."

ABBOTT AND COSTELLO MEET FRANKENSTEIN (Universal, 1948) 82 mins.

Producer, Robert Arthur; director, Charles T. Barton; suggested by characters created by Mary Shelley and Bram Stoker; screenplay, Robert Lees, Frederic I. Rinaldo, John Grant; art directors, Bernard Herzbrun, Hilyard Brown; set decorators, Russell A. Gausman, Oliver Emert; costumes, Grace Houston; makeup, Bud Westmore; music, Frank Skinner; orchestrator, David Tamkin; assistant director, Joseph E. Kenny; sound, Leslie I. Carey, Robert Pritchard; special effects, David S. Horsley, Jerome H. Ash; camera, Charles Van Enger; editor, Frank Gross.

Bud Abbott (Chick Young); Lou Costello (Wilbur Grey); Lon Chaney (Lawrence Talbot, the Wolf Man); Bela Lugosi (Count Dracula); Glenn Strange (Frankenstein's Monster); Lenore Aubert (Sandra Mornay); Jane Randolph (Joan Raymond); Frank Ferguson (Mr. McDougal); Charles Bradstreet (Dr. Stevens); Vincent Price (Voice of the Invisible Man); Harry Brown (Photographer); Paul Stader (Sergeant); Joe Kirk, George Barton, Carl Sklover, Joe Walls (Men); Howard Negley (Mr. Harris).

Screen comedians Bud Abbott and Lou Costello were in need of a good vehicle to rejuvenate their sagging box-office appeal, when Universal concocted the script which would pair them with

Frankenstein, Dracula, and the Wolf Man; all monsters whose film rights were owned by the studio. The result is a top notch film satire which still holds up quite well. Jim Mulholland observed in *The Abbott and Costello Book* (1975) that this motion picture ". . . is the best satire on horror movies ever made. . . . They [producer Robert Arthur and director Charles Barton] fashioned a film that adroitly blends the elements of humor and horror. The production is enhanced by stunning visual effects. Charles Van Enger's photography is first-rate and so is Frank Skinner's eerie musical score. The sets are superb." Made on an $800,000 budget, the film was a joyful finale to the studio's classic monster picture series which began with DRACULA (1931).

Florida shipping clerks Chick Young (Bud Abbott) and Wilbur Grey (Lou Costello) are assigned two crates to deliver to McDougal's House of Horrors, not aware that the boxes contain Count Dracula (Bela Lugosi) and Frankenstein's monster (Glenn Strange). Wilbur gets a call from Lawrence Talbot (Lon Chaney) warning them not to open the crates, but Wilbur does not heed the warning when pretty

Bud Abbott and Lon Chaney in ABBOTT AND COSTELLO MEET FRANKEN-STEIN (1948).

Sandra Mornay (Lenore Aubert) arrives, pretending to be in love with him. Actually she is a cohort of Dracula who is trying to get Wilbur's brain for the monster who has become too intelligent. The boys deliver the boxes to the museum and Dracula revives the monster. The two creatures leave before the owner (Frank Ferguson) appears. He has the delivery men arrested for stealing the crates' contents, but lovely Joan Raymond (Jane Randolph), who is an insurance investigator seeking missing museum exhibits, bails them out of jail. Talbot, actually the Wolf Man, takes a room at the boys' boarding house and convinces them that Dracula is out to revive the monster for his own nefarious ends. In the meantime, Sandra invites the duo to a masquerade ball and they stop at Dracula's castle to get her and the vampire who is posing as a research scientist. Chick and Wilbur accidentally find out the monster is hidden there, but end up accused of murdering the museum owner after the wolfman attacks him. Chased by a mob into the swamp, Dracula finds them and takes them back to his castle where he plans to place Wilbur's brain in the monster's head. Chick and Talbot come to his rescue and a fight ensues as Talbot turns into the Wolf Man and carries Dracula (in bat form) into the sea with him. The boys escape in a motor boat and the monster is entrapped in a pier fire started by Dracula's none-too-bright associate (Charles Bradstreet). Thinking they are now safe, the boys are nonplussed to discover their vessel also contains the Invisible Man (voice of Vincent Price). The adventure is not over. . . .

ABBOTT AND COSTELLO MEET FRANKENSTEIN is so good because it is both funny and horrific in well-proportioned doses; greatly enhanced by the casting of horror film stars Lon Chaney, Bela Lugosi, and Glenn Strange in their traditional monster assignments. The picture's commercial success resulted in several additional encounters for Bud and Lou with the horror and sci-fi genres: ABBOTT AND COSTELLO MEET THE KILLER, BORIS KARLOFF (1949), AFRICA SCREAMS (1949), ABBOTT AND COSTELLO MEET THE INVISIBLE MAN (1951) [q.v.], JACK AND THE BEANSTALK (1952), ABBOTT AND COSTELLO GO TO MARS (1953) [see: B/V], ABBOTT AND COSTELLO MEET DR. JEKYLL AND MR. HYDE (1954) [q.v.], ABBOTT AND COSTELLO MEET THE MUMMY (1955), and Lou's solo in THE THIRTY FOOT BRIDE OF CANDY ROCK (1959).

ABBOTT AND COSTELLO MEET THE INVISIBLE MAN (Universal, 1951) 82 mins.

Producer, Howard Christie; director, Charles Lamont; suggested by the novel *The Invisible Man* by H. G. Wells; story, Hugh

Wedlock, Jr., Howard Snyder; screenplay, Robert Lees, Frederic I. Rinaldo, John Grant; art directors, Bernard Herzbrun, Richard Riedel; music director, Joseph Gershenson; song, Frederick Herbert, Milton Rosen and Gershenson; makeup, Bud Westmore; special effects, David S. Horsley; camera, George Robinson; editor, Virgil Vogel.

Bud Abbott (Bud Alexander); Lou Costello (Lou Francis); Nancy Guild (Helen Gray); Arthur Franz (Tommy Nelson); Adele Jergens (Boots Marsden); Sheldon Leonard (Morgan); William Frawley (Detective Roberts); Gavin Muir (Dr. Philip Gray); Sam Balter (Radio Announcer); John Day (Rocky Hanlon); Syd Saylor (Waiter); Bobby Barber (Sneaky); Billy Wayne (Rooney); George J. Lewis (Torpedo); Frankie Van (Referee); Carl Sklover (Lou's Handler); Charles Perry (Rocky's Handler); Paul Maxey (Dr. Turner); Edward Gargan (Milt); Herbert Vigran (Stillwell); Ralph Dunn (Motorcycle Cop); Harold Goodwin (Bartender); Richard Bartell (Bald-Headed Man); Perc Launders (Cop); Edith Sheets (Nurse); Milt Bronson (Ring Announcer).

At the finale of ABBOTT AND COSTELLO MEET FRANKENSTEIN in 1948 [*supra*], the comedians have a brief encounter with the Invisible Man (voice of Vincent Price). The entanglement becomes full-blown in this amusing spoof which also interpolates gangsters and the fight racket into its merry plot.

Bumbling detectives Bud Alexander (Bud Abbott) and Lou Francis (Lou Costello) are hired by boxer Tommy Nelson (Arthur Franz) to help him prove his innocence in the murder of his manager. He takes them to the home of his friend, Dr. Philip Gray (Gavin Muir), who has been trying to perfect an invisibility serum he has inherited. He injects Tommy with the drug so he can elude the law, but it is discovered that the dosage could turn him into a madman. Tommy's girlfriend Helen Gray (Nancy Guild) tells the boys the murder was actually committed by gangster Morgan (Sheldon Leonard) because Tommy would not take a dive in a bout. To prove his innocence Tommy has Lou pose as a fighter with the invisible Tommy fighting alongside him in the ring. They plan to catch Morgan fixing the fight, thus leading to his arrest. Morgan signs Costello to a bout and orders him to take a dive. However, on the night of the match Gray, fearing for Tommy's sanity, locks him in his room. However, the boxer escapes in time to win the fight for Lou who has been taking a severe beating. Morgan and his thugs try to kill Abbott, and Tommy stops them. During the melee that follows, the gangsters are arrested.

This sci-fi takeoff is a fast-moving adventure and the comedians are well supported by an excellent cast. *Variety* noted the

". . . . team's stock double takes and bewhiskered gags are still fulsome, but the hackneyed quips achieve a new gloss in this entry." In *The Abbott and Costello Book* (1975), Jim Mulholland calls the feature " . . . a pleasant surprise. Many of the verbal gags misfire but the slapstick is often ingenious." Genre fans should note the photo of Claude Rains on the wall of Dr. Gray's laboratory, since it was Rains whose character first developed the invisibility formula in the classic THE INVISIBLE MAN in 1933 [see B/V].

THE ABERDEEN EXPERIMENT   see   SCARED TO DEATH.

THE ABOMINABLE SNOWMAN (OF THE HIMALAYAS) (Twentieth Century-Fox, 1957) 91 mins.

Executive producer, Michael Carreras; producer, Aubrey Baring; director, Val Guest; based on the teleplay *The Creature* by Nigel Kneale; screenplay, Kneale; production designer, Bernard Robinson; art director, Ted Marshall; makeup, Phil Leakey; music, John Hollingsworth; camera, Arthur Grant; editor, Bill Lenny.

Forrest Tucker (Tom Friend); Peter Cushing (Dr. John Rollason); Maureen Connell (Helen Rollason); Richard Wattis (Peter Fox); Robert Brown (Ed Shelley); Michael Brill (Andrew McNell); Arnold Marle (Lhama); Wolfe Morris (Kusang).

Yeti, the Abominable Snowman of the Himalayas, like America's Bigfoot, is a part of folklore which falls between science *fact* and science *fiction*. Many claim the creature is pure fantasy while others believe in its existence and that it is possibly "the missing link" between mankind and simian creatures. Whatever the truth, Yeti has certainly captured the imaginations of readers and moviegoers and has been the subject of several films, most notably THE SNOW CREATURE (1954), MAN BEAST (1956) [qq.v.], and this Hammer Films production, for Twentieth Century-Fox. The movie was based on Nigel Kneale's television script, "The Creature" and is said not to be as good as its source. Kneale also authored the TV scripts in the "Quatermass" series which were filmed as: THE CREEPING UNKNOWN, ENEMY FROM SPACE, and 20 MILLION YEARS TO EARTH [see: B/V].

The poster blurbs for THE ABOMINABLE SNOWMAN exclaim: "We Dare You To See It Alone! Each chilling moment a shock-test for your shock-endurance!" The title creature was described as "Demon-Prowler of Mountain Shadows . . . Dreaded Man-Beast of Tibet . . . The Terror of All That is Human!!" The story has botanist Dr. John Rollason (Peter Cushing) going to Tibet with an expedition hoping to find and capture the legendary Abominable Snowman. He joins forces with American Tom Friend (Forrest

Peter Cushing in THE ABOMINABLE SNOWMAN (1957).

Tucker) not knowing he has plans to exploit a captured Yeti. Friend manages to kill one of the creatures and they prepare to take the giant manlike being back to civilization but incidents occur in the hostile terrain which convince Rollason that they are being stalked by creatures with high intelligence. After Rollason and Friend have a falling out, the latter is killed by an avalanche and Rollason is left alone with the Yeti corpse. He takes refuge in a cave where he is confronted by one of the creatures and he realizes they only want to be left alone. Rollason returns to civilization without the dead being he had corralled.

Director Val Guest told Philip Nutman in an interview in *Fangoria* magazine (November, 1985), "I didn't like it, even then. If the budget had been larger and we'd had the opportunity to go and make it on location it would have been a far better picture. We were tied by the lack of money and the limited locations we could create in the studio. It wasn't sufficiently convincing. For that sort of film the budget was totally inadequate."

The film, with its Himalayan sequences shot in the French Pyrenees, is, however, a more than competent thriller with enough eerie suspense to sustain its storyline, heightened by the terror of the expedition being stalked by an unknown creature in hostile, snow-blown mountains. In addition, Peter Cushing and Forrest Tucker add to the trappings by their well-edged performances.

ADVENTURE UNLIMITED see WHITE PONGO.

THE ADVENTURES OF BUCKAROO BANZAI: ACROSS THE 8TH DIMENSION (Twentieth Century-Fox, 1984) C 103 mins.
Executive producer, Sidney Beckerman; producers, Neil Canton, W. D. Richter; associate producer, Dennis Jones; director, Richter; screenplay, Earl MacRauch; production designer, J. Michael Riva; art directors, Richard Carter, Stephen Dane; set designer, Virginia Randolph; set decorator, Linda De Scenna; music, Michael Boddicker; assistant directors, Gary Daigler, Katterli A. Frauenfelder; costume designer, Aggie Guerrard Rodgers; makeup supervisor, Bari Dreiband; stunt co-ordinator, M. James Arnett; assistant directors, Gary Dailer, Katterli A. Frauenfelder; sound designer, Bones Howe; special synthesized sound effects, Arne Schulze, Alan Howarth; electronic effects, Richard L. Thompson; electronic designer, Robin Dean Leyden; special visual effects supervisor, Michael Fink; visual effects co-ordinator, Linda Fleischer; animation visual effects supervisor, Peter Kuran; effects animator/designer for 8th Dimension sequence, John Van Vliet; visual effects, James Hegedorn, Beverly Bernacki, Colette Emanuel; matte paintings, Dream Quest Images; stop motion animator, Rick Heinrichs; miniatures supervisor, Mark Stetson; camera, Fred J. Koenekamp; editors, Richard Marks, George Bowers.
Peter Weller (Buckaroo Banzai); John Lithgow (Dr. Emilio Lizardo/Lord John Whorfin); Ellen Barkin (Penny Priddy); Jeff Goldblum (New Jersey); Christopher Lloyd (John Bigboote); Lewis Smith (Perfect Tommy); Rosalind Cash (John Emdall); Robert Ito (Professor Hikita); Pepe Serna (Reno Nevada); Ronald Lacey (President Widmark); Matt Clark (Secretary of Defense); Clancy Brown (Rawhide); William Traylor (General Catburd); Carl Lumbly (John Parker); Vincent Schiavelli (John O'Connor); Dan Hedaya (John Gomez); Mariclare Costello (Senator Cunningham); Bill Henderson (Casper Lindley); Damon Hines (Scooter Lindley); Billy Vera (Pinky Carruthers); Laura Harrington (Mrs. Johnson); Michael Santoro (Billy Travers); Kent Perkins (Mission Control); Jonathan Banks (Lizardo Hospital Guard); Robert Gray, Gary Bisig (Radar Blazes); Kenneth Magee (Duck Hunter Burt); James Keane (Duck Hunter Bubba); John David Ashton (Highway Patrolman); Yakov Smirnoff (National Security Adviser); Leonard Gaines (Artie Duncan); Francine Lembi (TV Anchorwoman); John Walter Davis (Star Surgeon); Red

THE ADVENTURES OF BUCKAROO BANZAI: ACROSS THE 8TH DIMEN-
SION (1984)

Morgan (Exhibitor); James Rosin (John Yaya); Raye Birk, Jane
Marla Robbins (Reporters); Kevin Sullivan (John Gant); Jessie
Lawrence Ferguson (Black Lectroid Commander); Radford Polinsky
(Marine Lieutenant); Sam Minsky, Robert Hummer (Kolodny Broth-
ers); Gerald Peterson (Rug Sucker).

   Buckaroo Banzai (Peter Weller), a noted Japanese-American
neurosurgeon/scientist/racing-car driver, is the leader of: 1) a band
of freedom fighters called the Hong Kong Cavaliers; 2) a group of
scientists; and 3) a rock star (Jeff Goldblum). While experimenting
in physics, Buckaroo and his futuristic vehicle are thrust through a
mountain into the eighth dimension where he discovers good-
intentioned aliens who want to stop a war between the United States
and the Soviet Union. At the same time, Buckaroo learns that evil
aliens have arrived on the scene to do battle with their counterparts:
all for control of the planet Earth. Lord John Whorfin, the leader of
the avaricious aliens, has taken over the body of a mad scientist, Dr.
Emilio Lizardo (John Lithgow), and plans to eliminate Lizardo with
the evil aliens taking over the bodies of earth people.

   Obviously, this high-tech, visually impressive feature (which its
director described as " . . . an outrageous comedy about a bunch of
guys in New Jersey") was to be the first in a series of films, since it
generated a mass merchandising campaign resulting in all kinds of

licensed paraphernalia, including: posters, toys, and various clothing items. However, THE ADVENTURES OF BUCKAROO BANZAI: ACROSS THE 8TH DIMENSION failed to generate the needed enthusiasm for moviegoers and no further madcap episodes of Buckaroo Banzai have been forthcoming.

Variety observed that the feature ". . . plays more like an experimental film than a Hollywood production aimed at a mass audience. It violates every rule of story-telling and narrative structure in creating a self-contained world of its own. . . . First-time director W. D. Richter and writer Earl MacRauch have created a comic book world full of references, images, pseudo scientific ideas and plain mumbo jumbo. It's half serious, half parody and half make believe [three halves!] with the parts adding up to more than the whole." Kim Newman commented in the British *Monthly Film Bulletin* that the film is ". . . . from the beginning to end, a non sequitur. Although it has inevitably found a small but devoted cult following in the States it was originally greeted with an overwhelming 'eh, what?' by audiences, and has several times failed to be released in Britain." Perhaps *TV Guide* summed up the film best when it decided, "Off-the-wall in concept, this wildly uninhibited 1984 adventure unabashedly mines the more sinister plot twists of such classic films as STAR WARS, DR. STRANGELOVE, and INVASION OF THE BODY SNATCHERS [see B/V for all three]. Some critics found the movie difficult to follow—and to swallow—but praised its genial wit and the imaginative production design of J. Michael Riva."

AELITA (Amkino, 1924) 120 mins.

Director, Yakov A. Protazanov; based on the novel by Alexei Tolstoy; screenplay, Fyodor Otzep, Alexei Faiko; art directors, Isaac Rabinoitch, Alexandra Exter, Viktor Simov, Sergei Kozlovski; camera, Yuri A. Scheljabuschsky, Emil Schunemann.

Yulia Solntseva (Aelita, Queen of Mars); Nikolai Batalov (Busev the Soldier); Nikolai Tseretelli (Los, the Inventor) Igor Illinsi (The Detective); Vera Orlova (The Servant Girl); and: Konstantin Eggert, Valentina Kuinzhi, Yuri Zavadsky.

Released in the United States in 1929 as REVOLT OF THE ROBOTS, this Soviet sci-fier is a visually captivating example of silent era cinematography and composition. Philip Strick noted in *Science Fiction Movies* (1976), "Full of zest and humour, and given bizarre perspectives by its expressionist sets, AELITA contains as much Flash Gordon as Tolstoy and deserves to be better known." The film was based on Alexei Tolstoy's novel (1922) with its expressionist sets created by Alexandra Exter of the Tairov Theatre.

John Baxter commented in *Science Fiction in the Cinema* (1970), "The design, with its strong compositions and startlingly grotesque costumes for the enslaved Martians, their heads bound in geometrical metal masks, obscured the fact Tolstoy's stories depended excessively on revolutionary doctrine for their impetus."

By inner-space camera, Aelita (Yulia Solntseva), the queen of Mars, observes Russian soldier Busev (Nikolai Batalov) and falls in love with him. When an eccentric inventor, Los (Nikolai Tseretelli) shoots his wife, he, Busev and a detective (Igor Illinsi) board the scientist's rocket ship and depart for the Red Planet. They land and Los romances Aelita while Busev is appalled at the conditions of the slaves on the planet. With the aid of a pretty servant girl (Vera Orlova), he causes a revolution which overthrows the existing power structure, turning the government over to the workers.

The Soviet Union was experimenting with sundry film genres in the mid-1920s in an attempt to use the cinema as propaganda for the Communist cause. Certainly AELITA is blatantly political but it also retains a naive charm bolstered by its outstanding visuals. Obviously the production cost a great deal of money and it is interesting that it should be made at a time when its homeland was just recovering from the horrendous 1921 famine. In the same year it was released, Josef Stalin ascended to power upon the death of V. I. Lenin. One wonders why the government chose to allocate the money necessary to produce this sci-fi propaganda opus when its budget might better have been spent feeding the hungry of Russia.

In his assessment of this film in *The Film Encyclopedia: Science Fiction* (1984), Phil Hardy noted, "As in so many of the Soviet silent films, the comedy is fast and well-timed, poking good-humoured fun at the more uncomfortable sides of life in their own country while enthusiastically parodying the West's 'decadent' aspects. . . . The next Soviet space opera was made over a decade later, the stodgy KOMITCHESKY REIS (1935)."

AIR HAWKS (Columbia, 1935) 68 mins.

Director, Albert Rogell; story, Ben Pivar; adaptors/screenplay, Griffin Jay, Grace Neville; camera, Harry Freulich; editor, Richard Cahoon.

Ralph Bellamy (Barry); Wiley Post (Himself); Tala Birell (Letty Lynn); Douglass Dumbrille (Arnold); Robert Allen (Lewis); Billie Seward (Mona); Victor Kilian (Tiny); Robert Middlemass (Drewen); Geneva Mitchell (Gertie); Wyrley Birch (Holden); Edward Van Sloan (Shulter); Bill Irving (Leon); C. Franklin Parker (Burbank); Peggy Terry (Blondie); Al Hill (Pete).

The Independent Air Lines, as well as other air operatives, are losing planes. Independent feels it is because of a mail contract sought by rival Arnold (Douglass Dumbrille). Government agent commander Barry (Ralph Bellamy) and news reporter pal Lewis (Robert Allen) find out planes are exploding in the air for no apparent reason. It develops that Arnold has hired mad scientist Shulter (Edward Van Sloan) to perfect a ray which causes the planes' engines to stop and then explode. Barry and Lewis bring Arnold to justice.

This programmer features famed pilot Wiley Post portraying himself in a small role. Post was killed in a plane crash with Will Rogers the same year this feature was issued. The film's only other entertaining angle is its sci-fi element involving a death ray.

The *New York Times* judged, "AIR HAWKS spends most of its time on the minor side of film entertainment. It belongs in the double-feature program, for which it has apparently been designed."

ALIEN (Twentieth Century-Fox, 1979) C 124 mins.

Executive producer, Ronald Shusett; producers, Gordon Carroll, David Giler, Walter Hill; director, Ridley Scott; screenplay, Dan O'Bannon; production designer, Michael Seymour; art directors, Les Dilley, Roger Christian; costumes, John Mollo; assistant director, Paul Ibbetson; music, Jerry Goldsmith; special effects, Brian Johnson, Nick Alider; camera, Derek Vanlint; editor, Terry Rawlings.

Tom Skerritt (Dallas); Sigourney Weaver (Ripley); Veronica Cartwright (Lambert); Harry Dean Stanton (Brett); John Hurt (Kane); Ian Holm (Ash); Yaphet Kotto (Parker).

The crew of the space freight ship *Nostromo,* led by Dallas (Tom Skerritt) and Ripley (Sigourney Weaver) are returning to Earth with cargo when they receive a signal from an unexplored planet. With orders to seek and bring back any alien life forms, they land and locate an ancient space craft. While exploring the catacombs beneath, one of the crew, Kane (John Hurt), is attacked by a mysterious being which penetrates his space helmet. He is brought back to the ship but kept quarantined as the thing stays sealed to his head. Suddenly the thing disappears and Kane is well again. After arguments between the various crew members, including Lambert (Veronica Cartwright), Ash (Ian Holm), Brett (Harry Dean Stanton), and Parker (Yaphet Kotto), Kane is allowed to rejoin the crew. However, during dinner he has a sudden attack and a reptile-like creature bursts forth from his stomach and takes refuge on the large ship. The crew wound the being, only to find it contains acid which nearly eats through the ship's hull. As the creature grows larger, the crew attempts to kill it, but finally all are destroyed except Ripley.

Tom Skeritt in ALIEN (1979).

She, along with the ship's cat, takes refuge in a space pod—only to discover the creature is there with them. Ripley places the cat in an air-tight container, puts on a space suit, and opens the pod door, releasing all the atmosphere in the vessel. The retreating air current sucks the alien into deep space.

Grossing $45,000,000 at the domestic box-office, ALIEN became a great favorite of sci-fi fans and a big merchandising campaign was built around the little seen (in the film) alien creature. Overall, the movie is a suspenseful affair, while obviously owing a great deal to IT! THE TERROR FROM BEYOND SPACE (1958) (see B/V). The alien's sudden attacks are the most exciting part of the film; its biggest letdown being the uninteresting, and somewhat grimy, characters who inhabit the cargo ship. Without likable people to cheer for, one's concern about the alien's activities is lessened, although the finale of Ripley (the most appealing character in the movie) having a battle of wits with the murderous creature is well-staged and exciting. Much was made by reviewers and social commentators about the emancipated, self-sufficient heroine being the unique pivotal character in the film, rather than a traditional brave, resourceful male. And the fact that this lead character was provocatively sexual and sensual gave the motion picture its special set of champions.

See: ALIENS.

ALIEN ENCOUNTERS see STARSHIP INVASIONS.

THE ALIEN ENCOUNTERS (Gold Key Entertainment, 1979) C 90 mins.

Producer, David E. Jackson; director/screenplay, James T. Flocker; music, William Loose; special effects, Becki Rosetti; camera, Holger Kasper; editor, Lawrence Ross.

Augie Tribuck (Allen Reed); Matt Boston (Steve Arlyn); Phil Catalli (Wally); Eugene Davis (Man in Black); and: Bonnie Henry, Patricia Hunt, Lukas Jackson, Chris Lee Jackson, Amy Dalton.

Set in desert country, this pseudo-speculation feature tells of a man Augie Tribuck (Allen Reed) who is trying to locate persons who have had encounters with alien beings. In investigating the disappearance of a scientist, he wins the trust of the man's teenage son (Matt Boston) and soon finds the man he is seeking, who actually has made contact with extraterrestrials. He and the boy try to re-establish this contact.

THE ALIEN ENCOUNTERS is a slow moving and poorly made docudrama which even manages to makes its intriguing premise seem flat. With the acting mediocre at best, the film examines such occurrences as: a haunted hotel, the death of a killer wolf— both blamed on aliens—along with the exploration of the Earth by UFOs. In its focus, the film becomes more of a sci-fi entry than the documentary film it pretends to be. Don Willis pinpointed the overall effects of the feature in *Horror and Science Fiction Films II* (1982) when he labeled it, "Unwitting minimal cinema."

ALIENS (Twentieth Century-Fox, 1986) C 137 mins.

Executive producers, Gordon Carroll, David Giler, Walter Hill; producer, Gale Anne Hurd; director, James Cameron; based on characters created by Dan O'Bannon, Ronald Shusett; story, Cameron, Giler; screenplay, Cameron; production designer, Peter Lamont; art director supervisor, Terence Ackland-Snow; conceptual designer, Ron Cobb; set decorator, Crispian Sallis; music, James Horner; additional synthesizer effects, Ian Underwood, Robert Garrett, Randall Frakes; orchestrator, Grieg McRitchie; music editors, Robin Clarke, Michael Clifford; costume designer, Emma Porteous; makeup supervisor, Peter Robb-King; stunt co-ordinator, Paul Weston; assistant directors, Derek Cracknell, Melvin Lind; visual effects camera, Harry Oakes, Leslie Dear; process camera, Charles Staffell, Roy Moores; video effects supervisor, Richard

Hewitt; certain special visual effects created by The L. A. Effects Group; visual effects supervisor, Robert Skotak, Dennis Skotak; special effects supervisor, John Richardson; original alien designer, H. R. Giger; alien effects creator, Stan Winston; mechanical armature designers, Doug Beswick, Phil Notaro; titles/video graphics designer, Tony White; supervising sound editor, Don Sharpe; camera, Adrian Biddle; editor, Ray Lovejoy.

Sigourney Weaver (Flight Officer Ripley); Carrie Henn (Rebecca Jorden [Newt]); Michael Biehn (Corporal Hicks); Paul Reiser (Carter J. Burke); Lance Henriksen (Bishop); Bill Paxton (Private Hudson); William Hope (Lieutenant Gorman); Jenette Goldstein (Private Vasquez); Al Matthews (Sergeant Apone); Mark Rolston (Private Drake); Ricco Ross (Private Frost); Colette Hiller (Corporal Ferro); Daniel Kash (Private Spunkmeyer); Cynthia Scott (Corporal Dietrich); Tip Tipping (Private Crowe); Trevor Steedman (Private Wierzbowski); Paul Maxwell (Van Leeuwen); Valerie Colgan (ECA Rep); Alan Polonsky (Insurance Man); Albie Parsons (Med Technician); Blain Fairman (Doctor); Barbara Coles (Cocooned Woman); Carl Toop (Alien Warrior); John Lees (Power Loader Operator).

Plans for a sequel to the commercial blockbuster ALIEN (q.v.) were formulated in 1983 but it required three years for the $15,000,000 project to be translated to the screen. The result, however, was a follow-up film that was superior to its original and which garnered an Academy Award nomination for star Sigourney Weaver and Oscars for Sound Effects and Visual Effects. As Judith Crist decided in *TV Guide,* "If you liked 1979's ALIEN, then you'll go ape for 1986's ALIENS, a terrific science-fiction thriller. . . ."

Warrant Officer Ripley (Sigourney Weaver) has drifted in space for fifty-seven years in a state of sleep and is unaged. She is rescued by a mining ship owned by the same company that had sent her first vessel, *Nostromo,* to the planet where the alien she finally killed had been discovered. Now that planet has been colonized but people have disappeared and this ship, commanded by Lieutenant Gorman (William Hope), along with android Bishop (Lance Henriksen) and company representative Carter J. Burke (Paul Reiser) is sent to investigate. Burke informs Ripley they plan to destroy the aliens and she agrees reluctantly to go along as a guide. On the planet they find only one survivor, a small, frightened girl named Newt (Carrie Henn). Deeper in the planet, troops led by Sergeant Apone (Al Matthews) fall prey to the aliens who have been using the bodies of the colonists as cocoons. In the fight, Gorman receives brain damage and Corporal Hicks (Michael Biehn) takes over the forces and plans to blow up the planet with a nuclear bomb. Their shuttle craft, however, is destroyed by the aliens and Bishop is sent to bring in the colonists' spaceship by radio. Ripley learns Burke intends to bring back specimens of the aliens, which was the reason for the mission in the first place. When the power in their quarters fails, the aliens attack the humans. The latter flee, but only wounded Hicks, Newt and Ripley survive. The little girl falls down a shaft and is captured by an alien, but Bishop returns to save Ripley and Hicks. Ripley arms herself and sets out to free Newt, whom she finds cocooned by the alien mother. She rescues Newt and joins Hicks and Bishop aboard the spacecraft just as the planet is detonated. It develops that the mother alien was attached to the escape shuttle craft and soon destroys Bishop. It attacks Ripley who, with the aid of a mechanical lifter, is able to toss the alien out of the craft and into deep space. The survivors return home.

John Pym wrote in the British *Monthly Film Bulletin,* "The creators of this efficient sequel have opted for a busier, less quirky formula: the plot is essentially unchanged . . . what the 's' in the title signals is that more is best." Dennis Fischer decided in *The Hollywood Reporter,* "The film suffers from a prolonged build-up which mistakes dragging things out for suspense, but after an initial encounter with the title character, [Director James] Cameron switches to high gear and reverts back to the relentless action and suspense approach that helped make THE TERMINATOR such a massive hit. Cameron isn't as concerned with scares or atmosphere, the staples of traditional horror films, as he is with setting up difficult situations for his characters to get out of, leaving audiences deliciously on edge." Comparing the sequel to its original, *Daily Variety* commented, "Technically, film is superior in all respects. Special effects are varied and always convincing, and behind-the-scene artisans have helped sustain the effective mood and tension all the way." Sheila Benson (*Los Angeles Times*) penned, "If the sequel doesn't equal ALIEN in cardiac-arrest value, it's only because stainless-steel teeth, repulsiveness and slime have gone about as far as they could go (with John Carpenter's 1982 THE THING [q.v.], then gone on to be a laughing matter in GHOSTBUSTERS. ('It *slimed* me' was Bill Murray's moan of nausea.). . . . Fortunately. . . . Cameron has shaped his film around the defiant intelligence and sensual athleticism of Weaver, and that's where ALIENS works best. In a funny way, she's become an image ripped from today's statistics: the Single Parent Triumphant—if not absolutely Rampant."

ALIENS grossed over $77,000,000 at the domestic box-office, and already ALIENS III and ALIENS IV are in the pre-production stage.

THE ALLIGATOR PEOPLE (Twentieth Century-Fox, 1959) 73 mins.

Producer, Jack Leewood; director, Roy Del Ruth; story, Orville H. Hampton, Charles O'Neal; screenplay, Hampton; music, Irving Gertz; art directors, Lyle R. Wheeler, John Mansbridge; sound, W. Donald Flick; camera, Karl Struss; editor, Harry Gerstad.

Beverly Garland (Jane Marvin); Bruce Bennett (Dr. Erik Lorimer); Lon Chaney (Mannon); George Macready (Dr. Mark Sinclair); Richard Crane (Paul Webster); Frieda Inescort (Mrs. Henry Hawthorne); Vince Townsend, Jr. (Toby); Ruby Goodwin (Lou Ann); Boyd Stockman (Paul's Double); John Merrick, Lee Warren (Nurses); Douglas Kennedy (Dr. Wayne McGregor); Bill Bradley (Patient); Dudley Dickerson (Porter); Hal K. Dawson (Conductor).

Two psychiatrists (Bruce Bennett, Douglas Kennedy) attempt to find out why nurse Jane Marvin (Beverly Garland) cannot remember a recent year in her life. They question her during hypnotherapy and record her responses as she relates about her marriage to Paul Webster (Richard Crane) and how he disappeared on their honeymoon. Through school records she traces his ancestry to the Louisiana bayous and goes there. She is met at a desolate train station by hook-handed Mannon (Lon Chaney) who has come to pick up radioactive material for his employers. She hitches a ride with him to a swampland plantation where her husband once lived. The owner, Mrs. Hawthorne (Frieda Inescort), insists she has never heard of Paul. Jane stays the night and wandering through the gloomy mansion finds the laboratory of Dr. Mark Sinclair (George Macready) who is experimenting on an alligator. Later she sees a fleeing man whom she recognizes as Paul. That evening she comes across him again and follows him into a storm and seeks sanctuary with Mannon who later tries to rape her. Paul stops him. She learns from Sinclair that he is working on experiments with reptiles in limb regeneration and that he has been attempting to help Paul who is becoming an alligator. That night Sinclair agrees to a final experiment on Paul, but Mannon arrives seeking revenge. In the scuffle, Paul turns into an alligator, Mannon is killed, and the house is set on fire. Paul dies fighting his own reptile kind. The two doctors agree not to tell Jane the truth about her story.

Despite its exploitation title and none-too-frightening alligator monster (played in most scenes by Boyd Stockman), THE ALLIGATOR PEOPLE is an atmospheric and entertaining sci-fi item. Karl Struss' steamy swampland cinematography is a real plus as is Roy Del Ruth's direction which keeps the film moving at a fast pace. George Macready is fine as the well-meaning, but inept scientist and Lon

Beverly Garland and Lon Chaney in THE ALLIGATOR PEOPLE (1959).

Chaney is a standout as the alligator-hating, hook-handed, filthy Mannon.

ANDROID (New World, 1982) C 80 mins.

Executive producers, Rupert Harvey, Barry Opper; producer, May Ann Fisher; associate producer, R. J. Kizor; director, Aaron Lipstadt; screen idea, Will Reigle; screenplay, James Reigle, Don Opper; music, Don Preston; art directors, K. C. Schelbel, Wayne Springfield; assistant director, Matia Karrell; sound, Mark Ulano; camera, Tim Shurstedt; editor, Any Orvitch.

Klaus Kinski (Dr. Daniel); Brie Howard (Maggie); Norbert Weisser (Keller); Crofton Hardester (Mendes); Kendra Kirchner (Cassandra); Don Opper (Max 404).

In the year 2036, on a far distant space station, scientist Dr. Daniel (Klaus Kinski) resides with a near human android, Max 404 (Don Opper), who helps him develop what he hopes will be the perfect android, the beautiful Cassandra (Kendra Kirchner) who will make Max 404 obsolete. Max, whose hobby is studying the 20th century via old records and films, wants to go to Earth where a one-time android revolt has caused his kind to be outlawed. Three escaped convicts (Brie Howard, Norbert Weisser, Crofton Hardester) arrive at the space station hoping to use it as a springboard back to Earth—and Max 404 wants to join them, especially when he learns Dr. Daniel plans to replace him with Cassandra. Trouble ensues when Max 404 falls in love with convict Maggie.

Filmed economically by Roger Corman's New World Pictures on sets left over from that studio's previous BATTLE BEYOND THE STARS (1980) (q.v.). ANDROID is a surprisingly good sci-fier which relies more on the interaction between the title character and his human counterparts than on a great deal of action, violence or sex. Don Opper, who appears as the android, also co-scripted the scenario.

"ANDROID is both one of the best low budget sci-fiers and the most interesting in house New World productions to come down the pike in some time. Making the most of its severe monetary limitations and consistently applying wit and intelligence to formulaic genre requirements, pic will particularly delight cognoscenti of futurism, ensuring cult status." (*Variety*). In the *Film Encyclopedia: Science Fiction* (1984), Phil Hardy called the production, "One of the wittiest, most pleasurable movies of its year regardless of genre. . . . The humanization of Max 404 is a slyly funny and acutely resonant process and the tyro film-makers . . . skillfully fit his superlative star turn into a telling network of relationships that speak volumes about knowledge and power (and even class). Though the genre hardware isn't shoddy, pure talent is the principal special effect on view."

ANDY WARHOL'S FRANKENSTEIN see FLESH FOR FRANKENSTEIN.

THE APE (Monogram, 1940) 80 mins.

Producer, Scott R. Dunlap; associate producer, William T. Lackey; director, William Nigh; based on the play by Adam Hull Shirk; screenplay, Curt Siodmak, Richard Carroll; art director, E. R. Hickson; music director, Edward Kay; camera, Harry Neumann; editor, Russell Schoengarth.

Boris Karloff (Dr. Bernard Adrian); Maris Wrixon (Frances Clifford); Gertrude Hoffman (Housekeeper); Henry Hall (Sheriff Jeff Holliday); Gene O'Donnell (Danny Foster); Jack Kennedy (Tomlin); Jessie Arnold (Mrs. Clifford); Dorothy Vaughan (Jane); I. Stanford Jolley (Trainer); George Cleveland (Townsman); and: Philo McCullough, Selmer Jackson.

After starring in five "Mr. Wong" detective entries for Monogram Pictures, Boris Karloff closed out his contract with that studio by headlining this horror/sci-fier, an economical remake of HOUSE OF MYSTERY (1934) which had been based on Adam Hull Shirk's stage play, *The Ape*. Outside of the title character, the Karloff version has little resemblance to the play although the 1934 film, produced by Paul Malvern, had been fairly faithful to its source, resulting in a flavorful mystery. William Nigh, who had directed the "Mr. Wong" mysteries, also helmed this offering which has a rawboned look about it. Its science fiction aspects are subjugated constantly to its horrific plotline by having Karloff carry out his grisly murders while masquerading as an ape.

Following the deaths of his wife and daughter due to a paralysis, eccentric Dr. Bernard Adrian (Boris Karloff) moves to remote Red Creek where he resides with a mute housekeeper (Gertrude Hoffman) and tries to produce a formula to stop the disease. He attempts to help pretty Frances Clifford (Maris Wrixon) who has been crippled by the same disease. A carnival visits the area and a killer ape escapes and commits a murder and then attacks Adrian who kills it. Clandestinely he removes the ape's skin and he wears it while committing murders to obtain spinal fluid for his experimental serum. The sheriff (Henry Hall) leads a posse to kill the ape. They corner it in front of Adrian's house and they kill the doctor thinking he is the simian. The serum, however, proves to be a cure for Frances who is free to marry fiancé Danny Foster (Gene O'Donnell), although the doctor's secret experiments have died with him.

The British *Kinematograph Weekly* termed the film a "Spectacular thriller. . . ." Kate Cameron was more on the mark when she assessed in the New York *Daily News*, "The story doesn't bear scrutiny at close range, but it does get over some good horror effects." Even more to the point was Don Miller in *B Movies* (1973), "It was laborious, stilted, but drew the customers."

THE APE MAN (Monogram, 1943) 64 mins.

Producers, Sam Katzman, Jack Dietz; associate producer, Barney Sarecky; director, William Beaudine; screenplay, Sarecky; art director, David Milton; camera, Mark Stengler; editor, Carl Pierson.

Bela Lugosi (Dr. Brewster); Wallace Ford (Jeff Carter); Louise Currie (Billie Mason); Minerva Urecal (Agatha Brewster); Henry Hall (Dr. Randall); Ralph Littlefield (Zippo); J. Farrell MacDonald (Captain); George Kirby (Butler); Wheeler Oakman (Brady); Emil Van Horn (The Ape); and: Jack Mulhall, Charles Hall.

A.k.a.: LOCK YOUR DOORS.

Between 1941 and 1944 Bela Lugosi starred in nine horror thrillers for Monogram Pictures producers Sam Katzman and Jack

Bela Lugosi and Henry Hall in THE APE MAN (1943).

Dietz; two being with the East Side Kids. Of the nine the worst is without doubt, THE APE MAN, followed by its sequel RETURN OF THE APE MAN (q.v.) in 1944. Not only does the movie have an inane plot which is explained away at the finale by its scripter (Ralph Littlefield) who has made fleeting, wise-cracking appearances throughout, but it totally wastes Bela Lugosi in a role which hides his face with simian hair and a fright wig and which forces him to spend practically all of his screen time walking in a stooped posture. In his book on Lugosi, *The Count* (1974), Arthur Lenning wrote of this production, "The results from an aesthetic point of view were abominable." He added, "The script is incredibly inept, and Lugosi is simply lost in the stupidity of it all."

Barney Sarecky's screenplay stars Lugosi as Dr. Brewster who due to his experiments has taken on the looks and posture of a human ape. Unhappy with this situation he develops a serum to counteract this effect but it requires human spinal fluid, resulting in death to the donor. When his associate Dr. Randall (Henry Hall) refuses to assist him, Brewster kills him and he and his experimental ape (Emil Van Horn) go on killing sprees which provide the needed fluid although the cure proves to be temporary. Know-it-all reporter Jeff Carter (Wallace Ford) and his talkative female photographer Billie Mason (Louise Currie) track down the source of the killings. Brewster knocks out Carter and abducts Billie, intending to use her fluids for his serum. But she releases the ape who murders the scientist as the police arrive to kill the simian.

The *Hollywood Reporter* had very mixed emotions about the film: "THE APE MAN is another of those films that cause the hair to stand on one's head. . . . Others will concede it to be a hilarious burlesque. . . ." Richard Bojarski determined in *The Films of Bela Lugosi* (1980), "Lugosi's reasons for his scientific experiments are unexplained . . . . Despite some interesting moments, its shock elements are weakened by lack of suspense and stereotyped characters. The drab production values not quite disguised by David Milton's art direction do contribute to the ominous atmosphere of the plot."

THE ASTRAL FACTOR   see   INVISIBLE STRANGLER.

AT THE EARTH'S CORE (American International, 1976) C 89 mins.

Executive producer, Harry N. Blum; producer, John Dark; director, Kevin Connor; based on the novel by Edgar Rice Burroughs; screenplay, Milton Subotsky; production designer, Maurice Carter;

art director, Bert Davey; music, Mike Vickers; camera, Alan Hume; editors, John Ireland, Barry Peters.

Doug McClure (David Innes); Peter Cushing (Dr. Abner Perry); Caroline Munro (Princess Dia); Cy Grant (Ra); Godfrey Janes (Ghak); Sean Lynch (Hooja); Michael Crane (Jubal); Bobby Par (Chief); Keith Barron (Dowsett); Helen Gill (Maisie); Anthony Verner (Gladsby); Andree Cromarty (Slave); Robert Gillespie (Photographer).

Edgar Rice Burroughs' novels about the underground world of Pellucidar came to life in three feature films produced in Great Britain and issued in the United States by American-International, with the trio all directed by Kevin Connor. AT THE EARTH'S CORE was the second of the set and perhaps the most rewarding, although it was still a " . . . half-hearted adaptation of the Edgar Rice Burroughs novel" (Ed Naha, *The Science Fictionary,* 1980).

Victorian scientist Dr. Abner Perry (Peter Cushing) invents an earth boring machine called the Iron Mole. He and his associate, David Innes (Doug McClure), experiment with it but the mechanism goes haywire and picks up speed. They end up at the planet's center in the strange world of Pellucidar. There they encounter prehistoric people being controlled by a race of highly intelligent pterodactyls, who use them as sacrifice. The two men meet Princess Dia (Caroline Munro) and set out to defeat the fearsome reptiles. Once they overwhelm the Mahars (the predators), the scientific team returns to the earth's surface.

AT THE EARTH'S CORE is a visually impressive feature, highlighted by good cinematography and colorful sets. The animation for the flying Mahars is particularly solid and the vicious reptiles are quite repulsive, especially when they sacrifice a young maiden. Still the picture is not overly satisfying and is hardly up to Burroughs' original work of 1922. Doug McClure seems bored with his hero's role and Peter Cushing is too addled as the scientist, a variation of his assignment as Dr. Who (see B/V) in that futuristic series. Comely Caroline Munro, however, is just fine as the heroine. Overall AT THE EARTH'S CORE is the best of a mediocre series. It was preceded by THE LAND THAT TIME FORGOT (q.v.) and followed by THE PEOPLE THAT TIME FORGOT (q.v.).

ATTACK OF THE CRAB MONSTERS (Allied Artists, 1957) 70 mins.

Producer, Roger Corman; associate producer, Charles Griffith; director, Corman; screenplay, Griffith; music, Ronald Stein; camera, Floyd Crosby; editor, Charles Gross, Jr.

Richard Garland (Dale Brewer); Pamela Duncan (Martha Hunt-

Caroline Munro in AT THE EARTH'S CORE (1976).

er); Russell Johnson (Hank Chapman); Leslie Bradley (Dr. Karl Weigand); Mel Welles (Jules Deveroux); Richard Cutting (Dr. James Carson); Beech Dickerson (Ron Fellows); Tony Miller (Jack Sommers); Ed Nelson (Ensign Quinlan).

Several people are stranded on a South Seas island after their plane crashes as it attempts to leave the atoll. An atomic bomb had been exploded near the isle and the radiation fallout has killed all the wildlife except for seagulls and crabs. As the humans explore the island they come to realize something mysterious is occurring. One of the party, Jules Deveroux (Mel Welles), hears the voices of allegedly dead sailors and is himself killed. Later the four remaining people—Martha Hunter (Pamela Duncan), Dr. Karl Weigand (Leslie Bradley), Dale Brewer (Richard Garland), and Hank Chapman (Russell Johnson)—hear Jules' voice as they enter his room. They eventually realize that the radiation overdose has given intelligence to two giant crabs who plan to take over the island and destroy the humans. The crabs detonate parts of the isle with dynamite and Karl and Hank die before the crabs are eventually destroyed.

Running little more than an hour, ATTACK OF THE CRAB MONSTERS is a well thought-out and entertaining little dualer (it was issued on a double bill with NOT OF THIS EARTH [see B/V]) and it moves quickly, holding audience interest with its twisting plot and its exploitable title monsters. Made on a $70,000 budget mostly at California's Bronson Canyon, the film grossed over $1,000,000 at the box-office. It was the first time producer/director Roger Corman utilized market research to select a provocative title. In *The Movie World of Roger Corman* (1979), edited by J. Philip di Franco, Corman stated why the film was so popular. "I believe its success was due to the combination of all these elements: the title, a strong story idea, the structuring of every scene for horror and suspense, and editing for rapid pace."

In 1989 a remake of the Corman feature was planned, to be filmed in the Bahamas with Jim Wynorski directing.

ATTACK OF THE GIANT LEECHES (American International, 1959) 62 mins.

Executive producer, Roger Corman; producer, Gene Korman; director, Bernard L. Kowalski; screenplay, Leo Gordon; art director Dan Haller; music, Alexander Laszlo; camera, John M. Nicholaus, Jr.; editor, Tony Magro.

Ken Clark (Steve Benton); Yvette Vickers (Liz Walker); Bruno Ve Sota (Dave Walker); Jan Shepard (Nan Greyson); Tyler McVey (Doc Greyson); Michael Emmett (Cal Moulton); Gene Roth (Sheriff Kovis); Dan White (Slim Reed); George Cisar (Lem Sawyer).

In the swamps near Cape Canaveral, one of the locals, Lem Sawyer (George Cisar), sees what appears to be a giant leech, but he cannot convince his friends of its reality. Rotund Dave Walker (Bruno Ve Sota) is married to beautiful Liz (Yvette Vickers), but she refuses to consummate the marriage and prefers the company of his buddy, Cal Moulton (Michael Emmett). Poachers have been working the area and a game warden, Steve Benton (Ken Clark), and his girlfriend, Nan Greyson (Jan Shepard), are looking for illegal traps when they find Lem dying from wounds caused by some kind of blood sucker. The sheriff (Gene Roth) refuses to do anything about the death. Meanwhile, Dave finds Liz and Cal making love and forces them into the swamp at gunpoint and the two are pulled underwater by giant creatures. Dave tells the sheriff what happened, but the lawman does not believe him and later Dave hangs himself in his cell. After two more men disappear, Steve and Nan's father, Dr. Greyson (Tyler McVey), search for the giant leeches and realize they are holed up in caverns under the swamp. Dave uses dynamite to blow up the monsters' den and their bodies float to the surface, as do the corpses of the citizens they had kept there for feeding. In the distance, however, the screech of the giant leeches can be heard.

At one point in ATTACK OF THE GIANT LEECHES (advertised simply as THE GIANT LEECHES and released in England as DEMONS OF THE SWAMP), Tyler McVey speculates that the title creatures might be the result of atomic energy used in the launching of rockets at Cape Canaveral. This is the only accounting for the arrival of the monsters who are rarely seen. Apparently the original monster suit costumes split during production, thus the practical need for only fleeting glimpses of the creatures. Co-star Bruno Ve Sota (who provides a well-shaded performance as the jealous, loutish Dave Walker) told actor/film historian Barry Brown in 1975, "If you took one close look, you'd laugh your head off. You see airtanks sticking out of the monster suits, you know?"

Besides Ve Sota, the main asset of this otherwise below par sci-fier is Yvette Vickers as the sluttish Liz. One of the sexiest women to appear in Hollywood movies, Vickers projects an "I can be easily had" portrayal. She is at her best in the scenes where she taunts Dave by wearing erotic underthings but will not allow him to touch her.

ATTACK OF THE KILLER TOMATOES (NAI Entertainment, 1978) C 87 mins.

Producers, Steve Peace, John De Bello; director, De Bello; screenplay, Costa Dillon, Peace, De Bello; music, Gordon Goodwin, Paul Sundfor; sound, Paul Wear; special effects, Greg Auer; camera, John K. Culley; editor, De Bello.

David Miller (Mason Dixon); George Wilson (Jim Richardson); Sharon Taylor (Lois Fairchild); Jack Riley (Agriculture Official); Rock Peace (Wilbur Finletter); Eric Christmas (Senator Polk); Al Sklar (Ted Swan); Ernie Meyer (President); Jerry Anderson (Major Milis); Ron Shapiro (Newspaper Editor).

Constructed to be a takeoff on all the monsters-on-the-loose low grade "B" features of yore, ATTACK OF THE KILLER TOMATOES has an amusing title with virtually no scenario substance. Advertised as "A New Musical-Comedy-Horror Show," the film provides none of these ingredients except a blaring, bad background score. Certainly there is little (intentional) comedy and absolutely no horror. No matter how classically inept some movies of the past were in this vein, *most* at least had some kind of horrific monster. However, the title fruit here is hardly scary, even in giant sizes!

San Diego is besieged suddenly by all sizes of intelligent tomatoes who molest people in a variety of ways, even committing murder and causing police cars and a helicopter to be wrecked. Government agent Mason Dixon (David Miller) is assigned to break the case and he orders captive tomatoes to be studied. He has a black agent infiltrate the tomatoes' headquarters disguised as one of them. But during a feast—in which the tomatoes take revenge on humans by roasting them—the agent asks for catsup and is captured. Dixon discovers that bad music will destroy the killer tomatoes and he uses it to succeed.

While it has taken on camp status and is a favorite on the midnight movie circuit, this motion picture has scant to offer except 87 minutes of near boredom. In *Horror and Science Fiction Films II* (1982), Donald C. Willis assesses it was, "A meant-to-be-comic monster movie, but not as funny as the accidental ones. . . ." Richard Meyer was right to the point when he wrote in *For One Week Only* (1983), "It takes a working knowledge of movies like THE NAVY VS. THE NIGHT MONSTERS (1966) and THE MONSTER THAT CHALLENGED THE WORLD (1957) [qq.v.] and all of the Godzilla pictures to really enjoy it—especially when the one Oriental character starts speaking in a badly dubbed American voice."

ATTACK OF THE MARCHING MONSTERS see DESTROY ALL MONSTERS.

AUTOMAN (Twentieth Century-Fox/ABC-TV, 1983) C 78 mins.

Executive producer, Glen A. Larson; co-executive producer, Larry Brody; producers, Donald Kushner, Peter Locke, Harker Wade; director, Lee H. Katzin; teleplay, Larson; music, Stu Phillips;

music supervisor, Lionel Newman; music theme, Dilly Hinsche, Phillips; art director, Russell Forrest; special effects, Donald Kuschner; camera, Frank Beascoechea; editors, Gene Ranney, John Dumas, Bud Hayes.

Desi Arnaz, Jr. (Officer Walter Nebicher); Chuck Wagner (Automan); Heather McNair (Officer Roxanne Caldwell); Robert Lansing (Lieutenant Jack Curtis); Gerald S. O'Loughlin (Captain E. G. Boyd); Gloria LeRoy (Miss Moneypenny); Patrick Macnee (Hamilton); Steven Keats (Collins); Robert J. Hogan (Peterson); James Antonio, Jr. (Cramer); Robert Dunlap (Chuck Wilson); Don Galloway (Martin Willis); Doug McClure (Smithers); Camilla Sparv (Tanya); Sid Haig, Mickey Jones (Gang Members).

Hamilton (Patrick Macnee), a power-hungry madman has been kidnapping famous scientists and forcing them to work for him in his Switzerland compound. An American policeman, Lieutenant Jack Curtis (Robert Lansing), and an Interpol agent, Tanya (Camilla Sparv), are entrapped by the man when they investigate his activities. A police computer expert, Officer Walter Nebicher (Desi Arnaz, Jr.), has created a holographic image called Automan (Chuck Wagner) which is aided by a small light called Cursor and the policeman uses them to fight crime. He is assigned to take his Automan to Switzerland to stop Hamilton and his henchman (Steven Keats). Eventually he brings the two to justice.

This TV movie is yet another in a series of futuristic outings which explored computer technology with a light touch. Although well produced, this telefilm is of more interest for its cast than for its premise as one quickly tires of the title character, Cursor, and Automan's supercar.

Variety commented, "Maybe there's an audience for this type of sheer escapism in primetime, but one has to doubt it—unless it be done with more ingeniousness than AUTOMAN brought to bear. The technological tricks were brought off reasonably well by the production staff, but eventually the gimmickry was self-defeating."

The forthcoming ABC-TV series lasted twelve episodes, with the final entry airing on April 9, 1984.

BACK TO THE FUTURE (Universal, 1985) C 116 mins.

Executive producers, Steven Spielberg, Frank Marshall, Kathleen Kennedy; producers, Bob Gale, Neil Canton; director, Zemeckis; screenplay, Zemeckis, Gale; production designer, Lawrence G. Paull; second unit director, Frank Marshall; assistant directors, David McGiffert, Pamela Eilerson; costume designer, Deborah L. Scott; art director, Todd Hallowell; set designer, Joseph E. Hubbard, Marjorie Stone McShirley, Cameron Birnie; makeup, Ken Chase;

music, Alan Silverstri; orchestrator, James Campbell; music supervisor, Bones Howe; music editor, Kenneth Karman; choreography, Brad Jeffries; sound, William B. Kaplan; visual effects, Industrial Light & Magic; special effects supervisor, Kevin Pike; special effects, Steve Suits, Kimberley Pike, Sam Adams, Richard Chronister, William Klinger; camera, Dean Cunde; editors, Arthur Schmidt, Harry Keramidas; supervising sound editors, Charles L. Campbell, Robert Rutledge.

Michael J. Fox (Marty McFly); Christopher Lloyd (Dr. Emmett Brown); Lea Thompson (Lorraine Baines); Crispin Glover (George McFly); Thomas F. Wilson (Biff Tannen); Claudia Wells (Jennifer Parker); Marc McClure (Dave McFly); Wendie Jo Sperber (Linda McFly); George DiCenzo (Sam Baines); Frances Lee McCain (Stella Baines); James Tolkan (Mr. Strickland); Jeffrey Jay Cohen (Skinhead); Casey Siemaszko (3-D); Billy Zane (Match); Harry Waters, Jr. (Marvin Berry); Donald Fullilove (Goldie Wilson); Lisa Freeman (Babs); Cristen Kauffman (Betty); Elsa Raven (Clocktower Lady); Will Hare (Pa Peabody); Ivy Bethune (Ma Peabody); Jason Marin (Sherman Peabody); Katherine Britton (Peabody's Daughter); Jason Harvey (Milton Baines); Maia Brewton (Sally Baines); Courtney Gains (Dixon); Richard L. Duran (Terrorist); Jeff O'Haco (Terrorist Van Driver); Johnny Green, Jamie Abbott (Scooter Kids); Norman Alden (Lou); Red Morgan (Cop); Sachi Parker, Robert Krantz (Bystanders); Gary Riley (Man); Karen Petrasek (Girl); Tommy Thomas, Granville Young, David Harold Brown, Lloyd L. Tolbert (Starlighters); Paul Hanson, Lee Brownfield, Robert DeLapp (Pinheads).

"It's easy to see why Universal executives were so excited by BACK TO THE FUTURE. The movie isn't just fun. It's fun at the speed of light, a whiz-bang time-travel adventure likely to result in some decidedly high-octane box-office dollars. . . . It's every kid's fantasy come true, and [director Robert] Zemeckis exploits its possibilities with delicious abandon, deriving considerable humor from the situation's unseen generation gap." (Kirk Ellis, *The Hollywood Reporter*)

Upset because his wimpy father, George McFly (Crispin Glover) will not stand up to his bully boss, Biff Tannen (Thomas F. Wilson), and by the fact his rock band has been snubbed by his school's prom night committee, Hill Valley teenager Marty McFly (Michael J. Fox) agrees to aid bizarre inventor/scientist Dr. Emmett Brown (Christopher Lloyd) test his time machine which he developed from a DeLorean auto. As they commence the experiment, Libyan terrorists break in and gun down Brown over a plutonium power play and Marty drives into the past—to the year 1955. There

Michael J. Fox and Christopher Lloyd in BACK TO THE FUTURE (1985).

he decides to change his future parents' lives. He meets Lorraine Baines (Lea Thompson), his future mother, and she is attracted to him and he has a week to make sure his parents meet and fall in love, because having contacted Brown again, he is assured of returning to the future at the moment a lightning bolt strikes the town hall. Marty takes Lorraine to the dance where bully Biff tries to molest her and at Marty's urging, George flattens him. To ensure Lorraine and George dance together, Marty takes over the band. He then drives back to 1985 and finds, thanks to his intervention, his family is quite affluent now and that he has a younger brother and sister. Brown, whom Marty has saved by a letter warning him to wear a bullet-proof vest, then returns from the year 2005 and insists Marty and his girlfriend, Jennifer Parker (Claudia Wells), go with him there to stop the havoc their children are wrecking on the future.

In analyzing the secret of its success, Blake Lukas wrote in *Magill's Cinema Annual* (1986), "It is as fantasy of a more traditional kind that the film finds its most meaningful context. The intervention of fantasy into the real world as a means of solving problems has many artistic precedents, notably in the American cinema, and classic films as beloved as THE WIZARD OF OZ (1939) and IT'S A WONDERFUL LIFE (1946) were in fact sometimes evoked in BACK TO THE FUTURE's initial reviews, in a very complimentary manner. . . . A more pervasive pleasure is also a vital element. When fantasy totally succeeds, it is rich in humor, enticing details, and flavorful characterization. Here is the surest measure of BACK TO THE FUTURE'S accomplishment."

Less esoteric, but almost as enthusiastic was Michael Dare in *L.A. Weekly*, "I swallowed all of this while I was watching it, even chewed it with gusto, but one hour later, eh!. . . . [Director Robert Zemeckis] wants you to get every joke, and you do, but the plot is so good that you wish the style were less of an assault and a bit more human. . . . I still could've used more [Francois] Truffaut and less [Stephen] Spielberg."

The public whole-heartedly endorsed this film and within six months after its release in the summer of 1985, it had grossed over $200,000,000 at the domestic box-office, and in the Oscar sweepstakes would win an Academy Award for best sound effects editing. The film side-stepped the potentially unpleasant Oedipal triangle situation it set up and skillfully blended sci-fi gadgetry with slapstick, nostalgia, and brisk performances by the ever-energetic Michael J. Fox as the teen-aged hero and the overshadowing performance of Christopher Lloyd's crazed inventor. As *Daily Variety* agreed, this blockbuster " . . . time-travel odyssey accelerates with wit, ideas and infectious, wide-eyed wonder. . . . the screen is constantly full of delightful comparisons: the old village-square movie house in '55 with a marquee showing Ronald Reagan in CATTLE QUEEN OF MONTANA has become a porno house in '85. The Studebaker lot is now peddling Toyotas. . . . None of these points are underscored but merely floating in the background as signposts of change. The most rousing and audience-grabbing scene of culture shock comes when Fox mounts the stage of a '55 high school band, says he's going to play an oldie, and digs into Chuck Berry's 'Johnny B. Goode' at the dawn of rock 'n roll. . . . .the mellow image of the fab '50s is the movie's nice, lingering image."

Recurrent industry rumors that BACK TO THE FUTURE II would become a reality have proven true.

BATTLE BEYOND THE STARS (New World, 1980) C 104 mins.

Executive producer, Roger Corman; producer, Ed Carlin; associate producer, Mary Ann Fisher; director, Jimmy T. Murakami; story, John Sayles, Anne Dyer; screenplay, Sayles; art director, Chip Radaelli; set decorator, John Zabrucky; music, James Horner; assistant directors, Henning Schellerup, Leon Dudevoir; costumes, Durinda Rice Wood; miniatures, Mary Schallock; miniature visual effects, C. Comisky; camera, Daniel Lacambre; editor, Michael Spence.

Richard Thomas (Shad); Robert Vaughn (Gelt); Darlanne Fleugel (Sadcor); George Peppard (Cowboy); Sybil Danning (St. Exmin); John Saxon (Sandor); Sam Jaffe (Dr. Hephaestus); Morgan Woodward (Cayman); Steve Davis (Quopeg); Earl Boen, John McGowans (Nestors); Larry Meyers, Laura Cody (Kelvins); Lynn Carlin (Nell); Jeff Corey (Zed); Julia Duffy (Mol); Eric Morris (Feh); Marta Kristen (Lux); Doug Carleson (Pok); Ron Ross (Dab); Terrence McNally (Gar); Don Thompson (Cush); Daniel Carlin (Pez) Ansley Carlin (Wok); and: Peter Liakakis, Debra MacFarlane, Max Robinson, Ocie Robinson, Michael Ruud, H. E. D. Redford, Chet Norris.

The evil Sandor (John Saxon) threatens the planet Akirian with destruction within one week if the inhabitants do not turn over all their riches to him. Shad (Richard Thomas), a young resident of the planet, vows to fight and hires a group of mercenaries to defend his homeland. He recruits a diverse team, including space cowboy (George Peppard), a hard-drinker; shootist Gelt (Robert Vaughn), and beautiful St. Exmin (Sybil Danning). Sandor musters his forces including his fantastic Stellar Converter and another vessel manned by Nestor, a manlike lizard and his quintet of white clones. Following a massive battle in space between the two, the forces of right prevail, although Gelt is killed in the conflict.

Costing $3,000,000, BATTLE BEYOND THE STARS was Roger Corman's outer space edition of the Japanese film THE SEVEN SAMURAI (1954) which had been translated into a classic Hollywood Western, THE MAGNIFICENT SEVEN (1960). In a homage to that version, Robert Vaughn repeated his role of the fatalist gunman. One third of the film's budget was allocated to special effects and they were the true highlight of the picture, a takeoff of STAR WARS (1977) (q.v.) and its ilk. Donald C. Willis noted in *Horror and Science Fiction Films* (1982) that the feature " . . . isn't quite funny enough for adults, but is probably fast and furious enough for kids. . . . The effects are hardly innovative, but they don't let up." Michael Weldon opined in *The Psychotronic Encyclopedia of Films* (1983), "Some of the gags were cut out and the editing could have been better, but it's a lot more memorable and more fun than THE EMPIRE STRIKES BACK [q.v.]." Phil Hardy weighed in *The Film Encyclopedia: Science Fiction* (1984), "The result is a film whose script presumably was inventive but which, in the course of its relatively expensive production, fell prey to the innate conservatism of Corman the producer."

Unused footage from BATTLE BEYOND THE STARS has emerged in such later Corman features as GALAXY OF TERROR (1981) and SPACE RAIDERS (1983) (qq.v.). The filmmaker, having built his own studio and special effects department for the film, later rented the facilities to others (e.g. ESCAPE FROM NEW YORK [q.v.]).

BATTLE BEYOND THE SUN (Filmgroup, 1963) C 75 mins.

Executive producer, Roger Corman; producer, Thomas Cochart; directors, A. Kozyr, M. Karyukov; story, Ed R. Korol; screenplay, A. Sazonov, Ye. Pomeshchikov; screenplay collaborator, M. Karyukov; English version adaptor, Francis Ford Coppola; art director, Yu. Shvets; set decorator, A. Borin; music, Yu. Meytus; assistant director, V. Fokin; costumes, G. Glinkova; makeup, Ye. Odinovich; sound, G. Parakhnikov; special effects, F. Semyannikov, N. Ilyushin, Yu. Shvets, G. Lukashov; camera, Nikolay Kulchitskly; editor, L. Mkhitaryants.

Ivan Pereverzev (Kornev); A. Shvorin (Gordiyenko); K. Bartashevich (Klark); G. Tonunts (Verst); V. Chernyak (Somov); V. Dobrovolskiy (Demchenko); A. Popova (Koreva); T. Litvienko (Lena); L. Borisenko (Olga); L. Lobov (Sashko); S. Filimonov (Troyan); M. Samoylova (Klar's Mother); Edd Perry; Andy Stewart.

The Soviets were pioneers in the sci-fi film field with AELITA (1924) (q.v.) although that film was basically propaganda for the Red

Edd Perry and Andy Stewart in BATTLE BEYOND THE SUN (1963).

cause. Russian science fiction features continued to be made to promote Communism as noted in their 1959 space opera NIEBO ZOWIET [The Heavens Call], which related the story of a race to Mars between the Russians and the Americans with the latter winning the race only to find they did not have enough fuel to get home and the Soviets coming to their rescue. With attractive color, the Soviet feature never got American release until producer Roger Corman obtained the rights to the production and hired Thomas Cochart to film new sequences for U.S. distribution by Corman's Filmgroup. Corman edited the Russian propaganda and the result was a dubbed, but not uninteresting, space melodrama.

Governments of the northern and southern hemispheres (thinly veiled references to the U.S. and Russia) are in a race to reach Mars. One group lands on the Red Planet but runs out of fuel necessary to return home and the others arrive to rescue them and they must fight a hostile environment, including dinosaurs. As a result of their cooperation, the astronauts find the Torch of Truth and return home determined to work together for the good of mankind.

Francis Ford Coppola wrote much of the American version

script for BATTLE BEYOND THE SUN and the rewrite had the Earth, sometime in the future, divided into two sections and competing for the conquest of space. Most memorable in his sequence with two monsters doing battle which he comically planned as a sendoff on sex films with the creatures blatantly engaged in a sex act. The ads for Corman's restructured release exclaimed, "SEE the incredible meteorites from Mars! The escape from the mysterious Sun! The space station run amuck in the Stars! The rocket cruisers in the last war of the Worlds!"

BATTLESTAR GALACTICA (Universal, 1979) C 120 mins.
    Executive producer, Glen A. Larson; producer, John Dykstra; supervising producer, Leslie Stevens; associate producer, Winrich Kolbe; director, Richard A. Colla; screenplay, Larson; music, Stu Phillips; art director, John E. Chilberg II; assistant directors, Phil Cook, Nick Marek; special effects, Apogee, Inc.; camera, Ben Colman; editors, Robert L. Kimble, Leon Ortiz-Gil, Larry Strong.
    Lorne Greene (Commander Adama); Richard Hatch (Captain Apollo); Dirk Benedict (Lieutenant Starbuck); Ray Milland (Uri); Lew Ayres (Adar); Jane Seymour (Serina); Wilfrid Hyde-White (Anton); John Colicos (Count Baltar); Laurette Spang (Cassiopea); John Fink (Dr. Paye); Terry Carter (Colonel Tighe); Herb Jefferson, Jr. (Lieutenant Boomer); Maren Jensen (Athena); Tony Swartz (Lieutenant Jolly); Noah Hathaway (Boxey); Ed Begley, Jr. (Ensign Greenbean); Rick Springfield (Lieutenant Zac); Randi Oakes (Young Woman); Norman Stuart (Statesman); David Greenan (Bridge Officer); Sarah Rush (Woman on Duty); David Matthau (Operative); Chip Johnson, Geoffrey Binney (Warriors); Paul Coufos (Pilot); Bruce Wright (Deck Hand).
    In the Seventh Millennia of time humans, in another galaxy, arrange a peace treaty with robots called Cyclons. Two council leaders (Lew Ayres, Ray Milland) find out too late the Cyclons have turned on them and the inhabitants of a dozen planets are eliminated as are their defensive space crafts. A rag-tag fleet of 220 ships escape the attack and led by the *Galactica,* commanded by Adama (Lorne Greene), the armada makes its way through space searching for its mystical thirteenth colony on Earth. The Cyclons, however, give chase, hoping to destroy the last of the human race. Aiding their commander in defending the fleet are Adama's son Apollo (Richard Hatch), pilot Starbuck (Dirk Benedict), Boomer (Herb Jefferson, Jr.) and Athena (Maren Jensen). Eventually the ships make it to Earth, but are still plagued by the Cyclons.
    Television's answer to STAR WARS (1977) (q.v.), BATTLESTAR GALACTICA was the two and one-half hour pilot for the teleseries

Lorne Greene in BATTLESTAR GALACTICA (1979).

of the same name. The telefilm pulled a huge rating and was issued theatrically where it grossed over $7,000,000. Garish, loud and imitative, the production was highlighted by producer John Dykstra's special effects and Ben Colman's cinematography. Donald C. Willis summed it up best in *Horror and Science Fiction Films II* (1982): "Good effects; nice score; tepid dramatics." Phil Hardy in *The Film Encyclopedia: Science Fiction* (1984) thought the production " . . . a strange mix of the fight of the Israelites from Egypt, the WAGON TRAIN teleseries and the views of Von Daniken whose 'God was an Astronaut' slogan the film literalizes."

The lame TV series ran on ABC-TV during the 1978-79 season for twenty episodes and again briefly in 1980 reemerged as GALACTICA 1980 for an additional nine segments. It produced sufficient footage for several cut-and-paste TV movies: CURSE OF THE CYCLONS, GREETINGS FROM EARTH, THE GUN ON ICE PLANET ZERO, THE LIVING LEGEND (also issued theatrically as MISSION GALACTICA: THE CYCLON ATTACK), LOST PLANET OF THE GODS, MURDER IN SPACE, PHANTOM IN SPACE, SPACE CASANOVA, SPACE PRISON, and WAR OF THE GODS.

BEAST OF BLOOD   see   BRIDES OF BLOOD.

THE BEAST OF HOLLOW MOUNTAIN (United Artists, 1956) C 81 mins.

Producers, William and Edward Nassour; directors, Edward Nassour, Ismael Rodriguez; screen idea, Willis O'Brien; screenplay, Robert Hill; additional dialogue, Jack DeWitt; music, Paul La Vista; special camera effects, Henry Sharpe; camera, Jorge Stahl, Jr.; editors, Holbrook Todd, Maury Wright, Fernando Martinez.

Guy Madison (Jimmy Ryan); Patricia Medina (Sarita); Eduardo Noriega (Enrique Rios); Carlos Rivas (Felipe Sanchez); Mario Navarro (Panchito); Pascual Garcia Pena (Pancho); Julio Villareal (Don Pedro); Lupe Carriles (Margarita); Manuel Arvide (Martinez); Jose Chavez (Manuel); Magarito Luna (Jose); Roberto Contreras (Carlos); Lobo Negro [Guillermo Hernandez] (Jorge); Jorge Trevino (Shopkeeper); Armando Guiterrez (Employee).

American rancher Jimmy Ryan (Guy Madison) is losing cattle mysteriously from his spread in Mexico and he suspects that Enrique Rios (Eduardo Noriega), his rival for the affections of Sarita (Patricia Medina), is responsible because the man also resents his partnership with Felipe Sanchez (Carlos Rivas). The locals, however, believe a terrible lizard allegedly living in the swamps near Hollow Mountain is responsible for the disappearing cattle. When more cattle disappear on the day she is supposed to wed Rios, Sarita leaves the man feeling he is responsible. A local child disappears and her father goes to the swamp to find her as does Sarita. Ryan and Rios follow. The beast, a prehistoric allosaurus, traps the young woman in a hut and kills Rios. Ryan leads the beast to a nearby swamp and it dies in quicksand.

Animator/writer Willis O'Brien wrote the original story for this film which also contains elements used in a later—and much better—dinosaur/Western, THE VALLEY OF GWANGI (1969) (q.v.). Utilizing the time warp gimmick, which provided the basis for so many sci-fi/horror films, this entry was an American/Mexican co-production and was filmed south of the border where it was issued as EL MONSTRO DE LA MONTA HUECA. The dinosaur herein is particularly effective and the battle scenes at the finale between it and hero Guy Madison are well done. Unfortunately they are preceded by about 70 minutes of nearly pure boredom.

Filming on THE BEAST OF HOLLOW MOUNTAIN commenced in 1954 and it was during this period that Guy Madison gained his greatest fame on television in the title role of the series "Wild Bill Hickok" and when this monster movie was finally released in 1956 it greatly benefitted from his box-office draw.

A.k.a. LA BESTIA DE LA MONTANA.

BEAST OF THE YELLOW NIGHT   see   BRIDES OF BLOOD.

BEAST WITH A MILLION EYES (American Releasing Corp., 1955) 78 mins.

Executive producer, David Kramarsky; producer, Roger Corman; director, Kramarsky; based on the story "The Beast" by William Fryer Harvey; screenplay, Tom Filer; music, John Bickford; special camera effects, Paul Blaisdell; camera, Everett Baker; editor, Jack Killifer.

Paul Birch (Allan Kelly); Lorna Thayer (Carol Kelly); Dona Cole (Sandy Kelly); Dick Sargent (Larry); Leonard Tarver (Tim); Chester Conklin (Old Man Webber).

"An Unspeakable Horror . . . Destroying . . . Terrifying!" screamed the poster blurb for THE BEAST WITH A MILLION EYES although the actual monster used for the finished product has only a mere two eyes. The title refers to the alien's capacity to take over the bodies of anything on earth: human, reptile, or any other animal. One famous anecdote relating to this production tells how exhibitors would not buy it because it had no special effects and how

American International Pictures head James Nicholson went into the editing room and with the use of scissors scratched the emulsion on the film in the scenes with the spaceship (actually a tank sunk in the sand with a propeller on top) and then colored in the scratches with an ink pen. The results, as projected on the screen, had the spaceship giving off lightning-type rays. It was surprisingly realistic!

In the desert Southwest, the Kelly family owns a dude ranch, but husband Allan (Paul Birch) and wife Carol (Lorna Thayer) are having marital troubles and they also do not get along with their teenage daughter Sandy (Dona Cole) nor her boyfriend Larry (Dick Sargent). Mysterious things begin to happen after a plane flies overhead. Actually it is a flying saucer which lands nearby. The alien in the craft can take over the mind of anything it wishes and it causes Sandy's dog to attack Carol, who kills it in self defense. A neighbor (Chester Conklin) is killed by his cow which then attacks Allan who shoots it. The ranch's mute helper (Leonard Tarver) comes under the control of the alien and he kidnaps Sandy but Allan and Larry pursue him and the kidnapper dies. Allan decides the alien feeds on hate and is hurt by love. The foursome unite to destroy the creature which dies as the spaceship leaves. The alien takes over the body of a rat, but is devoured by an eagle.

As with many (pseudo) science fiction tales, this story can be understood on many different levels, one of which is blatantly moralistic and patriotic (in the mid-1950s when fears of Communism and Soviet invasion/control of the United States was at its height.)

BEFORE I HANG (Columbia, 1940) 62 mins.

Producer, Wallace MacDonald; director, Nick Grinde; story, Karl Brown, Robert D. Andrews; screenplay, Andrews; art director, Lionel Banks; sound, J. S. Westmoreland; camera, Benjamin Kline; editor, Charles Nelson.

Boris Karloff (Dr. John Garth); Evelyn Keyes (Martha Garth); Bruce Bennett (Dr. Ames); Edward Van Sloan (Dr. Ralph Howard); Ben Taggart (Warden); Pedro de Cordoba (Sondini); Wright Kramer (Wharton); Bertram Marbrugh (Barclay); Don Beddoe (McGraw); Robert Flake (District Attorney); Kenneth MacDonald (Anson); Frank Richards (Kron).

Aging scientist Dr. John Garth (Boris Karloff) works on a rejuvenation formula. When he commits a mercy killing he is sentenced to be executed but is allowed to carry out his experiments in prison. He is assisted by the prison doctor (Edward Van Sloan) and injects himself with a serum from the blood of a convicted murderer. The result is that Garth is much younger in appearance

Bruce Bennett and Evelyn Keyes in BEFORE I HANG (1940).

and the prison doctor demands he too be injected with the serum. But the influence of the murderer's blood causes Garth to kill him and another prisoner. The authorities, however, believe the other prisoner killed the prison physician and Garth has his sentence commuted. He returns home to his daughter Martha (Evelyn Keyes) and again kills when his friends will not take the serum. Martha calls in her fiancé (Bruce Bennett) to stop Garth who is killed when he attempts to murder his arresting officer.

In the late 1930s and early 1940s Boris Karloff, on and off, headlined a series of programmers which had science fiction topics and this Wallace MacDonald production proved to be " . . . fanciful pseudo-science which builds to an exciting murder orgy." (*New York Post*). Here Karloff's mad scientist develops an immortality formula which is contaminated by the blood of a murderer thus turning its user into a homicidal maniac. When issued in Great Britain the film was trimmed by nine minutes. There the *Kinematograph Weekly* judged it a " . . . Grand Guignol thriller with a pseudo-scientific background. . . . Boris Karloff takes himself seriously as Garth and his sincere acting helps to cloak much of the incredibility of the part."

BELA LUGOSI MEETS A BROOKLYN GORILLA (Realart, 1952)
75 mins.

Producer, Maurice Duke; associate producer, Herman Cohen; director, William Beaudine; screenplay, Tim Ryan; additional dialogue, Ukie Sherin, Edmond G. Seward; music, Richard Hazard; art director, James Sullivan; camera, Charles Van Enger; editor, Phil Chan.

Bela Lugosi (Dr. Zabor); Duke Mitchell (Himself); Sammy Petrillo (Himself); Charlita (Nona); Muriel Landers (Salome); Al Kikume (Chief Rakos); Mickey Simpson (Chula); Milton Newberger (Bongo); Martin Garralaga (Pepe Bordo); Ramona the Chimp (Himself).

Bela Lugosi, and his name in the film's title, along with the "comedy" team of Duke Mitchell and Sammy Petrillo (Dean Martin and Jerry Lewis act-a-likes), are the sole assets of this strained, vapid sci-fi comedy which *Boxoffice* magazine charitably pegged a "broadly played farce" adding, "Neighborhood and small-town audiences will get some laughs." Actually there are no legitimate laughs to be had and it is sad to witness the aging, obviously ill Lugosi in this low-

Bela Lugosi in BELA LUGOSI MEETS A BROOKLYN GORILLA (1952).

end fare which does not even have the camp entertainment value of his 1940s Monogram thrillers. Director William Beaudine, who handled some of Lugosi's Forties' features, was unable to breathe life into the proceedings.

Nightclub performers Duke Mitchell and Sammy Petrillo (themselves) are entertaining servicemen on Guam when they fall out of a plane and land on an isle where mad Dr. Zabor (Bela Lugosi) is experimenting on turning gorillas into humans. Zabor lusts for pretty native girl Nona (Charlita) who finds the boys and takes them to her chieftain father (Al Kikume) who lets them live because his daughter likes Duke. Jealous, Zabor turns Duke into a gorilla and pal Sammy, who is persistently chased by a fat native girl, finally realizes what has happened. A mixup ensues when a real gorilla arrives on the scene and Sammy mistakes him for Duke. In a showdown with Zabor, Sammy steps in the way when the madman tries to shoot Duke. He awakes suddenly and realizes it was all a dream!

Nothing works in BELA LUGOSI MEETS A BROOKLYN GORILLA (issued in England as THE MONSTER MEETS THE GORILLA and shown on American TV as THE BOYS FROM BROOKLYN). Particularly annoying is Sammy Petrillo in his low grade imitations of zany Jerry Lewis. Former cowboy star Ray Corrigan plays the gorilla here, as he did in many other sci-fi features, but adds little fright potential to a feature already submerged in a mire of vapidity.

LA BESTIA DE LA MONTANA   see   THE BEAST OF HOLLOW MOUNTAIN.

BEYOND WITCH MOUNTAIN (CBS-TV, 2/20/82) 45 mins.

Executive producer, William Robert Yates; producer, Jan Williams; director, Robert Day; teleplay, Robert Young, B. W. Sandefur, Hal Kanter; art director, Mark Mansbridge; music, George Duning; camera, Jack Whitman.

Eddie Albert (Jason O'Day); Tracey Gold (Tia the Alien Girl); Andy Freeman (Tony the Alien Boy); Efrem Zimbalist, Jr. (Aristotle Bolt); J. D. Cannon (Deranian); Noah Beery, Jr. (Uncle Bene); Stephanie Blackmore (Dr. Adrian Molina); Peter Hobbs (Dr. Peter Morton); James Luisi (Foreman); William H. Bassett (Lowell Roberts); Hidi Lynn Hurtes (Reporter); Lola Mason (Lady Driver).

See: ESCAPE TO WITCH MOUNTAIN.

BIG CALIBRE (Supreme, 1934) 56 mins.

Producer, A. W. Hackel; supervisor, Sam Katzman; director,

Robert North Bradbury; screenplay, Perry Murdock; camera, William Hyer; editor, S. Roy Luby.

Bob Steele (Bob O'Neill); Forrest Taylor (Bentley); Peggy Campbell (June Bowers); John Elliott (Rusty Hicks); Georgia O'Dell (Arabella); Bill Quinn (Mr. Bowers); Earl Dwire (Sheriff); Frank Ball (O'Neill); Si Jenks (Dance Caller); Perry Murdock (Zenz/Gadski); and: Frank McCarroll, Blackie Whiteford.

Bob Steele's Westerns were hardly formula product, especially the ones made with his father, director/scripter Robert North Bradbury, who had a penchant for eccentric plot elements and picturesque locales. Their collaboration, HIDDEN VALLEY (1932), at Monogram Pictures, for example, included a lost valley, a forgotten Aztec civilization and the use of a zeppelin. BIG CALIBRE, one of the thirty-two starrers Bob Steele did for producer A. W. Hackel, uses science fiction elements, something novel in "B" oaters of the period.

Cowboy Bob O'Neill (Bob Steele) believes his father has been murdered and he sets out to find the killer, a chemist named Zenz (Perry Murdock). Bob and his foreman, Rusty Hicks (John Elliott) hunt for gold as they look for Zenz and in the desert Bob comes across what he believes is a human skeleton. He is later accused of killing rancher Bowers (Bill Quinn), whose ranch and pretty daughter June (Peggy Campbell) are sought by crooked banker Bentley (Forrest Taylor) who is in cahoots with the physically ugly assayer Gadski (Perry Murdock). The girl, however, believes that Bob is innocent. Jealous of her attention to the stranger, the banker incites the local citizens against him. Gadski tries to kill Bob with a vial of poison gas but Bob escapes and Rusty finds out the lawbreakers plan to rob the local bank. During the robbery Bentley turns on Gadski and knocks him out. Bentley then attacks June at the ranch but Bob saves her and unmasks Gadksi as Zenz. Bentley is captured. Zenz escapes in an auto/stage but Bob pursues him and in a perilous cliffside fight, the madman dies in a fall after breathing gas from his own weapon.

The use of a deadly gas and the hideous facial features of the villain add a sci-fi flavor to this actionful oater. Bob Steele's one-time vaudeville partner, Perry Murdock wrote the original screenplay as well as acted in the film.

THE BIG NOISE (Twentieth Century-Fox, 1944) 74 mins.

Producer, Sol M. Wurtzel; director, Mal St. Clair; screenplay, W. Scott Darling; art directors, Lyle Wheeler, John Ewing; set decorator, Al Orenbach; assistant director, Gaston Glass; music, Cyril J. Mockridge; music director, Emil Newman; special effects,

Fred Sersen; sound, Bernard Freericks; camera, Joe MacDonald; editor, Norman Colbert.

Stan Laurel (Himself); Oliver Hardy (Himself); Doris Merrick (Evelyn); Arthur Space (Alva Hartley); Veda Ann Borg (Mayme); Bobby Blake (Egbert); Frank Fenton (Charlton); James Bush (Hartman); Phil Van Zandt (Dutchy); Esther Howard (Aunt Sophie); Robert Dudley (Grandpa); Edgar Dearing (Motor Policeman); Selmar Jackson (Manning); Harry Hayden (Butler); Francis Ford (Station Attendant); Jack Norton (Drunk); Charles Wilson (Conductor); Ken Christy (Speaker); Beal Wong (Japanese Officer); Louis Arco (German Officer).

THE BIG NOISE was the fifth of six modestly-budgeted feature films Stan Laurel and Oliver Hardy made for Twentieth Century-Fox between 1941 and 1945. These films are often condemned in comparison to their classic work for Hal Roach in the late 1920s and throughout the 1930s but taken on their own, they have merit.

Mail order house detectives Laurel and Hardy (themselves) take a job guarding an experimental bomb developed by Alva Hartley (Arthur Space). The boys think the post will be an easy one

Oliver Hardy and Stan Laurel in THE BIG NOISE (1944).

but soon find themselves befuddled by the professor's ultra-modern house which includes push-button walls/furniture and meals in a pill. The inventor's widowed sister-in-law Aunt Sophie (Esther Howard), who has been married seven times, takes a liking to Oliver but he is disturbed by the fact that she walks in her sleep carrying a huge knife. Hoodlums learn of the bomb and plan to steal it and sell it to a foreign power. En route to Washington, D.C. Laurel and Hardy end up on a train and a remote-control plane before thwarting the gangsters, capturing an enemy submarine, and delivering the explosive to the government.

The film's best scenes involve the professor's futuristic house and a reworking of the train berth sequence from BERTH MARKS (1929).

BLACK FRANKENSTEIN   see   BLACKENSTEIN.

THE BLACK HOLE (Buena Vista, 1979) C 97 mins.

Producer, Ron Miller; director, Gary Nelson; story, Jeb Rosebrook, Bob Barbarsh, Richard Landau; screenplay, Rosebrook, Gerry Day; music/music director, John Barry; production designer, Peter Ellenshaw; art directors, John B. Mainsbridge, Al Roelofs, Robert T. McCall; set decorators, Frank R. McKelvy, Roger M. Shook; costumes, Bill Thomas; assistant directors, Tom McCrory, Christopher Miller, Joseph P. Moore; director of miniature camera, Art Cruickshank; miniature effects, Ellenshaw; camera, Frank Phillips; editor, Gregg McLaughlin.

Maximilian Schell (Dr. Hans Reinhardt); Anthony Perkins (Dr. Alex Durant); Robert Forster (Captain Dan Holland); Joseph Bottoms (Lieutenant Charles Pizer); Yvette Mimieux (Dr. Kate McCraw); Ernest Borgnine (Harry Booth): Captain S.T.A.R. (Tommy McLoughlin).

Astronomers and scientists have mixed opinions as to the actual existence of black holes but they continually grab the interest of sci-fi fans, resulting in this Disney organization film; the studio's first PG-rated thriller. It is speculated that black holes are formed by collapsing neutron stars and their gravity is so strong it sucks in even light, so they cannot be seen. It is believed a black hole may have been detected in the Cygnus X-1 binary star system.

Captain Dan Holland (Robert Forster) is in command of a spacecraft exploring the universe and his valiant crew includes Dr. Kate McCrae (Yvette Mimieux), Dr. Alex Durant (Anthony Perkins), Harry Booth (Ernest Borgnine), and Lieutenant Charles Pizer (Joseph Bottoms). They come across the *Cygnus,* a spaceship lost decades before. The ship is on the edge of a huge black hole and is commanded by insane Dr. Hans Reinhardt (Maximilian Schell) with a robot crew. The astronauts learn that Reinhardt has killed his crew and has used them for robots in his mad scheme to explore the black hole. Two of the robots aid the astronauts and they overcome Reinhardt, but by accident they are hurled through the black hole and wind up on the other side of the universe.

Grossing over $25,000,000 (which was a disappointment to the filmmakers after their extremely high production costs), THE BLACK HOLE was highlighted by excellent special effects. But overall, it was a mundane film. Phil Hardy noted in *The Film Encyclopedia: Science Fiction* (1984), "The film's most interesting element, the melding of man and machine, a recurring theme of modern Science Fiction, is hardly touched on in the . . . screenplay which simply alternates action with the most heavy-handed dialogue imaginable, made even more so by the constant stream of references to the like of Goethe and Cicero. Accordingly, the film's climax, the descent into the Black Hole, though spectacular, has no dramatic power at all."

BLACK OXEN (Associated First National, 1924) 90 mins.

Producer/director, Frank Lloyd; based on the novel by Gertrude Franklin Atherton; screenplay, Mary O'Hara; camera, Norbert F. Brodine.

Corinne Griffith (Madame Zattiany/Mary Ogden); Conway Tearle (Lee Clavering); Thomas Ricketts (Charles Dinwiddie); Thomas Guise (Judge Gavin Trent); Clara Bow (Janet Oglethorpe); Kate Lester (Jane Oglethorpe); Harry Mestayer (James Oglethorpe); Lincoln Stedman (Donnie Ferris); Claire McDowell (Agnes Trevor); Alan Hale (Prince Rohenhauer); Clarissa Selwynne (Gora Dwight); Fred Gambold (Oglethorpes' Butler); Percy Williams (Ogdens' Butler); Otto Nelson (Dr. Steinach); Eric Mayne (Chancellor); Otto Lederer (Austrian Advisor); Carmelita Geraghty (Ann Goodrich); Ione Atkinson, Mila Constantin, Hortense O'Brien (Flappers).

Corinne Griffith was billed as "The Orchid Lady" and she was without doubt one of the most beautiful women to grace the silent cinema. Her screen vehicles often reflected her looks and one of the most ingenious, and somewhat controversial, of these was BLACK OXEN, derived from Gertrude Atherton's best-selling novel of 1923. At the time the craze about physical rejuvenation via monkey gland transplants was at its height and Ms. Atherton herself claimed to have successfully undergone the treatment. The novel's title comes from lines from William Butler Yeats' poem "Countess Cathleen": "The years, like Great Black Oxen tread the world. And God the herdsman, goads them on behind."

Pretty Mary Ogden (Corinne Griffith) arrives in Manhattan and is mistaken for once popular socialite Madame Zattiany, but claims she is a relative of the woman who is now departed. Drama critic Lee Clavering (Conway Tearle) is attracted to Mary but also likes cute flapper Janet Oglethorpe (Clara Bow). Lee, however, chooses Mary and they plan to marry but a former boyfriend who knows her true secret informs Mary such a marriage would be a folly since she is really Madame Zattiany who had her youth restored at a sanitarium in Vienna. Mary realizes the man is correct and tells Lee the truth. She returns to Austria, leaving her beau to romance Janet.

Rejuvenation was a popular topic in the youth-conscious Roaring Twenties and BLACK OXEN was probably the most successful feature film to exploit this vintage sci-fi theme. (One of the most famous plays on this topic was Karel Capek's *The Makrophlos Case,* 1922.)

BLACKENSTEIN (Exclusive International, 1973) C 87 mins.

Producer, Frank R. Saletri; director, William A. Levy; suggested by the novel *Frankenstein* by Mary Shelley; screenplay, Saletri; music/sound effects, Walco Productions; assistant director, Paul Heslin; makeup, Gordon Freed; special electrical effects, Kenneth Strickfaden, Saletri; camera, Bob Caramico; editor, Levy.

John Hart (Dr. Stein [Dr. Frankenstein]); Joe De Sue (Eddie Walker); Ivory Stone (Winnifred Walker); Roosevelt Jackson (Malcolm); Andrea King (Eleanor); Nick Bolin (Bruno Stragor); James Cousar (Sergeant Jackson); and: Karin Lind, Bob Brophy, Yvonne Robinson, Liz Renay, Jerry Sousie, Beverly Haggerty, Daniel Faure, Andy "C", Cardella De Milo, Marva Farmer, Robert L. Hurd, Don Brodie, Dale Bach, the Doberman Dogs.

BLACKENSTEIN, also called BLACK FRANKENSTEIN, was perhaps the ultimate in the black exploitation film craze of the early 1970s, coming on the heels of the highly successful BLACULA (1972) and its sequel, SCREAM, BLACULA, SCREAM (1973). "Not Since FRANKENSTEIN Stalked The Earth Has The World Known So Terrifying a Day . . . Or Night" read the poster blurb for this production. For titillation value, the ad also featured a photograph of a screaming, near bare-chested young woman sporting an Afro hairdo.

Winnifred Walker (Ivory Stone) works for Nobel prize-winning scientist Dr. Stein (John Hart) who experiments in limb rejuvenation although one of his subjects has become part animal. Winnifred confides to Dr. Stein about her fiancee, Eddie Walker (Joe De Sue), who has lost all his limbs in an explosion in Vietnam. The doctor, who is really a descendant of the infamous Dr.

Frankenstein, agrees to treat him and as a result the patient develops new arms and legs. The doctor's other assistant, Malcolm (Roosevelt Jackson), lusts for Winnifred and in revenge for her liking Eddie, he injects the young man with a serum which turns him into an ugly, rampaging monster. After his killings, Walker returns to the doctor's castle and in doing so, is seen by witnesses who inform the police. When Malcolm tries to molest Winnifred, the monster kills him and he also kills two of the doctor's other patients (Andrea King, Nick Bolin). The doctor tries to stop him, but the monster murders him and scampers away to a graveyard where police dogs tear him to pieces.

Richard Meyers wrote in *For One Week Only* (1983), "Since the film had a ready-made monster mixture handy, it makes sense that it would also have a wide variety of women victims in various stages of undress for the monster to maul. This movie was accepted as the obvious rip-off it was, garnering almost no attention, few bookings, and less interest." In 1976, a sequel, BLACK FRANKENSTEIN MEETS THE WHITE WEREWOLF, was announced but mercifully never materialized.

BLADE RUNNER (Warner Bros., 1982) C 117 mins.

Executive producers, Brian Kelly, Hampton Fancher; producers, Michael Delley, Ridley Scott; associate producer, Ivor Powell; director, Scott; based on the novel, *Do Androids Dream of Electric Sheep?* by Philip K. Dick; screenplay, Fancher, David Peoples; music, Vangelis; production designer, Lawrence G. Paull; art director, David Snyder; set designers, Tom Duffield, Bill Skinner, Greg Pickrell, Charles Breen, Louis Mann, David Klasson; set decorators, Linda DeScenna, Tom Roysden, Leslie Frankenheimer; costumes, Charles Knode, Michael Kaplan; assistant directors, Newton Arnold, Peter Cornberg; special visual effects supervisors, Douglas Trumbull, Richard Yricich, David Dryer; visual futurist, Syd Mead; camera, Jordan Cornenweth; supervising editor, Terry Rawlings; editor, Marsha Nakashima.

Harrison Ford (Deckard); Rutger Hauer (Roy Batty); Sean Young (Rachael); Edward James Olmos (Gaff); M. Emmet Walsh (Bryant); Daryl Hannah (Pris); William Sanderson (Sebastian); Brion James (Leon); Joe Turkel (Tyrell); Joanna Cassidy (Zhora); James Hong (Chew); Morgan Paull (Holden); Kevin Thompson (Bear); John Edward Allen (Kaiser); Hy Pyke (Taffey Lewis).

"BLADE RUNNER is a visually arresting, futuristic *film noir,* a tour de force of technique which confirms director Ridley Scott's reputation as a stylist craftsman. Scott, an Englishman who came to feature films with an extensive background in television commer-

Harrison Ford in BLADE RUNNER (1982).

cials, made his directorial debut with THE DUELLISTS (1978). . . .
ALIENS (1979) [see B/V], the horror-thriller set aboard a spaceship, further established Scott as a director with a flair for striking
visual effects. BLADE RUNNER is his most ambitious, most visually exciting work to date. . . . yet while the film was lauded for its
look, critics charged that it was all stunning surface and no substance." (Pat H. Broeske, *Magill's Cinema Annual,* 1983)

In Los Angeles in 2109, reactivated Blade Runner Deckard
(Harrison Ford) is assigned to "retire" (destroy) a half-dozen
Replicants (intelligent robots designed for labor purposes) who have
been outlawed on Earth because of their mutiny on a space colony,
but who have snuck their way into the city. One of the robots is
Rachael (Sean Young) who is so advanced she has been programmed
not to know she is a Replicant. (This is part of the futuristic concept
of making the robots "more human than human.") At the 700-story

Tyrell Corporation building, Deckard meets Rachael and unaware she is one of his targets, the two fall in love. When the truth is discovered, the girl disappears for a time while Deckard rounds up the rest of the robots. Their leader, Roy Batty (Rutger Hauer), plans to eliminate him first in order to avoid his own destruction. The two eventually meet on a rooftop for a battle to the finish with Deckard winning and then returning to Rachael.

Based on Philip K. Dick's 1968 novel, the motion picture owes some of its plot to the works of William S. Burroughs. The film's stark vision of Los Angeles in the next century is frighteningly foreboding. Altogether it is visually stunning with its massive sky-scrapers and flying machines, all in direct contrast to the filth and poverty at street level: the city populated by teaming masses. The film's plotline is a throwback to the 1940s *film noir* detective films, overlayed with the technology and ambiance of the future. As in all substantial science fiction works, there is much philosophizing about the state of the human condition. Mankind depicted in BLADE RUNNER has reached a technical proficiency in which the robots are more humane than their creators; all of which makes the confrontations between the mechanical man Deckard and the warm robot Rachael so intriguing. There is more than irony in the verbal exchanges between Roy Batty, a combat model robot, and his creator, Tyrell (Joe Turkel), the head of the megacorporation which controls so much of the activities in Los Angeles and elsewhere on Earth. As suggested in its role model, FRANKENSTEIN (that man should not tamper with the creation process), so here the creator, Tyrell, has caused a warping of human value and life structure and is destroyed by his own creation —Batty.

Despite of, or because of its intellectualism and complex struc-ture, the film is hard to follow and too often degenerates into dull melodrama. Its downbeat plot and melancholy characters fail to interest. Made at a cost of $30,000,000 +, the film failed to recoup at the domestic box-office, earning only $14,800,000.

Variety, analyzing the pulse of the filmgoers, judged, "BLADE RUNNER undoubtedly constitutes the most riveting—and de-pressing—vision of the near-future since A CLOCKWORK OR-ANGE." The reviewer felt some of the film's faults were with the direction: "Scott and his collaborators have devoted considerable thought to virtually every other aspect of their undertaking, but haven't sufficiently adjusted or freshened up the basic narrative framework of the old-fashioned plot to make it jibe with their main interests."

BLOND GORILLA see WHITE PONGO.